The Rise of Ersatz Capitalism
in South-East Asia

The Rise of Ersatz Capitalism
in South-East Asia

Yoshihara Kunio

SINGAPORE
OXFORD UNIVERSITY PRESS
OXFORD NEW YORK
1988

Oxford University Press

Oxford New York Toronto
Delhi Bombay Calcutta Madras Karachi
Petaling Jaya Singapore Hong Kong Tokyo
Nairobi Dar es Salaam Cape Town
Melbourne Auckland
and associated companies in
Berlin Ibadan

Oxford is a trade mark of Oxford University Press

ISBN 0 19 588885 5 (B)
ISBN 0 19 588888 X (P)

British Library Cataloguing in Publication Data

Yoshihara, Kunio
The rise of ersatz capitalism in South-east Asia.
1. Asia. South-east Asia. Capitalism, 1900–1986
I. Title
330'.122'0959

ISBN 0-19-588885-5
ISBN 0-19-588888-X Pbk

Library of Congress Cataloging-in-Publication Data

Yoshihara, Kunio, 1939–
The rise of ersatz capitalism in South-East Asia/Yoshihara Kunio.
p.   cm.
Bibliography: p.
Includes index.
ISBN 0-19-588885-5:   ISBN 0-19-588888-X (pbk.):
1. Asia, Southeastern—Economic conditions.
2. Capitalism—Asia, Southeastern.   I. Title.
HC441.Y67 1988
330.959'053 — dc 19

87-34845
CIP

Printed in Malaysia by Peter Chong Printers Sdn. Bhd.
Published by Oxford University Press Pte. Ltd.,
Unit 221, Ubi Avenue 4, Singapore 1440

To Jun

Preface

THIS is a book on the superlayer of the economy in South-East Asia. My interest in this began in 1970 when I went to the Philippines, my first trip to the region. Since then, I have continued, intermittently, to collect relevant data and to write on this subject (see Bibliography under Yoshihara, Krirkkiat and Yoshihara, and Thee and Yoshihara). In a way, this book is a synthesis of my earlier writings, but it goes much beyond that. Here, I cover a country—Malaysia—I have not covered before, and I have broadened my focus from the manufacturing industry to include all sectors of the economy where there is big business.

The major stumbling block to this type of study is the paucity of data. The problem arises from the scarcity of printed information, especially in comparison with advanced countries such as Japan, where thousands of company histories and biographies and numerous business journals and newspapers are available. What is available in South-East Asia is often superficial and not always reliable. Attempts to make up for this lack of information through interviews are often frustrated because prominent businessmen are inaccessible. This is very different from the situation facing a social anthropologist who wants to interview peasants in a village (they always have plenty of time for anyone who wants to interview them). Even if businessmen are willing to be interviewed, they may not always tell the truth, for on the way to success they may, deliberately or otherwise, have resorted to questionable practices.

I do not wish to exaggerate the data problem. There is some literature on South-East Asian business (see Appendix 5 for a survey). And with some luck and a great deal of determination, it is possible to collect data through interviews and from unpublished sources (such as the files on people and companies held by banks or credit reference companies). While I could continue, almost endlessly, to build my data base, already certain patterns and problems have begun to surface. In places my data base may contain disinformation, elsewhere my information may be inadequate; but if I had waited indefinitely until I had built a better data base, I may have found myself unable to write anything except possibly a data book—an unexciting though necessary task—and the present book might never have been written. My real purpose in writing this book at this stage is to call attention to the emergence of an inefficient, at best lacklustre, superlayer of the economy, and to invite thought about the problems it poses to economic development in the future. These problems are difficult to detect and have received little attention, but the losses arising from them greatly exceed the sum allegedly embezzled even by such a corrupt politician as Ferdinand Marcos (reportedly $5–10 billion).

This book deals with the South-East Asian region as a whole, rather than its constituent countries chapter by chapter. I am fully aware that the level of economic development varies between countries and that the problems facing one country often differ in nature and degree from those facing another. While I therefore have to discuss differences between the countries to some extent, my emphasis is on the common problems faced by several countries, if not the entire region.

Since patterns and problems are the central issues of this book, biographical and corporate data are collected in Appendices 1–4 and are not much discussed in the text. Names are mentioned and sometimes explained, and facts are discussed in the text only as far as is necessary to develop themes.

I would like to acknowledge my appreciation to the various institutions in South-East Asia which acted as my hosts during my stay there. As a visiting professor, I stayed at the School of Economics, University of the Philippines, in 1970–1 and 1981–2; Department of Economics and Statistics, University of Singapore, in 1973–4; Faculty of Economics, Thammasat University, 1983–4; and Faculty of Economics and Administration, University of Malaya, in 1987. Under the sponsorship of JICA, I stayed with LIPI in Indonesia for three months in 1986. I have used these institutions as the bases for my data collection.

During these visits and on numerous short trips there, I received the help of a number of South-East Asian scholars in gathering data and developing conceptual frameworks. A few of them collaborated with me earlier in writing papers. Also, a number of non-academic people helped me. For example, a senior official in a government bank helped me gain access to its credit files. The head of a credit reference company opened its files on people and companies to me free of charge. The head of a government library gave me free access to its collection, including the classified materials. A business consultant, who has been following up business development in his country for the past two decades, spent numerous hours with me. Several librarians helped me to find references when I visited their libraries and have been corresponding with me ever since. These people made this study possible. Although I cannot name them individually, I wish to thank them all; all that I can offer in return is this volume.

Center for Southeast Asian Studies   YOSHIHARA KUNIO
Kyoto University
October 1987

Note

Throughout this study, all references to dollars ($) are to US dollars, unless otherwise specified. The word 'billion' is used to mean a thousand million.

Contents

Appendices

Tables

Chapter 1
Introduction

SINCE the term 'capitalist' has become a dirty word, those who play 'capitalist' roles do not usually want to be called by this term, and those who write about them often avoid doing so. Why the term has acquired derogatory connotations is not exactly clear, but perhaps Karl Marx's attacks on capitalism have been the most important contributing factor.

In the developed countries, with the progress of economic development, ownership has become fragmented and the Managerial Revolution has taken place, as a consequence of which capitalists have become a rare species. The major providers of capital there are now institutional investors (such as pension funds) and numerous individuals who invest for financial gain and do not want to participate in management. Managerial functions are undertaken by professionals who do not own the companies they manage.

In the developing countries, including those of South-East Asia, ownership and management are generally not separated, and the term 'capitalist', as understood in nineteenth-century Europe, is quite relevant; but because of its derogatory connotations, such terms as 'business élite', 'business executive', and 'entrepreneur' are often used instead. Here, however, the author wishes to reinstate the term 'capitalist' because it is useful from a comparative perspective. Those who were called capitalists in the nineteenth-century West or Japan are essentially the same 'species' as those whom the author wishes to call capitalists in South-East Asia. They command a large sum of capital, wield economic power, and can act as the vanguard of economic modernization.

One might argue that the term 'entrepreneur' is more neutral and better suited to academic writing. However, it does not capture some essential features of the term 'capitalist'. In the author's neighbourhood, there is a small grocery store. Its floor space is small (about ten by three metres), and its entire stock is worth no more than a few thousand dollars. The owner is an entrepreneur, in the same sense as those in Modjokuto (in East Java) whom the American anthropologist Clifford Geertz studied in the 1950s.[1] He cannot be a capitalist, since he commands only a small amount of capital and does not undertake the sort of complex operations that management of larger capital sums entails.

At this point, it is convenient to introduce the French historian Fernand Braudel's classification.[2] He divides the economy into three sectors: the subsistence economy, the market economy, and capitalism. The term for the first sector is self-explanatory: goods are produced for the producer's own consumption. In both the market economy and capitalism, economic activities are undertaken for the market; but in the former, economic activities are small-scale and utilize only a small amount of capital, while in the latter a considerable amount of capital is used and the scale of operation is large.

Capitalism is thus the sector in which the role of capital is pronounced. If capitalism can be considered as the sector of the economy which includes large businesses, then capitalist institutions are the individual economic enterprises which belong to this sector, and capitalists are the people who head such enterprises. How, then, does this definition relate to the conventional definition of capitalism? Implicit in the conventional definition of capitalism is the notion that capitalism is accompanied by a concentration of capital. This is especially so in the case of industrial capitalism, in which a large amount of capital is invested in fixed assets. The emphasis of the conventional definition is, however, on private property and free enterprise. Following this definition, if private property is a condition of capitalism, no government enterprises qualify as capitalist institutions, and 'state capitalism' becomes a self-contradictory term. In this study, the author wishes to retain this part of the conventional definition of capitalism.

In South-East Asia, the people the author calls 'capitalists' exist only in the ASEAN countries. Although not all means of production are nationalized in the non-ASEAN countries, and although considerable development has taken place in the market economy in Burma, a large concentration of capital is allowed only in the government sector. Thus, this book deals with the ASEAN countries, where the concentration of capital is observable in the private sector.

Borrowing the definition of capitalism from Fernand Braudel does not mean that the present writer agrees with his judgement on the economic performance of capitalism. Braudel argues that capitalists are speculators and monopolists who are in a position to earn large profits without undertaking much risk, and that innovations come largely from the market economy.[3] Most scholars who use the terms 'capitalist' and 'capitalism' today seem to agree with Braudel on this, but for the present writer, this is difficult. In Japan today, large corporations are, unlike many of their French and other Western European counterparts, innovative and competitive, and in many respects they are the modernizers of the economy. In the ASEAN countries, capitalism could play the same role; and from this perspective, this author has become interested in the capitalism of the region.

Unfortunately, what has occurred in South-East Asia is the emergence of ersatz capitalism. One might suppose that South-East Asian capitalism is dominated by foreign capital and ersatz for this reason. However, as shown in Chapter 2, South-East Asian capitalism is no longer controlled by foreign capital: in the past few decades there has been considerable development of South-East Asian capital, and as a whole, foreign capital has declined in importance.

What is ersatz about South-East Asian capitalism derives from the fact that the development of South-East Asian capital has been largely confined to the tertiary sector. This does not mean, however, that the non-tertiary sector is still dominated by foreign capital. In the manufacturing sector, many large South-East Asian-owned factories have been set up, and in terms of ownership, foreign capital has become insignificant. This is true for the manufacturing sector of the region as a whole, though foreign capital is still important in a few industries, and foreign capital is still dominant in Singapore. Despite such progress, however, South-East Asian industrial capital cannot act as the vanguard of economic development because it does not have export capability. Any dynamism in this sense comes from the market economy, not from capitalism. This is because large industrial capitalists are comprador capitalists (acting as the agents of foreign manufacturers in their own countries), or they depend on foreign technology in a broader sense, or they are not efficient enough to compete in the international market.

South-East Asian capitalism is ersatz for other reasons. To the Muslim fundamentalists and chauvinistic nationalists, it is ersatz because it is dominated by Chinese capitalists. Although this has become less true under government policies that encourage indigenous entrepreneurship, Chinese capitalists still retain a virtual control of South-East Asian capitalism (to be more exact, its non-foreign portion).

To *laissez-faire* economists, South-East Asian capitalism is ersatz because it is dominated by rent-seekers. In fact, there are strange breeds of capitalists such as crony capitalists and bureaucratic capitalists. In addition, there are political leaders, their sons and relatives, and royal families involved in business. What they seek is not only protection from foreign competition, but also concessions, licences, monopoly rights, and government subsidies (usually in terms of low-interest loans from government financial institutions). As a result, all sorts of irregularities have flourished in the economy.

Also, there are a number of speculators. In itself, speculation is not wrong: there is, in fact, a place for it in capitalism. What is wrong is that many business leaders have a short time-horizon and go after quick profits. A number of industrialists have diversified into real estate and non-manufacturing fields, instead of concentrating on technological improvement and slowly building up industrial empires. In Singapore and Malaysia, where the stock markets are fairly well developed, there are, as in the American corporate world, 'paper entrepreneurs' who pursue relentlessly opportunities for acquisitions, mergers, restructurings, and leveraged buy-outs. In their restructuring schemes, manufacturing is often sacrificed for other activities which turn quicker profits.

This book is about the capitalists who have created ersatz capitalism in South-East Asia. However, it is not intended primarily as a denunciation. In a way, they have become what they are, by having operated within the given environment. More important and constructive is to understand what this environment is and how they developed within it. This leads in turn to the question of how to create a dynamic capitalism. A prescription for this is offered in Chapter 6, although obstacles to its implementation arise from the social and political conditions of South-East Asia. In fact, these conditions are largely responsible for having created the environment of the present situation of capitalism, and unless they change, it is unlikely that capitalism will become more dynamic in the future.

1. Clifford Geertz, *Peddlers and Princes*, Chicago, University of Chicago Press, 1963.

2. Fernand Braudel, *Civilization and Capitalism, 15th–18th Century*, Vol. 1: *The Structures of Everyday Life*, New York, Harper & Row, 1981, Introduction.

3. 'A Chat with Fernand Braudel', *Forbes*, 21 June 1982. See also Fernand Braudel, *Civilization and Capitalism, 15th–18th Century*, Vol. 3: *The Perspective of the World*, New York, Harper & Row, 1984, pp. 619–32.

Chapter 2
Foreign Capital

The Patterns of Investment

Multinational Expansion

THE most familiar pattern of foreign investment in South-East Asia today is the investment of a foreign-domiciled company. For example, a Japanese manufacturing company may find it necessary to set up a factory in a South-East Asian country, or an American company may decide to carry out oil exploration in the region. In such a case, capital comes from the foreign company, as does the necessary management team. If the company does not have enough capital, it may borrow money from a bank or other sources, but it is the initiator of investment.

Foreign investment may be of a horizontal, vertical, or conglomerate type, depending on the type of operation the foreign company undertakes in the region.

A horizontal investment is undertaken to finance an operation which the foreign company also undertakes in its domicile. For example, if the Japanese car manufacturer, Toyota, decides to set up an assembly plant in South-East Asia, it is a horizontal type of investment, since Toyota is engaged in assembling in Japan.

This type of investment is not confined to manufacturing but extends to the primary sector. Examples are Caltex's investment in oil drilling, Weyerhaeuser's investment in logging, and INCO's investment in nickel production (all in Indonesia). Foreign companies in the service sector have also invested in South-East Asia. The investments of the American engineering companies Atlantic, Gulf & Pacific, and Honiron in the Philippines are among the earliest. More recently, Japanese department stores and supermarkets have invested in Singapore, Thailand, and Malaysia.

Nevertheless, the horizontal type of investment by a manufacturing company is the most typical. It was started in the pre-war period by Western companies which found it more profitable to undertake production in the region either because of the high costs of transportation of their products or because of the availability of raw materials for their products. For example, because of transport costs, the Dutch beer company, Heineken, set up its factory in Indonesia, while the American motor vehicle manufacturer, Ford, set up an assembly plant in Singapore. On the other hand, Procter & Gamble began production of soap and margarine in Indonesia and the Philippines because coconut oil, the main raw material, was readily available there.

Such import-substitution investments (so named because they resulted in the substitution of newly made local products for imports) were, however, induced mostly by trade barriers. In the pre-war period, because the colonial governments had vested interests in encouraging the import of manufactured products from the home countries, there were few artificial trade barriers. Thailand remained independent, and in the 1930s, it began imposing trade barriers to encourage industrial production within the country. This induced, for example, British–American Tobacco to set up a cigarette factory there.

In the post-war period, all the colonies gained independence, and the new governments began pursuing nationalistic policies. They reasoned that their underdevelopment was due to the pre-war trade pattern, namely, the import of manufactured goods and the export of primary products, and that the best way to promote development was by industrialization. However, since the industrial base was weak, it was necessary to protect it from foreign competition. For this purpose, high tariffs were imposed on certain categories of manufactured products, and if tariffs were not enough, imports were subjected to quotas or even banned outright.

Many of the foreign manufacturing companies which had been exporting their products set up local factories to get around the trade barriers. Examples abound. It is difficult to trace the sequence of such investments, but the first major investments were in textiles, followed by the assembly of household electrical appliances and motor cars. These areas are now largely exhausted, and investment has been channelled into capital-intensive or technologically sophisticated areas.

The change in policy between the pre-war and the post-war periods is noteworthy. It is reflected not only in the imposition of trade barriers, but also in the regulation of foreign investment. Unlike in the pre-war period, foreign companies have not been free to invest as they pleased in the post-war period. Often they are not allowed to invest if the domestic response in the particular field is sufficient. Even if they are allowed to invest, they usually have to share equity with local investors.

There is another type of horizontal investment called export-oriented investment, so named because it leads to production for export. One of the earliest examples is the American cordage manufacturer, Tubbs Cordage, which set up a rope manufacturing plant in the Philippines in the early 1920s. More recent examples are the participation of Japanese aluminium smelters in the Asahan project in Indonesia and Kawasaki Steel's sintering plant in the Philippines.[1] In Kawasaki Steel's case, the main raw material (iron ore) is brought from abroad for processing, but most other investments of this type came to South-East Asia to process local raw materials.

Non-resource-based export-oriented investments were pioneered by American semiconductor manufacturers (such as Texas Instruments and Fairchild) in the late 1960s. They brought the necessary materials to Singapore for assembling and shipped back finished products to the United States. Electronics investment of this type later expanded into Malaysia, Thailand, and the Philippines.

Japanese manufacturers also began undertaking export-oriented investments in the mid-1970s, when the rising cost of production in Japan and the revaluation of the yen forced them to look for an offshore base. They went first to Singapore and a little later to the export-processing zones of Malaysia and the Philippines. The largest investment of this type undertaken thus far is Sumitomo's chemical complex in Singapore. In the mid-1980s, the sharp revaluation of the yen has again spurred Japanese manufacturers to go offshore. For example, Matsushita is expanding its production capacity in Singapore and plans to produce goods for export worth over S$1 billion within a few years.[2] Unlike American investors, however, most Japanese investors have been using their overseas subsidiaries for export to third countries such as the United States.

The number of vertical investments is smaller, but their beginnings predate import-substitution investments. In the early 1910s, for example, Western tyre manufacturers invested in rubber plantations: Dunlop in Malaya, Goodyear in Sumatra, and United States Rubber Co. (the predecessor of Uniroyal) in Malaya and Sumatra. In the late 1910s, the American sugar manufacturer, Spreckels, invested in the Philippines to obtain raw sugar for its refineries in California; and in the mid-1920s, Unilever came to the Philippines to acquire coconut oil, the raw material for soap production in its American factories.

Another typical vertical investment is the establishment of sales offices. In the pre-war period, Western manufacturers who did not want to rely on trading companies for marketing set up their own sales offices in the region. Examples include cigarette manufacturers, oil companies, tyre manufacturers, pharmaceutical companies, and machinery producers. In the post-war period, with distribution often being reserved for national companies, it became more difficult to set up sales offices, but many manufacturers (Western as well as Japanese) are still engaged in marketing through liaison offices. Foreign manufacturers also sometimes set up purchasing offices, although examples are rarer than those of sales offices. One of the earliest is International Harvester's purchase of a trading company in the Philippines at the beginning of the twentieth century. The trading company dealt mainly in abaca, which International Harvester needed for its reaper.

Japanese *sogo shosha* (general trading companies) have also undertaken a number of vertical investments. To secure a supply of the commodities they handle, they have invested in resource exploitation, resource processing, and manufacturing. Sometimes they have invested in conjunction with other Japanese companies, sometimes on their own. The largest of these investments is that made by Mitsubishi Shoji in liquefied natural gas (LNG) plants in Sarawak and Brunei. The trading companies have been the major Japanese investors in logging and other resource exploitation and processing. They also made many import-substitution investments together with Japanese manufacturers. In these cases, they have been minority partners, for their interests usually lie in being purchasing agents for the raw materials the joint ventures require. Nevertheless, recently, they have started participating in export-oriented industrial ventures.[3]

Lastly, there are the conglomerate investments. In Malaysia, a Japanese sugar manufacturer has invested in a large hotel. Its Malaysian partner in the sugar business diversified into hotels, so the Japanese sugar manufacturer decided to join him in one of his hotel projects. In the pre-war period, the Nomura *zaibatsu* decided to go into plantations in Indonesia. Its main activities in Japan had been in banking and securities, but Nomura had been looking for areas into which to diversify. Since profitable areas within Japan had been pre-empted by the older zaibatsu (such as Mitsui and Mitsubishi), late starters like Nomura had to go overseas. While the other late starters went to China, Nomura went to South-East Asia.

The expansion of a bank or a trading company into the region does not fall neatly into any of the above three categories. In the case of a bank, it is rather like a horizontal expansion, since a branch in South-East Asia undertakes various activities which it undertakes in its domicile. But for a horizontal expansion, there is too strong a linkage between branches, for a branch in South-East Asia acts as an integral part of its global network. This is especially true in the case of a trading company. This type of expansion should constitute its own category, which may be called network expansion.

Organizing for South-East Asian Ventures

In the pre-war period, multinational corporate expansion was not the rule. Most of the capitalist institutions at that time were formed specifically for South-East Asian ventures.

Some of the institutions were set up by Western merchants in the region as family companies or partnerships. They came originally either as independent merchants or as employees of commercial organizations, who later became independent. They started operation in a small way in South-East Asia, and if necessary, extended it to their home countries. Initially, their capital was small, but their business was profitable, so they were able to grow with the passage of time by reinvesting their profits. This was how they became large concerns, although they eventually went public and became linked to the financial market at home. British trading companies (Guthrie and Boustead) and soft-drink bottler Fraser & Neave in Malaya, Dutch trading companies (Jacobson van den Berg, Borsumij, and George Wehry) in Indonesia, and the British trading company Warner, Barnes & Co. in the Philippines fall into this category. Ishihara Sangyo (which mined iron ore in pre-war Malaya) is a Japanese example.

Other companies were organized by Western merchants and residents in South-East Asia. Before there was a stock exchange, a group of merchants sometimes organized a joint-stock company through an informal network. After a stock exchange was formed, it became easier to organize a company locally and some companies were organized in that way, especially in the Philippines and Singapore. In time, however, as these Western merchants and residents in South-East Asia retired to their home countries, it became more convenient to list such companies on the stock exchanges of the home countries. Also, it was necessary to do this when a larger amount of capital had to be mobilized. Examples of locally organized joint-stock companies are Straits Trading, Straits Steamship, and Tanjong Pagar Dock in Malaya; Nederlandsch-Indische Escompto Maatschappij (NIEM), Koninklijke Paketvaart Maatschappij (KPM), and Java Bank (or Javasche Bank) in Indonesia; and the Bank of the Philippine Islands and Benguet Consolidated in the Philippines.

There are also joint-stock companies organized at home for South-East Asian ventures. The initiative for this sometimes came from investors at home. In the case of the Philippines, Tabacalera was formed in Spain in 1881 to take over the export of leaf tobacco and cigar and cigarette production from the Spanish colonial government which had decided to end the tobacco monopoly. In the case of Indonesia, several financial institutions were formed in the Netherlands in the last quarter of the nineteenth century after the Dutch colonial government decided to abolish the Culture System and develop Indonesia with private capital, including Handelsvereeniging Amsterdam (HVA), Koloniale Bank, Nederlandsch-Indische Handelsbank (NIHB), and Internatio. These financial institutions got into trouble during the sugar crisis of the early 1880s and came to specialize in commercial banking or investment banking (this latter category of banks were called culture banks). Internatio was, however, reorganized as an international trading company.

Nederlandsche Handel-Maatschappij (NHM) was also a company organized at home, but it differed from other capitalist institutions in its being promoted by the Dutch King to increase trade with Indonesia. Although the bulk of its capital came from the private sector, the King was an important shareholder, and the company was given various privileges during the culture period.[4] Later, especially after the Culture System was abolished, it began to function more and more like a purely private company, and moved out of trading into banking (commercial and investment).

The culture banks were the most important investors in pre-war Indonesia. They owned sugar factories and coffee, tea, and rubber plantations. They invested particularly heavily in sugar, which was then Indonesia's major export. In the early 1930s, their factories accounted for about 60 per cent of sugar production. They were much less heavily involved outside sugar, but still the producers under their control accounted for 27 per cent of coffee, 14 per cent of tea, and 9 per cent of rubber produced in the early 1930s.[5]

In Britain, too, a number of companies were organized for South-East Asian ventures, but the initiative came mainly from outside. Typical of these were the rubber companies. These were registered in Britain and capital was raised there, but they did not run the plantations in South-East Asia (usually in Malaya but sometimes in Sumatra). They were 'no-staff' companies—investment funds interested only in returns.

How this came about is related to how these companies were organized. When a British trading company (such as Guthrie) started or bought a plantation, or linked up with a planter who had started a plantation, the plantation was floated in Britain. By the beginning of the twentieth century, there were plenty of investors in Britain who were willing to risk part of their capital in a new venture, provided they had assurance that it was potentially profitable. This assurance could come only from someone trustworthy—often a long-time trader in Malaya, sometimes in association with retired former high officials of the Malayan

Civil Service. Such a trader was in a good position to mobilize capital for investment in South-East Asia. He organized a company in Britain, became its secretary, found a manager for its plantation in South-East Asia, and handled its purchasing and marketing requirements. Because his trading company acted as the agent of the rubber company, it was often called an agency house.[6] In the early 1950s, the five largest agency houses controlled more than 60 per cent of the European-owned plantations in Malaya.[7]

Initiatives also came in different ways or resulted in a different organizational set-up. For example, the trading firm East Asiatic Co. was formed in Denmark in 1897 through the merger of H. N. Andersen's trading experience and connections in Thailand with capital in Copenhagen. The British trading company, Borneo Co., was similarly formed: it was the merger of the trading experience of Robert MacEwen in South-East Asia with capital in London. Royal Dutch Co., which later merged with Shell Trading and Transport to become Royal Dutch Shell, was formed on the initiative of A. J. S. Zijlker, who had discovered oil in Sumatra. Deli Maatschappij, a large tobacco plantation company, was formed on the initiative of Jacob Nienhuys, who had experimented with tobacco cultivation in East Sumatra. NHM helped Nienhuys in forming the company, but its role was less important than that of the British trading companies in the formation of rubber plantation companies.

Such mobilization of foreign capital into South-East Asia is now exceptional; and most of the companies thus created in the pre-war period failed to adjust to the age of nationalism that followed independence. They were either nationalized or taken over by South-East Asian interests. Some of the survivors have virtually withdrawn from the region (for example, Ishihara Sangyo), and the few which still operate in the region do so as international companies (for example, Shell). In the post-war period, multinational corporate expansion has become the dominant pattern of foreign investment in South-East Asia.

Western Capital

Genesis

The Dutch East India Company and English East India Company may be thought of as the first capitalist institutions in South-East Asia. If they are so considered, then the origin of capitalism can be placed as far back as the early seventeenth century, when these companies were formed. In Europe, the East India Company was undoubtedly a capitalist institution: its capital came from traders and financiers, not from the state; and it was formed for economic enterprise—to trade with the East. But in South-East Asia, it was more than a capitalist institution: it was a trade regime with various governmental functions. For example, it had military forces to protect and expand its trading interests, or to coerce people into submission. Since a capitalist institution is normally one specializing in economic activities, it is best not to consider the East India Company in South-East Asia as one.

By the nineteenth century, the Dutch East India Company had monopolized the external trade of Indonesia, so that practically no independent Dutch or European merchants operated there.[8] On the other hand, at that time the English East India Company had virtually ceased its activities in South-East Asia, and it was not until the early nineteenth century that Britain became a significant force in the region again. In the Philippines, the dominant external trade was that between Manila and Acapulco. There, unlike in Indonesia, individual merchants participated; but the Manila–Acapulco trade was government-supervised, with limited opportunity for individual initiative. Despite this, some merchants seem to have earned large profits; but if they did, they returned to Acapulco and later possibly to Spain, leaving Manila without any lasting commercial institutions that had a concentration of capital.[9] In Thailand, external trade was dominated by the Court, which, if it needed help from traders, relied on the Chinese, leaving little room for Western traders.[10]

Early in the nineteenth century the government-dominated trading situation began to change. In 1800, for example, the Dutch Government dissolved the Dutch East India Company. It did not, however, abolish a government monopoly (this was reinstituted under the Culture System from 1830), although it did begin relying on private initiative for the exploitation of Indonesia. The English East India Company was not dissolved until the mid-1850s, but it set up Singapore as a free port, allowing European, Chinese, and indigenous merchants to engage in trade free from government interference. In the Philippines, the Spanish colonial government began opening up its ports to non-Spanish merchants; while in Thailand, under pressure from the English East India Company, the Court began lifting restrictions on Western traders, and, in 1855, signed the Bowring Treaty, which opened up the country for free trade.

As a result, the presence of Western merchants increased in the nineteenth century (the number of European trading firms in Singapore increased from 14 in 1827 to 22 in 1846, 44 in 1858, and 52 in 1864).[11] However, none of their businesses were large organizations, being either family companies or partnerships. Guthrie, for example, was one of the largest Western trading houses in Singapore around 1870, but its office consisted of four Europeans (headed by Thomas Scott) and a few Chinese.[12] It probably did not command much capital either, since typically the trading houses of this time received goods from Europe on commission and delivered in return not money but Straits produce.[13]

One major problem was that the East was still far. In the mid-1860s, including stops, it took about 120 days to sail from England to Singapore. To increase the volume of trade with Europe, the region had to be integrated more effectively with Europe, but this required two things: the improvement of the steamship, and the opening of the Suez Canal.

In the first half of the nineteenth century, steamships were still slow and expensive to build, so it was cheaper to use sailing boats for cargo. But the design and the performance of the marine engine were being improved, and the steamship eventually dominated the world's shipping. The beginning of the steamship age roughly coincides with the opening of the Suez Canal in 1869, which cut the distance between London and Singapore by one-third (to about 8,000 miles).[14]

The expansion of capitalism came with the development of the steamship and the opening of the Suez Canal, but even before that, in the freer economic environment, the establishment of large business enterprises had begun. The first of these were not, however, purely capitalist institutions. NHM, which was established in the Netherlands in 1824 with capital of 37 million guilders, was promoted by the King and given special privileges in Indonesia under the Culture System. Java Bank, which was set up a few years later with capital of 4 million guilders, was promoted by the colonial government and acted as a sort of central bank of the colony. Semi-official status was also attached to the first large-scale enterprise in the Philippines, the Bank of the Philippine Islands, which was set up in 1851. It was similar to Java Bank in its functions, but differed in being promoted not by the government but by a private group. Nevertheless, it was not a typical private company: besides being closely connected with the government (acting as a sort of central bank), its main financier was the Catholic Church (or, more precisely, its investment funds, Obras Pias).

Some companies were formed on a purely private basis. Several were formed in England and invested capital in Singapore (for example, Singapore Gas Co. and Johore Steam Saw Mills). A few British banks (formed either in London or India) moved into Singapore, starting in 1846 with the Oriental Bank. One company was formed in Singapore by resident merchants (Tanjong Pagar Dock Co.). In Indonesia, Dutch residents of Jakarta established NIEM in 1860, and a few years later, Dutch financiers established three more banks (NIHB, the Rotterdam Bank, and Internatio). A month before the Suez Canal was opened, the Dutch tobacco planter, Nienhuys, formed the large plantation company Deli Maatschappij, together with NHM and Dutch financiers. With the rise of these capitalist institutions, the structure of the South-East Asian economy gradually changed.

Expansion

Western capital first moved into South-East Asia mainly to produce primary commodities. The first major export of the period was sugar. In 1870, the Dutch Government passed the Agrarian Law, which practically ended the Culture System and allowed Western capital to move into estate production on a large scale.[15] Its effects on the mobilization of Dutch capital were not immediate, but in the 1880s, the number of large plantation companies began increasing (for example, the number of estate companies listed on the Amsterdam Stock Exchange increased from zero to 102 between 1881 and 1895).[16] A large part of the Dutch capital was channelled into sugar production in Java, which in subsequent years became one of the world's major sugar centres. The central role in this capital transfer was played by culture banks. Around 1880, HVA and Koloniale Bank were formed, by which time NHM had become a large investment house and phased out its original trading activity.

The Philippines was another centre of sugar production, although less important than Java. During the Spanish period, the colonial government was not very keen to develop the Philippines: after all, Spain was backward for a European country, and its business sector was neither strong enough to press the government nor possessed of enough capital to start estate production in the colony. The next colonizer, the United States, had capital, but was not very interested in exploiting the country for commercial advantages. If it wanted sugar, it had Hawaii and Puerto Rico. In the very early years of its involvement, the United States imposed a 1 000-hectare limitation on land-ownership, which made it difficult for American capital to move into sugar production. Nevertheless, a few American-owned plantations were born, and some sugar mills were set up with American capital, but far less American capital was invested in the Philippines than Dutch capital was in Indonesia. Even if the sugar mills and plantations owned by Spanish residents are included, the amount of foreign capital involved was limited. On the other hand, unlike in Indonesia, a substantial indigenous entrepreneur group emerged in the Philippines and participated in sugar production.[17]

Tin was another major export developed in the nineteenth century. Malaya was the main tin-producing area of the region, but until the mid-1880s, little foreign (or British) capital was involved. Rather, tin mining and smelting were undertaken by the Chinese on a small scale. At that time, alluvial deposits were rich and could be easily exploited with manual labour, so large-scale tin mining was not a paying proposition. In the mid-1880s, however, British capital (Straits Trading) gained entry into smelting with a more efficient capital-intensive operation employing modern technology. Then, around 1910, the rich tin-bearing ground became exhausted, and a large-scale dredging method began to pay off; and with this, British capital set up a number of dredging companies. It was also around this time that the second British-owned smelter was set up (Eastern Smelting in Penang). [18]

Rubber did not become a major export until the twentieth century, but once it did, it quickly surpassed tin in export value. The rise of the motor car industry created a large demand for rubber, and Malaya became the centre of rubber production with British capital. Estate production of rubber then spread to Sumatra. Western tyre manufacturers were among the largest investors.

Other primary products also attracted Western capital. Royal Dutch Co. was formed to exploit oil in Indonesia, and this evolved into Royal Dutch Shell, which became the dominant producer of oil in pre-war Indonesia. Stanvac also started oil production in Indonesia. A few companies were formed by the resident Americans in the Philippines to mine gold, which became especially attractive after 1933, when the United States raised the gold price. Tobacco and coffee production in Sumatra also attracted European capital, as did logging (teak) in Thailand. In the Philippines, coconut-oil production attracted Unilever; tobacco production, Tabacalera; rope production (from abaca), Tubbs Cordage; and pineapple production, Castle & Cooke (Dole) and California Packing (Del Monte).

With the rise of primary production, the need to import Western manufactured goods increased. Machines and other manufactured inputs were needed for production and processing; and the growth of the Western population in the region and the enrichment of segments of the Chinese and indigenous population created a greater demand for Western industrial goods. The linchpin of this export and import trade was the trading companies. Some of them, especially some of the British trading companies, also acted as the organizers of many plantation companies in South-East Asia.

Increased trading necessitated banking facilities. In Indonesia, NHM acted also as a commercial bank; NIHB specialized in commercial banking, transferring investment banking to its subsidiary, Nederlandsch-Indische Landbouw Maatschappij (NILM); and NIEM concentrated on commercial banking from the beginning, with little involvement in investment banking. Java Bank was also involved in some commercial banking operations. These four Dutch banks dominated the commercial banking in pre-war Indonesia, despite the presence of British and other foreign banks.

In Malaya, the Chartered Bank and the Hongkong and Shanghai Bank were the most important of the commercial banks. They were little involved in investment banking, but offered exchange and other commercial banking services to Western enterprises in the colony. They were also among the earliest banks established in Thailand and the Philippines, as well as having branches in Indonesia, and were probably the two largest foreign banks in pre-war South-East Asia. The only American bank operating in the region (in Singapore and the Philippines) was the National City Bank of New York (the predecessor of Citibank).

Other service companies also operated in the region. There were, for example, public utilities companies (e.g. Meralco and PLDT in the Philippines), railroad companies (e.g. Deli Spoorweg Maatschappij in Sumatra and Paknam Railway in the Bangkok area), and shipping companies (e.g. KPM and Straits Steamship). There were also manufacturing companies (e.g. Procter & Gamble in the Philippines and Indonesia; Ford in Singapore; Heineken, Bata Shoes, and General Motors in Indonesia; and British–American Tobacco in Thailand and Indonesia). However, the plantation companies, tin smelters, tin-dredging companies, banks, and trading companies were the major force in creating capitalism in South-East Asia; and the period up to the Pacific War was the golden age of Western capital.

Decline

The political independence that sooner or later followed the Pacific War changed the business environment for Western capital. The change was most dramatic in Indonesia, more gradual in the Philippines, and even later in Malaysia; but the end result was the same: few Western enterprises are left today. Some were nationalized (this was the case in Indonesia under Sukarno), some were taken over by South-East Asian business groups, and others were bought out by South-East Asian governments (this was especially the case in Malaysia under the New Economic Policy (NEP) from the early 1970s).

In Indonesia, after the four years of civil war that followed the Pacific

War, most of the pre-war Dutch companies came back, but they found that the environment had changed drastically. The monetary environment was unstable, there were more regulations on business activities, and the government's policy was, in general, nationalistic as well as socialistic. However, for several years, although some 'key' companies were nationalized (for example, Java Bank) and nationalistic policies (such as the Benteng programme) reduced somewhat the relative importance of Dutch companies, most of the large pre-war companies continued to operate. Then, in late 1957, they were obliterated when the government decided to nationalize them in connection with the West Irian dispute. Several years later, when Britain and the United States supported the formation of Malaysia by the Federation of Malaya, Singapore, and the British territories of British North Borneo (Sabah) and Sarawak in north Borneo, the Indonesian Government nationalized British and American enterprises.[19] Under the New Order government of Suharto, government policy changed in favour of foreign capital, but with the exception of some British and American companies, most of the foreign concerns nationalized by Sukarno (especially Dutch companies) were not returned to their original owners.

In the Philippines, transition to independence was smoother, although the country was embroiled in bitter fighting during the Pacific War. In the mid-1930s, the Philippines obtained autonomy status and was promised independence ten years later. At this time, some American companies began withdrawing (for example, Insular Sugar Refining and Calamba Sugar Estate), but after the war, since, under the Bell Trade Act and later under the Laurel-Langley Agreement, American companies were given national treatment, namely the same rights as Filipino companies, there was no immediate large withdrawal of American capital. But with the Laurel-Langley Agreement scheduled to expire in 1974, some large American companies began in the 1960s to transfer ownership to Filipino interests (for example, Meralco and PLDT);[20] by the time the Agreement expired, most large pre-war American companies had ceased to be American-owned (for example, the last major pre-war American company, Benguet Consolidated, was Filipinized in the last few years before the expiration, in accordance with the requirements of the Constitution).

In Malaysia, the withdrawal of British capital was slow until the implementation of the NEP in 1971. Until then, the government had largely refrained from intervening in the economy, but with the rise of Malay expectations, the non-interventionist policy became untenable and was replaced by a more pro-Malay economic policy called the New Economic Policy. Although this policy was far from radical (requiring the *bumiputra* stake in the economy to be raised to 30 per cent of ownership and management by 1990), British investors began to sell their holdings. This was made easier by the fact that the Malaysian Government, flush with petrodollars, was willing to buy British holdings in order to increase the Malay share in the corporate sector of the economy. Most of the major pre-war British companies in plantations and tin mining have been bought by the government (for example, London Tin, Sime Darby, and the plantations under Harrisons & Crosfield and Guthrie). As a result of these buy-outs, few pre-war British companies are left in Malaysia.[21]

The other problem Western capital faced was Japanese competition. In the post-war period, because of the rise of economic nationalism, various limitations were imposed on foreign capital, and new foreign entries became difficult. The exception was manufacturing industry. To attain the pace of industrialization it thought desirable, South-East Asia needed supplementary technological expertise and capital from outside, and so allowed a number of Western manufacturing companies to enter. Under the import-substitution programme, Western car makers, pharmaceutical manufacturers, tyre producers, household electrical appliance makers, oil companies (for refining), etc., started production.[22] However, later, as Japanese products became popular, many of these companies withdrew from the region. For example, there are few Western auto and household electrical appliance manufacturers left now, though their products dominated the region in the 1950s and early 1960s.

Of course, a number of Western companies are still operating. For example, British and American banks (especially the former) have branches in the region. But as South-East Asian governments restricted their operations and encouraged domestic banks to grow, their position declined sharply in the post-war period. In Malaysia, where promotion of domestic companies started relatively late and was pursued with some caution, the Chartered Bank and Hongkong and Shanghai Bank still remain important; but as of September 1983, there were three bigger domestic banks (in terms of assets) and a few were close behind.[23] In the Philippines, as of the same date, the Western banks (there were four) accounted for only about 13 per cent of the total deposits of the commercial banks.[24] In Indonesia, where state banks dominate commercial banking, Western banks accounted for only about 5 per cent of the total assets of the commercial banks in 1984;[25] and in Thailand, where domestic banks started expanding earlier (in the mid-1940s), the share of foreign banks in deposits is less than 2 per cent.[26]

In manufacturing, Japanese companies are not very competitive in pharmaceuticals, toiletries, and food, and in these fields, some Western companies remain. Japanese companies are also weak in petroleum refining, but in this case, Western companies faced a different problem. Some South-East Asian governments considered oil to be a key industry and set up state oil companies (Pertamina, Petronas, and Philippine National Oil Co.).[27] Sometimes taking over foreign refineries, sometimes starting their own, these state enterprises increased their share in petroleum refining and marketing. In addition, there are some export-oriented Western manufacturing companies (mostly electronics firms) which do not compete directly with Japanese companies.

Singapore is the only country where Western capital is still significant. In the past two decades, the government has been pursuing an economic policy of making the country a regional centre and its economy export-oriented. There was not enough capital and expertise in the country for this, so the government encouraged foreign companies to come in; today, there are a few Western oil companies operating large refineries, several electronics firms, a dozen offshore banks, and a number of other service companies. But even in Singapore, many of the pre-war Western companies are gone (for example, Fraser & Neave, Straits Trading, Straits Steamship, Malayan Breweries, and United Engineering). They have been bought out by local interests (in a few cases, by the government). The few that remain (like banks) have lost their pre-war eminence due to restrictions placed on their operations and the rise of local firms.

For Western capital in the pre-war period, Thailand was a backwater in South-East Asia. Some trading companies were set up, and a few banks moved in to finance foreign trade; but in general, it was difficult for Western countries to operate there, and the inflow of Western capital was limited. Apart from a few tin-dredging companies in southern Thailand (such as Tongkah Harbour Tin Dredging), no large-scale Western companies were formed for production of primary products. In the post-war period, therefore, there were few Western companies that the government could nationalize or take over; and although there was no strong negative reaction to foreign capital, the government was, and remains, generally cautious about allowing it in, making, like the other governments, manufacturing industry the only major exception. Western capital moved into this area, but much of it later withdrew in the face of Japanese competition. As in the other countries, Western companies are still left in pharmaceuticals, toiletries, petroleum refining, and other minor areas where Japanese competition is weak. In addition, there are a few American electronics firms undertaking the assembling of components for export.

Japanese Entry

Unlike the comparable policy in China, the isolation policy of Tokugawa Japan was strictly enforced, so that there were practically no Japanese in South-East Asia before the mid-nineteenth century. The Meiji Restoration of 1868 freed Japanese to travel abroad, with the result that in about 1890 Japanese emigration to the region began to increase, and by the late 1930s the number of Japanese residents there reached about 40,000 (most of them came from Western Japan).[28] They were engaged in various occupations, such as agriculture (especially in abaca production at Davao in Mindanao, the Philippines), fishing, and trading. Practically all of them came with little capital, and few of their businesses went beyond the market economy to join capitalism. The notable exceptions are Ishihara Sangyo, which mined iron ore in Malaya, and Ohta Kogyo, which operated a large abaca estate in Davao.[29]

In the pre-war period some Japanese capitalist institutions were organized for South-East Asia, but they were much fewer than their European counterparts. Examples are the plantation companies organized by wealthy individuals (e.g. those of the Mitsuis and Iwasakis (of Mitsubishi)). Unlike Western capital, the most typical Japanese capital institution in the region was the branch or subsidiary of a company in Japan. For example, Mitsui Bussan, the largest trading company in pre-war Japan, opened an office in Singapore in 1891 to sell coal, and soon this led to expansion into Surabaya where it bought sugar as a return cargo for the ship which brought coal from Japan (Miike mines in Kyushu).[30] Then, around 1900, this coal business led the company to Manila where more steamships began coming under the new American rule. By the late 1930s, Mitsui had offices in Singapore, Manila, Bangkok, Surabaya, Jakarta, Iloilo, Cebu, Davao, Medan, Palembang, and Semarang. Another large Japanese trading company, Mitsubishi Shoji, also moved into the region, starting with an office in Singapore in 1917. By the late 1930s, it had set up offices in Surabaya, Bangkok, Jakarta, and Manila. Besides these two giants, there were lesser trading companies such as Daido operating in pre-war South-East Asia.

There were other instances of corporate expansion. Yokohama Specie Bank (the predecessor of the Bank of Tokyo) began operations in South-East Asia as the number of Japanese increased and trading companies became active. Its first branch was set up in Singapore in 1916, and in the following two decades it moved into Bangkok, Surabaya, Jakarta, Semarang, and Manila. Two other banks were also involved in the region. Mitsui Bank had a branch in Surabaya; and the Bank of Taiwan, a Japanese 'national policy' bank set up to finance Japanese ventures in South China and South-East Asia, came to the region a little earlier than Yokohama Specie Bank and set up an extensive network before the Pacific War.[31]

One should not, however, overestimate the importance of Japanese investment in pre-war South-East Asia. According to one estimate, total Japanese investment in 1937 was 204 million yen. This amounted to less than a third of American investment, a little less than 20 per cent of British investment, and about 3.5 per cent of Dutch investment.[32]

In the post-war period, Japan had to start all over again, since its pre-war assets were taken over by the South-East Asian governments (Japan abandoned its rights to those assets when it signed the San Francisco Peace Treaty). In the pre-war period, under Western colonial governments, the Japanese had not fared as well as Western investors, but the investment climate in the post-war period was worse. For one thing, there were a number of regulations barring new foreign entry. Some of the firms remaining from pre-war years, like the Western companies, were exempted from such regulations, but they were fully applicable to those which wanted to newly enter the region.

In particular, entry into banking was difficult, and was permitted to some only on the basis of the principle of mutuality. The Bank of Tokyo established branches in Singapore in 1957, in Kuala Lumpur in 1959, in Bangkok in 1962, and in Jakarta in 1968. Mitsui Bank also managed to re-enter the region, setting up a Bangkok branch in 1952 and a Singapore branch in 1963. But even at the time of writing, no Japanese banks have entered the Philippines. Besides branches, there are several joint ventures in which Japanese banks participate on a minority basis. The most significant among them is Bank Perdania in Indonesia, in which Daiwa Bank and Ishihara Sangyo together hold a 49 per cent interest.

For trading companies, re-entry was easier. The new nationalistic governments of South-East Asia did not think much of trading, and wanted to restrict foreign entry to this field; but there were a few leverages Japanese trading companies could use to re-enter. The main one was the difficulty national trading companies faced in exporting local produce. Export requires connections in addition to capital, and it was more pragmatic to let Japanese trading companies take on the promotion of exports. Of course, when local produce (like rubber) was already being exported, Japanese trading companies were not allowed to handle it. Indent business was also restricted, since it was thought that, being a simple intermediary business, it could be handled by South-East Asian companies.[33] But as a whole, the South-East Asian governments needed Japanese trading companies, and so allowed them to come in from relatively early post-war years. For example, C. Itoh set up its Jakarta office in 1951, and by the end of the decade it had offices in Bangkok, Singapore, Manila, Kuala Lumpur, Medan, and Surabaya.

It is, however, in manufacturing that Japanese investment has been most noticeable and relatively large. The governments of post-war South-East Asia, considering industrialization to be the key to economic development, have been promoting it by offering subsidies and protection; but unlike other fields (such as trading and banking), technology has stood as a barrier. To overcome this problem, the South-East Asian governments let foreign companies in, usually on a joint-venture basis. Japanese manufacturing companies were willing to invest on this basis, in order to protect their markets that would be threatened under the protection programme. Many of them, however, being inexperienced in operating abroad, needed the assistance of Japanese trading companies, and invested together with them; thus, the South-East Asian governments also needed Japanese trading companies to promote industrialization.

Direct foreign investment was not a happy solution for some South-East Asian governments. To Sukarno of Indonesia, it was an instrument of imperialism; and it was not until he was replaced by the more pragmatic Suharto that foreign (including Japanese) direct investment really began. In the Philippines, Japanese investors faced a different problem. As the after-effect of bitter fighting in the country during the Pacific War, there were strong anti-Japanese feelings in the post-war period, and it was not until 1967 (a little over 20 years after the war) that the first direct investment was approved. Even since then, the Philippines has been rather reluctant to let Japanese companies in.[34]

The first wave of Japanese investment went into Thailand, a country where anti-Japanese feelings were relatively absent. It was not, however, until the late 1950s, when Sarit Thanarat came into power and began taking measures to encourage foreign investment, that Japanese investment really began. During this time, Thailand gave a great deal of freedom to foreign investors in manufacturing, allowing 100 per cent foreign ownership, tax exemptions on the import of industrial machinery, five-year tax holidays on corporate profits, and relatively free entry of foreign technicians. Later, regulations on foreign investment became a little stricter, but until the mid-1970s, when the Thanom–Praphat regime (which continued Sarit's policy) fell, foreign investment was relatively free.

In the late 1960s, under the New Order government, Japanese investment in Indonesia began in earnest. With a devastated economy under Sukarno, the New Order government had little choice but to offer liberal incentives to foreign investors. Taking advantage of these incentives, a large number of Japanese manufacturing companies invested in Indonesia. Since Indonesia is a large country, it offered a large market for some basic industrial products; and though its level of income was the lowest among the five ASEAN countries, this was enough to entice a number of Japanese companies. Despite the late start, as of March 1984, Japanese investment in Indonesia was about two times that in Thailand, and two-thirds of it was in textiles.[35]

Japanese investment in Singapore and Malaysia began a little before the formation of Malaysia. Japanese manufacturers who went to Singapore, however, were disappointed when the Malaysian common market did not materialize, and after Singapore's withdrawal from the Federation, many of them got into difficulties, since they could not sell their products in Malaysia free of import duty and the Singapore market was too small. But some survived, either because the Singapore market was enough to support their operations, or because they exported their products. However, those who initially survived on domestic demand had later to face reduced protection and could continue to survive only by being relatively efficient.

The bulk of investment in Singapore today is export-oriented. It began with Ishikawajima-Harima's establishment of Jurong Shipyard in 1963. This was set up for ship-repairing, and five years later Ishikawajima-Harima established the shipbuilding company, Jurong Shipbuilders. Then, in the early 1970s, two more shipbuilding companies invested in Singapore: Hitachi Zosen set up Hitachi Zosen-Robin Dockyard, and Mitsubishi Heavy Industries set up Mitsubishi Singapore Heavy Industries. About ten years later Mitsubishi pulled out, but the three others are still operating.

The largest export-oriented investment in Singapore is the petrochemical complex of the Sumitomo group. The flagship of the complex is Petrochemical Corporation of Singapore, which produces ethylene and a few other products (such as propylene). In addition, there are three companies which produce ethylene derivatives: one produces low-density polyethylene; another, high-density polypropylene; and the third, ethylene oxide and ethylene glycol. The total amount of Japanese capital committed to this project was roughly 110 billion yen (at the then exchange rate, about $500 million). The Japanese Government also participates in this project, but in contrast to the Asahan project in Indonesia, the major Japanese commitment was made by the private sector (Sumitomo). The Singapore Government also participates in this project.[36]

Some household electrical appliance makers have chosen Singapore as their production base for export. Among them, Matsushita Electric has been the largest investor. Matsushita Refrigeration Industries produces compressors for refrigerators; Matsushita Electronics, radios and other audio equipment; Matsushita Electric Motor, precision electric motors; Matsushita Electronic Components, various electronic components; and Matsushita Denshi, semiconductors. The first of these was the compressor company set up in 1972, and the others followed by the end of the decade. With the recent revaluation of the Japanese yen, Matsushita has been stepping up its production in Singapore, and has set its export target for 1989 at one billion Singapore dollars.[37]

Some of the export-oriented investment went to Malaysia, although much less than to Singapore. First, some household electrical appliance makers set up factories for export-oriented production. For example, Matsushita is producing air-conditioners in Selangor, and Sony is producing radios and other audio equipment in Penang. Needing components, these companies also induced Japanese components producers (such as Mitsumi Electric) to invest in Malaysia. However, the Japanese semiconductor producers who came to Malaysia (for example, Hitachi in Penang and Shin-Estu Handotai in Selangor) are exporting most of their products directly. Among the Japanese shipbuilders, Sumitomo Shipbuilding and Machinery is the only one in Malaysia. Together with the Malaysian Government (more specifically, Heavy Industries Corp. of Malaysia (HICOM)), it set up Malaysian Shipbuilding & Engineering Corporation in Johor Bahru. Also, Toray Industries has set up a few textile companies for export (e.g. Penfabric, Penfibre, and Pentex).

Japanese investment in import substitution in Malaysia was limited until the mid-1970s. For one thing, although the level of income is higher in Malaysia than in Thailand, the Philippines, and Indonesia (currently about twice that of Thailand), it has a small population (about 16 million) and a relatively small domestic market. For another, its connections with Britain, Singapore, and Hong Kong (the latter two Chinese connections) obviated the need for Japanese capital to a large extent. But in the past decade, under the NEP, Japanese investors have become more active, especially in some of the capital-intensive projects the government has promoted. Notable examples are Nippon Steel's participation in Perwaja Trengganu (a sponge-iron plant in Terengganu) and Mitsubishi Motor's participation in the national car (Proton Saga) project.

The Philippines began approving direct Japanese investment in 1967, but in the first several years it was cautious in doing so. As of 31 March 1974, Japanese manufacturing investment in the Philippines stood at

$20 million on an approval basis, which was about 10 per cent of the sum invested in Indonesia and 23 per cent of that in Thailand;[38] and, under the more positive foreign investment policy of the martial law regime, Japanese investment increased. Kanegabuchi Chemical (together with Takeda Chemical) set up Biophil to produce yeast using sugar molasses (to be used for Takeda Chemical's pharmaceutical product); Isuzu joined General Motors in setting up an assembly plant; Marubeni and two other Japanese trading companies participated in the copper-smelting plant, Philippine Associated Smelting & Refining Corp.; Kawasaki Heavy Industries, together with a subsidiary of the Philippine National Bank, set up a shipyard (Philippine Shipyard & Engineering); Kawasaki Steel set up a sintering plant (Philippine Sinter); Kao Soap set up Pilipinas Kao to produce coco-based chemicals; and Noritake set up Porecelana Mariwasa to produce porcelain ware. Of these, the largest was Kawasaki Steel's investment in the sintering plant (the total project cost was 1.6 billion pesos, or a little over $200 million at the exchange rate then). However, compared with the other ASEAN countries, Japanese investment in the Philippines is the smallest. Moreover, the recent economic troubles in the Philippines have caused a number of Japanese companies to withdraw, notably Kanegabuchi Kagaku and Isuzu.

Thailand has been attracting export-oriented investment from Japan since the mid-1980s. There has been some Japanese involvement in the recent increases in exports of garments, toys, ceramics, plastic products, frozen shrimp, and chicken. Some of this investment went into companies which were originally set up for the domestic market and later became export-oriented (notably some textile companies). In addition, some machinery and parts producers have invested in Thailand. For example, a ball-bearing manufacturer (Minebear) is producing miniature bearings as well as some electronic components for export; Mitsubishi, Isuzu, Toyota, and Nissan are planning to start production of engines and other motor vehicle parts for export; and a manufacturer of household electrical appliances, Sharp, is planning to set up an export centre. The perception of Thailand by Japanese investors has improved remarkably in the past few years, and it will soon become a major centre of export-oriented production by Japanese companies in the region.[39]

The Relative Position of Foreign Capital Today

Although capitalism in South-East Asia was created by Western capital and was dominated by it for about a century, the situation has changed dramatically in the past few decades. Recently, for example, a number of Western companies have withdrawn in the face of mounting competition from Japanese companies, which emerged as the most dynamic force in the world economy after the Second World War. There is no question that the days of Western supremacy are over, but has there simply been a substitution of Japanese for some Western capital, so that foreign capital still dominates South-East Asian capitalism?

The answer is definitely negative. What emerged as the dominant element in the post-war period is South-East Asian capital. Political independence after the Pacific War changed the environment for foreign capital. The new governments restricted the entry of foreign capital and created state enterprises, either newly or by taking over foreign companies (sometimes resorting to the extreme measure of nationalization). They gave protection and subsidies to private domestic capital and made it an important element of South-East Asian capitalism.

It is difficult to show quantitatively how foreign capital stands in the superlayer of the present-day South-East Asian economy. One problem is that financial data on a large number of companies are not published

TABLE 2.1

The Relative Position of Foreign Capital

Industry	Foreign Capital	Private Domestic Capital	State Capital
Banking	minor/ moderate	substantial	moderate/ substantial
Property Development		substantial/ dominant	moderate
Construction	moderate/ substantial	substantial	minor
Mining	minor/ moderate	substantial	substantial
Oil Exploration	dominant		
Plantation Agriculture	minor	moderate	substantial
Export/Import Trade	moderate/ substantial	moderate	moderate
Manufacturing	moderate	substantial	substantial
Light Industries	minor	substantial	minor
Machinery	moderate/ substantial	moderate	moderate
Metals & Petrochemicals	minor		substantial

(this is especially the case in Indonesia). Another, less serious than the first, is the problem of aggregating financial data in terms of different national currencies into a common denominator (for example, the US dollar). At this stage, the best that can be done is to give qualitative, somewhat impressionistic, indicators, as in Table 2.1.

'Foreign companies' are defined as those over which foreign-domiciled companies exert control through equity holdings. They do not include companies in which foreign-domiciled companies hold minority interests, nor those over which they have some control through licence without equity participation. In a foreign company, although ownership may be shared with South-East Asian investors, the foreign shareholder(s) has to have management control. In a number of cases, even management is shared (for example, the local side takes care of marketing, the foreign partner production). In these cases, although there is a risk of over-estimating the importance of foreign capital, the company was considered foreign.

In Table 2.1, the relative positions of foreign and domestic companies are measured on a ten-point scale. If there is no entry, the score is less than 1.0; 'minor', 1.0–2.4; 'moderate', 2.5–3.9; 'substantial', 4.0–7.4; 'dominant', 7.5 and above.

Banking

The relative importance of foreign banks is between 'minor' and 'moderate' (this means that it is in the upper end of the 'minor' range or the lower end of the 'moderate'product).

In banking, Japanese concerns are not very significant. What count here are Western banks (especially British and American). In the post-war period, their operation was restricted in a number of ways (for example, setting up a new branch became extremely difficult), and their relative importance declined sharply as new South-East Asian banks were created.[40] In Thailand, foreign banks are now of minor importance. At the end of 1985, the largest foreign bank was Mitsui Bank (in terms of assets), but it was smaller than 15 of the 16 Thai commercial banks (only one is a state bank in the sense commonly understood). In the other countries, however, foreign banks are more important. In Malaysia, the Chartered Bank and Hongkong and Shanghai Bank are still among the largest (though not the largest). In the Philippines, Citibank is much smaller than the Philippine National Bank (PNB), but it is the largest of the private banks. In Indonesia, too, Citibank is the largest private bank. But there are a number of large state banks today, and they surpass those foreign banks in importance. For example, in Indonesia, there are seven state banks which are not only bigger than Citibank but also dominate commercial banking (in 1984, they accounted for about 80 per cent of the total assets).[41]

Property Development and Construction

In property development, foreign entry is highly restricted and foreign capital is hardly significant. But in construction, where there is the problem of technical know-how and a highly cyclical demand, foreign companies are allowed in. Especially in the early 1980s, when many large construction projects were undertaken, foreign (especially Japanese) construction companies were important (probably in the 'substantial' category), but in the mid-1980s, due to the economic slow-down, their importance has declined, and a number of them have left.

Between private and state enterprises, the former seem more important in both property development and construction. In Indonesia and Malaysia, state enterprises (or their subsidiaries) are moderately important. In Indonesia, for example, the City of Jakarta is the major shareholder in the construction company, PT Pembangunan Jaya; and in Malaysia, Pernas and a few other government bodies (such as the Urban Development Authority, UDA) are engaged in construction and property development (through subsidiaries). Nevertheless, even in these countries, there are a number of large private construction and property development companies (e.g. Teknik Umum of Indonesia and Ipoh Garden and Landmarks Holdings of Malaysia). In Thailand, Singapore, and the Philippines, state enterprises are much less signifi-cant (excluded are the companies taken over by the Philippine Govern-ment because of their default on loans from its financial institutions, especially Construction & Development Corporation of the Philippines).

Mining

In the Philippines, all major American companies had been taken over by private Filipino interests by 1974 when the Laurel–Langley Agree-ment expired. In Malaysia, many of the large tin-dredging companies are now Malaysian-owned. The companies under London Tin, former-ly the largest British mining agency in Malaysia, now form the state enterprise, Malaysia Mining Corp. (MMC). In Indonesia, all Dutch mining companies (especially tin) were nationalized and are now state enterprises. In the south of Thailand, where there is tin mining, there has been no significant transfer of ownership, but its importance in the mining industry of South-East Asia as a whole is small. Some Western companies have remained in Malaysia and southern Thailand, and a few Western companies have newly entered the region (nickel mining in Indonesia and tin mining in southern Thailand); but their overall significance is between 'minor' and 'moderate'. Private and state enterprises seem to be almost equally important for the region as a whole. In Indonesia, of course, state enterprises are far more important; but in the Philippines, the reverse is true. In Malaysia and southern Thailand, they seem roughly equal in importance: government-owned mines are counterbalanced by private (almost all Chinese) mines.

Oil Exploration

Oil exploration requires a large amount of capital and sophisticated technology, and at the same time it is highly risky, so Indonesia, Malaysia, and Thailand—especially Indonesia—where major oil exploration is going on, leave it mainly to Western oil companies. The national oil companies of Indonesia, Pertamina, and Malaysia, Petronas, undertake some exploration activities, but they are still largely at the learning stage.

Plantation Agriculture

In Indonesia, all Dutch plantation companies were nationalized in 1957. In the early 1980s there were still a couple of American and a few European plantation companies left, but in the mid-1980s one of them (Uniroyal Sumatra) sold its interest to an Indonesian group (Bakrie). State enterprises dominate this sector, though there are some private domestic plantation companies (besides the Bakrie group, the Astra group has entered this industry).

In Malaysia, practically all of the major British companies seem to have withdrawn. Dunlop sold its interest to Multi-Purpose Holdings, and Sime Darby, Harrisons & Crosfield, and Guthrie sold theirs to the Malaysian Government. Practically no major foreign plantations remain. State enterprises tend to dominate this industry, but there are some private plantation companies; besides Multi-Purpose Holdings, Kuala Lumpur–Kepong (henceforth K.L.–Kepong) is privately owned.

In the Philippines, a few American plantations remain. Unlike rubber and palm-oil, the canned pineapple of the American plantations is marketed under well-known brands ('Dole' and 'Del Monte'), so it is difficult for the Philippine Government to force these companies to transfer majority ownership to Filipinos. Nevertheless, even if these companies are added to the few in Indonesia, the relative importance of foreign companies in the region as a whole is 'minor'.

Export/Import Trade

There are a number of state and private South-East Asian trading companies. Examples of the former are Intraco of Singapore, various state trading companies in Indonesia (Pantja Niaga, etc.), and Pernas of Malaysia. Private trading companies include Hong Yiah Seng, Metro, and SCT (Siam Cement Trading) of Thailand; Mulpha International Trading of Malaysia; Elizalde & Co. of the Philippines; Hong Leong and Lee Rubber of Singapore; and Waringin Kencana and Astra International of Indonesia. All these companies tend to be smaller than the Japanese and Western trading companies operating in the area, which the South-East Asian governments have to allow because of their international networks, but they are by no means dominated by the foreign companies. In addition, many of the manufacturers and primary producers of the region conduct overseas trade directly, and this has further eroded the position of foreign trading companies. Many textile companies, for example, sell their products abroad directly or through sales subsidiaries. However, Japanese trading companies are involved in the export of major primary products such as oil and LNG, and their business is still considerable. As a whole, their relative position is probably between 'moderate' and 'substantial'.

Manufacturing

This is another area over which the South-East Asian governments do not have complete control: they need the capital and technology of foreign manufacturing companies. A number of foreign companies have therefore been established (more precisely, they are usually foreign-controlled joint ventures). Initially, since the South-East Asian countries lacked experience in manufacturing, the industry appeared to be dominated by foreign companies; but as shown in Table 2.1, their importance in the mid-1980s is only 'moderate'.

There are at least two main reasons for this. One is economic nationalism, which led to the proliferation of state enterprises. In Indonesia, many were created by the nationalization of Dutch enterprises in 1957, and more were newly created to 'spur' industrialization. For example, Pertamina set up new refineries and the integrated steel mill, Krakatau Steel Mills, and the Indonesian Government set up new cement and fertilizer plants.[42] In Malaysia, through HICOM, Petronas, and other public enterprises, the government is heavily involved in industrialization. Even in the Philippines and Singapore, there is some government involvement. For example, the Singapore Government is the major shareholder in two large shipyards (Keppel and Sembawang); while the Marcos government also got involved in a number of capital-intensive projects, such as copper smelting, ship-repairing, steel, and petroleum refining. In the capital-intensive steel and petrochemical industries (including refining), although a few Western-owned refineries and one Japanese petrochemical complex operate, their position in the region as a whole is 'minor': it is state enterprises that are dominant.

In light industry, the reason is different. Here, the relative position of state enterprises is 'minor'. What caused the decline of foreign capital was the emergence of private domestic companies. For example, in the mid-1960s, textiles (especially integrated textile production) in Thailand was dominated by Japanese companies, but two decades later, privately owned Thai companies dominate. The same is true for Indonesia, although Japanese and other foreign investment there started later (in the late 1960s). In Indonesia, after the first oil crisis, oil money was channelled through state banks into industry. By early 1986, the share of foreign companies in spinning had declined to about 27 per cent.[43] In Thailand (possibly more so than in Indonesia), as technology was mastered, profits were accumulated, and capital became more abundant, a number of new Thai textile companies were established, and the position of private domestic companies rose dramatically. In some Japanese joint ventures, through the process of capital expansion (and thus increase in equity), the Thai partners came to hold majority shares and eventually phased out their Japanese partners (for example, the Sukri group).

In machinery, there is greater foreign participation. Japanese companies are involved in several shipyards in Singapore, Malaysia, and the Philippines. About a dozen Japanese motor vehicle and household appliance makers operate assembly plants in the region, some of which are producing for export, and their investments have increased sharply in the past few years with the revaluation of the yen (for example, Matsushita operates several plants in Singapore, and a few Japanese car producers are starting parts production in Thailand). There are also a number of semiconductor factories. In Singapore, American companies (such as Texas Instruments and Fairchild) pioneered semiconductor production for export, but later expanded into other countries (recently, into Thailand in particular). Semiconductors are also produced for export by some Japanese companies (especially in Malaysia by Hitachi and a few others).

There are also a number of South-East Asian companies in this field. In Singapore, the government owns two shipyards; in Malaysia, the government is heavily involved through HICOM (for example, the

Proton Saga motor car project); and in Indonesia, the government is involved in shipbuilding (e.g. PAL Surabaya) and general machinery (e.g. Barata Indonesia). In addition, there are a number of privately owned assembly plants which produce under licence. In the Philippines, most household electrical appliance companies are Filipino-owned (for example, Philacor); in Indonesia, there are a number of privately owned vehicle assembly plants (the largest of them being the Astra group); in Malaysia also, there are a few privately owned car assemblers (for example, UMW); and in Thailand, the Siam Cement group operates a foundry which produces machinery and parts, and there are some private car assemblers and household electrical appliance makers (e.g. Siam Motor, Tanin Industrial). In view of the existence of such South-East Asian companies, the relative position of foreign companies in machinery cannot be dominant or even 'substantial'. It is probably between 'moderate' and 'substantial'.

There are a number of industries which are not covered in Table 2.1. One might argue, for example, that pharmaceuticals is foreign-dominated. If one takes a specific industry, it is not too difficult to come up with an example of one that is foreign-dominated; but in a broader category, this is difficult to do. The only exception is oil exploration. Even pharmaceuticals is far from foreign-dominated, with the largest companies tending to be South-East Asian-owned: United Laboratories in the Philippines, Osothsapha in Thailand, Haw Par Brothers International in Singapore, and Kalbe Farma in Indonesia are all the largest pharmaceutical companies in their respective countries. If they need technology from abroad, they can tie up with foreign companies and produce under licence, and in some cases, they can pirate their patents.

The large-scale retail trade (department stores and supermarkets) is believed by some to be dominated by foreign companies. In Thailand, for example, Daimaru was once the target of anti-Japanese demonstration. Recently, a few more Japanese department stores have moved in (Tokyu and Sogo), along with one supermarket (Jusco). In Singapore and Malaysia, there are also several Japanese department stores and supermarkets (e.g. Isetan, Yaohan). But in the other countries, there are no foreign-owned department stores. For example, the largest department stores in Indonesia and the Philippines—the Sarinah and Sarinah Jaya Department Stores of Indonesia, Rustan of the Philippines—are all South-East Asian-owned. Even in Thailand and Singapore, despite the presence of foreign companies, the response of their entrepreneurs has been remarkable. The Thai-owned Central Department Store is larger than any foreign-owned department store; while in Singapore, Metro and other Singapore-owned department stores and supermarkets are offering a strong challenge to foreign-owned ones.

As a whole, the relative importance of foreign companies is no more than 'moderate': there are too many South-East Asian companies for it to be 'substantial'. However, to some South-East Asian nationalists, even this moderate level of foreign participation may be too high. After all, in Japan, for example, there was not even a 'minor' level of foreign participation in the process of development. If foreign investment was significant there, it was in terms of loans, not as direct investment. Thus, their claim that South-East Asia should further reduce its dependence on foreign capital is understandable; but there is no factual basis for arguing that foreign capital is still dominant. In the post-war period, there has been a remarkable increase of South-East Asian-owned companies. The next three chapters focus on these companies, which, if not 'dominant', constitute at least a 'substantial' part of the superlayer of the South-East Asian economy today.

1. In the cases of the Asahan project and Kawasaki Steel's sintering plant, the distinction between vertical and horizontal expansion is not clear-cut, for what they started in South-East Asia has been gradually phased out in Japan, so that they have become vertically integrated to their operations in Japan.

2. *Asian Wall Street Journal*, 27 and 28 February 1987.

3. For further discussion on sogo shosha, see Yoshihara Kunio, *Sogo Shosha: The Vanguard of the Japanese Economy*, Tokyo, Oxford University Press, 1982.

4. Clive Day, *The Policy and Administration of the Dutch in Java*, reprinted Kuala Lumpur, Oxford University Press, 1966, pp. 240–2.

5. J. T. M. van Laanen, *Changing Economy in Indonesia*, Vol. 6: *Money and Banking 1816–1940*, The Hague, Martinus Nijhoff, 1980, p. 37.

6. Tin companies were organized in different ways, though how this was done is not entirely clear since there is little writing on this subject. Some tin-mining companies were organized by Osborne & Chappel, one of the major mining agencies operating in Malaya. Osborne and Chappel were engineers who came to Malaya around 1900, and promoted a company in London whenever they found a deposit worth exploiting. They did not invest their money in mining (originally, they probably did not have capital), but they managed in Malaya the companies they promoted in England. In a way, they played the same role in tin mining as some British trading companies did in rubber. The major difference was that Osborne & Chappel did not have trading interests. (Interview with Abdullah bin Yusof, executive director of Osborne & Chappel International, 30 July 1987.)

In the case of the companies under Anglo-Oriental (Malaya), the pattern of mobilization of capital seems to have been different. As in the case of Osborne & Chappel, Anglo-Oriental (Malaya) was a mining agency, and managed a number of tin-mining companies incorporated in England (in fact, Anglo-Oriental (Malaya) had been the biggest tin-mining agency for a few decades before the withdrawal of British capital in the mid-1970s). However, Anglo-Oriental (Malaya) had an investment company as the parent company, whose primary task was to finance tin mining in Malaya. This parent company (probably called Anglo-Oriental Mining Corp.) seems to have floated a company when Anglo-Oriental (Malaya) found a deposit worth exploiting, and become a main shareholder of the company at the same time. In 1937, Anglo-Oriental was absorbed into London Tin, another company which was formed in England (in 1925) to finance tin mining. At some stage, London Tin seems to have become related to Consolidated Tin Smelters (and thus to the Patino group), for London Tin and Eastern Smelting (Consolidated Tin's subsidiary) began appearing together as the major shareholders of some tin-mining companies in Malaya.

7. J. J. Puthucheary, *Ownership and Control in the Malayan Economy*, reprinted Kuala Lumpur, University of Malaya Cooperative Bookshop, 1979, p. 27.

8. On the Dutch East India Company, see C. R. Boxer, *The Dutch Seaborne Empire, 1600–1800*, London, Hutchinson & Co., 1965, and Day, op. cit.

9. William Schurz, *The Manila Galleon*, reprinted Manila, Historical Conservation Society, 1985, p. 293.

10. On the organization of foreign trade in Thailand before the Bowring Treaty, see John Bowring, *The Kingdom and People of Siam*, reprinted Kuala Lumpur, Oxford University Press, 1969; John Crawfurd, *Journal of an Embassy to the Courts of Siam and Cochin China*, reprinted Kuala Lumpur, Oxford University Press, 1967; and Pannee Ouansakul, 'Trade Monopoly in Ayudhya', *Social Science Review* (Bangkok), 1976.

11. Wong Lin Ken, 'The Trade of Singapore, 1819–69', *Journal of the Malayan Branch of the Royal Asiatic Society*, Vol. 33, Pt. 4 (1960), p. 167.

12. Sjovald Cunyngham-Brown, *The Traders: A Story of Britain's South-East Asian Commercial Adventure*, London, Newman Neame, 1971, p. 102.

13. Wong Lin Ken, 'The Trade of Singapore, 1819–69', p. 163.

14. D. J. M. Tate, *The Making of Modern South-East Asia*, Vol. 2: *The Western Impact, Economic and Social Change*, Kuala Lumpur, Oxford University Press, 1979, pp. 2–3, and Francis Hyde, *Far Eastern Trade: 1860–1914*, London, Adam & Charles Black, 1973, pp. 17–21.

15. On the Agrarian Law and its effects, see Day, op. cit., p. 335, and W. M. F. Mansvelt *et al.*, *Changing Economy in Indonesia: A Selection of Statistical Source Material from the Early 19th Century up to 1940*, The Hague, Martinus Nijhoff, Vol. 3, pp. 11–19.

16. Mansvelt *et al.*, op. cit., p. 12.

17. Yoshihara Kunio, *Philippine Industrialization: Foreign and Domestic Capital*, Quezon City, Ateneo de Manila University Press, and Singapore, Oxford University Press, 1985, Chapters 4 and 6.

18. On the tin-mining industry up to the early twentieth century, see Wong Lin Ken, *The Malayan Tin Industry to 1914*, Tucson, University of Arizona Press, 1965.

19. On the economic policy of the Indonesian Government under Sukarno, see Lance Castles, 'Socialism and Private Business: The Latest Phase', *Bulletin of Indonesian Economic Studies*, No. 1, 1966; Frank Golay *et al.*, *Underdevelopment and Economic Nationalism in Southeast Asia*, Ithaca, Cornell University Press, 1969, Chapter 3; Douglas Paauw, 'From Colonial to Guided Economy', in Ruth McVey, ed., *Indonesia*, New Haven, Southeast Asian Studies, Yale University, 1963; and John Sutter, *Indonesianisasi: Politics in a Changing Economy, 1940–1955*, Data Paper No. 36, Southeast Asian Program, Cornell University, 1959.

20. On the decline of American capital in the Philippines up to the early 1970s, see Yoshihara, *Philippine Industrialization*, Chapter 4.

21. Consolidated Tin Smelters, which controls Datuk Keramat Holdings, one of the two smelters in Malaysia (formerly known as Syarikat Eastern Smelting), is often mis-

takenly thought to be British-owned, since it is a company incorporated in Britain. For some time after its incorporation, it was British-owned, but it was taken over by the Patino group based in Bolivia, and then later by the German mining company, Preussag A. G. Datuk Keramat Holdings is still German-owned today.

There is no comprehensive treatment of the transfer of British companies to Malaysian interests, since major buy-outs are fairly recent. However, the following sources are useful: E. K. Fisk and H. Osman-Rani, eds., *The Political Economy of Malaysia*, Kuala Lumpur, Oxford University Press, 1982, and Sieh Lee Mei Ling and Chew Kwee Lyn, 'Redistribution of Malaysia's Corporate Ownership in the New Economic Policy', in *Southeast Asian Affairs 1985*, Singapore, Institute of Southeast Asian Studies, 1985.

22. There are a number of references on Western manufacturing companies in the post-war period. For example, see Lim Mah Hui, *Ownership and Control of the One Hundred Largest Corporations in Malaysia*, Kuala Lumpur, Oxford University Press, 1981; Junid Saham, *British Industrial Investment in Malaysia, 1963–1971*, Kuala Lumpur, Oxford University Press, 1980; Akira Suehiro, *Capital Accumulation and Industrial Development in Thailand*, Bangkok, Chulalongkorn University, 1985; Thee Kian-wie and Kunio Yoshihara, 'Foreign and Domestic Capital in Indonesian Industrialization', *Southeast Asian Studies*, March 1987; Kunio Yoshihara, *Foreign Investment and Domestic Response: A Study of Singapore's Industrialization*, Singapore, Eastern Universities Press, 1976; and Yoshihara, *Philippine Industrialization*.

23. Bank Negara Malaysia, *Money and Banking in Malaysia*, Kuala Lumpur, 1984, p. 160.

24. Philippine National Bank, *Philippine Commercial Banking System in 1983*, Manila, Table 2.

25. *Informasi Financial Profile 84/85*, Jakarta, Pusat Data Business Indonesia, 1985, pp. 38–9.

26. *Taikoku Keizai Gaikyo 1986–87 Nen-ban*, Bangkok, Bangkok Nihonjin Shoko Kaigisho, n.d., p. 180.

27. In Thailand, there is a major refinery called Thai Oil Refinery. It is not a state enterprise in the usual sense, but a joint venture with foreign oil companies (Shell and Caltex) in which the government holds 51 per cent of the equity.

Petronas did not nationalize any existing refineries, but Pertamina and Philippine National Oil Co. took over some existing refineries. Pertamina bought out the refineries of Stanvac and Shell and built new ones, whereas Philippine National Oil Co.'s refineries are those formerly owned by Stanvac and Gulf Oil.

28. Ministry of Finance (of Japan), 'Nihonjin no Kaigai Katsudo ni Kansuru Rekishi-teki Chosa: Nanpo-hen' (unpublished), 1947, p. 127. On the background of Japanese emigration to and investment in South-East Asia, see the following works by Yano Toru: *Nihon no Nanshin to Tonan Ajia*, Tokyo, Nihon Keizai Shinbun-sha, 1975; *Nihon no Nanyo Shikan*, Tokyo, Chuokoron-sha, 1974; *Nanshin no Keifu*, Tokyo, Chuokoron-sha, 1975.

29. On Ishihara Sangyo, see Appendix 1. On Ohta Kogyo, see Furukawa Yoshizo, *Davao Kaitaku-ki*, Tokyo, Furukawa Takushoku Kabushiki Kaisha, 1956.

30. On the overseas expansion of Mitsui Bussan and other Japanese trading companies, see Yoshihara, *Sogo Shosha*, Chapter 3.

31. On the expansion of the three Japanese banks to South-East Asia, see *Taiwan Ginko-shi*, Tokyo, Taiwan Ginko-shi Hensan-shitsu, 1964; *Yokohama Shokin Ginko-shi*, Yokohama, Yokohama Shokin Ginko, 1920; and *Mitsui Ginko Hyakunen no Ayumi*, Tokyo, Mitsui Ginko, 1976.

32. Ministry of Finance (of Japan), op. cit., p. 135.

33. Another leverage used by Japanese trading companies was their connections with Japanese manufacturing companies. To attract the latter, which, in general, did not know how to operate abroad, it was necessary to invite Japanese trading companies which could co-operate with them in foreign ventures.

34. On the background to the resumption of Japanese investment in the post-war period, see Kunio Yoshihara, *Japanese Investment in Southeast Asia*, Honolulu, University Press of Hawaii, 1978, Chapter 3.

35. Yoshihara, *Japanese Investment in Southeast Asia*, p. 66.

36. MITI, *Keizai Kyoryoku no Genjo to Mondaiten 1983*, Tokyo, Tsusho Sangyo Chosa-kai, 1984, pp. 422–3. Although the private sector largely bore the risk on the Japanese side, three-quarters of the funding came from the two government financial institutions (Export–Import Bank of Japan and Overseas Economic Cooperation Fund).

37. At present, faced with increased production costs in Japan due to the recent revaluation of the yen, Matsushita is planning to increase the share of overseas production in the total from 14 to 25 per cent. *Asahi Shinbun*, 18 March 1987.

38. Yoshihara, *Japanese Investment in Southeast Asia*, p. 66.

39. There is no data on how Japanese investment stands *vis-à-vis* American or European investment. It is not impossible to come up with some comparative figures from published data, but there is a problem of reliability. In manufacturing industry, it would be safe to state that Japanese investment now exceeds American and European investment. This is definitely true for Indonesia, Thailand, Malaysia, and the Philippines. In Singapore, where there are a few Western-owned refineries, a big gap once existed between Japanese and Western investment, but in the past several years Japanese investment has been stepped up considerably, and the gap, if not yet closed, must have narrowed. It is therefore unlikely that the Singapore situation would change the overall picture.

What is not clear is how Western investment in oil exploration offsets the difference in manufacturing industry. A large part of the investment went to Indonesia, the major oil-producing country of the region, and the remainder to Malaysia. It seems unlikely that this investment would compensate for the difference in manufacturing. However, even if it did, the strength of Japanese industry in the world economy, which has, for example, brought about the recent revaluation of the Japanese yen, will continue to induce Japanese companies to shift their production abroad, to South-East Asia in particular, and is bound to make Japan the largest investor in the region.

40. On the change in the environment for a British bank in Malaysia, see Chee Peng Lim *et al.*, 'The History and Development of the Hongkong and Shanghai Banking Corporation in Peninsular Malaysia', in Frank King, ed., *Eastern Banking: Essays in the History of the Hongkong and Shanghai Banking Corporation*, London, The Athlone Press, 1983.

41. See *Informasi Financial Profile 84/85*, Bank Negara Malaysia, Philippine National Bank, and *Taikoku Keizai Gaikyo 1986–87 Nen-ban*, cited in notes 23–26.

42. See Thee and Yoshihara, op. cit.

43. ASPI (Asosiasi Industri Pemintalan Indonesia).

Chapter 3
Chinese Capital

The Chinese

Who the Chinese are is a complicated question, which it is not proposed to settle here. However, it will be dealt with to some extent, for there cannot be a discussion of Chinese capital until there is a shared understanding of the concept of the Chinese. At the same time, readers who are not familiar with the complexity of the definition might get a glimpse of it in the following few pages.

The Chinese in this book come close to the people who are called 'ethnic Chinese'. They are neither Chinese nationals nor Chinese immigrants; for the vast majority of them have citizenship in their country of residence. Their place of birth is not a good criterion, either. A large number of people who are normally regarded as Chinese were born in South-East Asia. Examples are legion: Tan Chin Tuan of Singapore; Tan Siew Sin, Tan Cheng Lock, and Robert Kuok of Malaysia; Udane Techapaibul and possibly Chin Sophonpanich of Thailand; Alfonso Yuchengco and Albino Sycip of the Philippines; and William Soeryadjaya, The Ning King, and Ciputra of Indonesia.

Who, then, are the ethnic Chinese? It is tempting to say that they are bearers of Chinese culture. But the problem with this definition is the difficulty in defining 'Chinese culture'. This leaves language as a major criterion, but this excludes all those who do not speak Chinese (whether Mandarin or a local dialect such as Hokkien). Undoubtedly, Chinese-speakers form the core of the ethnic Chinese, but there are a number of people who do not speak Chinese but are regarded as Chinese by the indigenous population (especially in Malaysia and Indonesia), because they still observe certain Chinese customs, have some Chinese personal ties (such as clan associations), or have some Chinese values.

In a macro study like this, it is not possible to check whether a particular person speaks Chinese, and if he does not, whether he observes any Chinese customs. There are too many people involved, spread over time as well as space. A more practical guide is therefore needed—

in particular, a guide to whether or not a particular capitalist can be considered Chinese.

The guide used for the pre-war period is relatively simple: practically all people who were worthy of the appellation 'Chinese' had Chinese surnames. There are, of course, a few exceptions. In the Philippines, some prominent businessmen bore Filipinized names. They belonged, however, to Chinese organizations and mingled with other Chinese (more specifically, with those who bore Chinese names), and so they could be easily included with the Chinese (for example, Albino Sycip in China Banking Corporation).

Another complication in the Philippines is that some of those who had Chinese surnames cannot be regarded as Chinese. In general, people in important posts in the government or government institutions in the pre-war period cannot be regarded as Chinese, whether or not they had Chinese names, for the fact that they held such posts meant that they were accepted by indigenous society as full-fledged members. Of course, Chinese employees of colonial governments, which did not have the support of the indigenous population, have to be excluded from this consideration, especially the Capitan China who worked for the Dutch and British colonial administrations. It was in Thailand, and in the Philippines after the establishment of the Commonwealth Government, that the government was indigenous. In Thailand, however, there were none who served the government in important posts while retaining Chinese names. In the Philippines, though, there were some such people (for example, Vidal Tan, a professor at the University of the Philippines and later its president). They were few, however, and in view of the importance of personal ties in Chinese business success in the pre-war period, it is highly unlikely that such people attained prominence in business.

Chinese names are not as useful a guide for the post-war period as for the pre-war period. It is only in Singapore and Malaysia that it is still safe to use the pre-war guide: that is, to regard only those who have Chinese surnames as Chinese. In Indonesia also, Chinese surnames can be a criterion, but not as reliably as in Singapore and Malaysia, because many so-called Chinese have adopted Indonesian names. The simplest thing to do in this case is to include all children of people who had Chinese names in the pre-war period. At that time, as in present-day Singapore and Malaysia, those who were regarded as Chinese bore Chinese names (although not all of them spoke Chinese). This criterion will lose much relevance in the future when one has to deal with the next generation. It also compels the inclusion of those who are well assimilated to indigenous society and are treated in many ways as being indigenous (like Bob Hasan). Thus, there may be the risk of being too inclusive, but the criterion is functional today, and it avoids the complicated problem of sorting one from another.

The situation in the Philippines and Thailand is similar to that in Indonesia: many of the so-called Chinese no longer bear Chinese surnames. Thus, as in Indonesia, all those whose parents had Chinese names in the pre-war period are regarded as Chinese. In the Philippines, this criterion forces the inclusion of people whose parents had Chinese names in the pre-war period but could not be regarded as Chinese for the reason pointed out earlier, but as in the pre-war period, it is highly unlikely that such people attained prominence in post-war business.

The Chinese thus include three groups. One comprises immigrants from China who speak Chinese; another, those who were born in South-East Asia and speak Chinese; and the third, possibly the largest, consists of people who were born in South-East Asia (sometimes in China) and do not speak Chinese, but who may have Chinese values (or the values of their Chinese fathers, which are substantively different from those of the indigenous population) and/or personal ties with the first two groups, which they may use to advantage in business.

Not all of those who qualify as Chinese are full-blooded Chinese. Of course, the immigrants from China are, but many of those who were born in South-East Asia, including some who speak Chinese fluently, have mixed blood. In such cases, their mothers (sometimes, their grandmothers) are indigenes. Most of the so-called *peranakan* in Indonesia and the *Baba* Chinese in Malaysia are of this type. Many Chinese Filipinos also have mixed blood, and they can be called 'mestizos', but one must be careful in using this appellation, for it also applies to Chinese of mixed blood who were assimilated to Philippine society and are no longer regarded as Chinese. Among the Thai Chinese, too, there are a large number of mixed parentage. It is only the Singapore Chinese who seem to be predominantly pure-blooded.

The immigrants came largely from South China, mainly from Fukien and Kwangtung. It is from these two provinces that the four major dialect groups (Hokkien, Teochiu, Cantonese, and Hakka) came. In the late 1930s, the largest group was Teochiu, constituting 32 per cent of the total Chinese population in South-East Asia. The next largest was Hokkien (25 per cent), the third was Cantonese (16 per cent), and the fourth was Hakka (13 per cent).[1] The Teochiu were the largest group because of their predominance in Thailand, but in the other ASEAN countries, the Hokkien were the largest group.[2]

As for the percentage of the Chinese in the total population, Victor Purcell gives the following estimates for 1960: 10 per cent for Thailand;

37 per cent for Malaysia (more precisely, the then Federation of Malaya); 75 per cent for Singapore; 2.9 per cent for Indonesia; 0.67 per cent for the Philippines; and 6 per cent for the region as a whole.[3] On the other hand, Wu and Wu's estimates for 1974 are slightly different: 8.5 per cent for Thailand; 36 per cent for Peninsular Malaysia; 72 per cent for Singapore; 2.5 per cent for Indonesia; 1.4 per cent for the Philippines; and 5.6 per cent for the region as a whole.[4] The differences between these estimates are not entirely due to the difference in the years of estimation. More importantly, they seem to be due to the difference in the definition of 'Chinese'. Nevertheless, precise figures are not very important for this study; from these estimates, some idea may be obtained about the relative size of the Chinese population.

Genesis

Chinese capitalist institutions have been predominantly the creation of Chinese immigrants and their descendants. Before the Pacific War, there were some subsidiaries and branches of capitalist institutions in China (for example, the Bank of Canton), but they were exceptional and appeared in South-East Asia relatively late, probably from the late 1910s.[5] Prior to this, possibly going back several centuries in some cases, there were representatives or agents of merchant houses (or groups) in China; but up to the mid-nineteenth century, it is highly unlikely that there were large-scale operators among them.

Chinese began coming to the region a long time ago (probably as far back as the dawn of history) to exchange such Chinese goods as silk and porcelain for aromatics, drugs, and other exotic and rare goods of the region.[6] Some of the silk sold in the region was taken to the West by Indian and Arab merchants, destined finally for Europe; and thus the trade between China and the region formed the eastern portion of the sea route for the silk trade between China and Europe. Over time, some of the Chinese traders began settling in major port cities, and when the Europeans arrived in the sixteenth and early seventeenth centuries, they found Chinese traders thinly but widely scattered throughout the region. In the next few centuries, they acted as trade intermediaries or worked as labourers and small-scale producers, first for the colonial administrations (the Court in Thailand) and then for Western merchants; and as their numbers increased, they came to dominate the market economy of the region.[7]

In the mid-nineteenth century, some Chinese merchants began to rise above the rest, among them Tan Kim Seng, Tan Tock Seng, and Whampoa of Singapore. These people understood English and grew through their business relations with European merchants or officials. For example, Tan Kim Seng's firm, Kim Seng & Co., sold tin and other Malayan produce to Western merchant houses and bought from them Western goods for local distribution. At this time, trading profits were large, so they must have made a fortune by contemporary standards; but as in the case of Guthrie discussed in the previous chapter, they were at this stage still running relatively small-scale operations (in terms of the number of employees and the amount of capital committed).

It would be best to consider the rise of Chinese capitalist institutions as a spin-off of the vast economic change that started around 1870. As discussed in the previous chapter, this was the time of the Transportation Revolution (the opening of the Suez Canal and the arrival of the steamship age), which brought Europe closer to the region. Also by this time, the environment for economic activities had changed considerably. Singapore had been a free port from its establishment in 1819; the Philippines had begun opening up to European merchants; the Bowring Treaty had established free trade in Thailand; and in Indonesia, the Agrarian Law of 1870 assured Western capital of unrestricted entry to estate agriculture. As the result of these institutional–legal and technological changes, Western capitalist institutions began to mushroom, and the market economy expanded rapidly.

The first Chinese capitalist institutions to appear in Malaya involved tin mining, and in Indonesia, sugar. These products were in great demand in the West in the late nineteenth century, so easy profits awaited those who could supply them. Their large-scale production was made possible for the Chinese by the new institutional–legal order which the colonial administrations created primarily for Western capital.

Thailand, on the other hand, had a weaker linkage with the West, being an independent country (with its own institutional–legal order) and having no attractive mineral resources. The Philippines also had a weak linkage, not with the West in general (after all, Spain is a Western country) but with the major sources of Western capital, for the Spanish Administration did not feel any urgency to develop the country with Western capital. Therefore, in both of these countries, economic change in the late nineteenth century was slower, and Chinese capitalist institutions appeared there later than in Malaya and Indonesia.

The big tin miners (such as Chung Thye Phin, Foo Choo Choon, Loke Yew, and Eu Tong Sen) and large sugar producers and traders (such as Kian Gwan of Oei Tjie Sien and his son, Oei Tiong Ham) appeared in the late nineteenth century.[8] Then, in the decades up to the late 1920s, the first wave of Chinese capitalist institutions emerged. They spread from sugar and tin to other commodities and economic activities and from Malaya and Indonesia to Thailand and the Philippines. They were not then, of course, as dynamic and powerful a force as their Western counterparts; but their rise was a significant historical event: for the first time, Chinese capital entered the superlayer of the economy which had been monopolized hitherto by Western capital.

Two types of Chinese capitalist institution emerged in this period. One was created through business relations with Western institutions (mostly business institutions). Tin and sugar were just noted; and, as described in the previous chapter, rubber became a major export in the twentieth century, attracting a large amount of Western capital into rubber plantations. Some Chinese also moved into this field (for example, Tan Chay Yan, Quek Shin, and Tan Kah Kee of Malaya, and Tjong A Fie of Sumatra). Some were large contractors for Western institutions such as plantations and governments; examples include Tjong A Fie, Chang Pi Shih of Indonesia and Malaya, and Wong Ah Fook of Singapore. Tjong A Fie and Chang Pi Shih supplied coolies for Western plantations as well as doing some contract work for them. Chang Pi Shih also acted at one time as a major provisioner for the Dutch Army during the Aceh War. Wong Ah Fook was a building contractor in Singapore and Johor Bahru and, like Tjong A Fie, also went into plantations (in his case, in Johor). These men had at their command a group of coolies, whom they used to develop their own plantations when rubber production proved to be a profitable proposition.

Some made money and developed a large organization through trading relations with Western merchants and producers. Tan Kim Seng, Tan Tock Seng, and Whampoa were the forerunners of this group. They sold the produce of the region to Western merchants and bought Western goods from them. Then, in the early twentieth century, some Chinese began developing direct contacts with merchants and producers in the West, thus bypassing Western merchants in the region.[9] In rubber trading, Tan Ean Kiam and Tan Kah Kee of Singapore, in sugar, Oei Tiong Ham of Indonesia, and in general imports, Oei Tiong Ham and the Sycip brothers (Alfonso and Albino) of the Philippines were the pioneers of direct trade. There were not enough Western merchants to represent Western manufacturers (this was especially true in the Philippines); and, besides, some Chinese merchants proved to be far more competent.

The other type of Chinese capitalist institution operated largely within the Chinese sphere. The rice traders and millers in Thailand (such as Arkon Teng and, a little later, Tan Wanglee) and in Singapore (such as Khoo Cheng Tiong, Khoo Kok Wah, and Tan Kim Ching) may have bought some rice directly from indigenous farmers (if not from other Chinese distributors), but they sold rice largely to other Chinese (either in the region or in China).[10] Then, Chinese banks began appearing to meet the financial needs (e.g. foreign exchange, short-term loans) of Chinese merchants. In Malaya, Kwong Yik Bank (1903), Sze Hai Tong Bank (1907), China Commercial Bank (1912), Ho Hong Bank (1917), and Oversea-Chinese Bank (1919); in Indonesia, Oei Tiong Ham Bank (1906) and Batavia Bank (1918); and in the Philippines, China Banking Corporation (1920) were set up in this period.[11] In Thailand, there were money-changers and pawnbrokers, but, except for a small bank (Sino-Siamese Funds, which operated for several years from 1907), no Chinese banks were set up until the early 1930s;[12] rather, Chinese banks set up in other countries moved in and met the financial needs of Chinese (such as Oversea-Chinese Bank and Sze Hai Tong Bank). Some large food and liquor producers (such as Carlos Palanca, who operated the distillery La Tondena in the Philippines, and Go Boon Kwan, who operated Ho Ho Biscuit in Singapore) also dealt primarily with small Chinese distributors, although some of their products were ultimately consumed by non-Chinese (predominantly, the indigenous).

There were also mixed types. Even the large Chinese trading companies had to deal with the small Chinese traders who collected the goods they sold to the West or distributed the goods they imported, though it was largely in their ability to deal directly with the West that their strength lay. However, in the case of large Chinese coastal and inter-island shipping companies which emerged in this period (such as Eastern Shipping, Ho Hong Steamship, and Heap Eng Moh Steamship), the demand for services came from both Chinese and Western traders.

The rise of Chinese capitalist institutions was made possible largely by the economic expansion generated by the massive inflow of Western capital that followed the Transportation Revolution and the change in the institutional–legal order. The Chinese, who had dominated the market economy, were now split into a superclass and the masses. Those who made it had business acumen, organizational ability, and personal characteristics which won them trust among the Chinese community. But in their ascent, many were helped by political patronage and monopoly concessions from the government (such as tax-farms). Especially in Indonesia and Thailand, these government connections were important in the initial phase of capital accumulation (as exemplified by the cases of Arkon Teng of Thailand and Oei Tiong Ham of Indonesia who had profitable tax-farms).[13]

Some Chinese institutions were born out of competition with Western institutions. Initially, banking services were offered to the Chinese by

Western (mostly European) banks. Language was a major barrier for Western bankers seeking direct access to Chinese traders, but they solved this problem by using Chinese compradors who could act as financial intermediaries. However, as the market economy expanded and certain trust relations developed within the Chinese community (more specifically within Chinese speech-groups such as the Hokkien group), it became possible (though difficult) to mobilize capital within the community.[14] This development enabled Chinese to set up banks, in competition with Western ones, to meet the financial needs of their community.

Initially the Chinese had little skill in banking. But to compensate, the Chinese organizers could recruit Chinese who were working in Western banks or hire Westerners for managerial positions.[15] Foreign exchange was more tricky, and some Chinese banks burned their fingers, but it was only a matter of time before the Chinese learnt this operation and did as well as Western bankers.[16] The major problem lay in setting up a non-family organization and making it a going concern, which was by no means an easy task for Chinese who were used to family organization and the primacy of family interests. The banks which emerged in this period were those which somehow managed to overcome this organizational problem (although some of them got into trouble later).

To get into direct trade was not terribly difficult, for there were a large number of Western manufacturers who were not represented in the region by Western trading houses. This was especially so in the Philippines, where there were not enough American merchants (unlike British merchants in Malaya and Dutch in Indonesia). For the Chinese, language was a major barrier; but this they could overcome by learning on their own, or by having their children educated in the West or at local Western-language medium schools.[17] In import trade, finance was another problem, but as the market economy expanded, capital became more plentiful, and the Western banking institutions could be used to make financial settlements with the suppliers in the West (if not directly, a Western bank could be used at least indirectly through a Chinese bank). There was, of course, some know-how involved in direct trade, but for those who had the determination to break into it, it was quite possible.

It was, however, difficult for Chinese to break into fields where some technology was involved and the optimum scale of production was large. Even in trading, it was difficult for Chinese to deal in technical goods because it required engineering knowledge (in order to offer a repair service). In tin mining in Malaya, although the Chinese were dominant while the tin-bearing ground was rich and could be exploited by labour-intensive techniques, around 1910, when the rich surface deposits became scarce and it became necessary to rely on dredging machines to rework the old mines or operate in the swampy areas where it was difficult to use manual labour, they lost ground to British capital, being unable to raise the large initial capital required for the large optimum scale of a dredging operation.[18] Their community was still relatively capital-poor (at least in comparison with the business community of the West).

The disadvantage of the Chinese with regard to capital and technology had manifested itself earlier in tin smelting, which turned out to be more efficient by capital-intensive methods than by traditional methods (this was proven by the ascent of Straits Trading). Also, the optimum scale for sugar-cane production and sugar milling was large, so only a few Chinese could break in. In rubber production, although the economy of scale was not so absolute as in tin smelting and tin mining (after the rich surface deposits were exhausted), there were certain advantages in estate production, and again, capital acted as a barrier to the Chinese.

The barrier to the Chinese was not so much the size of capital as the amount of initial capital required for entry. This is clearly demonstrated in the ascent of the Chinese in rice milling in Thailand.[19] After the Bowring Treaty, Western merchants brought rice-milling machines to Thailand, and initially had the upper hand over the Chinese, to whom power-driven machines were unfamiliar and expensive. However, the technology of rice milling was not complex; and after solving the initial technical problems by hiring European technicians, the Chinese soon mastered the necessary skills. Furthermore, the optimum scale of rice milling was relatively small (smaller at least than those of tin smelting, sugar milling, and tin dredging), so that the Chinese could start with relatively small capital, and if successful, they could expand production (so owning several mills). The Chinese monopolized rice distribution, but this was not an absolute factor in their ascent in rice milling, for if it had been, the same thing should have happened in tin smelting in Malaya where, despite the Chinese monopoly of tin supply, small Chinese tin smelters lost out to the two large European tin smelters, Straits Trading and Eastern Smelting.[20]

The problems Chinese capital faced in competition with Western capital were partly caused by the discriminatory policy of the colonial administrations. For example, in Malaya, the government granted the new tin smelter, Straits Trading, a monopoly of tin ore exports from Selangor and Sungei Ujong in its first several years of operation.[21] Also, in the early years of the twentieth century, it became no longer possible to open a mine without a licence, and in issuing licences to dredging companies, the government favoured British capital.[22] Furthermore, the land regulations of 1897 operated against Chinese and in the interests of British capital in setting up plantations.[23] After all, this was the colonial period, and in the fields where Chinese and Western capital were in competition, the colonial administrations adopted discriminatory policies. Although the discrimination was not as blatant as some would claim, it was clearly an important factor inhibiting the growth of Chinese capital.

Expansion

The Great Depression which started in 1929 not only stopped the expansion of Western capital in South-East Asia, it also affected Chinese capital. The environment of economic expansion had been an important contribution to the rise of Chinese capital, so the Depression could only be a negative factor for Chinese capital in the 1930s. But, in retrospect, it seems to have had rationalizing effects on Chinese capital and functioned as a positive factor later, when the economy began expanding again. Even in the 1930s, it did not prevent Chinese capital from expanding in the areas on which the Depression had little direct impact.

It was true, of course, that a number of Chinese businesses folded up during the Depression. In Singapore, for example, some banks, especially those engaged in foreign exchange, were hit hard and dissolved shortly afterwards; Tan Kah Kee's business empire got into trouble and was finally liquidated in 1934; the Ho Hong group, which had been slowly declining since its height in the late 1910s, virtually disappeared after the Ho Hong Bank got into difficulties and merged with other banks. In their place, however, emerged more viable Chinese companies. For example, the Oversea-Chinese Banking Corporation (OCBC) was formed in 1932 as the result of the merger of three banks which were facing financial problems; and Lee Kong Chian's Lee Rubber really got off the ground at this time by taking over the factories and businesses of rubber traders in trouble (like Tan Kah Kee). Both OCBC and Lee Rubber became dynamic capitalist institutions in the post-war period, but this would not have been possible without the Depression which forced them to make innovations and blend them with traditional Chinese ownership and management practices.

Some Chinese companies seem to have adjusted better to the Depression than Western companies. For one thing, since they had few professional managers, they had lower overhead costs. And being owner–managers, they had more flexibility in restructuring management and mapping out a new strategy. Kian Gwan, for example, which was hard hit by the Depression because of its heavy reliance on sugar, managed to produce profits even in sugar from the mid-1930s, and also expanded into other products such as pepper and rubber.[24]

Areas not directly affected by the Depression saw the birth of new capitalist institutions. In Thailand, for example, some large Chinese traders began moving into banking: it was in the first half of the 1930s that Wanglee Bank (then called Wanglee Chan Bank), Tan Pen Choon Bank, Thye San Bank, and a few others (altogether about seven banks) were set up. Many of them were rice traders like the Wanglees, who had grown in rice trading and later expanded into real estate and other fields. In the case of the Wanglees, banking was not the only modern business into which they went. In the 1930s and the early 1940s, they formed a shipping company and two insurance companies (Thai Commercial Insurance and Luang Lee Insurance, which was later renamed Wanglee Insurance).[25]

If the Depression stopped the expansion of Western capital, the Pacific War administered a devastating blow. With the Japanese occupation of the region, all remaining Westerners were imprisoned, and the assets of all Western companies were confiscated, if they had not already been destroyed or transferred abroad. It is true that the Western powers returned after Japan was defeated, but the Pacific War was not merely a short-term, disruptive event in South-East Asian history. It set in motion political forces that ultimately caused the decline of Western political influence and the eventual political independence of the former colonies.

Even the imminent possibility of war began having effects on Western capital in the late 1930s. In the Philippines, for example, the American owners of Pacific Commercial Co. decided to liquidate the company in 1939, and its agencies were transferred to other trading companies. One of the beneficiaries of this was Yutivo Sons Hardware which obtained part of its agency for the distribution of General Motors. From this, Yutivo went on to become its exclusive distributor in the early post-war period, and its assembler when the import-substitution policy began.[26]

Thailand saw little fighting during the Pacific War, and because it had depended less on Western capital for its development in the pre-war period, the war created less disruption there than in the other South-East Asian countries. A great deal of activity was therefore going on in the market economy, and towards the end of the war, the demand for banking services could not be met by the few Thai banks that had been set up in the pre-war period (most of the Chinese banks had been liquidated before the war). Thus, in 1944 and 1945, the Bangkok Bank of Commerce, Bangkok Bank, Bank of Ayudhya, and Thai Farmers Bank were set up. In the post-war period, these banks developed under the protection of the government to become the country's major banks (today, Bangkok Bank is the largest Thai bank, and Thai Farmers Bank is the second largest private bank).

As explained in Chapter 2, the post-war period has been one of decline for Western capital, but for Chinese capital, it has been one of expansion. Being an element of domestic capital, it benefited from the nationalization of Western capital, restrictions on the entry and operation of foreign capital, and protection and promotion of domestic capital—the measures the South-East Asian governments launched after independence to put the economy on a new development path. It is true that it was a target of discrimination at one time or another (except in Singapore), but it received distinctly better treatment than Western capital.

Examples of how the government measures promoted Chinese capital are many and span many industries (e.g. banking, insurance, real estate, plantation agriculture, manufacturing). To cite just a few: Indocement in Indonesia is headed by the Chinese capitalist, Liem Sioe Liong, who built his first cement plant in 1975 and seven more in the next decade, resulting in a total capacity of 7.7 million tons a year in 1987. The eight plants are in one location (Cibinong near Jakarta) and constitute the biggest cement complex in Asia. The total investment in this project is estimated to have been around $1 billion. There are three foreign companies producing cement, but their combined total production capacity of 3.2 million tons a year is less than half that of Indocement.[27] There are many reasons why Liem could build such a large cement group, but the key was his ability to get funding from state banks. The Indonesian Government was flush with petrodollars in the 1970s and early 1980s and offered part of it as industrial loans. Liem was a large beneficiary of this. More recently, when he found that his plants were suffering from overcapacity (in 1985, the utilization rate of his cement plants was less than 50 per cent), he asked the government for relief from his interest payments, which, with such low utilization rate, had become a terrible burden despite being at well below the market rate, and the government responded by buying 35 per cent of Indocement's equity.

In banking, Thailand offered the most favourable environment for Chinese capital. In 1938, there were more foreign banks than Thai banks. About ten years later (1949), the situation was reversed, with 13 Thai banks and 10 foreign banks. The turnabout was even more remarkable in terms of the number of branches: the 13 Thai banks had 41 branches whereas the 10 foreign banks had only 11 branches (both include their head offices). In the following thirty-five years, the number of foreign banks has increased to 14 with 20 branches, whereas Thai banks have increased to 16 with 1,816 branches.[28] Most of these banks are Chinese banks (e.g. Bangkok Bank, Thai Farmers Bank, Bangkok Metropolitan Bank). As noted in Chapter 2, foreign banks are insignificant in Thai banking today. What made this dramatic transformation possible is, besides the business acumen of the Chinese, the government restriction on the entry and operation of foreign banks.

In manufacturing, protection from import competition, restriction on foreign entry, low-interest loans from government financial institutions (and government guarantees of foreign loans carrying lower interest), and other incentives (such as tax exemption) were a great inducement for Chinese capital. For foreign companies with a clear advantage in technology, entry restriction meant that they had to share it with South-East Asian, especially Chinese, capitalists. In some cases, this meant licensed production without foreign equity participation. In others, it meant a joint-venture agreement. In the latter, when the level of technology involved was not high, the Chinese capitalist often came eventually to control the company by buying out the equity of his foreign partner; examples include Sukri Bodhiratanangkura in Thailand (textiles) and The Ning King in Indonesia (textiles and steel).[29]

Although far less important than the government measures to protect and promote South-East Asian capital, Japanese entry helped Chinese capital to forge ahead. In the early post-war years, Japanese trading companies either had not yet returned or were handicapped *vis-à-vis* Western trading companies in terms of the amount of capital they could command or the degree of freedom given them by South-East Asian governments. Thus, Japanese manufacturers had to depend on Western or Chinese trading companies to penetrate the market, but it was more difficult to depend on the former, which had established connections with Western manufacturers. On the other hand, less well-established Chinese capitalists were more willing to link up with Japanese manufacturers, who were still groping their way in the region. For example, the Siam Motor group of Thailand and the Hong Leong group of Singapore made contact with Japanese companies at that time and grew with them in the subsequent years. More recently, with the increased popularity of Japanese products, Western trading companies have started to distribute some Japanese products; but as shown in UMW's take-over of the Toyota agency from Inchcape in Malaysia, some Chinese companies have snatched the distribution rights of

Japanese products from Western trading companies. If, for example, Toyota executives, like those of Western manufacturers, had had closer personal ties with the executives of Inchcape, having often wined and dined with them, UMW's coup would have been more difficult.[30]

The rise of some Chinese companies had nothing to do with government protection of domestic capital. Some Singapore Chinese (such as Lee Kong Chian, Tan Lark Sye, Ko Teck Kin, and Ng Quee Lam) became dominant forces in rubber trading in the 1950s—when Singapore was still under British rule. In addition to rubber trading, Lee Kong Chian had large interests in rubber production, rubber processing, pineapples, sawmills, oil-mills, and biscuits (Lee Rubber Estates, Lee Pineapple, Lee Sawmills, Lee Oil-mills, Lee Biscuits, etc.).[31] Also in the 1950s, OCBC expanded under the chairmanship of Lee Kong Chian, and the OCBC group took over such British companies as Fraser & Neave, Malayan Breweries, and Great Eastern Life Assurance.

The combination of Chinese business acumen and the governments' nationalistic policy seems to have made Chinese capital the most important element of capital in South-East Asia, although it is difficult to show this quantitatively, for the reasons pointed out in connection with Table 2.1. Thus, at this stage, the best one can do is to give qualitative, somewhat impressionistic indicators. This is done in Table 3.1, where the relative positions of foreign, Chinese, and private indigenous capital are measured on a ten-point scale. As in Table 2.1, no entry indicates a score of less than 1.0; 'minor', 1.0–2.4; 'moderate', 2.5–3.9; 'substantial', 4.0–7.4; 'dominant', 7.5 or above.

In no major area is private indigenous capital more important than Chinese capital. At best, it is of equal importance in a few areas. In comparing the two, however, one has to keep in mind differences between countries. In Singapore, it is not surprising that Chinese capital completely dominates indigenous capital, for the Chinese constitute three-quarters of the population.[32] In Thailand, the Chinese, though a minority group, dominate its capitalism. If the Siam group (Siam Cement and Siam Commercial Bank) is not regarded as a purely private group since it is controlled by the Crown Property Bureau, there are only two significant capitalist institutions left: a brewery (Boon Rawd) and a construction company (Italian–Thai Development Corp.).

In Indonesia, indigenous capitalists are more important, but they are much less significant than Chinese: for example, among the top ten private banks, there is only one indigenous-controlled bank (Bank Niaga), and among the large manufacturing companies, Bakrie is the only major group, though there are several other more obscure

TABLE 3.1

The Relative Position of Chinese Capital

Industry	Foreign Capital	Chinese Capital	Private Indigenous Capital
Banking	moderate	substantial/ dominant	moderate/ substantial
Property Development		substantial	substantial
Construction	moderate	moderate	moderate
Mining	moderate	moderate/ substantial	moderate
Oil Exploration	dominant		
Plantation Agriculture	minor	substantial	moderate/ substantial
Export/Import Trade	substantial	substantial	minor
Manufacturing	substantial	substantial	minor
Light Industries	minor	dominant	minor
Machinery	substantial	substantial	minor
Metals & Petrochemicals	dominant	minor	

indigenous-owned manufacturing companies.[33] The indigenes (called *pribumi*) are, however, more significant in construction and the oil service industry—the industries which are tied to the government (in the latter case, to Pertamina, the state oil company).[34]

In Malaysia, since the New Economic Policy was launched in 1971, a number of new indigenous (called bumiputra) capitalists have emerged and become more prominent, especially in finance and real estate; but apparently the Chinese still have the upper hand. As late as 1983, bumiputra investors owned only 7.6 per cent of the equity of the corporate sector, whereas the Chinese owned about 45 per cent.[35]

It is only in Philippine capitalism that the indigenous may be more significant than the Chinese. In banking, for example—although it is somewhat difficult to determine which banks are still private, since some are now under government receivership (either as a result of financial trouble in the past few years or because their controlling shares were owned by cronies of former President Marcos)—out of the top ten which seem still to be in private hands, seven are owned by the indigenous and three by the Chinese.[36] The relative position of Chinese capital in Philippine capitalism as a whole is more difficult to determine, since there has been a great shake-up in corporate owner-ship in the past few years due to economic trouble and the govern-ment's sequestration of Marcos's cronies' equity. However, in view of the existence of a number of indigenous groups (topped by the Ayala group), indigenous capital in the Philippines is much stronger than in the other South-East Asian countries.[37]

The superiority of Chinese capital over foreign capital is less clear-cut than its superiority over indigenous capital. But as a whole, Chinese capital seems to be a more important element of South-East Asian capital than foreign capital. This is clear, as shown in Table 3.1 in terms of industrial coverage. Because foreign capital has been restricted in entry as well as in operation, it is only in areas where it has distinct advantages over South-East Asian capital that it is allowed on a sub-stantial scale and is equivalent or even superior to Chinese capital in importance. These advantages, which are based on technology, capi-tal, or marketing, explain the roughly equal significance of Chinese and foreign capital in construction, export/import trade, and manufacturing. In capital-intensive steel production and petrochemicals (including petroleum refining), foreign capital is dominant, though some Chinese capital is involved (in steel). But this is greatly offset by Chinese domi-nance in light industry. Certainly, the amount of capital involved in, for example, a single textile mill may not be very much, but when there are many such mills controlled by the Chinese (this is especially the case in Indonesia, Thailand, and the Philippines), the total sum must be substantial. There is also the large investment in Indocement (discussed earlier), which was larger than the total Japanese capital committed to the petrochemical complex in Singapore.[38] In undertaking such large industrial ventures, as discussed earlier, the Chinese were greatly helped by the governments' willingness to channel petrodollars, general government revenues, and development assistance as well as to guarantee private foreign loans to manufacturing industry.

Advantages

If economic nationalism caused the decline of foreign capital and the rise of domestic capital, the question naturally arises: why did indigenous capital, the more favoured element of domestic capital, not do as well as Chinese capital? It is not, however, only in capitalism but also in the market economy that the Chinese fare better, so the question can be rephrased as why the Chinese do better in economic competition with the indigenous. One answer is that the Chinese have long had well-structured, extensive business networks. For example, the present

Prime Minister of Malaysia, Mahathir Mohamad, attributed the absence of the bumiputra in business before the NEP to their lack of networks.[39] And Lance Castles, in studying the Chinese take-over of the *kretek* cigarette industry in Kudus, Java, once a pribumi domain, cited the availability of a better business network as a major reason.[40]

Networks

The lack of a business network was, until recent years, a major obstacle even to an indigene with the personal attributes required for business success. In starting business, for example, he would have no one who could help him to get training, for his father and his relatives would probably be peasants. If he approached an established business organization and actually managed to get a job, it would be a lowly one, the experience of which would hardly be sufficient to embark on any significant business on his own.

Capital was also a major problem for the indigene, unlike for the Chinese, who had a network through which to find someone who could help him get started in business. In pre-war Malaya and Indonesia, for example, there was no bank to which the indigenous could go for help. He could not approach a Chinese bank, since the Chinese did business only among themselves. Even if he could find someone willing to lend him money, he had to pay higher interest rates. It was also difficult for the indigene to obtain supplies on credit, since it was the Chinese who monopolized the distribution network and they did not trust indigenous traders.

In some areas where the Chinese did not penetrate, either by choice (this was especially so in the Philippines where the Chinese had to concentrate on lucrative areas because their number was small due to restricted immigration) or because of exclusion by the colonial government, indigenous traders emerged and developed their own networks, but these were weak compared with Chinese networks. For one thing, an indigenous network tended to be location-specific, since it could not easily transcend an ethnic group. In contrast, a Chinese network could much more easily link up with a national or even an international network. A Hokkien network in a town in East Java, for example, could be linked to another Hokkien network in a town in Sumatra, and if necessary, to the one in Singapore or any other place where there were Hokkiens.[41]

In understanding Chinese networks, it is important to bear in mind that, in the pre-war period, these excluded not only the indigenous but also many other Chinese. The broadest group was a speech-group

(Hokkien, Teochiu, etc.). In addition, there were narrower groups based on other ties, such as native place. In the post-war period, these ties loosened and new ties formed in the new places of residence, resulting in networks having a broader base than the speech-group, though not usually broad enough to include non-Chinese.

In the pre-war period, not every one who spoke, for example, Hokkien, could belong to a Hokkien network. Of course, ability to speak Hokkien and possession of a 'Hokkien personality' were necessary conditions for entry to that network, but a number of other conditions had to be met. The most crucial of these was what the Chinese call *shinyung* (trustworthiness).[42] This was important because business was often done with a verbal promise and because even if there was a contract, its enforcement was inefficient and costly when it was broken (at least, this was how the Chinese perceived the administrative justice in their countries of residence).[43] A Chinese with shinyung would not break a promise or contract, so only such people were kept in the network.

None had shinyung from the beginning. Those who wanted to enter business had to go through a training period, and only those who finished it successfully could enter a network with the endorsement of their masters. Then, in the course of their career, they could either lose shinyung and drop out of business, or win greater shinyung and establish themselves as traders. There was always a possibility that someone with a certain amount of shinyung could cheat the network or fail it unwillingly, but it was minimized by the fact that the Chinese formed a close, minority community. Being a minority, business and social life were so intertwined that severe social sanctions were imposed on those who were dishonest in business. But at the same time, gossip was exchanged at social gatherings and at the meetings of trade and other business associations, and any worthwhile information (often negative) was fed back to the network so that it could adjust its evaluation of its members' shinyung.

As pointed out above, the organizational basis of networks changed over time, and what was true in the pre-war period no longer holds.[44] But Chinese business networks still exist, and they still operate on the basis of shinyung. The indigenous, who have never been given a chance to prove themselves, are excluded from these networks and cannot compete with the Chinese on an equal basis. In the post-war period, some South-East Asian governments established banks, trading companies, and other institutions to break the Chinese monopoly on networks, but these efforts were not enough to counterbalance the disadvantages the indigenous face in competition with the Chinese.

One might think that if the indigenous were barred from Chinese networks, they could have used a foreign network. In general, this was difficult before the government began taking measures to promote indigenous entrepreneurship, but in the Philippines, it was possible even in the pre-war period. The Philippine situation was unique in some ways. First of all, the Chinese population was small because the American Administration restricted Chinese immigration to prevent the Chinese from using the Philippines as a gateway to the United States.[45] As a consequence, the Chinese could not penetrate all sectors of the economy. Secondly, the United States, having little experience in colonization, was both a little naïve and idealistic, so that as a colonizer, it did a great deal to help the Filipinos become an independent nation. One consequence of this was that a number of university-educated Filipinos worked with American companies and later started their own businesses. Thirdly, the indigenous group included the mestizos, who were more willing to take advantage of new opportunities (including commercial opportunities) than the non-mestizo indigenous group. Some of these people mingled freely with the foreign business community and were helped by foreign contacts.[46]

Institutional Constraints

Although the Philippine situation was somewhat unique, the indigenous could not, in general, develop business networks. In Thailand, one reason for this may have been the constraints the government imposed on the Thais and the liberal treatment it accorded Chinese immigrants. In particular, the government required peasants to perform corvée labour, which meant that they could not leave their villages for the entire year. It can be argued that this corvée obligation handicapped the Thais who wished to enter business. At the same time, the Chinese were more lightly taxed than the indigenous, because the government wanted to induce Chinese immigration; and this tax discrimination may also be argued to have also worked against the Thais.[47]

These constraints may have discouraged Thais from entering business; but similar constraints were absent in the other South-East Asian countries, where there were, in fact, more constraints on the Chinese than on the indigenous. In those countries, restrictions were placed, for example, on Chinese travel and residence: the Chinese were required to live in designated areas and to obtain permits to travel to other areas. It is true that these were gradually removed, but in Java, they remained until as late as 1919 (and this freedom was extended to the Outer Provinces in 1926).[48] There were also similar restrictions in the Philippines during the Spanish period, though they were removed earlier than in Java (in the mid-nineteenth century).[49]

If tradition can be considered an institutional factor, it may be thought that underdevelopment of the indigenous market economy before the sixteenth century was a constraining factor. Because of such underdevelopment, one might argue that the colonial administrations and the Thai Government encouraged more experienced and dynamic Chinese to come to the region, thereby nipping in the bud the potential of the indigenous to expand the market economy. As a consequence, the argument goes, business tradition could not evolve among the indigenous to serve them as a useful guide or instrument.

Two objections can be raised against this argument. One concerns the assumption that the indigenous market was underdeveloped before the sixteenth century. Some might argue that there were indigenous traders operating not only in local markets but also in international circuits.[50] In particular, the robustness of trade in Melaka in the fifteenth century does not seem to accord well with the postulate that the market economy of the region was underdeveloped. In general, though, the underdevelopment thesis seems correct for the region as a whole.

The point here is not whether the market economy existed, but whether or not it was developed. It seems to have been underdeveloped compared with, say, the contemporary market economy of China. As a market economy develops, the quantity of money in circulation increases; instruments of credit (such as promissory notes and bills of exchange) appear and proliferate; contracts are signed when agreements are reached; written records are kept of commercial transactions and a method of bookkeeping develops; and devices to simplify and speed up calculation become widely used. All these had taken place in China (and India and Japan) by the fifteenth century, but not in South-East Asia (at least, there is no evidence to this effect). So, it seems that the market economy which existed in the region at that time was based mainly on barter trade and was of limited extent, for a greater volume of exchange would have necessitated the developments just outlined.

Objection could also be raised against the assumption that the Chinese were more dynamic in business than the indigenous. This is another way of saying that the Chinese were more responsive to commercial opportunities and more willing to work hard to exploit them for profits. Many observers have held this assumption to be true and considered it to be the major reason for Chinese business success.[51]

One thing that has to be remembered, however, is that the Chinese are not innately commercially oriented and hard-working. Certainly, the majority of Chinese in China were not like that. But the Chinese in South-East Asia may have had these qualities, at least more so on the average than the indigenous in the pre-war period, partly because the bulk of them were immigrants who were lured by better economic opportunities and wanted eventually to return to China. Of course, they did not start from scratch but were helped by existing networks and this makes it difficult to determine how independent their value orientation was. It appears to have been an important factor, however. In the Philippines, for example, the Chinese mestizos (who were treated like the indigenous by the Spanish Administration) tended to dominate business whenever the number of Chinese shrank due to expulsion and restriction of immigration, and to be displaced from the areas the Chinese re-entered when they were allowed to return.[52] In Malaya, the Chinese took over tin mining from the Malays in the mid-nineteenth century, which again seemed to have little to do with networks.

Another factor is the nature of indigenous society, which is also related to the underdevelopment of the indigenous market economy. As discussed earlier, the dominance of the Chinese in the market economy was possibly due to the initial underdevelopment of the indigenous market economy; but the underdevelopment itself may have been due to the value orientation of the indigenous, who emphasized leisure and the adaptation of man to nature. Historically, the population density of the region was low, and nature was bountiful, so that there was no need for the indigenous to work hard for a living—at least not as hard as the Chinese in South China, which had a higher population density and was sometimes stricken by natural disasters. This South-East Asian environment could, under different circumstances, have led to an abundance of surplus goods and the development of the market economy; but possibly because of the humid tropical climate, people seem to have preferred to do less physical work and be content with fewer material comforts.

After a long period of stay, and also from the second generation onwards, the Chinese tended not to work hard for money. After all, such a life was not enjoyable, and a number of Chinese opted, at least partially, for an indigenous way of life.[53] In Thailand and the Philippines, this could be accomplished relatively easily by marrying and being absorbed into indigenous society (absorption did not often follow marriage for the first generation, but from the second generation, it was quite common, even if the father remained within the Chinese community). Nevertheless, in the pre-war period, a constant influx of new immigrants kept alive the work ethic and commercial orientation of the Chinese community. In the early post-war years, the inflow of Chinese stopped (which is bound to have serious effects on the value system of the Chinese in the long run), but the work ethnic and commercial orientation were kept alive as a matter of survival in the countries where the Chinese were discriminated against, their lives and properties were threatened, and their future was uncertain.

In sum, the Chinese had tremendous advantages over the indigenous because they had networks which helped them to get training, a start in business, and credit, supplies, and information. These networks were formed initially by speech- and native-place groups, but in the post-war period, as the Chinese began developing an identity with their places or countries of residence in South-East Asia, the organizing principles of networks changed. Nevertheless, networks still exist, still exclude the indigenous, and their importance should not be underestimated. However, they do not seem to be the only reason for Chinese strength in business. The built-in bias of indigenous society against plain money-making and toward non-materialistic aspects of life; the fact that the Chinese communities were, until recently, constantly being replenished with immigrants who were willing to work hard to make money; and the social pressure which forced the Chinese from the second generation onwards to adopt the value system of their immigrant ancestors as a matter of survival—these seem to have conjoined to make the Chinese a more dynamic element of the South-East Asian economy.

Government Reaction

While Chinese dominance in capitalism and the market economy has presented no problems to the government of Singapore, where the Chinese constitute a large majority, the governments of the other four countries, where the Chinese are a minority, have not always been happy about it and have taken discriminatory measures at one time or another.

The earliest reaction came from the Thai Government. From the late 1930s to the mid-1950s, under Phibul Songkhram, the government intervened in the economy to reduce dependence on foreign (including Chinese) capital. Thai Rice Co., which was set up in 1938 to take over the Chinese-controlled rice industry, then the kingdom's major industry, was the first major state enterprise. In the following years government intervention accelerated, and by the mid-1950s there were numerous state-owned or state-controlled companies in manufacturing, public utilities, commerce, and services. It was, however, in manufacturing that government involvement was most extensive. Directly through its ministries or through the National Economic Development Corp., the government monopolized tobacco, spirits, and playing-cards, dominated timber, sugar, paper, and gunny sacks; and had large stakes in cement, glass, pharmaceuticals, batteries, and textiles.[54]

Philippine reaction was different. Instead of state enterprises, the Philippine Government promoted the private indigenous sector: for example, it restricted the allocation of foreign exchange to the Chinese (the Import Control Act of 1950) and barred the Chinese from certain sectors of the economy (the Retail Nationalization Law and Rice and Corn Nationalization Law). In implementing these laws the Philippine Government was quite legalistic, unlike the Indonesian Government, which will be discussed shortly. The Chinese targets of this legislation were those without citizenship. This approach would not have worked if there had been too many Chinese with citizenship; but at the time of independence, most Chinese did not have Philippine citizenship, and in the following years, the Philippine Government imposed tough requirements for naturalization. Citizenship was based on *jus sanguinis*, so that people of Chinese parentage remained Chinese. Those who were wealthy enough could secure naturalization, and though they faced some discrimination, they were treated more or less like Filipinos in dealings with the government (to obtain licences, financial assistance, etc.). The majority, however, could not obtain citizenship and suffered under those nationalistic laws until the mid-1970s, when President Marcos, during the martial law period, liberalized naturalization requirements.[55]

In the first several years, the Indonesian Government also tried to reduce dependence on the Chinese by promoting indigenous entrepreneurship. Like the Import Control Act of the Philippines, the Benteng Programme, which started in 1950, gave preference to pribumi traders in the allocation of foreign exchange. The Chinese discriminated against in Indonesia, however, included Indonesian citizens, not just those without citizenship as in the Philippines. Then, in the mid-1950s, having turned away from the policy to explicitly promote indigenous entrepreneurship, the Indonesian Government decided to statize the economy, thus preventing the Chinese from dominating the economy even after foreign capital was expelled. This, apparently, was not enough to quell fear of the Chinese. In November 1959, the government issued a directive, called Regulation No. 10, barring Chinese traders from the rural areas. Although not enforced throughout the country, it was quite disruptive; and in West Java, where the Sundanese suffered from competition with the Chinese, its implementation was rather thorough. Furthermore, in 1961, the government nationalized the then largest Chinese concern, Kian Gwan.[56]

Soon after Suharto came into power, Chinese capital became part of domestic capital, and discrimination stopped (at least in business). As a result, the Chinese again became a dynamic element of the Indonesian economy, expanding into various fields which the new economic policy opened up. The Chinese did so well in this period that anti-Chinese feelings again heightened among the pribumi. Combined with other factors, this led to the Malari Riot during Japanese Prime Minister Tanaka's visit in January 1974. This incident forced the government to revise its economic policy and announce a pribumi policy as one of the remedial measures. This still remains in effect (though less explicitly than in the mid-1970s when it was first announced); but it lacks clear-cut programmes like those of the New Economic Policy in Malaysia and has not been very effective in reducing the Chinese position in the Indonesian economy.[57]

In Malaysia, the government took its first steps to promote indigenous entrepreneurship in the 1960s: for example, it discriminated against the Chinese in favour of the bumiputra in areas where government licences were needed (such as timber concessions, taxis, and land transportation), and it set up a state-owned bank, Bank Bumiputra, for bumiputra businessmen, who had hitherto been neglected by the Chinese banks. Otherwise, the government remained generally non-interventionist.[58] It was only after the May 1969 riot that it started thinking seriously about speeding up bumiputra participation in the modern sector of the economy; and its new policy, commonly referred to as the New Economic Policy, was enunciated for the first time in the Second Malaysia Plan (1971–5). Compared with the other South-East Asian countries, government reaction was late in Malaysia; but when it came, the government acted forcefully. It set 1990 as its target year to achieve 30 per cent bumiputra participation in the corporate sector of the economy, and began setting up a number of state enterprises (such as Pernas, Petronas, and HICOM) and channelling petro-dollars and tax revenues to newly fostered bumiputra entrepreneurs. This pro-bumiputra policy remains in full force.[59]

In Thailand, anti-Chinese policy was abandoned in the late 1950s, and the Chinese are now treated as full-fledged members of Thai society. In the Philippines, discrimination continued until the mid-1970s, but thereafter, with naturalization liberalized, more and more Chinese became Philippine citizens and came to be treated like other Filipinos in business. Today, the bulk of the former Chinese have been naturalized. In the Philippines, however, unlike in Thailand, anti-Chinese feelings remain, especially in social fields, though it is not as strong as in Malaysia and Indonesia.

In Thailand and the Philippines, the Chinese problem has subsided partly because the dividing line between the Chinese and the indigenous is not as clear-cut as in Malaysia and Indonesia, where Islam is often perceived to be a divisive factor. In Thailand and the Philippines, religion plays no such role. There are a number of Chinese Buddhists in Thailand, and, in the view of the Chinese community, Buddhism is not as demanding a religion as Islam (for example, there is no prohibition on pork, which the Chinese like to eat). In the Philippines, Catholicism, the major religion of the Filipinos, has also attracted a number of Chinese. As a consequence, in both Thailand and the Philippines, the dividing line is considerably blurred (more so in Thailand than in the Philippines). [60]

The need for economic rationality may have been an additional factor. The unavailability of mineral and forest resources in Thailand and the Philippines must have increased these economies' dependence on the Chinese and suppressed discrimination. In the Philippines, for example, the sharp increase in oil prices and the depletion of mineral and forest resources in the mid-1970s seem to have been major, albeit possibly indirect, factors behind the government's decision to liberalize naturalization requirements in order to better utilize Chinese manpower. In Indonesia and Malaysia, on the other hand, the availability of oil and other resources probably reduced the need for economic rationality.

Of course, economic rationality cannot provide a full explanation. In Indonesia and Malaysia, Chinese policy has changed over time, despite the fact that Islam continues to be perceived as a clear dividing line between the indigenous and the Chinese and that resources have been, at least potentially, available for export. This policy change has to be explained by other factors. Why, for example, has Suharto been more liberal towards the Chinese than Sukarno was? And why did government policy have to change around 1970 in Malaysia? Need for economic rationality cannot answer these questions, but it has acted as a constraint on the government in shaping economic policy, at least in the past two decades.

Indonesia has oil and other resources, but at the same time there is a huge, inefficient state sector. The availability of resources has kept this sector not only alive but expanding (at least until the early 1980s when oil prices began to drop), but the government could not be too wasteful in managing the economy. To counterbalance the inefficient state sector, the country needed a dynamic private sector, in which the Chinese have been indispensable. At the same time, the existence of a large state sector has prevented the Chinese from dominating the superlayer of the economy, which has exonerated the government from the charge that the Chinese dominate the economy.

In Malaysia, anti-Chinese discrimination has been stronger in the past fifteen years or so than in any other South-East Asian country. This does not mean, however, that economic rationality is disregarded. When the government started the New Economic Policy, Malays owned only 1.0 per cent of the total equity of the corporate sector. Even if government and other Malay interests were added, Malay ownership increased only to 2.0 per cent.[61] What the government did, then, was to change the rules of the game such that Malays could acquire their 'due' share of the economy. This, of course, has appeared strongly discriminatory to the Chinese, who had been used to a non-interventionist government. Probably rightly, they fear that this type of policy might escalate, for example, with the target for Malay corporate ownership being raised well over the 30 per cent set forth in the Second Malaysia Plan.[62] Comparatively, though, Chinese discrimination has been less severe than in Indonesia during the Sukarno period or in the Philippines in the 1950s and 1960s. The Malaysian Government cannot disregard economic rationality, or at least has not done so thus far. This factor gains added significance whenever natural resources become scarce or their prices in the world economy decline. The recently announced postponement of the target year (to achieve 30 per cent bumiputra ownership) can be best understood within this framework.

One can then argue that need for economic rationality has constrained the South-East Asian governments from radically changing ownership structure; and this constraint, despite the fact that the Chinese are not fully acceptable to the indigenous (perhaps Thailand is an exception), has enabled the Chinese to dominate the capitalism of South-East Asia. Economic rationality is, of course, bounded rationality. It has been accepted as almost imperative in countries without resources, but it has been diluted in countries with resources. Even the latter, however, have been able to depend on resources for economic management only to a limited extent, beyond which economic rationality has come into play.

1. D. J. M. Tate, *The Making of Modern South-East Asia*, Vol. 2: *The Western Impact, Economic and Social Change*, Kuala Lumpur, Oxford University Press, 1979, p. 20. The author has not seen more recent figures.

2. Suyama Taku *et al.*, *Kakyo*, Tokyo, Nihon Hoso Shuppan Kyokai, 1972, p. 72. The original source is *Huaqiao Jingji Wenti*, Taipei, 1963.

3. Victor Purcell, *The Chinese in Southeast Asia,* reprinted Kuala Lumpur, Oxford University Press, 1980, p. 3.

4. Yuan-li Wu and Chun-hsi Wu, *Economic Development in Southeast Asia: The Chinese Dimension,* Stanford, Hoover Institution Press, 1980. For other estimates, see Lea E. Williams, *The Future of Overseas Chinese in Southeast Asia,* New York, McGraw-Hill, 1966; and G. William Skinner, 'Report on the Chinese in Southeast Asia', Southeast Asian Program, Cornell University, 1950.

5. The Bank of Canton established a branch in Bangkok in 1918. This was possibly the first South-East Asian branch of a capitalist institution in China. Other Chinese capitalist institutions which expanded to the region were Bank of China and Bank of Communications.

6. There are a number of writings on Chinese trade with South-East Asia. For example, see John S. Guy, *Oriental Trade Ceramics in South-East Asia: Ninth to Sixteenth Centuries,* Singapore, Oxford University Press, 1986; and on a more recent period, Sarasin Viraphol, *Tribute and Profit: Sino-Siamese Trade, 1652–1853,* Cambridge, Council on East Asian Studies, Harvard University, 1977. On the trade between South-East Asia and the Arab world (and Europe), see Fernand Braudel, *Civilization and Capitalism, 15th–18th Century,* Vol. 2: *The Wheels of Commerce,* New York, Harper & Row, 1982, pp. 114–34.

7. In Manila, for example, Legaspi found about 150 Chinese when he arrived there in 1571. The number increased to 24,000 in 1596, 40,000 in 1749, 67,000 in 1886, and 100,000 in 1896. Gregorio Zaide, 'Contribution of Aliens to Philippine Economy', *Fookien Times Yearbook 1954,* Manila. For Singapore, Melaka and Penang, see Mak Lau Fong, *The Sociology of Secret Societies: A Study of Chinese Secret Societies in Singapore and Peninsular Malaysia,* Kuala Lumpur, Oxford University Press, 1981.

8. Yap Ah Loy is not included because his success in tin mining depended heavily on his ability to command a secret society to fight for his interests. In his time, the British had not established law and order in Kuala Lumpur, in whose vicinity he operated. On the other hand, the tin miners mentioned here operated under British law and order. This, however, is unlikely to have been sufficient to protect their interests or settle internal disputes within their organizations, and they too must have depended for success on their connections with secret societies, though perhaps not as heavily as did Yap Ah Loy. Thus, as in the case of the Dutch East India Company, which was a trading regime with government functions (including the use of military power to protect or expand its business interests), it is possible to argue that their businesses were not pure capitalist organizations. On Yap Ah Loy, see S. M. Middlebrook, 'Yap Ah Loy, 1837–1885', *Journal of the Malayan Branch of the Royal Asiatic Society,* July 1951.

9. In Malaya, direct contact with the West started as far back as 1883. See G. C. Allen and Audrey Donnithorne, *Western Enterprise in Indonesia and Malaya,* London, George Allen & Unwin, 1954, p. 237.

10. Singapore rice merchants depended heavily on rice merchants in Saigon and Bangkok, although some had their own operations in these places. See Appendix 4 for the names of the rice dealers mentioned in the text.

11. Tan Ee Leong, 'The Chinese Banks Incorporated in Singapore and the Federation of Malaya', in T. H. Silcock, ed., *Readings in Malayan Economics,* Singapore, Eastern Universities Press, 1961; 'China Banking Corporation: Golden Anniversary', *Chronicle* Business Report, 16 August 1970; and Mantetsu Toa Keizai Chosa-kyoku, *Ranryo Indo ni okeru Kakyo,* Tokyo, [published by the author], 1940, p. 222.

12. Hiizumi Katsuo, '"Tai no Kakyo" ni tsuite no Arekore Part 13,' *Shoho* (of the Japanese Chamber of Commerce, Bangkok), August 1985, p. 53; and Mantetsu Toa

Keizai Chosa-kyoku, *Taikoku ni okeru Kakyo*, Tokyo, [published by the author], 1939.

13. On revenue-farms in Indonesia, see James Rush, 'Opium Farms in Nineteenth Century Java: Institutional Continuity and Change in a Colonial Society, 1860–1910', Ph.D. thesis, Yale University, 1977; and in Thailand, Lysa Hong, *Thailand in the Nineteenth Century: Evolution of the Economy and Society*, Singapore, Institute of Southeast Asian Studies, 1984.

14. The banks of this period were formed within dialect groups. The founders of Kwong Yik Bank were Cantonese; those of Sze Hai Tong Bank were Teochius; and China Banking Corporation, Ho Hong Bank, and others were founded by Hokkiens.

15. China Banking Corporation, for example, had Westerners as its general managers from its establishment (1920) to 1936. 'China Banking Corporation: Golden Anniversary', p. 10.

16. Ho Hong and Oversea-Chinese Banks established branches in other South-East Asian cities in their early years, and were engaged in foreign exchange operations. Partly because of this, however, they got into trouble, and merged with another bank, Chinese Commercial Bank, to form the Oversea-Chinese Banking Corporation.

17. The number of Chinese who could handle European languages increased in the colonies. For example, Tan Keong Saik once worked at Borneo Co. and later served as a director of the British-controlled Straits Steamship Co. in Singapore; and Albino Sycip, shortly after returning to Manila with a law degree from the University of Michigan, went into trading business with his brother, Alfonso.

18. On the rise of dredging, see Lim Chong-yah, *Economic Development of Modern Malaya*, Kuala Lumpur, Oxford University Press, 1967, pp. 50–1; and Wong Lin Ken, *The Malayan Tin Industry to 1914*, Tucson, University of Arizona Press, 1965, pp. 216–18. The use of dredges began increasing around 1910, and in 1928, they accounted for about a third of tin production. See Allen and Donnithorne, op. cit., p. 297.

19. On the rise of the Chinese in rice milling, see G. William Skinner, *Chinese Society in Thailand: An Analytical History*, Ithaca, Cornell University Press, 1957, pp. 144–5.

20. On the rise of British capital in tin smelting, see Wong Lin Ken, *The Malayan Tin Industry to 1914*, pp. 164–5; and K. G. Tregonning, *Straits Tin: A Brief Account of the Straits Trading Company Limited, 1887–1962*, Singapore, The Straits Times Press, 1962, pp. 89–90.

21. Wong Lin Ken, *The Malayan Tin Industry to 1914*, p. 164.

22. Li Dun Jen, *British Malaya: An Economic Analysis*, reprinted Petaling Jaya, Institute for Social Analysis, 1982, p. 67.

23. Mohamed Amin and Malcolm Caldwell, eds., *Malaya: The Making of a Neo-Colony*, Nottingham, Bertrand Russell Peace Foundation, 1977, p. 23.

24. Liem Tjwan Ling, *Raja Gula: Oei Tiong Ham*, Surabaya, published by the author, 1979, p. 25.

25. Peter Beal, 'The Empire Builders', *The Investor*, February 1981, p. 15.

26. Yoshihara Kunio, *Philippine Industrialization: Foreign and Domestic Capital*, Quezon City, Ateneo de Manila University Press, and Singapore, Oxford University Press, 1985, p. 91.

27. The source of data on the cement industry is Asosiasi Semen Indonesia (ASI). Indocement's investment was estimated from the fact that its capacity is about ten times as large as Semen Nusantara's (ASI), and that the total investment needed for Semen Nusantara was about $100 million (interview with Mr Kawakami Shigeru, Vice-President of Semen Nusantara, May 1986). Since Indocement's capacity is ten times larger, it was estimated that ten times as much as capital was needed.

28. *Taikoku Keizai Gaikyo 1986–87 Nen-ban*, Bangkok, Bangkok Nihonjin Shoko Kaigisho, n.d., p. 178.

29. Sukri Bodhiratanangkura set up several joint ventures with Japanese companies, including Thai Blanket Industry, Thai Iryo, Thai Synthetic Textile Industry. Initially, he held minority interests, but eventually gained control of most of them. In Indonesia, The Ning King set up Budidharma Jakarta (to produce structural steel) and Kuraray Manunggal Fiber Industries (to produce polyester fibre) with Japanese companies holding minority interests, but recently he has bought out the Japanese shares and now controls these companies. The difficulties for Japanese companies are government regulations on foreign investment, which, for example, require foreign investors to reduce their holdings over time to below 50 per cent.

30. For UMW's Toyota coup, see M. G. G. Pillai, 'Ecstasy at UMW over Eric Chia's Toyota Coup', *Insight*, December 1981.

31. J. J. Puthucheary, *Ownership and Control in the Malayan Economy*, reprinted Kuala Lumpur, University of Malaya Cooperative Bookshop, 1979, p. 134.

32. It is assumed here that even as a minority, the Chinese are the dominant element of South-East Asian capitalism, so as a majority group, they would more or less monopolize it. Why they do so much better in the economy is discussed in the next section.

33. There are pribumi industrialists in shipbuilding and repairing (for example, the Ibnu Sutowo family), textiles (Haji Muhammad Joesoef), and a few other industries, but they are not many.

34. Pribumi capitalists are more visible in these fields. Examples are: in construction, Probosutedjo and Eddi Kowara; and in the oil service industry, Tony Ardie, Iman Taufik, Arifin Panigoro, and Suryo Bambang Sulisto.

35. *Mid-term Review of the Fourth Malaysia Plan, 1981-1985*, Kuala Lumpur, Government Press, 1984, p. 101.

36. Out of the ten, the seven Filipino-owned banks are Bank of Philippine Islands, Consolidated Bank, Family Savings Bank, Far East Bank, Manila Banking Corp., Phil. Commercial and Industrial Bank, and Security Bank; and the three Chinese-owned banks are China Banking Corp., Metro Bank, and Rizal Commercial Banking Corp.

37. There were a few Chinese among Marcos's cronies (for example, Lucio Tan and Ralph Nubla), but most of them were Filipinos (such as Roberto Benedicto, Eduardo Cojuangco, Herminio Disini, Antonio Floirendo, Ricardo Silverio, and Bienvenido Tantoco). In addition, there are Marcos's in-laws, the Romualdezes, who were also active in business. Today, they are gone, but Filipinos are still strong in such fields as sugar and cement besides banking. Definitely, they are much more broadly represented and more active than their counterparts in the other South-East Asian countries.

38. As noted earlier, the total Japanese investment in the petrochemical complex in Singapore was about $500 million, whereas Indocement's investment was about $1 billion.

39. Mahathir bin Mohamad, *The Malay Dilemma*, Kuala Lumpur, Federal Publications, 1970, p. 53.

40. Lance Castles, *Religion, Politics, and Economic Behavior in Java: The Kudus Cigarette Industry*, New Haven, Southeast Asian Studies, Yale University, 1967, p. 88.

41. In the pre-war period, the Minangkabaus probably had the best business network among the indigenous groups of South-East Asia, but because they were not as widespread as the Chinese, even in Indonesia, their network was not very extensive. At that time, particularly in business, Indonesia's indigenous groups could not transcend their ethnicity.

42. On the importance of shinyung, see Clifton Barton, 'Trust and Credit: Some Observations Regarding Business Strategies of Overseas Chinese Traders in South Vietnam', in Linda Y. C. Lim and Peter Gosling, eds., *The Chinese in Southeast Asia*, Vol. 1, Singapore, Maruzen Asia, 1983. This article is not on an ASEAN country, but there is no reason to think that the working of shinyung is different.

43. For an economic theory of shinyung, see Janet Landa, 'The Political Economy of the Ethnically Homogeneous Chinese Middleman Group in Southeast Asia: Ethnicity and Entrepreneurship in a Plural Society', in Linda Y. C. Lim and Peter Gosling, eds., *The Chinese in Southeast Asia*, Vol. 1, Singapore, Maruzen Asia, 1983.

44. On the changing character of Chinese organizations in Singapore (though not a network in particular), see Cheng Lim Keak, *Social Change and the Chinese in Singapore*, Singapore, Singapore University Press, 1985.

45. Around 1931, the Chinese population in the Philippines was 72,000, whereas it was 445,000 in Thailand, 1,704,000 in Malaya, and 1,900,000 in Indonesia (Purcell, *The Chinese in Southeast Asia*, p. 3).

On the restriction of Chinese immigration, see Khin Khin Myint Jensen, 'The Chinese in the Philippines during the American Regime: 1896–1946', Ph.D. thesis, University of Wisconsin, 1956.

46. On the circumstances surrounding the rise of indigenous entrepreneurship in the Philippines, see Yoshihara, *Philippine Industrialization*, Chapters 5 and 6.

47. On the privileged position of the Chinese in Thailand, see Tate, *The Making of Modern South-East Asia*, Vol. 2: *The Western Impact*, p. 544.

48. Purcell, *The Chinese in Southeast Asia*, p. 446.

49. Edgar Wickberg, 'The Chinese Mestizo in Philippine History', *Journal of Southeast Asian History*, 1964, pp. 63–8.

50. The following references deal with early indigenous trade and traders: Syed Hussein Alatas, *The Myth of the Lazy Native*, London, Frank Cass, 1977; Guy, op. cit. (particularly Chapter 7); Kenneth Hall, *Maritime Trade and State Development in Early Southeast Asia*, Honolulu, University of Hawaii Press, 1985; *Indonesian Sociological Studies: Selected Writings of B. Schrieke*, Part One, The Hague, W. van Hoeve, 1957; M. A. P. Meilink-Roelofsz, *Asian Trade and European Influence*, The Hague, Martinus Nijhoff, 1962; Anthony Reid, 'Pre-colonial Economy of Indonesia', Paper presented to the Conference on Indonesian Economic History in the Dutch Colonial Period, Australian National University, 16–18 December 1983; J. C. van Leur, *Indonesian Trade and Society*, The Hague, W. van Hoeve, 1955.

51. For the observations of Westerners during the colonial period, see, for example, John Crawfurd, *Journal of an Embassy to the Courts of Siam and Cochin China*, reprinted Kuala Lumpur, Oxford University Press, 1967, pp. 20, 343–4, and 555; Clive Day, *The Policy and Administration of the Dutch in Java*, reprinted Kuala Lumpur, Oxford University Press, 1966, pp. 345–8, 356–7, and 361; James Low, *The British Settlement of Penang*, reprinted Singapore, Oxford University Press, 1972, pp. 8–9; Ernest Young, *The Kingdom of the Yellow Robe*, reprinted Kuala Lumpur, Oxford University Press, 1982, pp. 9, 138, and 206; J. H. Boeke, *Indische Economie*, Vol. 1, Haarlem, H. D. Tjeenk Willink, 1940, p. 19; F. A. Swettenham, *British Malaya*, London, Allen & Unwin, 1955, p. 136; and C. G. Warnford-Lock, *Mining in Malaya for Gold and Tin*, London, Crowther & Goodman, 1907, pp. 32–3. Also, the positive views on the Chinese (*vis-à-vis* the indigenous) held by Governor Bort (the Dutch Governor of Malacca), Francis Light and John Crawfurd are cited in Victor Purcell, *The Chinese in Malaya*, Kuala Lumpur, Oxford University Press, 1967, pp. 31, 52–3, 260, and 291.

One might argue that their views on the indigenes were biased, and that many of them also had negative views on Japan and the Japanese in the mid-nineteenth century (which have since proved to be wrong, since the Japanese are doing better than the West in the world economy today); but there were some who were impressed with the work ethic and craftsmanship of the Japanese (for example, Commodore Perry of the United States Navy), while none of the Western observers who left written records praised the work ethic of the indigenes in South-East Asia. For Commodore Perry's view, see S. Morison, *'Old Burin': Commodore Matthew C. Perry, 1794–1858*, Boston, Little, Brown & Co., 1967, p. 428.

In the post-war period, the network theory has become popular, but the value system of the Chinese is still often regarded as a major factor for their success in business. For writings on the subject by non-indigenous writers, see, for example, Donald Wilmott, *The Chinese of Semarang: A Changing Minority Community in Indonesia*, Ithaca, Cornell University Press, 1960, pp. 69–73; Lim Chong-yah, op. cit., pp. 120–2; and Tham Seong Chee, *Malays and Modernization*, 2nd ed., Singapore, Singapore University Press, 1983, various pages.

Even some indigenous writers admit the value system is a relevant factor. The earliest among them appears to be Jose Rizal who wrote 'The Indolence of the Filipinos' (which appears in E. Alzona, trans. and ed., *Selected Essays and Letters of Jose Rizal*, Manila, Rangel & Sons, 1964). More recent writers have not put the problem as strongly as Jose Rizal did, but they still give some credit to the value theory. See, for example, Mochtar Lubis, *The Indonesian Dilemma*, translated by F. Lamoureux, Singapore, Graham Brash, 1983, pp. 33–4; and Mahathir, op. cit., pp. 20–8 and 85.

52. Wickberg, 'The Chinese Mestizo in Philippine History', pp. 90–1.

53. On the assimilation of the Chinese to indigenous society, see, for example, Botan, *Letters from Thailand*, translated by Susan Fulop Morell, Bangkok, D. K. Book House, 1977.

54. International Bank for Reconstruction and Development, *A Public Development Program for Thailand*, Baltimore, The Johns Hopkins Press, 1959, pp. 90–1.

55. On anti-Chinese discrimination in the Philippines before martial law, see Jacques Amyot, *The Manila Chinese: Familism in the Philippine Environment*, IPC Monographs, No. 2, Quezon City, Ateneo de Manila University, 1973, pp. 74–8; Frank Golay *et al.*, *Underdevelopment and Economic Nationalism in Southeast Asia*, Ithaca, Cornell University Press, 1969, Chapter 2; and Yoshihara, *Philippine Industrialization*, pp. 84–8.

56. On anti-Chinese discrimination in Indonesia during the Sukarno period, see Golay *et al.*, op. cit., Chapter 3; and Douglas Paauw, 'From Colonial to Guided Economy', in Ruth McVey, ed., *Indonesia*, New Haven, Southeast Asian Studies, Yale University, 1963, p. 210.

57. It is sometimes said that the dichotomy of the pribumi and the non-pribumi was abandoned in 1984 in favour of the economically strong and the economically weak, but when it comes to concession and loan applications, the government still makes sure that substantial pribumi interests are involved.

58. On government policy in the 1960s, see Golay *et al.*, op. cit., Chapter 6.

59. On the New Economic Policy, see Benjamin Higgins, 'Development Planning', in E. K. Fisk and H. Osman-Rani, eds., *The Political Economy of Malaysia*, Kuala Lumpur, Oxford University Press, 1982.

60. On Chinese assimilation in Thailand, see Skinner, *Chinese Society in Thailand*, pp. 299–300.

61. *Second Malaysia Plan, 1971–1975*, Kuala Lumpur, Government Press, 1971, p. 40.

62. For example, Deputy Prime Minister Ghafar Baba has stated that bumiputra should own at least 50 per cent of Malaysia's corporate sector by the year 2000 if 'real equality in all respects' with the non-bumiputra is to be meaningful. *ASEAN Forecast*, May 1987, p. 60. Ghafar Baba later issued a statement saying that he meant 50 per cent of the local equity, i.e. after the foreign equity position had been discounted.

Chapter 4
Rent-seekers and Speculators

Rent-seekers

THE capitalists who try to establish government connections for business advantage can be called rent-seekers because they are essentially seeking opportunities to become the recipients of the rent the government can confer by disposing of its resources, offering protection, or issuing authorization for certain types of activities it regulates. 'Rent' is here defined as the difference between the market value of a government 'favour' and what the recipient pays to the government and/or privately to his benefactors in the government (if he does not pay at all, the entire market value is rent, or more precisely, economic rent).

South-East Asia today has a large number of rent-seekers. In the Philippines, the term 'crony capitalist' was coined during martial law for those who benefited greatly from having close relations with President Marcos. In Thailand, some scholars have borrowed the term 'bureaucratic capitalist' from China studies and applied it to a certain type of rent-seeking capitalist. Below, other categories of rent-seeking capitalists are created based on the way they developed their relations with government, and each is explained with some examples.

Royal Capitalists

There are royal families in Thailand, Malaysia, and Indonesia (but not in Singapore and the Philippines). In Malaysia and Indonesia, sultans and/or their families, and in Thailand, the King (more precisely, the Crown Property Bureau, which manages the property and investment of the royal household) are involved in business. Of the three countries, royal involvement in business is least significant in Indonesia, for there are only a few sultans left, and among them, only the Sultan of Yogyakarta (Sri Sultan Hamengkubuwono) is involved extensively. He owns, for example, about half the equity of Bank Dagang Nasional Indonesia, one of the largest private commercial banks; and he owns or holds interests in a number of other companies (such as PT Duta Merlin, a shopping complex in Jakarta).

In Malaysia, nine of the thirteen states have their own sultans, and they wield more political power than do the sultans of Indonesia.[1] In many cases, the sultans of Malaysia tie up with Chinese and bumiputra capitalists and act more as *rentier* than as capitalists, but in some cases, their investments are directly managed by their families and personal staff. For example, in the case of Negeri Sembilan, the members of the royal family are quite active in business: Tunku Abdullah ibni Almarhum Tuanku Abdul Rahman, a brother of the Yang Dipertuan Negeri, owns the Melewar group, while Tunku Imran, a nephew of Tunku Abdullah, owns the Antah group. In the case of Pahang, Tengku Ariff Bendahara, a brother of the Sultan, established the TAB group, which he headed until his death in 1987.

In Thailand, during the period of absolute monarchy (which ended in 1932), there was no clear separation between the government and the royal household. During that time, businessmen approached the king for financial assistance as they do the government today. Also, as the government often does today, the king took the initiative in forming a company.[2] But when the monarchy became constitutional, the royal household was separated from the government, and its corporate holdings were placed under the Crown Property Bureau (CPB). Today, the CPB holds controlling interests in Siam Commercial Bank and Siam Cement Co., two leading companies in Thailand, and also owns pieces of valuable property in business districts in Bangkok.

Presidential Families

In Indonesia, President Suharto is said to have invested in business, particularly in Liem Sioe Liong's companies, but there is no way to verify this since he has not done so in his own name. His family, however, is extensively involved in business. His half-brother, Probosutedjo, heads the Mertju Buana group of companies. He shares a monopoly on clove import with Liem Sioe Liong; is a major contractor of government projects; and is a major supplier to the state oil company, Pertamina. Suharto's foster brother, Sudwikatmono, often acts as a frontman for Liem Sioe Liong, but he also has his own group of companies (the Subentra group). Furthermore, Mrs Suharto's brother, Bernard Ibnu Hardjojo, owns the Gunung Ngadeg Jaya group of companies, which is involved in logging, cement distribution, foreign trade, and offshore supply.[3]

President Suharto's three sons are also involved in business.[4] The newest 'debutant' is Tomy (Hutomo Mandala Putra), the youngest son. He owns a trading company called PT Humpus, which has been given the exclusive agency right for the methanol and purified terphtalic acid (PTA) that Pertamina began producing in 1986. Methanol is used by adhesive producers and paint manufacturers, while PTA is used by synthetic fibre makers. Methanol is required for production by about 71 companies, so arguably a trading company is needed to distribute it; but if Pertamina wanted to do it itself, it could do so. PTA is used by only five makers, so there is no need for an intermediary like PT Humpus. It is said that Pertamina gave Tomy the agency right for the two products as a 'graduation present'.

Suharto's oldest son, Sigid Harjojudanto, often ties up with one of his father's close associates, Bob Hasan. They are involved together in plywood, tin plates (Nusamba), offshore supply, and car assembling (Nissan). Sigid is also involved in business with Liem Sioe Liong; for example, he owns a 10 per cent share of the Sinar Mas Inti Perkasa group, which is involved in estate agriculture, cooking-oil production, and shipping (the famous cooking-oil producer, Bimoli, is a member of this group). Furthermore, Sigid is one of the key figures in the Hanurata group, which bids for logging concessions and government projects.

Of the president's three sons, the second, Bambang Trihatmodjo, is the most systematic and appears to be the most determined to succeed in business. Together with his brother-in-law, Indra Rukmana Kowara (a son of the pribumi entrepreneur, Eddi Kowara, who heads PT Teknik Umum, a large private construction company), Bambang set up a business group called Bimantara, which comprises about 30 companies. These companies cover such fields as LNG transportation, general cargo shipping, and petrochemical manufacturing.

In the Philippines, former President Marcos was probably the biggest capitalist in the country before his overthrow, in the sense that he held large shares in a number of major companies through dummies and investment companies (which were exposed after his overthrow). He is alleged to have obtained most of these shares through extortion or as 'payments' from the companies which benefited from his favours. He was not, however, active in business himself.

Several of his relatives on his own side of the family were involved in business (for example, his brother, Pacifico Marcos, and his nephew, Mariano Marcos II), but they were not as extensively involved or conspicuous as his in-laws.[5] Imelda Marcos's younger brother, Benjamin Romualdez, headed First Philippine Holdings, which controlled Eugenio Lopez's former flagship, Manila Electric Co. (whose controlling shares Marcos forced Eugenio Lopez to sell); and he also obtained a controlling interest in the former American mining company, Benguet Consolidated. Another brother of Imelda's, Alfredo, was given a monopoly on casinos in Manila and other major cities; he also took over Philippine Jai-Alai & Amusement Corp. and was the key figure behind Bataan Shipyard and Engineering. Imelda's sister, Alita, together with her husband (Rudolfo Martel) and his brothers, owned the Marsteel group, set up Harrison Plaza, and was a major shareholder of Century Park Sheraton.

Crony Capitalists

Crony capitalists are private-sector businessmen who benefit enormously from close relations with the head of a state. Capitalists such as Roberto Benedicto, Eduardo Cojuangco, Rodolfo Cuenca, Herminio Disini, Antonio Floirendo, and Ricardo Silverio have often been referred to as Marcos's cronies. Many of Marcos's cronies had established businesses before martial law. For example, Ricardo Silverio was the assembler and distributor of Toyota cars, while Rodolfo Cuenca was the head of the construction company, Construction and Development Corp. of the Philippines. Of course, they expanded their business interests tremendously during martial law.

Some, however, made fortunes from almost nothing. Herminio Disini is an example. Philippine Tobacco Filters Corp., the first company he set up (in 1970), attracted little attention until 1975, when it gained control of the cigarette filter market because Marcos did him the favour of imposing a 100 per cent import duty on acetate tow, the main raw material of filters, while Disini paid only 10 per cent. In the following years, he set up a number of companies which used government connections for business advantage or served as a front for Marcos. These companies formed the Herdis group.

There were also some Chinese cronies, although they were less conspicuous and less important than Filipino cronies.[6] The best known among them were Ralph Nubla, who was Marcos's classmate at the University of the Philippines and served as President of the Federation of Filipino-Chinese Chambers of Commerce and Industry during the martial law period; Jose Campos (also known as Jose C. Yao) of United Laboratories, the largest drug company in the Philippines; and Lucio Tan of Allied Banking Corp.

The rise of Lucio Tan was meteoric. In the early 1960s, he was an obscure employee at a cigarette factory. Then, in the mid-1960s, he set up a small cigarette factory; shortly thereafter he tied up with a small American cigarette maker; and by the time martial law was imposed, he had succeeded in making it a major cigarette manufacturing company in the Philippines. This was made possible by a great deal of irregularities with the government, on which he came to rely even more during martial law. In 1977, he took over an obscure bank in trouble (which was renamed Allied Banking Corp.), and in the following years, with Marcos's backing (with which he could obtain special loans from the Central Bank and also special considerations for the opening of new branches), he made it a top commercial bank.

One can argue that there were cronies even before the martial law period, but the cronies and the more general government-connected capitalists should be distinguished. One thing unique to the martial law period is that the President enjoyed far greater power then than previously and was willing to use it for his own or his supporters' economic benefit. Also, because he stayed in power for a considerable period, the economic benefit which accrued over time to some of his supporters was enormous. Thus, it seems better to apply the term 'crony capitalists' only to those who were closely connected with Marcos during the martial law period, while attaching different labels to those who enjoyed government privileges at a much reduced level either during the martial law period or before.

The term 'crony' has its origins in the Philippine setting, but as just defined, it can also be applied to some of the Indonesian capitalists who have close relations with President Suharto—for example, Liem Sioe Liong and Bob Hasan. Liem's relations with President Suharto go back to the late 1950s when he was with the Diponegoro Division. It was at this time that he won the confidence of Suharto through business dealings, and after Suharto came into power in 1965, he obtained a number of monopolies and enjoyed government privileges. With these, he went on to build the country's biggest business empire with interests in banking, steel, real estate, cement, motor vehicles, and trading.

Bob Hasan's relations with President Suharto seem also to have started during his time with the Diponegoro Division. Initially at least, Bob Hasan had better credentials to win Suharto's confidence, being an 'adopted' son of Gato Subroto, a military leader who had close ties with Suharto. After Suharto came into power, Bob Hasan obtained a number of logging concessions and has built a big business group based on logging and wood processing. He is also involved in shipping, manufacturing, trading, and construction.

Bureaucratic Capitalists

The term 'bureaucratic capitalist' was coined in relation to China and has since assumed several different meanings; but here, it is more specifically defined.[7] First, those who qualify as bureaucratic capitalists once held or still hold bureaucratic posts, which they used for their initial capital accumulation. Second, if they no longer hold bureaucratic posts, they may still maintain close connections with the government and use these for their business. Third, they have their own businesses and run them as any other capitalist does.

The last condition excludes many retired military officers in Indonesia from the group of bureaucratic capitalists. After retirement, in order to supplement their pensions, high military officers (generals, etc.) often tie up with Chinese and secure a handsome income by obtaining facilities from the government for their Chinese partners. In this case, they are acting more as rentier than as capitalists: they are needed and paid for their influence on the government.

Some businesses are run by the Indonesian military without Chinese or other outside help (for example, Propelat of the Siliwangi Division of the Indonesian Army).[8] The military needs these businesses in order to obtain extra income and to provide its officers with opportunities to earn extra income after retirement. These businesses would qualify as bureaucratic capitalist institutions, but the people who run them should be regarded more as managers than as capitalists, since the businesses they run are not their own.

As defined above, bureaucratic capitalists are far fewer in number than is generally thought.[9] In Thai economic history, the term is applied to Chinese capitalists who obtained government posts with money and used them for business advantage. They became tax-farmers or provincial governors, and were engaged in business at the same time.[10] Examples are Arkon Teng who founded Kim Seng Lee & Co. and Khaw Soo Cheang and his son, Khaw Sim Bee, of southern Thailand. However, the purchase of government posts has become rarer over time, and there are practically no capitalists in the 1980s who correspond to the bureaucrats-cum-capitalists of the early years of the twentieth century.

In their place, a different type of bureaucrat-cum-capitalist emerged in the late 1930s and became conspicuous in the next 20 years. Especially in the early post-war years, high-ranking serving military officers such as Phin Choonhavan, Sarit Thanarat, and Praphat Charusathien set up their own businesses to obtain funds for advancing their interests in the military, which dominated Thai politics at that time. For example, Sarit Thanarat owned Bangkok International Trading Co., which had a large quota on rice export; Dhipaya Insurance, which sold policies to government employees; and Vichitra Construction Co., which was given many government contracts without bidding.[11]

On the other hand, it is difficult to find examples of bureaucrats-turned-capitalists (that is, bureaucrats who have resigned from their posts to go into business and succeeded). By reason of their training and temperament, officials in the civil administration were better fitted to take advantage of government connections than military officers; and, in fact, King Chulalongkorn encouraged them to go into business. But among those who tried, few succeeded. The only notable exception is Phraya Bhirombhakdi, the founder of Boon Rawd Brewery, which produces 'Singha' beer.

In Malaysia, bureaucratic capitalists are more numerous. When the NEP sowed the seed for a burgeoning of bumiputra capitalists, the Malaysian bureaucracy proved to be the most fertile ground, for in the absence of other attractive fields, it contained the largest number of professional bumiputra. Bumiputra capitalists who once worked for the government include Abdul Aziz bin Mohamed Zain of Renong Tin; Azman Hashim of Arab-Malaysian Development; Ikmal Hisham Albakri of Kumpulan Akitek; Raja Khalid of Malayan Commercial Services; Haji Shamsuddin bin Abdul Kadir of Sapura Holdings; and Shahrani Haji Abdullah of Shapadu Holding. Especially in the case of Shamsuddin, business success seems to have depended directly on the connections cultivated while working for the government. He once worked for the Telecommunications Department as director-general and is now a large contractor for Syarikat Telekom Malaysia (which took over telecommunications services from the government in January 1987). Even in the case of Shahrani, although he did not occupy a high post when he left the Ministry of Works, his connections there seem to have been used in getting contracts from the Ministry for his group (e.g. the North Kelang Expressway).

In Indonesia, the foremost among the bureaucratic capitalists is probably Ibnu Sutowo, who headed the rich national oil company, Pertamina, until 1976 and seems to have accumulated a large personal fortune at that time. Today, he heads the Nugra Santana group of companies. His influence declined somewhat after he left Pertamina, but there are still many people in the government who feel indebted to him or are obliged to appease him because of the secret dealings they had with him during his presidency of Pertamina.

Those who can be considered bureaucratic capitalists in Indonesia came mostly from the military. Ibnu Sutowo was a lieutenant-general in the army when he retired from Pertamina. General Soemitro, who was forced to resign after mishandling the Malari Riot of early 1974, went into business and now heads the Rigunas group; from the very beginning, he has depended heavily on government concessions and contracts. Ardi Sose, a former colonel who currently heads the

Marannu group, has also depended on government finance. The former Permesta rebel, Herman Nicolas Sumual, who heads the Konsultasi Pembangunan group, depended heavily on government facilities early in his business career, but his joint ventures with Japan have recently become a major focus of his business operation. However, his government connections are still substantial.

Arnold Baramuli is one of the few non-military bureaucrats who succeeded in business in Indonesia. While he was with the Ministry of Interior, he got involved in business, but he resigned in 1972 to concentrate solely on business. Through his government connections, he obtained logging concessions and, a little later, went into manufacturing together with Japanese companies (Toray and Mitsui Toatsu Chemical). Today he heads the Poleko group of companies. His formal relations with the Ministry of Interior ended with his resignation, but informally he appears to remain on close terms. There is a rumour that the Department of Interior is the real owner of the Poleko group.[12]

Politicians-turned-capitalists

There are not many politicians-turned-capitalists. First, politicians' power has been limited. In Indonesia, the military has played a central role in government, at least in the New Order period. In Thailand, it is only in the past decade that politicians have begun to wield some power: before that, the military long dominated Thai politics. Secondly, because of either their education or their mental make-up, politicians have generally been more reluctant to go into business than bureaucrats.

There are, however, some exceptions. In the Philippines, Jose P. Laurel, a prominent politician in the pre-war and early post-war periods (his son, Salvador Laurel, is Vice-President of the country today), founded Philippine Banking Corporation in the mid-1950s. For him, entry into business came towards the end of his life. However, Ramon Durano, a politician of long standing, went into business relatively early in his political career. In Danao, about 30 kilometres north of Cebu City, he has built a political and business empire on which most Danao residents depend directly or indirectly for their living—on his sugar mill, cement factory, and many other businesses. There are also schools and hospitals bearing his name. During the Marcos period, Durano was the President's ardent supporter; in return, he received various rewards, including government loans for his businesses.

In Malaysia, Syed Kechik bin Syed Mohamed can be regarded as a politician-turned-capitalist. After getting a degree in law, he was drawn into politics and became Assistant Secretary of the Kedah Alliance in 1964. In the following year, he was sent by Tunku Abdul Rahman, then Prime Minister, to arrest the centrifugal tendency in Sabah in the aftermath of Singapore's separation from Malaysia. There, he helped Tun Mustapha Harun to power and served as his political adviser. During this time, he is said to have accumulated capital through logging concessions. On leaving Sabah, he went to Kuala Lumpur, where he enjoys good relations with UMNO élites. With the money from the Sabah period and good government connections, he went into business and has become one of the top bumiputra capitalists.

Tan Sri Haji Mohamed Noah bin Omar can be considered another politician-turned-capitalist. In 1970, after 20 years in politics, he went into business, often tying up with Chinese capitalists (for example, with Lim Goh Tong in Genting Highlands Hotel). With two sons-in-law who became Prime Minister (Abdul Razak Hussein and Hussein Onn), he was one of the most sought-after bumiputra capitalists by Chinese and foreign investors under the NEP. Another Malay politician, Ghafar Baba, also got involved in business (for example, he once headed Kompleks Kewangan and Goodyield Plaza). He was more of a politician-cum-capitalist than a politician-turned-capitalist, although he is probably not so now that he is serving as Deputy Prime Minister. His son, Tamrin, however, is active in business.

Although there are state and military enterprises in other South-East Asian countries, it is only in Malaysia that a political party owns a business group. The ruling Malay party, the UMNO, owns the Fleet group, whose assets are estimated to amount to a billion dollars. The holding company of the group, Fleet Holdings, owns New Straits Times Press (which publishes the leading English language daily, *New Straits Times*, the Chinese daily, *Shin Min*, and the Malay daily, *Berita Harian*); Faber Merlin (which owns the country's biggest hotel chain and is also a major property developer); Peremba (a large property developer); Idris Hydraulic (which owns two finance companies, an insurance company, and a few joint ventures); Pan Pacific Hotel; and Kwong Yik Bank (indirectly through Idris Hydraulic). Under the management of Daim Zainuddin, in the early 1980s Fleet Holdings became actively involved in banking, insurance, leasing, property development, and other service industries. It seems that the UMNO originally set up the company in order to gain greater direct control over the mass media through which its views could be aired, but since Daim took over its management, it became more business-oriented and expanded into new fields.[13]

Capitalists-turned-politicians

In the Philippines, a number of capitalists have entered politics. Advancement of their business interests may not have been their sole reason for entering politics, but it was probably an important consideration. One of the earliest capitalists-turned-politicians is probably Melicio Cojuangco, who was elected to the Philippine Assembly in 1907. He was the son of Jose Cojuangco and the brother of Ysidra Cojuangco, who built the Cojuangco empire in Tarlac. A more recent example is Gil Puyat, who is the son of prominent Filipino capitalist Gonzalo Puyat, and who entered politics in the early 1950s. Another is Fernando Lopez, the brother of Eugenio Lopez, who owned sugar haciendas and Meralco (Manila Electric Co.), the largest power company in the Philippines. With his brother's financial backing, Fernando became a powerful member of the Nacionalista Party and served as Vice-President of the Philippines before martial law was imposed. In addition, there have been a number of capitalists (such as Salvador Araneta and Joaquin Elizalde) who were drafted by the government to serve as ministers or advisers.

In Malaysia, too, a number of capitalists have entered politics. Tan Cheng Lock and Henry Lee Hau Shik are probably among the earliest (they were active in politics in the 1950s). Tan Siew Sin, the son of Tan Cheng Lock, is a more recent example. These people were not, however, as conspicuous as those businessmen who entered politics in the past decade. The most prominent examples of the new breed are Tan Koon Swan and Kee Yong Wee. Tan Koon Swan was convicted on charges brought against him and sentenced to a prison term in Singapore, while Kee Yong Wee has been charged with criminal breach of trust in connection with the management of the Chinese co-operative Komuda, which is now in government receivership. Both were capitalists-cum-politicians rather than capitalists-turned-politicians, for they were active in business as well as in politics. While heading Supreme Corp., a conglomerate with subsidiaries in housing development, plantations, and finance, Tan Koon Swan was also active in the Malaysian Chinese Association (MCA) and succeeded in becoming its president in 1986. Kee Yong Wee was also active in politics while heading a real estate and finance conglomerate (Malaysian Resources Corp.); and in 1981, he was elected to the Central Committee of the MCA and appointed a senator in the following year. For both, politics was an indispensable part of business.

In Indonesia, several pribumi capitalists entered politics or served the government in an important capacity during the Sukarno period, though they were fewer in number and less important than other types of rent-seekers. For example, the capitalist based in Medan, T. D. Pardede, served as a Minister of Berdikari in the Sukarno government. They virtually disappeared, however, once the military started to dominate the government in the New Order period.

In Thailand, the military dominated the government until the early 1970s, and there was no scope for capitalists to enter politics and influence government decisions in their favour. But since then, especially in the past few years, the military has been sharing power with politicians, many of whom are involved in business. In the first Prem government, 46 per cent of his ministers were from the business community; in the second, the percentage went down to 30, but in the third, it rose again to 42.[14] In the general election of 1986, about a quarter of those elected to the National Assembly come from the business sector (one example is Chavalit Techapaibul, Udane Techapaibul's nephew, who was involved in Suramaharas, which now has a monopoly on whiskey production).[15]

Other Government-connected Capitalists

This last category includes all other capitalists who have government connections and use them for business advantage. The government can grant a monopoly, a logging or mining concession, or a sought-after licence; give protection from foreign competition, financial assistance, and a large government contract; appoint a special purveyor; give special consideration to an application for the re-classification of land usage; and sell government property at concessionary prices. Those who have connections with high government officials are in a position to take advantage of these government privileges since they are given a great deal of discretion in decision-making.

The capitalists in this category differ from those in the previous five categories in the following ways. First, unlike presidential and royal families, they do not have an advantage based on blood ties. Secondly, unlike cronies, they do not enjoy very close relations with the head of a state, and the benefits they derive from government connections are not as large or as long-lasting; in an extreme case, they may seek government privileges only at certain phases of their careers. Thirdly, unlike bureaucratic capitalists and politicians-turned-capitalists, they have never been professional bureaucrats or politicians: instead, they started their careers in the private sector and developed government connections in non-official capacities.

In short, this category is the most inclusive of the six categories in this section. It is a little difficult to come forward with an example for Singapore; but because some enjoy more government privileges than others (for example, in getting a banking licence or a licence to open a new branch), it cannot be argued that there are no government-connected capitalists in the island-state. In Thailand, where the government has enjoyed more discretion in decision-making, it is easier to come up with examples of government-connected capitalists. These include Amphorn Bulpakdi, who enjoyed a large rice-export quota in the early 1950s through Sarit Thanarat, who served as chairman on the board of directors of the rice-trading firm, Thanya Thai Co.; Chin Sophopanich, who obtained government financial assistance at one stage of the growth of Bangkok Bank and long enjoyed special relations with the government; and Sawang Laohathai, who diversified from trading to fertilizer, flour, and steel production with government protection and financial assistance.

In Indonesia and Malaysia, where government economic intervention is both more extensive and intensive, there have been a large number of government-connected capitalists. The best connected one in Malaysia today is probably Daim Zainuddin, who enjoys the confidence of Prime Minister Mahathir Mohamad. In Indonesia, during the Benteng Programme, numerous indigenous capitalists (such as Hasyim Ning and Abdul Ghany Aziz) enjoyed government favours in foreign exchange allocation. In the New Order period, such capitalists as Go Ka Him, Go Swie Kie, Achmad Bakrie, and Eddi Kowara enjoy various government privileges. The first two have been acting as the purchasing agents of Bulog, the government food agency; the third is a major supplier of steel pipes to the government oil company, Pertamina; and the last, whose son Indra is married to President Suharto's daughter, heads the construction company, Teknik Umum, one of the largest recipients of government contracts.

In the Philippines also, there have been a large number of government-connected capitalists. The first batch were born during the Commonwealth period and include Vicente Madrigal, who had close ties with President Manuel Quezon. After the Pacific War, with independence, the government gained more power, and over time, the ethics of politicians and bureaucrats deteriorated, so that use of government connections for business became more widespread. Amado Araneta and his brother-in-law, Jose Yulo, who used government loans to buy sugar mills, were among the government-connected capitalists of the early post-war years. Jose Marcelo, who built steel factories with the low-interest loans from the Development Bank of the Philippines

(DBP), is an example from the 1960s (though he began borrowing from the DBP in the early 1950s, the amount was small at that time).[16] Then with martial law came crony capitalists. It should be noted, however, that there was a large number of non-crony, yet government-connected capitalists during the martial law period, though their connections were often with Marcos's lieutenants (if their connections were with Marcos, they were not as strong as those of the so-called cronies).

Speculators

If a speculator is defined as someone who takes a risk for the chance of profit, any businessman becomes a speculator, since any investment is bound to involve risk. To qualify as a speculator, he has to take large risks on the chance of large profits. The businessman who goes to a casino with a lot of money is archetypical. It is said that many people who go to casinos in the Philippines and Malaysia (also in Indonesia until 1981) are businessmen. Those who are not satisfied with these casinos go to Macao or even as far as Las Vegas. Earlier, when there were no casinos, many Chinese gambled at social clubs such as the Ee Hoe Hean and Tanjong Rhu Clubs in Singapore.[17]

In early 1981, the Chinese capitalist, Dewey Dee, fled the Philippines, leaving behind a debt of about $83 million, apparently having lost most of it not in the textile business he was involved in (his family owned Continental Manufacturing Corp.) but in gambling and speculation. It is said that he not only frequented casinos in Manila but also went abroad to gamble. He also speculated on commodities and stock, and seems to have lost especially heavily on sugar and gold futures. Apparently, he took advantage of financial institutions' confidence in his family to keep borrowing, in the hope of recouping his previous losses.[18]

Although sheer gambling may be uncommon, speculation in the commodity futures market is not. Many Chinese capitalists are traders, and many find it difficult not to speculate. Ordinarily, they make money from the margin between buying and selling prices, and it is possible to gradually accumulate large assets by normal buying and selling (that is, selling what they have bought); the owners of some department stores (e.g. the Chirathivat family of Central Department Store) are one such example. However, in order to earn a large profit within a short period, it becomes necessary to buy and sell in the commodity futures market. If one relies on this over a long period of time, the chances are high that even if he gains today, he will lose some day; but some have profited by resorting to speculation from time to time. Rubber traders like

Tan Lark Sye and Ko Teck Kin seem to have resorted to speculation periodically, and made large profits during the Korean War boom,[19] while the meteoric rise of Robert Kuok in Malaysia seems to have had something to do with speculation in the sugar futures market.

Speculation can also take place in the foreign exchange and stock markets. For example, in Indonesia, where the foreign exchange rate is maintained at a certain level by the Bank of Indonesia, whenever a rumour circulates that devaluation will take place due to deterioration in the balance of payments, there is heavy buying of the US dollar. It is not very clear who the parties engaged in this are, though it is often said that Chinese banks, which dominate the private commercial banking sector, are willing participants.

In Singapore and Malaysia, the stock market is well developed *vis-à-vis* the level of overall economic development. According to one estimate, the ratio of the size of the stock market to GDP was roughly 70 per cent in 1986, which was considerably higher than the 6.2 per cent in the Philippines, 7.5 per cent in Thailand, and 0.6 per cent in Indonesia.[20] Thus, in those two countries, there is active trading in the stock market, and there is considerable temptation to buy or sell on margin—which is a form of speculation since, while the number of shares contracted to buy or sell greatly increases (how much depends on the margin requirement), the cash deposit can be quickly wiped out if the price moves in the wrong direction. These speculators are, however, relatively innocuous participants. The real villains seem to be the securities brokers who borrow from financial institutions to engage in margin trading. For example, they were mainly responsible for the closure of the Kuala Lumpur and Singapore Stock Exchanges that was precipitated by the bankruptcy of Pan Electric Industries in late 1985.[21]

In those two countries, there are a number of capitalists who use the stock market in some other ways. For example, suppose there is a manufacturing company listed on the stock exchange (Kuala Lumpur or Singapore), whose controlling shareholder wants to sell his interests. One way in which a capitalist can make use of this situation to get rich quickly is to take over this company and use it as a corporate vehicle for raising capital to get into real estate, finance, or some other service where fast money can be made. Manufacturing is slow in earning profit, so it is either divested or scaled down, and after a few years, the original company becomes a service-centred conglomerate. For example, Kee Yong Wee's real estate and finance conglomerate, Malaysian Resources Corp., used to be a carbide manufacturer; and Tan Koon Swan's Pan Electric Industries, the property and hotel giant, was originally a manufacturer of refrigerators and fans.[22]

The first hurdle to clear on this road to success is getting started. The manufacturing company is attractive because it is already listed on the stock exchange, whereas to start a new company and get it listed would be time-consuming and troublesome (there are some listing requirements). But if it is attractive to the speculator, why is it not so to the present owner? The speculator must have something which raises the worth of the company. For example, if the company has a competitor which is causing it financial trouble and this competitor is also facing some problems, the speculator can increase the company's worth if he can somehow arrange its merger with the competitor and get it approved by the government. Alternatively, the company may be facing problems due to bad management (despotic management or family-dominated top management), and its worth may be increased by the appointment of professional management. The company's owner could also be a foreigner who wants to pull out because he feels uneasy under the conditions prevailing in the country.

The next hurdle is to raise capital in the stock market. This is an attractive method since there is no interest burden, but in order to do so, the purchaser has to be able to sell newly issued shares to investors at a high price. If the price is low, the amount of capital that he can raise is that much smaller. Alternatively, the full amount required for a corporate take-over need not be raised in the market directly. The owners of the target company may accept new shares (usually with some cash), although for this take-over bid to be successful, the shares have to be attractive. Either way, it is important to maintain the share price at a fairly high level. Part of the task may be accomplished in the initial take-over stage if the market responds positively to the merger or the introduction of a professional management team. But this is not enough for a speculator; he wants to do more, for example, by leaking disinformation to the public to manipulate the share price.

A publicly listed company has to issue periodically a financial statement disclosing certain information. For general investors, this is an important basis for investment decision, so the financial statement has to look good if the share price is to remain high. Theoretically, bad financial results are reflected in the statement, which will, in turn, lower the share price. It is required by law that these results be reported in the financial statement, but there are ways to make them appear much less significant than they actually are. For example, loans which cannot be collected for some reason (e.g. the borrowers are in financial difficulty, hovering between existence and liquidation) have to be wiped out as losses, but they can be kept as assets. In the worst case, for which its executives can be charged with criminal breach of trust, the company reports profits when it actually suffered losses. Although there are some checks on such dishonest financial reporting (such as requiring an audit by a chartered accountant), they sometimes do not work. Thus, there is some truth in the saying in South-East Asia that 'an audited financial statement does not mean a thing'.

Another way to obtain quick returns is to borrow for investment. Even borrowing heavily to expand a manufacturing facility can be regarded as a speculative activity, since the company will be saddled with heavy interest payments if the expected results do not materialize. The most conservative strategy would be not to borrow at all and meet all financial requirements with the company's own funds, but this may be a little anachronistic in the present fluid situation. The next most conservative strategy would be to borrow for working capital but not for long-term investment. To a trader, for example, borrowed capital is recovered when the goods it bought are sold, so even if things do not go as expected, the damage can be minimized; but if he builds a big building with borrowed funds, the interest payments will become a heavy—perhaps even crippling—burden in the event of a prolonged recession.

Speculative borrowing goes further beyond that. In comparison, the borrowing of a trader to build a headquarters or of a manufacturer to expand his plant looks respectable. Speculators borrow heavily and invest the money in areas where they can expect quick returns. A typical area of investment is real estate; another is hotels. Since the mid-1970s, many high-rise buildings were built for offices and hotels in the ASEAN countries; for example, along Jalan Thamrin and Jalan Sudirman in Jakarta and in the Golden Triangle in Kuala Lumpur. In fact, Kuala Lumpur has more high-rise buildings than Tokyo. As a result of this and of the economic recession brought about by the decline of oil prices, the rental price of office floor space in Kuala Lumpur fell to less than half of what it was at its peak. A somewhat similar situation exists in Singapore and Metro Manila, where hotel room rates are especially depressed. Those who have entered housing development are finding themselves in the same predicament: the land they bought and the houses they built do not sell at the expected prices. They cannot even recover the sunk cost, let alone make profits.[23] Thus, those who have invested in real estate and hotels with borrowed capital are now facing serious financial problems. Some have already pulled out or gone bankrupt: for example, Hendra Rahardja of Indonesia, who invested in hotels in Singapore; John Gokongwei, who built hotels in Metro Manila, and Chong Kok Lim, who built Sungei Wang Shopping Plaza and Regent Hotel in Kuala Lumpur.[24] Many are, however, still surviving, having managed to roll over their loans, but this has caused problems for financial and other creditor institutions, which cannot easily foreclose the property offered as security since its market value has dipped below the sum advanced to the speculators.

A mystery for those who are familiar with sound corporate financing is that high leverages (debt–equity ratios) of several to one are common in South-East Asia. How is this possible? To any sensible financier, equity is a rough ceiling on loan; but in South-East Asia, loan often exceeds equity by more than two to one. This is possible because financial institutions in the region accept as collateral, the asset which is to be bought with the borrowed money. They are willing to do this for respectable investors who have a proven track record, since there are not many of them and the alternatives are equally unattractive, or even less attractive.

There are also other reasons. As pointed out in the previous two chapters, state banks are important in the ASEAN countries, especially in Indonesia and Malaysia. In general, they appear to be less professionally managed and under heavy political pressure. Those with strong government connections often manage to obtain a big loan for a respectable-looking project, by pledging the asset to be bought with the loan as security. Many of the buildings along Jalan Thamrin and Jalan Sudirman in Jakarta and in the Golden Triangle of Kuala Lumpur were financed with loans from state banks.

It is not, however, only investors in real estate and hotels who rely on state banks for new, large ventures. Some who are short of capital borrow heavily from state banks by using government connections for quite respectable business ventures (such as manufacturing, which qualifies as a pioneer project under the government's industrialization programme in some countries), and use as equity capital the 'commissions' they receive from their contractors or suppliers. This may be a more conscientious type; in a worse case, the company set up with government money is made a milch cow for the organizer and his family. It is said, for example, that a number of Filipino capitalists have done this.[25]

In the mid-1980s, several private commercial banks have run into trouble (for example, Asia Trust Bank in Thailand, National Bank of Brunei, and Pan Indonesia (Panin) Bank in Indonesia). These were serving essentially as money machines for the owner families. The money collected in the banks was channelled to their other family businesses, often without proper collateral. The worst of these was the National Bank of Brunei. Malaysian capitalist Khoo Teck Puat, who had a controlling interest in the bank, diverted about $600 million (about 90 per cent of the total portfolio) to his other businesses in such fields as hotels, real estate, and banking. By appointing members of the Brunei royal family to top executive posts, Khoo made it appear that the bank was state-related, if not state-owned, and deceived international bankers into giving it inter-bank loans. In 1986 the Brunei Government arrested his son who had been serving as its chairman; and it is also putting pressure on Khoo Teck Puat to repay the loans.[26] Interestingly, in the mid-1960s, he had tried to use Malayan Banking Berhad, a bank he founded in Malaysia, for the same purpose. He partly succeeded, but when word of what he was doing leaked out and a run on the bank ensued, he eventually lost control to the Malaysian Government, which mounted a rescue operation. While he was heading Malayan Banking Berhad, he bought hotels in Singapore.[27]

That there is considerable room for speculators in South-East Asia results partly from the fact that the financial markets are well developed *vis-à-vis* the level of economic development. The stock markets in Singapore and Malaysia have already been referred to; and another well-developed financial market is the money market. For example, in the Philippines during the Marcos period, finance companies were active in discounting commercial papers. In effect, they were quasi-banks: although they could not accept demand deposits and engage in some other operations allowed for commercial banks, they could accept time-deposits, and, in order to attract deposits, they offered higher interest rates than commercial banks. With these deposits, they bought commercial papers.

The risky part of this operation was that the commercial papers they bought carried more risk than those offered to commercial banks. Companies which had exhausted their line of credit with commercial banks came to finance companies. They were willing to pay higher interest rates, but the fact that they had exhausted their credit meant that they were poor risks. The finance companies which bought their commercial papers were therefore assuming more risk than were the commercial banks, but they needed to buy these papers because they were paying higher interest rates to depositors. The danger implicit in this operation was not apparent when the Philippine economy was faring well, but it came to a head in early 1981 when Dewey Dee absconded. The major finance companies of that time (for example, Bancom and Atrium) had lent heavily to him; after he fled the country, they were saddled with the worthless sheets of paper he had signed. When this became known, it started a run on them, and soon afterwards they went bankrupt.[28]

Among the capitalists in South-East Asia, questionable characters appear to outnumber speculators. Some capitalists, when in need of money, seem to be willing to set fire to their factories to collect the insurance. Particularly in the Philippines and Indonesia, some of the frequent factory fires must be due to arson.[29] Other capitalists resort to smuggling. In the Philippines and Indonesia, one often hears about institutionalized smuggling with the tacit approval of government officials. In Indonesia, Chinese capitalists often tied up with military officers during the Sukarno period.[30] Some of them moved to Singapore and smuggled rubber out of Sumatra during the Confrontation period, again allegedly with the tacit approval of the military commanders in the region.[31] For many cigarette and liquor manufacturers, it is far simpler to make money by evading taxes than to make efforts to reduce production costs, for taxes constitute a large part of their prices. Evading taxes is so important that they are willing to bribe government officials or keep influential ones in their pay for protection. Some who have good government connections even seem to offer protection to those who are undertaking illegal activities (for example, the tax cheater, the smuggler, and the organizer of a black market dollar ring). Rightly or wrongly, it is charged in the Philippines and Indonesia that most of those who resort to these illegal activities are Chinese.

The Socio-political Environment

Dictatorship has been the most fertile ground for rent-seekers in South-East Asia, for, since there are no effective checks on the use of political power under that system, the government can dispose of economic resources under its control or intervene in the economy with impunity. On the dictators who emerged in developed countries in the course of modern history, war (or its threat) imposed a certain rationality, but on the state-making of South-East Asia in the post-war period, it has been a much weaker constraint. Furthermore, in developed countries where dictators had to impose taxes for state financing, the way in which state revenue could be spent was more constrained than in the dictatorships of contemporary South-East Asia which obtain a large part of state revenue from sale of natural resources (such as oil) to multinational companies and/or can depend on economic aid and external borrowing for financing state or state-sponsored activities.

The Marcos government from late 1972 until his downfall in early 1986 was a dictatorship. Soon after he declared martial law in late 1972, he proceeded to destroy or considerably weaken the political institutions which could act as checks on his power. In succeeding in these tasks, Marcos came to assume almost absolute power. Unfortu-

nately for him, by the time of martial law, the Philippines had few forest and other natural resources left, so he brought the two leading
exports, sugar and coconut, under state control. He also obtained a
large amount of economic aid from the United States, Japan, and some
other developed countries, and at the same time borrowed extensively
from international lending agencies. These government monopolies,
economic aid, and international borrowings created an inordinate
amount of economic rent for his cronies. Of course, he himself pocketed
a lot of money: he is alleged to have embezzled $5–10 billion, and
appeared in the recent Guinness Book of World Records as the biggest
thief in the world.[32] Corruption pervaded the Philippine bureaucracy.
His lieutenants, such as Juan Ponce Enrile and Gregorio S. Licaros,
are alleged to have had some share in the spoils.[33] They too attracted
rent-seekers, whose rake-in was, of course, smaller than that of
Marcos's cronies. With such pervasive corruption, business morale
deteriorated dramatically; to establish government connections and
use them to manipulate the environment became the dominant strategy
for any aspiring businessman.

   Indonesian dictatorship under President Suharto is structurally
different from Marcos's martial law regime.[34] Suharto, who has
headed the Indonesian Government for the past two decades, has
never had such absolute power as Marcos did; rather, he has shared
power with other military leaders.[35] Of course, he has been the
strongest leader and has the largest 'fief', but the other military
leaders also have their own 'fiefs' (ministries or regions), within which
they exercise power with a considerable degree of freedom.[36] There
has been a great deal of change among Suharto's military supporters in
the past two decades (some have died and others have lost power),
but the *modus vivendi* has not been seriously disturbed. This has enabled the military leaders to wield political power with a great deal of
discretion, and in the economic field, create cronies and a large
number of other rent-seekers. From the viewpoint of aspiring capitalists, rent-seeking has been the most logical strategy since the government not only wields its power with discretion but also controls a huge
amount of capital through its banks and other state enterprises (a large
part of that capital has been oil money). Thus, as in the Philippines
during martial law, they have sought powerful patrons who could
assist them in their approach to the government.[37]

   Democracy has not necessarily done better than dictatorship; it too
has created many rent-seekers. In the Philippines under the Aquino
government, and in Malaysia under the NEP, although the use of
government connections for business is not as blatant as under

dictatorship, rent-seeking activities are prevalent.[38] The situation was also similar in the Philippines before martial law and in Indonesia in the early 1950s.[39] One major problem of democracy is that politicians have to seek votes, and in so doing, they make promises to their supporters. When they are elected to office, they have to deliver on their promises. And if they do, they can count on the same support when they next run for office.

What they can deliver is what they can do with their political power. It may be a government licence, public works project, loan from a government financial institution, protection from foreign competition, foreign exchange allocation, land conversion, logging or mining concession, monopoly, government approval, or anything with economic value which the government can deliver. Being politicians, they cannot do many of these things by themselves: they need the co-operation of the bureaucracy. They therefore try to bring it under their control, and in the process, destroy its autonomy. Appointment, tenure, and promotion in the bureaucracy become politicized, so decision-making within the bureaucracy becomes highly penetrated by the interests of politicians who have selfish motives. Their stake in the bureaucracy becomes much higher with the inflow of economic aid, the availability of external funds with government guarantee, and the extremely high prices fetched by natural resources in the international market (especially *vis-à-vis* their shadow prices in the domestic economy).

Rent-seekers are not, however, a unique phenomenon of South-East Asia. In Japan and the West, there are also a number of rent-seekers; and in the past century or so, there have been considerably more who have played significant economic roles. In Meiji Japan, rent-seeking activities became so widespread that the term '*seisho*' was coined for conspicuous rent-seekers. The Mitsubishi and Mitsui zaibatsu were the largest and best-known seisho of pre-war Japan. One might therefore argue that the South-East Asian situation is a repetition of what happened in Japan and the West and will resolve automatically in the process of capitalistic development. However, rent-seeking is by far more pervasive in South-East Asia today, and there are no indications (at least for the immediate future) that it will decline. In Japan and the West, although they had different types of government (Japan had an authoritarian government whereas the West had a democracy in the developing stage), war-making and the need to tax people for the bulk of state revenue imposed rationality on governments and greatly reduced the scope for rent-seeking.

The situation in South-East Asia, of course, differs from one country to another. Rent-seeking activities are not prevalent in Singapore.

One major reason for this is Lee Kuan Yew's style of political leadership. He succeeded in making the PAP the dominant party without tying politics to business (at least not to any significant extent); and although he has had almost complete authority, he has not abused it for economic gain, nor let his ministers and other high government officials do so.[40] He set a growth-oriented, clean, strong government as his goal, and has been largely successful in realizing it. A great deal of the credit for this must go to his wisdom, determination, and political skills.

There were, however, conditions that allowed one such as Lee Kuan Yew to emerge as the dominant political leader in Singapore. First, the population is largely Chinese, and the Chinese could do fairly well in business on their own. It was not absolutely necessary for politicians to make many personal promises to businessmen or for the government to make special allowances to nurture the entrepreneurship of its supporters. Furthermore, the fact that Singapore is a small island and a predominantly Chinese state seems to have been another favourable factor for Lee Kuan Yew. In the 1950s, the Chinese were being discriminated against in Indonesia, the Philippines, and Thailand. The situation has dramatically improved in Thailand since then, but there are still strong anti-Chinese feelings in the other two, and in the 1970s, Malaysia joined them with the NEP. Thus, the leading Singapore Chinese seem to have developed a siege mentality, which has acted as a powerful centripetal force.

In Thailand also, rent-seeking activities have considerably declined. In the 1950s, politics dominated business, and so, for protection as well as for business advantage, it was imperative for capitalists to find patrons among the high-ranking military officers who dominated Thai politics. Many of them sat on the board of directors of their client companies.[41] With the passage of time, however, these patron–client relationships declined in importance, and the capitalists emerged as an independent force.[42]

Why did this happen? One favourable factor was the existence of the King, who could act as a check on the military. The King lost absolute power in 1932, but he retains both high prestige among the Thai people and some actual powers (such as approval of the promotion of high military officers). Thus, for political stability, the military needed the support of the King, who could, in turn, restrain them from abusing their power. If a protest movement developed and threatened political stability, the King could act as a balancing factor. Alternatively, a protest movement could aim from the beginning to replace the military government with a new political system that retained the King as a constitutional monarch. From the viewpoint of military leaders, this meant that if they mismanaged matters and a protest movement developed, they could not suppress it by force alone (at least not for too long). Furthermore, because of the prolonged military conflict in Indo-China, the threat of external aggression appeared quite real to the Thai military on a number of occasions. Thus, because of both the King's presence as a balancing factor and the military threat from Indo-China, there was fairly strong need for rationality in government policy.

Since Thailand did not have oil or other mineral resources, the government had to rely essentially on labour productivity for the economic management of the country. For this, the most effective group was the Chinese. Fortunately, because the Chinese in Thailand were better integrated than elsewhere in South-East Asia, the government's reliance on them for economic development did not arouse strong emotional reaction from the indigenous Thais.[43] Furthermore, because they accounted for a substantial proportion of the population (about 10 per cent or more), the Chinese had the potential to become a powerful force for economic development. So, as the military withdrew from the economy and gave the Chinese a free hand, the economy improved; and this forced the military to withdraw further.

The fact that the Chinese are fairly well integrated into Thai society also allowed them to participate in politics, and recently they have emerged as a powerful force in Thai politics. The Chinese capitalists now share political power with the King and the military. Theoretically, this makes it easier for them to penetrate the government and influence its policy in their favour. Some have done so, but the government maintains a considerable degree of autonomy, and the relationship between business and the government seems merely to be part of the normal process of capitalistic development: compared with Japan of a few decades ago, for example, rent-seeking in Thailand does not seem excessive.

On the other hand, the degree of rent-seeking in the Philippines, Malaysia, and Indonesia is excessive, and rent-seekers dominate the capitalism of those countries. One might cite the greater government involvement in the economy as the major reason for this, and for the last two countries, explain it in terms of the availability of oil revenue. Undoubtedly, oil money did increase the scope for government involvement. Nevertheless, a more fundamental reason is that the Chinese are less well integrated into indigenous society, so that the government has had to step in to create indigenous capitalists; but, because of either their dependency on government patronage or their lack of business expertise, indigenous capitalists have not become a political force to exert a rationalizing influence on the government.

Take, for example, the case of Indonesia. The Chinese dominate the capitalism of the country, but they cannot become a political force. Because they are not well integrated into indigenous society, its members (or pribumi) will not accept their participation in Indonesian politics, which, like Islam, they view as sacrosanct and reserved for themselves. Thus the possibility of economic power becoming political power, which exists in Thailand, is blocked in Indonesia. The Indonesian military, which monopolizes power, feels no urgency to change the situation. As long as it is only the Chinese who dominate Indonesia's capitalism, the military need not fear that someday they may have to share power with them and eventually hand it over—which is a distinct possibility in Thailand. There are some pribumi capitalists, but they are so dependent on the grace of the government that they have no chance of becoming an independent force.

In Malaysia, under Tunku Abdul Rahman, there was little government intervention in the economy, and rent-seeking activities were at a moderate level.[44] However, with the inauguration of the NEP in 1971, the government began intervening extensively in the economy and has created a large number of government-connected capitalists. Here again, a basic problem is the lack of integration of the Chinese and the weakness of indigenous capitalists. To the political élites of the UMNO, the dominant force in Malaysian politics, the Chinese ceased to be acceptable as full-fledged domestic capitalists after the May 1969 riot, and it became imperative to promote indigenous capitalists. To do this, the Malaysian Government changed considerably the rules of the game of business. Though it was not the government's intention, the NEP enabled well-connected Malays to get rich quickly; and as a consequence, Malays who aspired to be capitalists expended much effort on establishing such connections and using them for business advantage. This in turn affected the business ethics of Chinese capitalists. By working closely with Malay capitalists or Malay politicians, it became possible to make a large sum of money—an accomplishment that would take decades even for the most successful Chinese capitalists before the NEP. The rise of such capitalists as Tan Koon Swan was both disgusting to and demoralizing for the old Chinese towkay, who had made every cent of their money through hard work. Few of them made the transition to the NEP period and the new rules of the game, so that a new breed of Chinese capitalist (such as Lim Goh Tong, Robert Kuok, and Khoo Kay Peng), many of whom are rent-seekers, has become dominant.

In the Philippines today, with the economy at such a depressed level, everything goes round in a vicious circle. The major problems were created largely by Marcos during the martial law period. The question then boils down to why Marcos was able to declare martial law and abolish democracy. One answer is that the economy was not dynamic enough to support democracy. Not a few people were disillusioned with democracy's performance, especially its economic performance, and welcomed martial law as a solution to the problems at that time. The economy was not faring well partly because many Chinese could not obtain citizenship and were so discriminated against that they could not contribute their full potential to the economy. The Filipino capitalists who emerged at their expense or at the expense of American investors were more mature than their counterparts in Indonesia and Malaysia, partly as the result of the promotion policy of the American Administration in the pre-war period, but many of them thrived on quota allocation (foreign exchange quotas in the 1950s and sugar quotas throughout the period), government financial assistance, monopolies, and other government favours, and became a burden on the economy. To prop up the economy, the government became more interventionist; and as a consequence, rent-seeking activities became more rampant and the economy suffered so much more.

Many of the rent-seekers are speculators. They share one common feature: both seek quick returns. For example, many of those who had access to government financial institutions borrowed money to invest in real estate. Many of the high-rise buildings in the Golden Triangle of Kuala Lumpur and along Jalan Thamrin and Jalan Sudirman in Jakarta could not have been built without cheap government loans. Investment in property development appeared profitable since property prices had been rising and earlier investors were making handsome profits. Despite the possibility that property prices would decline in an economic recession, which might cause serious financial problems, investors were willing to take a chance, since the risk was small and the potential reward was large. If something went wrong, they might lose some money, though often not much, since most of the money spent on such projects was government money. (The land and property to be developed were mortgaged when money was borrowed from government financial institutions. If this was not enough, additional properties were mortgaged at inflated values.)

Government financial institutions became sitting ducks for government leaders and the rent-seekers connected with them.[45] If these institutions ran out of funds, the rent-seekers went bearing government guarantees to international financial institutions. Part of the debts of South-East Asian countries is of this nature. The government guarantee means that if projects do not go well, the government assumes the liability. For example, the Development Bank of the Philippines and Bank Pembangunan Indonesia (Bapindo) have taken over a number of internationally financed projects started by rent-seekers.

It is not only real estate development that attracts the speculative interest of rent-seekers. It may be any field which looks promising. For example, Suharto's son, Bambang, ventured into shipping (Trikora Lloyd) with the money he raised abroad with Bapindo's guarantee; Liem Sioe Liong of Indonesia borrowed heavily from government banks to build a huge cement complex (Indocement); Ricardo Silverio of the Philippines borrowed heavily from the PNB to expand his assembly plant in the 1970s; and another Marcos crony, Rodolfo Cuenca, went into shipping (Galleon Shipping Corp.) with money borrowed from foreign banks with government guarantee. To them, it did not matter whether they had expertise in their fields of investment: in fact, Bambang and Cuenca knew nothing about shipping, and Liem Sioe Liong knew nothing about cement. Their logic was that in countries where capital is short, a big sum of money is a monopoly power, and investment of such a sum in new areas is bound to bring huge profits.

The prevalence of speculative activities is also related to the insecure position of the Chinese in South-East Asia. In Indonesia, for example, many Chinese apparently feel insecure: this is reflected in the saying one sometimes hears, that the rich Chinese send capital and children abroad (for education at first and settlement after graduation), the middle-class Chinese send only children since they do not have capital for investment, and the poor Chinese have money neither for investment nor children's education, and so are stuck in the country. The Chinese in Malaysia also seem to be feeling insecure about their present and future status because of the socio-economic changes wrought at their expense in the 1970s and the recent rise of Islamic fundamentalism which aims at the establishment of an Islamic state in Malaysia (which would be a deadly threat to their way of life).[46] Some of the capitalists in these countries have extensive investments abroad (for example, Robert Kuok of Malaysia and Liem Sioe Liong of Indonesia). There are those who regard this as multinational expansion and thus a sign of capitalistic progress, but it seems to be more a case of capital flight.

To a number of Chinese, especially in the regional cities of Indonesia, the military appear more as racketeers than a legitimate government institution.[47] As Chinese have been the target of violent attacks by

Indonesians, those who have tangible assets are willing to make contributions to the military if they can offer protection. This arrangement for protection, however, takes the form of organized crime when the military threaten the Chinese either directly or indirectly by inciting private anti-Chinese groups.[48] Many of the big capitalists who are well connected with the government in Jakarta do not suffer this problem, and benefit greatly from the government, but they too seem uncertain about their own and their families' future, since an undercurrent of anti-Chinese feeling remains in Indonesian society. In Malaysia, the situation is not as bad as in Indonesia, but there is also a feeling of insecurity and concern about the future.[49] In such a setting, it is difficult to formulate long-term business strategy: the most reasonable course of action is to make money as quickly as possible and invest a substantial portion of it abroad or leave with it.

1. The remaining four states are headed by a governor.

2. For example, the King took the initiative in forming Siam Commercial Bank and Siam Cement Co. For their evolution and further references, see Appendix 4.

3. Sukamdani Sahid Gitosardjono, head of the Sahid group, which is involved in hotels, construction, and trading, is sometimes said to be related to Mrs Suharto, but if there is a blood relationship between them, it must be distant.

4. For more details on their involvement in business, see *Asian Wall Street Journal*, 24–26 November 1986.

5. The involvement of Marcos's side of the family in business is discussed in the paper entitled 'Some are Smarter than Others', which was privately circulated in 1979. It is commonly known as 'the octopus paper', because the title page carries a picture of an octopus (probably symbolizing Marcos's 'tentacles' reaching into many businesses).

6. The Chinese are often said to be better accomplices in corruption. For example, Benigno Aquino thought that for Marcos, Chinese were more important allies than Filipinos (Fred Poole and Max Vanzi, *Revolution in the Philippines: The United States in a Hall of Cracked Mirrors*, New York, McGraw-Hill Book Co., 1984, p. 264). However, the evidence gathered so far shows that Marcos relied more extensively on Filipinos than on Chinese.

7. For various meanings of the term 'bureaucratic capitalist', see Karl Wittfogel, *Oriental Despotism*, New Haven, Yale University Press, 1957, Chapter 7, Section 5.

8. PT Admiral Lines is controlled by the navy; Tri Usaha Bhakti by the army; and Yayasan Dharma Putra by Kostrad. For details, see Richard Robison, *Indonesia: The Rise of Capital*, North Sydney, Allen & Unwin, 1986, pp. 260–6. Military officers on active duty sit on the board of directors of these military enterprises, but they cannot participate in management. However, retired officers can. In some cases (such as Yayasan Dharma Putra), there is active Chinese participation in management.

Until the late 1950s, there were a number of military enterprises in Thailand. See Sungsidh Piriyarangsan, 'Thai Bureaucratic Capitalism, 1932–1960', Master of Economics thesis, Thammasat University, 1980, Chapter 4.

9. This concept is relevant only to Malaysia, Indonesia, and Thailand. In Singapore, there are none who can be called bureaucratic capitalists. In the Philippines, although government connections have been important, the Philippine bureaucracy has been weak, so few capitalists have emerged among the former bureaucrats. Fanny Cortes Garcia, who founded Pacific Cement in the mid-1960s, is one of the few exceptions.

10. On tax-farmers in Thailand, see Chatthip Nartsupha and Suthy Prasartset, eds., *The Political Economy of Siam, 1851–1910*, Bangkok, The Social Science Association of Thailand, n.d.; Chatthip Nartsupha *et al.*, eds., *The Political Economy of Siam, 1910– 1932*, Bangkok, The Social Science Association of Thailand, [1978]; and Hong Lysa, *Thailand in the Nineteenth Century: Evolution of the Economy and Society*, Singapore, Institute of Southeast Asian Studies, 1984.

11. Sungsidh, op. cit., Chapters 3 and 4.

12. For example, see Robison, *Indonesia*, p. 359.

13. For more details on the Fleet group, see *Asiaweek*, 3 May 1987.

14. Krirkkiat Phipatheritham, 'The Push and Pull of Economics and Politics in Thailand' (unpublished).

15. *Asahi Shinbun*, 29 July 1986.

16. Yoshihara Kunio, *Philippine Industrialization: Foreign and Domestic Capital*, Quezon City, Ateneo de Manila University Press and Singapore, Oxford University Press, 1985, pp. 134–40.

17. Tan Ee Leong's interview transcript, Oral History Programme, Archives & Oral History Department, Singapore, p. 159; Mantetsu Toa Keizai Chosa-kyoku, *Eiryo Marei Biruma oyobi Goshu ni okeru Kakyo*, Tokyo, [published by the author], 1941, pp. 554–6.

18. This paragraph is based on the so-called financial white paper which circulated privately in 1981. Reputedly, it was written by the Bank of Philippine Islands. Its exact title is 'Recent Developments in the Chinese Community'. Hereafter, it is referred to as 'the Philippine financial white paper'.

19. Tan Lark Sye's and Ko Teck Kin's businesses declined after their death. It seems that those businesses were essentially one-man organizations dependent on their speculative instinct.

20. *Asian Wall Street Journal*, 19 March 1987.

21. On the closing of the Kuala Lumpur and Singapore Stock Exchanges in late 1985, see *Far Eastern Economic Review*, 12 December 1985.

22. The number of Malaysian-based companies listed in the Kuala Lumpur Stock Exchange's property section has doubled to 14 since 1979. Many of these were formerly manufacturing or mining companies. *Far Eastern Economic Review*, 2 April 1987. For further discussion on stock market manipulation (as well as other speculative activities) in Malaysia, see also Khor Kok Peng, *Malaysia's Economy in Decline*, Penang, Consumers' Association of Penang, 1987.

23. According to one estimate, a typical high-rise building needs to be sold for at least M$350 per sq. ft. to break even, but it is currently worth only about M$200 per sq. ft. The Singapore market for high-rise buildings is similarly depressed. *Far Eastern Economic Review*, 12 March 1987.

24. Besides Paper Products, two other property companies, Sri Hartamas and Duta Consolidated, seem to be in serious trouble. A number of other property companies in Malaysia are also said to be in difficulties.

25. Recently, the Jacinto family asked the Philippine Government to return to them the control of Iligan Integrated Steel Mills, which Marcos had forced them to sell in the mid-1970s. An investigation into this matter by the government revealed a number of

irregularities by the Jacinto family during their management of the steel mill. *Sunday Times*, 3 August 1986.

26. On Khoo Teck Puat's involvement in the National Bank of Brunei, see *Far Eastern Economic Review*, 11 and 18 December 1986; and *Asian Wall Street Journal*, 21–22 and 24 November 1986 and 2 February 1987.

27. On Khoo Teck Puat's involvement in Malayan Banking Berhad, see Bank Negara Malaysia, Economics Department, *Money and Banking in Malaysia*, Kuala Lumpur, 1984, pp. 74–7 and 270–3.

28. In Thailand, too, a large finance company called Raja Finance collapsed in the late 1970s. See *Business in Thailand*, June 1979.

29. The Philippine financial white paper alleges that Dewey Dee and his Chinese friends (the so-called Magnificent Seven) resorted to arson, smuggling, tax evasion, and foreign exchange dealings in the black market.

30. During the Sukarno period, the military sponsored smuggling in order to raise money, because economic decline prevented the government from providing an adequate budget. See Ruth McVey, 'The Post-Revolutionary Transformation of the Indonesian Army', *Indonesia*, No. 11 (1971), pp. 152–3.

Even during the New Order period, smuggling has not apparently stopped (especially with regard to imports). One still hears about large-scale smuggling of household electrical appliances (for example, in early 1986, a number of household electrical appliances which were not produced in the country and not allowed to be imported, were being sold in Jakarta). Some have been caught: for example Robby Sie, who was smuggling expensive European cars into the country in the mid-1970s.

31. Ko Teck Kin is an example. Tan Ee Leong's interview transcript, p. 165.

32. There are a number of writings on Marcos's plunder. For example, see Primitivo Mijares, *The Conjugal Dictatorship of Ferdinand and Imelda Marcos I*, San Francisco, Union Square Publications, 1976; *San Jose Mercury News*, 23 June 1985; *Asian Wall Street Journal*, 20 August 1986, 13 October 1986, and 2 February 1987; and Poole and Vanzi, op. cit.

33. A corruption charge against Juan Ponce Enrile was reported in *Asahi Shinbun*, 2 November 1986. Licaros is mentioned in the Philippine financial white paper.

34. Sukarno may have been a dictator during Guided Democracy, but the number of rent-seekers he created and the largess they received were held down by his anti-capitalist orientation. On the rent-seekers of this period (such as Aslam and Markam), see Robison, *Indonesia*, pp. 91–2.

35. On the structure of political power in Indonesia under Suharto, see David Jenkins, *Suharto and His Generals: Indonesian Military Politics 1975–1983*, Ithaca, Cornell Modern Indonesia Project, Monograph No. 64, 1984; Harold Crouch, *The Army and Politics in Indonesia*, Ithaca, Cornell University Press, 1978; and Karl Jackson and Lucian Pye, eds., *Political Power and Communications in Indonesia*, Berkeley, University of California Press, 1978.

36. The biggest of the 'fiefs' 'owned' by Suharto's lieutenants was Ibnu Sutowo's Pertamina. Sutowo, however, left Pertamina in 1976, taking responsibility for its payment crisis (under his management, Pertamina incurred debts of $10.5 billion despite a large oil price increase in the preceding several years). On the Pertamina scandal, see *Asian Wall Street Journal*, 23 May 1980 and 17 July 1980.

37. On the effect on business ethics, see Nono Anwar Makarim, 'Companies and Business in Indonesia', Doctor of Juridical Science thesis, Harvard Law School, November 1978, p. 276.

38. On new cronyism under Aquino, see *Far Eastern Economic Review*, 26 March

1987. In Malaysia also, some high government officials are alleged to be involved in corruption or ethically dubious practices. For example, see the report of Bumiputra Malaysia Finance Ltd. (Hong Kong) Committee of Enquiry (published by Bank Bumiputra Malaysia in 1986) and *Far Eastern Economic Review*, 2 April 1987.

In Malaysia, the state governments grant timber concessions and permits to change the designated usage of land. In nine of the thirteen states, the Menteri Besar (Chief Minister), who heads the majority party of the state legislature (Legislative Assembly), is appointed by the Sultan as the chief executive (the other four states have a governor). For a state government to function smoothly, the Menteri Besar must have a good working relationship with the Sultan (whose signature is needed, for example, for a bill passed by the state legislature to become law). His family and private businessmen can approach him to use his influence with the state government when they apply for timber concessions or conversion of land usage.

39. On corruption in the Philippines before martial law, see the bibliography in Ledivina Carino, ed., *Bureaucratic Corruption in Asia*, Manila, College of Public Administration, University of the Philippines, 1986. On Indonesia in the 1950s, see John Sutter, *Indonesianisasi: Politics in a Changing Economy, 1940–1955*, Data Paper No. 36, Southeast Asian Program, Cornell University, 1959, pp. 1053–5 and 1240–4; and Douglas S. Paauw, 'From Colonial to Guided Economy', in Ruth McVey, ed., *Indonesia*, New Haven, Southeast Asian Studies, Yale University, 1963.

40. The Singapore Government has not been completely free from corruption. On a recent scandal involving the Minister of National Development, Teh Cheang Wan, see *Far Eastern Economic Review*, 29 January 1987. In February 1987, the Malaysian newspaper, *The Star*, insinuated that the Teh case is merely the tip of an iceberg and that corruption is quite widespread in Singapore.

41. On patron–client relationships in Thailand in the 1950s, see G. William Skinner, *Leadership and Power in the Chinese Community of Thailand*, Ithaca, Cornell University Press, 1958, pp. 191–3.

42. See John Girling, *The Bureaucratic Polity in Modernizing Societies: Similarities, Differences, and Prospects in the ASEAN Region*, Singapore, Institute of Southeast Asian Studies, 1981, pp. 25 and 38; and John Girling, *Thailand: Society and Politics*, Ithaca, Cornell University Press, 1981, pp. 197–8.

43. On the integration of the Chinese in Thailand, see G. William Skinner, *Chinese Society in Thailand: An Analytical History*, Ithaca, Cornell University Press, 1957; Victor Purcell, *The Chinese in Southeast Asia*, reprinted Kuala Lumpur, Oxford University Press, 1980; and Cristina Blanc Szanton, 'Thai and Sino-Thai in Small Town Thailand: Changing Patterns of Interethnic Relations', in Linda Y. C. Lim and Peter Gosling, eds., *The Chinese in Southeast Asia*, Vol. 2, Singapore, Maruzen Asia, 1983.

44. The state of Sabah enjoys a considerable degree of autonomy. Tun Mustapha Harun, who dominated Sabah politics for about a decade until 1976, created such rent-seekers as Syed Kechik by handing out logging concessions. See Bruce Ross-Larson, *The Politics of Federalism: Syed Kechik in East Malaysia*, Singapore, published by the author, 1976; and Ed Hunter, *Misdeeds of Tun Mustapha*, [Hong Kong?], Ed Hunter Enterprise, [1976].

45. On the bad debts of the Indonesian state banks, Bank Bumi Daya and Bapindo, see Makarim, op. cit., p. 275.

46. On the rise of Islamic fundamentalism and its political implications, see Diane Mauzy and R. S. Milne, 'The Mahathir Administration: Discipline through Islam', in Bruce Gale, ed., *Readings in Malaysian Politics*, Petaling Jaya, Pelanduk Publications, 1986.

47. A similar situation prevailed in Bangkok in the 1950s. See Skinner, *Leadership and Power in the Chinese Community of Thailand*, pp. 303–4; and Fred Riggs, *Thailand: The Modernization of a Bureaucratic Polity*, Honolulu, East-West Center Press, 1966, Chapter 9.

48. For the view that a state can run a protection racket, see Charles Tilly, 'War Making and State Making as Organized Crime', in Peter Evans *et al.*, eds., *Bringing the State Back In*, Cambridge, Cambridge University Press, 1985.

49. Chang Ming Thien's move to Hong Kong is probably the best-known example of Chinese capital flight from Malaysia. He disposed of his controlling interests in United Malayan Banking Corp. in the early 1980s. Robert Kuok still has substantial interests in Malaysia, but he seems to have moved his headquarters to Hong Kong. George Tan, the key figure behind the Carrian affair which surfaced in Hong Kong in 1982, had little capital when he moved there from Singapore, but he soon managed to find access to Chinese flight capital from South-East Asia, and from Malaysia in particular, and used it to build up the Carrian group in its initial phase.

Chapter 5
Industrialization without Development

The Engine of Growth

IN response to those who believe that capitalism in South-East Asia is dominated by foreign capital (and is therefore ersatz), one can point to the rise of South-East Asian-owned banks as counter-evidence. As shown in Table 2.1, South-East Asian banks are far more important than foreign banks today, in contrast with the pre-war period, when foreign banks dominated the banking industry. It is true that the rise of South-East Asian banks has been made possible largely by government protection, but this does not necessarily mean that they are less efficient than foreign banks. The leading banks of the region (such as Bangkok Bank and OCBC) are quite modern in ownership and management (e.g. they are usually public companies managed largely by professionals) and seem to offer equally good banking services as (if not better services than) foreign banks. The organizers and managers of those banks have shown that they can learn what the Westerners are doing and can do equally well, thus destroying many of the stereotypes held of them.

The power of these banks is symbolized by their buildings. At Raffles Place, Singapore, stands the tallest building in Asia, the 65-storey OUB Centre. It is the headquarters of Overseas Union Bank (OUB), one of the three largest commercial banks in Singapore. Not far from Raffles Place, on Chulia Street, stands another tall (52-storey) building called OCBC Centre, the headquarters of another commercial bank, OCBC (Oversea-Chinese Banking Corp.). The 32-storey headquarters of UOB (United Overseas Bank) in Raffles Place is now dwarfed by the new building its rival constructed (OUB Centre), so it is planning to build an even taller building in the near future. In Bangkok, the tallest building in its business centre (on Silom Street) is the 31-storey headquarters of Bangkok Bank. In Metro Manila, Jakarta, and Kuala Lumpur, the headquarters of commercial banks are also conspicuous.

Banking is not the only sector in which modern, dynamic South-East Asian-owned capitalist institutions have been created. In Thailand,

Central Department Store, which is owned by the Chinese family, the Chirathivats, has several branches in Bangkok and is now the country's largest department store—bigger than Daimaru and other Japanese department stores operating there. Also, it gives better service to its customers (especially in terms of price and variety of merchandise). In other capitals of South-East Asia, there are also well-run South-East Asian-owned department stores (e.g. Metro in Singapore and Sarinah Jaya in Jakarta).

Another respectable South-East Asian-owned capitalist institution is the Ayala group. Besides banking (Bank of the Philippine Islands), it is engaged in insurance (Insular Life Assurance and FGU Insurance Corp.), real estate (Ayala Corp.), investment finance (Ayala Investment and Development Corp.), and hotels (Davao Insular Hotel, Calatagan Resort). In particular, the Ayala group is known as the developer of Makati. A few years after the Pacific War, Joseph McMicking of the Zobel family, which controls the Ayala group, came up with the idea of converting the family's Makati hacienda into a modern multizone sub-city, and, in the next 25 years, implemented it with great success. In property as well as insurance and banking, the Ayala group has excelled, and is respected for it by many Filipinos.

When OCBC, OUB, Bangkok Bank, Central Department Store, and Ayala Corp. are cited as evidence of the progress of capitalism in South-East Asia, a socialist economist might counter that they are mostly in unproductive fields. In the national accounting system of a socialist country, banking, real estate, and some of the other service industries in which South-East Asian capitalists tend to excel are not included. The socialist economist would therefore ask for evidence from manufacturing or other producing sectors of the economy if someone were to try to convince him that South-East Asian capitalism has made substantial progress.

One might question the Marxist theory of value which underlies the national income accounting system of a socialist state, but it has to be realized that the goods-producing sectors of the economy (that is, the primary (e.g. agriculture) and secondary (manufacturing) sectors) have different growth potentials from the service sector of the economy (such as banking, real estate, etc.). This is because the goods-producing sectors can act as an engine of growth, dragging the service sector along with them, but not vice versa. At best, the service sector can facilitate the growth of the goods-producing sector, but it cannot act as a locomotive of the economy.

Why? The reason is that only goods are tradable, but not services.[1] Tradable goods generate trade, which can act as an engine of growth.[2]

In trade, one tends to view export as good and import as bad for the economy. At least, that is what Keynesian economics teaches; but in growth economics, import is the objective of trade and export is its means. Imports enable a country to obtain the goods it cannot produce efficiently and the new machinery it cannot produce because it does not have the necessary technology. Exports earn the foreign exchange necessary to make such imports possible. In addition, foreign exchange earnings from exports enable a country to import patented technology which is not embodied in machinery and send engineers and scientists abroad for further training.

Even without trade, a country can grow—but only very slowly. Japan's successful economic development is unthinkable without trade, and so is the recent rapid growth of Taiwan, Hong Kong, and Korea. Then, one might ask, if these countries could use trade to their great advantage, why not others? The main reason is that they have been able to keep expanding their exports. Export expansion was important for their growth not because it increased their aggregate demand (as Keynesian economics teaches), but because it enabled them to import the goods (such as raw materials) which they produced inefficiently or not at all and the new machinery which appeared in the world market. Import composition changes over time, as the structure of the economy changes in the course of development, but what is important is to sustain the expansion of import (which has to be fed into the expanding economy) with an expansion of export (which meets ever-increasing foreign exchange requirements).

The next question is how to sustain an expansion of export over time. Here lies the importance of industrialization. England, which pioneered modern economic growth, the late starters such as Japan which followed England, and the Newly Industrializing Countries such as Taiwan and Korea in the recent period—all these countries sustained an increase of export with manufactured goods. Primary goods are also tradable, and theoretically it is possible to develop a country depending on their export, but in practice it is difficult. As Myrdal and Prebisch argued, the terms of trade for primary goods tend to deteriorate over time.[3] There may be exceptional periods and exceptional goods (because their supply is limited by nature's endowment), but in general, primary producers tend to suffer from such a deterioration and find it increasingly difficult to sustain an increase of export. This is because entry into production of primary goods (such as agricultural goods) is relatively free and their supply can thus be increased; or if supply cannot be expanded, as in the case of mineral resources, a resource-saving technology develops and reduces demand.

The point, however, is not necessarily manufactured versus primary goods. What is important is a country's ability to generate new exports one after another, or, as a Japanese economist put it, in a flying-geese pattern.[4] This enables the country to move on to a new product which fetches a better price when the old product ceases to be an attractive export (and eventually cannot be exported) either because of increased costs (due to increased wages) or new competition (from new entry or new products). This ability, however, can be more easily created by 'technologyful' industrialization. The major barrier to moving into a new product is usually technology. Once a technological base is created in industrialization, it is quite possible for one technology to lead to another, thus enabling a country to create production and export in a flying-geese pattern.

Industrial Achievements

The most dramatic post-war change in the economic structure of South-East Asia is the rise of the manufacturing industry. From being predominantly agricultural in the pre-war period, the region's manufacturing industry now accounts for about 20 per cent of its national income.[5] Primary processing (such as sugar milling, production of coconut oil, tin smelting, rubber processing, etc.) was the first major manufacturing industry to emerge in the region. Some primary products (such as oil) could be exported without processing, but in the case of others, processing before export was preferable, since transportation cost was saved or better quality resulted. Thus, around the turn of this century, machines were imported from the West for processing these products, and a large-scale machine-based manufacturing activity got off the ground.

In the pre-war period, industrial progress outside the processing industry was modest. The ideal candidates for import substitution (local production of manufactured goods which were formerly imported) were those for which there was a fairly large demand in the region, of which local production did not present difficult technical problems, whose main raw materials were available in the region, or in which transportation cost weighed heavily in their prices if imported. Beer, soft drinks, liquor, footwear, textiles, toiletries, and cement are examples. The inducement to local production was, in the case of beer, soft drinks, and cement, high transportation cost; in the case of liquor, footwear, and toiletries, the availability of raw materials in the region (sugar molasses for liquor, rubber for footwear, and coconut oil for soap); and in the case of textiles, large domestic consumption.

In general, however, import-substitution production did not advance very far in the pre-war period. In the post-war period, when the South-East Asian countries gained the freedom to chart their own courses of development, they gave top priority to import-substitution industrialization. This expanded the import-substitution industries which had started in the pre-war period, and enabled them not only to meet the domestic demand but also to export some of their products abroad. For example, although production of textiles had begun in the pre-war period, the demand was still being met largely by imports. In the post-war period, however, a large number of textile factories were set up with government help, and self-sufficiency was soon achieved (although this was delayed in Indonesia until the 1970s). Now, even the bulk of synthetic fibres (especially nylon and polyester fibre), needed as a raw material for textile production, is produced in the region.

The post-war import-substitution policy also led to production of a wide variety of new manufactured goods. As a result, industrial production is no longer confined to simple consumer goods. Consumer durables such as motor cars and household electrical appliances and a variety of components, parts, and intermediate products are produced. In addition, capital-intensive production (such as petroleum refining, production of petrochemicals, and integrated steel production) is undertaken.

One might ask whether such industrial activities are directed by foreign capital. Of course, some are. In Singapore, in particular, foreign capital dominates petroleum refining, production of petrochemical products, assembling of semiconductors, and assembling of household electrical appliances. However, the majority of industrial activities in the region are now undertaken by domestic capital. As argued in Chapter 2, the South-East Asian governments of the post-war period took various measures to promote domestic capital in the manufacturing field and succeeded in making it the major agent of industrialization.

With the rise of a manufacturing industry, a number of industrial capitalists emerged in the region. Examples include: in the Philippines, Ang Tuan Kai (textiles), Jose Campos (pharmaceuticals), Manuel Elizalde (paint, steel, and sugar), Guillermo Guevara (chemicals), Vicente Madrigal (cement), Jose Marcelo (steel), Aurelio Montinola (construction materials), and Gonzalo Puyat (furniture, steel, and flour); in Thailand, Suree Assadathorn (sugar), Sukri Bodhiratanangkura and Damri Darakananda (both in textiles), Dhanin Chiaravanont (agribusiness), Thiam Chokwatana (toiletries and other consumer goods), Taworn Pornprapha (motor cars), Kiatri Srifuengfung (sheet glass), Sawang Laohathai (steel and fertilizer), Udane Techapaibul (liquor), and Phraya Bhirombhakdi (beer); in Malaysia, Robert Kuok (sugar), Eric Chia, Chua Cheng Bok, Loh Boon Siew, and Tan Yuet Foh (all in motor vechicles); in Singapore, Aw Boon Haw (pharmaceuticals), Brian Chang (oil equipment), Chew Choo Keng (flour), Goh Tjoei Kok (steel), Kwek Hong Png (construction materials), and Robin Loh (shipbuilding); and in Indonesia, Ang Kok Ha (textiles and motor cars), Bob Hasan (plywood), Liem Sioe Liong (cement), Sjamsul Nursalim (motor vehicle tyres), William Soeryadjaya (motor vehicles), Tan Siong Kie (sheet glass, detergent, and food seasoning), The Ning King (textiles and steel), Handoko Tjokrosaputro (textiles), Surya Wonowidjojo (cigarettes), Rukmini Zainal Abidin (pharmaceuticals), Achmad Bakrie (steel pipes), Thayeb Gobel (household electrical appliances), Sjarnoebi Said (motor vehicles), and Wirontono (ball bearings).

Some of these industrial capitalists have done fairly well in competition with foreign multinationals. For example, Surya Wonowidjojo, who was operating a small kretek cigarette business in the early 1960s, succeeded in making it the biggest cigarette company during the New Order period in Indonesia. He and other kretek cigarette manufacturers foresaw the latent demand among Indonesians for the distinctive taste of their cigarettes and, by modernizing production and marketing, built large cigarette companies (besides Gudang Garam, they are Bentoel, Djarum, and Sampoerna).[6] These companies are faring much better than two foreign companies (BAT Indonesia and Faroka), which produce such internationally known brands as 'Dunhill' and 'Lucky Strike'. Also in Indonesia, Tan Siong Kie has been competing successfully in the detergent market. His company brand, 'Dino', seems to have gained the upper hand of Unilever's 'Rinso'. In the market for mono-sodium glutamate, which is dominated by the Japanese company, Ajinomoto, in the other South-East Asian countries, Tan Siong Kie's 'Sasa' brand has the largest share. In the market for dry-cell batteries, soft drinks, and cosmetics in which foreign brands tend to have the upper hand, Indonesian local brands are also doing well.[7] Outside Indonesia, local brands are also competing well in Thailand, where Thiam Chokwatana, for example, has been successful in marketing his consumer products under local brands.

In export, the leaders of agribusiness in Thailand are doing particularly well in the mid-1980s. A little over a century ago, in the mid-nineteenth century, Thailand exported sugar; but after the signing of the Bowring Treaty, cheaper sugar was imported from Java and the Philippines, and Thailand became a sugar-importing country. Then, in the mid-1920s, the Thai sugar industry started to revive; and during the Pacific War, it received a further boost when imports stopped.[8]

In the post-war period, it made further progress, helped by the decline of the sugar industry in Java, which had been the major supplier to the region in the pre-war period (this decline was caused by the deterioration in the environment for and the eventual nationalization of the Dutch capital that had dominated the sugar industry in the pre-war period).[9] Today, sugar groups like Suree Assadathorn's Thai Roong Ruang are the leading sugar exporters of the region. Such a dramatic rise is not confined to sugar. For example, Thailand is now the leading canned-pineapple exporter of the region, having overtaken the Philippines.[10] In addition, agribusiness groups such as Charoen Pokphand (CP) have an integrated operation for chicken production (with their own feed-mills, chicken farms, meat-processing plants, etc.) and are exporting their chicken, especially to Japan.

The rise of textile exporters is also part of the dramatic industrial transformation that has been going on in Thailand. In its first few decades, the Thai textile industry was largely inward-looking, and the infrastructure for textile export was still poorly developed. Then, in the early 1970s, the Thai Government began belatedly to encourage textile producers who had periodically suffered from overproduction to export their products, by streamlining the export procedure as well as giving incentives to exporters. Japanese joint ventures and trading companies (sogo shosha) took advantage of this new policy and began exporting their products to the Middle East and Africa. In 1976, for the first time, textile exports exceeded imports, and Thailand became a net textile exporter. Later, Thai companies, led by garment manufacturers, joined the export drive by modernizing production facilities and improving product quality.[11]

That this was accomplished in a short time can be seen from the rapid rise of Saha-Union, which is today engaged in textile distribution and production ranging from spinning to garment manufacturing (through subsidiaries). Damri Darakananda, who has headed Saha-Union since its inception, was in the late 1950s operating a small importing business which handled, among other things, YKK zips from Japan. In the early 1960s, he set up a joint venture with YKK, which was the beginning of his ventures into production of such inputs for garments as thread, buttons, elastic webbing, etc. In 1972, these operations were put under the newly incorporated Saha-Union. In 1977, it took over a textile mill and finally became an integrated textile producer. Over the next several years it grew quickly, and is now Thailand's largest textile conglomerate and exporter. This dramatic growth seems to have been related to Damri's new approach to business. In a number of ways, Saha-Union differs from the traditional textile companies. For one thing, it is one of the first Thai companies to have gone public to raise capital in the newly created stock market; for another, it relies on professional managers to a great extent. With this modern approach, it has won the confidence of large financial institutions such as Bangkok Bank, which funded a large part of the capital needed for its rapid plant expansion.

After the Pacific War, the Western colonialists probably did not foresee the speed with which industrialization would take place in the next few decades. The rise of South-East Asian capitalists (mostly Chinese) in the pre-war period may have given them an inkling of their further progress in trade and finance, but probably not in the manufacturing industry, especially the heavy-chemical industry, which requires technological expertise and large capital. There is no question that they underestimated the capability of South-East Asian, especially Chinese, capitalists to undertake industrial activities, but they were right in thinking that manufacturing was more difficult than trading or banking. Yet, industrialization took place on a much larger scale than they expected. This is because they could not foresee the extent to which the newly formed South-East Asian governments would be willing to promote industrialization at the expense of efficiency. The governments have poured a huge amount of capital into industry, and protected it with tariffs, quotas, and foreign exchange regulations. As a result, apart from a few bright spots, the industrial capital that emerged has generally become a burden on the economy rather than a propelling force as in the experience of the West and Japan.

Inefficiency

Inefficiency is bound to be reflected in higher prices, so the best indicators of the inefficiency of South-East Asian industry are probably the ratios of domestic prices to c.i.f. prices. The ratio exceeds one for a large number of industrial products, especially goods which require expensive machines for their production. Exceptions are the goods for which transportation cost weighs heavily in their prices (such as beer and soft drinks), those for which labour is the major input and capital cost is not a large part of production cost (such as garments and simple rubber products), and goods whose major raw materials are more cheaply available within the country (such as plywood, sugar, and some other processed primary products). Other products (such as plastic goods) can compete with imports even without protection, with lower quality but lower prices. However, of the goods for which substitution of quality for price is limited and whose production depends heavily on imported materials or is capital-intensive, the domestic prices tend to be higher than the c.i.f. prices.

One of the most glaring examples of inefficiency is passenger cars. In South-East Asia, they are usually two to three times more expensive than in Japan.[12] This imposes a heavy burden on the consumers. Although public transportation is reasonably well developed in the capital cities of most developed countries so that cars are not an absolute necessity, in the capitals of South-East Asia (where most cars are sold) public transportation is poor, so the middle classes want to have their own cars. But these are so expensive relative to wages that married women often join the labour force, working full-time and sacrificing time with their families, in order to pay the instalments on their cars. Even if cars were available without trade barriers, the low wages in South-East Asia would make buying one difficult; but at two to three times the price in Japan, the task becomes herculean.[13]

A number of intellectuals have criticized this unsatisfactory situation and questioned the wisdom of the government in promoting the car industry in South-East Asia. For example, Malaysian economist Chee Peng Lim expresses his criticism as follows:

With hindsight we now know that [the] decision [to promote the car industry] was wrong because the motor car assembly industry has been a dismal failure . . . the motor vehicle assembly industry, which was supposed to have ushered us into a new age of industrialization[,] turned out to be an illusion. The minimal benefits that we obtained were hardly commensurate with the cost we had to pay.[14]

If it is not the consumers who benefit from such industrialization, who does? Chee Peng Lim answers:

. . . the only beneficiaries in the motor vehicle assembly programme were the government and the assemblers. The former managed to collect vast sums of money by gradually increasing its import duties on completely-built-up (c.b.u.) cars while the latter profited from the heavy protection imposed on the motor vehicle industry.[15]

Who benefits more, the industrial capitalists or the government? In most cases, it seems to be the former. Even in Thailand, where government economic policy has been more rational than in the other South-East Asian countries (except Singapore), the industrial capitalists, especially the traders-turned-capitalists who are producing for the domestic market, are enjoying large benefits from government protection and subsidies, at the expense of the consumers. Indignant at this situation and the inroads that such industrial capitalists are making into politics to promote their own interests, army commander Gen. Chaovalit Yongchaiyuth once said that it would be better for Thailand to become an agricultural, instead of industrial, superpower.[16]

An apologist for South-East Asian industrialization would say that the region has just started to industrialize and that the situation will improve in the future. But how soon? It does not seem likely in the near future. It has to be remembered that the history of industrialization in South-East Asia is not as recent as the apologist would have us believe. In the Philippines, for example, promotion of the textile industry started around 1950, more than thirty-five years ago; but it has not yet become an export industry, nor it is likely to become one in the near future. If textiles were allowed to be imported freely, many Philippine textile companies would go bankrupt, and this is why some manufacturers find it more profitable to smuggle in textiles than produce them.

It is true that a number of textile companies in the region are exporting their products; Saha-Union and other Thai-owned textile companies discussed in the previous section are examples. But they are exceptions. Practically all the rest which have export capability are foreign-owned. For example, some Indonesian textile companies are exporting their products; but Indonesian-owned (actually mostly Chinese-owned) companies cannot export because the poor quality of their products allows them to be sold only for the domestic market. Nevertheless, these companies seem to be quite satisfied with this.[17]

Inefficiency results also from extensive government involvement in industry. In defence of state enterprises, however, it should be stated at the outset that they need not be inefficient and that even if they are not very efficient, they need not have adverse effects on other industrial sectors. Given the gap between them and the developed countries, it is unrealistic to expect the governments not to get involved in industry at all. In fact, Japan had some large state enterprises (such as an integrated steel mill, Yahata Steel Works), as does Taiwan today.[18] In Singapore and Thailand, there are a number of state enterprises, but they do not seem to be particularly inefficient (although the Singapore Government, which is more involved in the economy than the Thai Government, is thinking of privatizing some state enterprises). However, in Indonesia, the state sector is out of proportion to the private sector, dominating in particular the capital-intensive upstream sector of industry (especially petrochemicals and steel), which sells high-cost or low-quality products to the downstream private sector. In addition, it has a monopoly on fertilizer production, it dominates shipbuilding, and it has a large stake in cement and pulp production.[19] Despite access to low-interest loans from government banks and various other privileges (including some monopoly rights), many of these state enterprises are running at a loss.

Consider the case of Krakatau Steel Mills, an integrated steel mill and the largest in South-East Asia. Its main products are steel plate and other steel products used mostly in the construction and shipbuilding industries. Recently, it diversified into production of tin plate by setting up Pelat Timah Nusantara together with a state mining company (Tambang Timah) and the Bob Hasan group (tin plate is sold to the producers of tin cans). In addition, it is due to start production of steel sheet through Cold Rolling Mill Indonesia Utama (a joint venture with the Liem Sioe Liong group and a Western steel company), for use in the motor vehicle and household electrical appliance industries. The problem of Krakatau Steel and its joint ventures is that they were badly planned initially and poorly managed once operations began. To protect them, the Indonesian Government gave Krakatau Steel an import monopoly on products which compete with their own, but they do not seem to be charging the full cost to the domestic users, since this would reveal their inefficiency. In mid-1986, they were charging only about 10–20 per cent more than c.i.f. prices. Fortunately (from their point of view), they are not required to disclose their financial statements, though they seem to be operating at a substantial loss. So far, the problem has been confined to higher prices, but when Krakatau Steel starts to supply steel sheet, the problem of quality may arise, since sheet (which is thinner than plate—usually thinner than 0.3 mm, and that made into galvanized iron sheet is as thin as 0.18 mm) requires more precision than plate (which is used for construction and shipbuilding).[20]

The fact that Krakatau Steel exports its products from time to time should not be taken as a sign of efficiency. Krakatau Steel, and, for that matter, most other state enterprises which can export (for example, Nusantara Aircraft Industry, which is planning to export helicopters), can export their products because they do not charge their full cost; that is, they are satisfied if their prices cover only variable costs (but not capital cost). However, this type of export cannot persist, because they are allowing their production facilities to deteriorate.

Malaysia is following the Indonesian path. In 1974, the Malaysian Government set up the national oil company, Petronas, which is engaged in petroleum refining, marketing, LNG and fertilizer production (it is the Malaysian counterpart of Pertamina in Indonesia). The Malaysian Government also set up the national trading company, Pernas, which is now involved in a number of manufacturing fields on a joint-venture basis. The most recent addition is Heavy Industries Corp. of Malaysia (HICOM), through which the government planned to set up cement plants, sponge-iron plants, a cold rolling mill, a methanol plant, a pulp and paper plant, a fertilizer plant, and a motor vehicle assembly plant.[21] However, since the prices of oil and other major Malaysian exports declined soon after HICOM was set up, the government has had to shelve some of its plans, though it could still implement others. Two of HICOM's well-publicized ventures are the motor vehicle company Perusahaan Otomobil Nasional (which produces the Proton Saga) and the sponge-iron plant, Perwaja Trengganu. Neither of these, however, is economically viable: the former has been losing money while the latter ran into technical problems and has ceased to operate.[22]

In the Philippines, the Marcos government became heavily involved in industry. It took over a steel mill (Iligan Integrated Steel Mills) from Fernando Jacinto and created National Steel Corp.; it set up a copper smelter (Philippine Associated Smelting and Refining Corp.) and the first shipyard which could repair ocean-going vessels (Philippine Shipyard and Engineering Corp.); and it created Philippine National Oil Co., which, besides getting into petroleum marketing, took over two foreign-owned oil refineries (Bataan Refining and Filoil Refining). In addition, the government took over numerous companies in trouble.

Government entry into the sugar and coconut-oil industries was devastating to their producers. In the case of sugar, the government did not get involved in production, but it monopolized distribution through the Philippine Sugar Commission and by mismanagement and a 'skimming' operation, it considerably reduced the incentives for producers. In the case of coconut oil, the government, through the Coconut Producers Federation (COCOFED), set up United Coconut Oil Mills (UNICOM) and, by refusing to pay subsidies to uncooperative mills, brought most of the major oil mills under UNICOM's control.[23]

The government monopolies on sugar and coconut oil were rescinded after Marcos lost power, but the Philippine Government still has a large number of companies under its control. Some are state enterprises created during the Marcos period; others are companies which the government took over from Marcos and his cronies after Marcos fled; and the majority are companies which defaulted on the loans given or guaranteed by government financial institutions (in particular, Development Bank of the Philippines and Philippine National Bank). The government is now a dominant force in Philippine industry. It says it will privatize, but this seems difficult since Filipino capitalists have been greatly debilitated by the economic turmoil of the past few years. Thus, the government is likely to stay in industry.

The inefficiency of state enterprises is sometimes justified on the grounds of equity. If the government were not involved, the argument goes, the South-East Asian portion of the superlayer of the economy would be dominated by the Chinese, which would be intolerable for the indigenous élites. Alternatively, it might be argued that to leave capital-intensive industry to the private sector would give monopoly profits to a small number of capitalists, which is not fair from the distribution point of view. Government involvement might also be justified on the ground that private capital was too hesitant to move into strategic industries, so that the government had to set an example. Whatever the justification might be, government involvement has gone too far in Indonesia, Malaysia and the Philippines, aggravating the already acute problem of inefficiency.

The political leaders of these countries have not faced up to the gross distortion of efficiency created by heavy government involvement in industry. In their defence, it should be made clear that their motives were not necessarily unsavory. Marcos may have been somewhat exceptional in that he sought to enlarge the financial base for his 'skimming' operation by sponsoring large industrial projects, but even he considered these projects to be a sign of industrial progress and promoted them with national interests in mind. This is even more true in the case of Suharto in Indonesia and Mahathir in Malaysia. However, the trouble is that the national leaders do not realize that true industrialization is based on an economic system that encourages people to strive for innovation and creativity. These features are invisible and difficult to understand, and the system takes time to build up, while new, large factories can be quickly built with petrodollars or money from foreign lending agencies, and they can be shown to people as a concrete sign of development under their government. Private capital built some factories at the government's persuasion, but since it was often sceptical about their economic feasibility, the government has assumed the major responsibility and built most of them on its own; but instead of becoming the concrete proof of progress, as was intended by the political leaders who sponsored them, the large, capital-intensive factories now stand as monuments to their economic naïvety.

'Technologyless' Industrialization

The other major problem of South-East Asian industrialization is that it is 'technologyless'. If this is true, one might ask, how were certain South-East Asian capitalists able to set up sophisticated industries? For example, such capitalists as Taworn Pornprapha of Thailand, Eric Chia, Loh Boon Siew, and Tan Yuet Foh of Malaysia, William Soeryadjaya and Sjarnoebi Said of Indonesia are engaged in motor vehicle and motor vehicle parts production. Their activities appear quite technologically sophisticated, and they are sometimes hailed as industrial pioneers; but the fact is that they are Japanese compradors. Taworn Pornprapha and Tan Yuet Foh are Nissan's compradors; Eric Chia and William Soeryadjaya are Toyota's; Loh Boon Siew is Honda's; and Sjarnoebi Said is Mitsubishi's. Most of the major components are supplied by the Japanese companies, and some which are produced locally are made under the technical supervision of the Japanese companies. The South-East Asian capitalists are essentially the distributors of Japanese cars, with the difference that they have assembling plants. Technologically, however, they are almost 100 per cent dependent on their Japanese licensers, and, under the present set-up, it would be impossible for them to become technologically independent and start exporting their products. Their technological dependency is not temporary but, being structural, semi-permanent.

One might say that there are a number of industrial capitalists who are not compradors. For example, pharmaceutical producers in South-East Asia (like Jose Campos of United Laboratories in the Philippines and Svasti Osathanugraph of Osothsapha in Thailand) produce drugs under licence from foreign countries, but they are far more independent than the motor vehicle producers. Although they use foreign patents, they do not depend on one company, and often they tie up with more than just a few companies. Sometimes they pirate foreign patents and produce generic products, which is not illegal in Thailand and Indonesia. They therefore have a great degree of freedom; but there is little technology involved in much of what they do. A large part of their operations is to mix imported chemicals (according to the formulas supplied by their foreign licensers) and bottle the products.

Those in textiles, steel, cement, and petrochemicals (especially downstream products) have no foreign licensers and accordingly enjoy a greater degree of freedom in the procurement of raw materials and the marketing of their products. At the same time, their operation is fairly capital-intensive and appears technologically quite sophisticated— a sign of industrial progress. However, it is the machines which make their operations appear sophisticated. Raw materials are fed into the machines, and the final products come out. If there is any technological sophistication in the operation of such plants, it is in the making of machines. But the machines are imported, so there is nothing sophisticated in what these industrial capitalists are doing.

One might say that this was also true in Japan in its early phase of development and in Korea and Taiwan not so long ago. But Japan, Korea and Taiwan were not as totally dependent on foreign companies as South-East Asian countries are at present. If they could not produce the machines they needed, they had to import them, and in fact, they imported a great deal; but that is all they did. Unlike South-East Asian capitalists, Japanese capitalists did not depend on foreign companies for the layout of their factories or installation of machines. At that time, there was no concept of 'plant export', but now a South-East Asian capitalist can essentially buy a plant from a foreign company as a turnkey project. If his staff do not know how to operate it, he can enlist a foreign engineering company to give the necessary training before the plant is completed; and if this is not enough, he can hire its technicians to stay on at the plant. Even if this is unnecessary, he may later have to depend on the engineering company or the supplier of the machines when something goes wrong, for his technical staff may lack the ability to make complicated repairs.

Although technical capability differs from one plant to another, the situation described above is not exceptional. Industrial capitalists are able to run manufacturing plants that require technical competence far beyond what they can muster within their own countries because foreign companies can fill the gap—for a fee, of course. They are willing to undertake this because it is profitable, as the government, in its eagerness to promote industrialization, provides protection and subsidies. In Japan, Korea, and Taiwan, the government also offered protection and subsidies to industrial capitalists, but their industrialization was more commensurate with their own technological progress.

Why cannot South-East Asia promote technological progress as well as the East Asian countries? An answer one sometimes hears is that industrial capitalists were formerly traders so that they have neither technical training nor interest in technical matters: all they are interested in is quick profits. The pattern of entry into manufacturing is more complicated than that, but it is true that many traders became industrialists with the implementation of the import-substitution policy.[24] Some traders went into manufacturing because the goods they were importing could no longer be imported. For them, entry into manufacturing was a strategy for survival. Others went in seeing a great opportunity to make profits under the protection and incentives offered by the government. These traders had little technical knowledge when they went into production.

It is not, however, only traders who ventured into manufacturing. Some went into it with an engineering background (for example, Jose Marcelo of the Philippines and Sawang Laohathai of Thailand), but it is difficult to prove that such people have a longer time-horizon in corporate planning and a more technically competent staff than those with a trading background. For one thing, former traders can hire engineers and skilled workers; they do not have to be technically competent themselves. Also, it is expensive to depend on foreign companies for patents, maintenance, repairing, and other technical services, so it is to their advantage to make use of local technology and technicians when possible. In fact, many industrial capitalists in the East Asian countries were weak in technical matters and depended on their staff.

The basic reason for the technical weakness of industrial capitalist institutions in the region is the low overall level of technical competence. Because of this, capitalists who aspire to be industrialists have to depend on foreign technology even though it is extremely expensive. There is no effective local substitute for the technology needed for the advanced industrial activities the government is promoting. The situation was different in the East Asian countries: technology had to be imported, but this was minimized by substituting local technology whenever possible. They could do this because there were a number of better trained engineers and skilled workers; and it paid to train them further because it was more likely to lead to technological independence, product innovation, and cost reduction.

Japan is often cited as a model of technological development for developing countries, but the technological gap was much narrower when Japan was developing. Up to the first few decades of the twentieth century, much of what the West invented could be understood without much scientific education and reproduced without much research expenditure. For example, Toyoda Sakichi, an uneducated carpenter, was intrigued by a British weaving machine exhibited at Tokyo and went on to build one himself. Eventually, he invented a first-rate weaving machine, which contributed to the progress of the Japanese textile industry.[25] Of course, his success did not come instantly but after many years of trial and error; but what is important is that he could achieve it with little education and without a large research expenditure. However, someone from a developing country who saw a robot making a sunny-side-up at the Science Expo at Tsukuba in 1985 would not be able to reproduce it without many years of advanced scientific education and good research facilities. In the past several decades, industrial technology has become increasingly more dependent on basic sciences and large research expenditure.[26]

Today's large technological gap frustrates in many ways South-East Asian efforts to catch up with the technology of developed countries. This problem should not be overemphasized, however, for against similar odds, Korea has been catching up rapidly. But none of the South-East Asian countries is making comparable technological progress. The gap may even be widening. According to the estimate of Roger Posadas, Dean of the College of Science at University of the Philippines, in science and technology, the Philippines is 20–30 years behind Taiwan and Korea, and 50–75 years behind Japan, the United States, and other developed countries.[27]

For a long time, Thailand also cared little about science and technology; but in the late 1970s, in order to demonstrate to the people that the country needs to make more rapid progress in these fields, the government created the Ministry of Science, Technology, and Energy. It has, however, amounted to no more than a gesture. With little budget, the ministry came to be referred to as the 'cemetery ministry', and in July 1985, its minister, Damrong Lathaphipat, committed suicide. He may have had other reasons for taking his own life, but his act was seen as a protest against the Sixth National Economic and Social Development Plan which gave science and technology the cold shoulder.[28] This incident was interpreted by some people as showing that if one became serious about science and technology in Thailand, one would end up killing oneself as Damrong did.

There are a number of indicators of the technological backwardness of South-East Asia. Indonesia's textile industry, which is one of the most mature industries, employs a number of foreign technicians (many from Taiwan and some from Japan and Korea) because there are not enough competent Indonesians. The Philippine textile industry, which the government began promoting in the early 1950s, has not 'matured', partly because textile machines are not properly maintained and often break down (thus reducing the utilization rate of machines in which capital has been sunk). Also, there are no privately owned shipyards in the region which can build ships greater than a few thousand tons, despite the importance of ocean transport. Shipbuilding is not like a turnkey project, in which imported machines play a central role; it is more like building a house.[29] Each ship has a different design and requires various kinds of skilled workers at different stages of production; and unless jobs are done properly, it may sink. However, even though building a large ship is technologically more complicated than, say, melting scrap iron and making steel products or producing cement from limestone and clay, by present-day standards it does not require much scientific and technological sophistication. Even so, there are no South-East Asian capitalist institutions capable of building a large ship even for the domestic market.

Singapore is often regarded as a model of capitalism in South-East Asia, but it is certainly not a model of industrial capitalism. Practically all industrial capitalist institutions which have export capability there are foreign-owned. Although there are Singaporean industrial capitalists, they are mostly inward-looking, producing food and construction materials (such as steel products, cement, etc.) for the domestic market. If some export their products, it is only a small part of their sales. Despite the government's encouragement, the capitalists of Singapore have been reluctant to move into manufacturing industry on their own (some have done so with foreign companies, e.g. Robin Loh of Hitachi Zosen-Robin Dockyard). Trading, finance and property development have been their familiar turf, and they seem to feel that the level of technology in the country is not sufficiently high to entice them to invest in a manufacturing venture.

Brian Chang almost proved them wrong. After studying engineering in England, he returned to Singapore and worked for a few foreign companies. Then, in the early 1970s, he set up a company called Promet to assemble offshore oil equipment (oil rigs in particular). This business boomed as oil exploration activities intensified in the region after the first oil crisis. This gave a big boost to Promet, and Brian Chang became one of Singapore's leading industrialists. He did not, however, confine himself to manufacturing for long. In particular, tying up with Ibrahim bin Mohamed, an influential bumiputra lawyer, he went into construction and property development in Malaysia. Initially, Promet made a lot of money in these new ventures, but in the early 1980s, when the prices of primary products began declining and Malaysia lapsed into recession, Promet began facing difficulties, and a few years later (1986), it faced ruin. Non-manufacturing activities such as property development are so attractive that they tempt even a successful industrialist; but if he gets hurt by entering these fields, he destroys his potential to make his manufacturing venture a long-lasting capitalist institution.

Singapore cannot build dynamic industrial capitalism of its own. One reason is that foreign companies with superior technology compete with Singaporean companies for technicians and engineers. Another is that its service sector makes a much bigger demand on well-educated manpower than that of an ordinary country. This is because, being a city-state unlike the other South-East Asian countries, Singapore can make its service sector tradable by serving as a trading, financial, and tourist centre in the region. In one sense, it is an 'oasis' for the region and in another, it is the service centre of the region (for example, it serves as the regional headquarters of many foreign financial insti-tutions). Thus, Singapore has to provide a congenial environment for the service sector. Finally, the small size of the country limits its ability to finance government expenditure on science and technology; and it limits the scope for industrial diversity, which allows the cross-fertilization and inter-industry co-operation that are essential for technological innovation. These considerations make it difficult to foresee the emergence of Singaporean industrial capitalists who will act as a loco-motive of the economy.

Some people say that Singapore has already joined the group of Newly Industrializing Countries (NICs) and that Thailand will do so in a few years. But this is not true. Although Singapore enjoyed rapid growth until the early 1980s and achieved a high level of income, it has been suffering from low growth rates (negative growth in 1985) in the past few years, while the other Asian NICs have been enjoying high growth. Singapore's high level of income is largely due to its service sector (as discussed above), and if there is any dynamism in its industry, it is due to foreign capital. Unlike such NICs as Korea, it does not have indus-trial capitalists of its own who can compete in the export market. If there is anything 'industrializing' about Singapore, it is because it serves as the offshore centre for foreign capital.

If 'NIC status for Thailand is less than a few years away', as stated by Snoh Unakul, Secretary-general of the National Economic and Social Development Board and former Governor of the Bank of Thailand, it can only be through foreign capital.[30] Like Singapore, Thailand does not have dynamic industrial capitalists of its own: technologically, they are dependent on foreign companies. As a new development on the Thai industrialization scene that augurs Thailand's attainment of NIC status, some might point to the plan of some Thai companies to export cars and motor vehicle parts (such as engines), but these are all foreign (Japanese) joint ventures. Damrong's suicide, as discussed above, is symbolic of Thailand's technological backwardness as well as its un-willingness to push for technological progress. The only things Thai industrialists can export are processed primary products, garments, textiles, and other labour-intensive products.

One might ask what is wrong with those products. Is it not also true that Japan depended on silk and textiles in the initial stage of industrial-ization in the Meiji period, and that more recently, so did Korea? However, while Japan was depending on silk and textiles, Mitsubishi, Sumitomo and other technologically sophisticated companies were growing up, and in Korea more recently, Hyundai, Samsung, and other companies were developing in the field of heavy industry while it was exporting textiles. But in Thailand, there are no such companies. The industrial sectors in which Thai companies have developed export capability are technologically blind alleys, and cannot act as a pivot for technological diversification. This means that when Thai wages in-crease, which is necessary for its development, Thailand cannot develop new industrial exports and thus upgrade the composition of its industrial products.

The relatively good economic performance of the ASEAN countries after the first oil shock in late 1973 gave some economists grounds for optimism about their future growth and for arguing that they would soon be joining the NICs and would catch up with Japan and other developed countries in the not-too-distant future. But it turned out that Indonesia's and Malaysia's growth depended on high oil prices, and the Philippines' on international borrowing, while Singapore's growth depended greatly, if not entirely, on the prosperity of Malaysia and Indonesia, for which it acts as a service centre and an 'oasis'. Thus, soon after the economic growth of these two countries plunged, so did Singapore's. The fact that foreign capital which has set up offshore production, centres there, gives it some independence from these two countries, but that sort of industrialization is dependent rather than autonomous, as it is in the more genuine NICs of East Asia. Thailand has pursued more independent industrialization, but in trying to upgrade its exports and thus join the NICs, it has begun to do what Singapore has been doing for some time, that is, depend on foreign capital. Thus, none of the ASEAN countries can join the NICs on their own because they lack their own technological bases. Their industrialization has been largely 'technologyless' because they failed to commit themselves to progress in science and technology.

Dependent Capitalism

In the West and Japan, the advent of capitalism is often equated with the Industrial Revolution. This is not strictly true, however, since there were capitalist institutions before the Industrial Revolution. For example, the Houses of Mitsui and Sumitomo in Japan fully qualified as capitalistic institutions even during the Tokugawa period.[31] In the West, Braudel traces back the origin of capitalism to the rise of Italian cities in the eleventh century.[32] Nevertheless, the Industrial Revolution tends to be regarded as the beginning of capitalism, because sustained long-term growth, which Kuznets called modern economic growth, began with the Industrial Revolution.[33] After this, industrial capitalists became the vanguard of capitalistic development and pulled along with them merchant and financial capitalists. The reason why they could become such a dynamic force was, as explained on pp. 100–2, their ability to expand foreign trade and use it as an engine of growth.

The South-East Asian governments, after gaining the freedom to chart their own courses of development, pushed industrialization, and in the process, created industrial capitalists who were expected to play a dynamic role. But their contribution has been much less than expected. Among the efficient industrial capitalists are some who produce for the domestic market (offering good quality goods at reasonable prices); examples include some manufacturers of kretek cigarettes (in Indonesia), soft drinks, and beer. Others, especially those in agribusiness and textiles (in Thailand), can export their products. But the majority of the industrial capitalists have depended on the government for finance and protection and on foreign companies for technology. They have been a burden on the economy more than anything else.

This is not necessarily entirely their fault: blame should also rest on the environment which created them. First of all, governments gave protection and subsidies to those who were willing to venture into manufacturing; and governments also became directly involved, thereby creating an inefficient industrial system. Second, governments did little to promote technological and scientific progress, as a consequence of which the newly created industrial capitalists became technologically dependent on foreign companies. Such technological dependence made it impossible for South-East Asian industrialists to generate exports one after another in a flying-geese pattern and play a leading role in economic development.

If industrial capitalism was not a dynamic force, what was the driving force of capitalistic development in South-East Asia? It was largely the royalties from resources exploitation (oil in particular) and the dynamism of the market economy (as defined by Fernando Braudel). Some capitalist institutions were created for resource exploitation (especially in logging), but they tend to be predatory and are unlikely to become long-lasting institutions. Much of resource exploitation was carried out by foreign companies, and the royalties they paid to South-East Asian governments funded industrial projects and fuelled economic growth. Moreover, in a country like Thailand, the market economy produced major exports (such as rice, rubber, garments, etc.) and acted as a propelling force of the economy. In many ways, such financial capitalist institutions as, for example, Bangkok Bank are the creation of the market economy.

Was it not true that in the developed countries, capitalism also depended on the market economy in the early phase of development? In Japan, which started industrialization much later than England, industrial capitalists needed protection and subsidies from the government to make up for their disadvantage in technology and capital, and did not act as an engine of growth for some time. In the meantime, the market economy produced major exports (such as silk) and acted as the driving force of economic development. A more or less similar situation prevailed later in Korea and Taiwan. One might therefore argue that the situation in South-East Asia is not unusual—something to be expected in the initial stage of economic development of such late starters as the South-East Asian countries. However, as discussed on pp. 106–18, inefficiency and technological dependence makes the South-East Asian situation different from that in Japan, Korea, and Taiwan. Despite a relatively long history of industrialization (the Philippines has a longer history of industrialization than either Korea or Taiwan), industrial capitalism is still dependent and likely to remain so. As a result, capitalism as a whole remains dependent and will continue to be so in the foreseeable future.

1. Services are exportable also, but not to a great extent in a developing stage. The only exception would be a small city-state like Singapore which serves as an entrepôt trade centre or a regional centre.

2. For further theoretical discussion of this, see Denis Robertson, *Essays in Monetary Theory*, St. Albans, Staples Press, 1948, p. 214.

3. Raul Prebisch, *Towards a New Trade Policy for Development*, New York, United Nations, 1964, and Gunnar Myrdal, *International Economy*, New York, Harper & Row, 1956.

4. Every export commodity passes through a cycle of growth and eventual decline. Expansion of export has therefore to be sustained by the successive emergence of new export goods. When the rises and falls in volumes of export commodities are plotted against time, the resultant graph resembles a flock of geese flying in formation. This finding is attributed to the Japanese economist Akamatsu Kaname.

5. The share of manufacturing in national income is a little lower in Indonesia (about 15 per cent). For the others, it ranges from about 19 to 25 per cent.

6. For further details of the Indonesian kretek cigarette industry, see *Asian Wall Street Journal*, 2 May 1985.

7. For further discussion on the competition between Indonesian and foreign brands, see Thee Kian-wie and Kunio Yoshihara, 'Foreign and Domestic Capital in Indonesian Industrialization', *Southeast Asian Studies*, March 1987.

8. On the history of the sugar industry in Thailand, see Phitsanes Jessadachatr, 'A History of Sugar Policies in Thailand: 1937–75', Master of Economics thesis, Thammasat University, 1977.

9. During the American period, sugar became the major industry of the Philippines; but since the preferential treatment it received in the American market made it unnecessary to strive for efficiency and compete in the world market, Philippine sugar was not much exported to markets other than the United States. On the history of the Philippine sugar industry, see Carlos Quirino, *History of the Philippine Sugar Industry*, Manila, Kalayaan Publishing Company, 1974.

10. *Asian Wall Street Journal*, 13–14 March 1987.

11. This paragraph is based on an interview with Mr Fujinaga Takahiro, President of Marubeni Thailand (January 1987). He has been dealing in Thai textiles since his posting there in the mid-1960s.

12. The Center for Southeast Asian Studies, Kyoto University, of which the author is a staff member, maintains offices in Bangkok and Jakarta, for which a new car is bought every several years. For this, a budget proposal is submitted to the Japanese Government (Kyoto University is a state university). The amount requested for the Jakarta

office is roughly three times more than is needed to buy the same car in Japan (the car is usually a Toyota) and two times more in the case of the Bangkok office.

13. The rate of protection on consumer durables is one of the highest, but other locally produced goods are also well protected. For further details, see Mohamed Ariff and Hal Hill, 'Protection for Manufactures in ASEAN', *Asian Economic Journal*, March 1987.

14. Chee Peng Lim, 'The Proton Saga—No Reverse Gear: The Economic Burden of Malaysia's Car Project', in Jomo, ed., *The Sun Also Sets: Lessons in 'Looking East'*, Petaling Jaya, Institute for Social Analysis, 1985, p. 388.

15. Ibid.

16. *Far Eastern Economic Review*, 9 April 1987, p. 24.

17. Interview with Mr Okubo Hiroaki, President Director, PT Century Textile Industry.

18. The Korean Government has privatized many of the former state enterprises and is now less involved in industry than is the Taiwan Government. The largest steel mill at Pohang is one of the few still under government control, but even this is scheduled to be privatized.

19. On the involvement of the Indonesian Government in industry, see Thee and Yoshihara, op. cit.

20. This paragraph is based partly on Nippon Tekko Renmei, 'Indonesia', 1984 (Nippon Tekko Renmei is the association of steelmakers in Japan), and partly on interviews with Japanese steel executives in Jakarta (May 1986).

21. *Investors Digest*, May 1985, and *Far Eastern Economic Review*, 16 June 1983.

22. An up-to-date, comprehensive discussion of state enterprises in Malaysia is yet to be published. On the rise of state enterprises until the end of the 1970s, see Bruce Gale, *Politics and Public Enterprise in Malaysia*, Singapore, Eastern Universities Press, 1981.

23. For further discussion on the sugar and coconut industries during martial law, see Gary Hawes, *The Philippine State and the Marcos Regime: The Politics of Export*, Ithaca, Cornell University Press, 1987.

24. On the pattern of entry into manufacturing in the Philippines, see Yoshihara Kunio, *Philippine Industrialization: Foreign and Domestic Capital*, Quezon City, Ateneo de Manila University Press, and Singapore, Oxford University Press, 1985, Chapters 5 and 6.

25. Toyoda Sakichi, after succeeding in weaving machines, started motor vehicle production with his eldest son, Kiichiro. This later (in 1937) led to the formation of Toyota Motor Co. 'Da' of 'Toyoda' and 'ta' of 'Toyota' are two variations in the pronunciation of the same Chinese character, *'tian'*, meaning a rice-field.

26. Nylon and synthetic rubber, whose commercial production began in the 1930s, are among the earliest products invented by the application of basic science.

27. *Business Day*, 15 October 1985.

28. *ASEAN Forecast*, September 1985, p. 132.

29. This analogy was suggested to the author during an interview with Mr Kitajima Jun, the representative in Jakarta of Mitsui Engineering & Shipbuilding Co. (June 1986).

30. Dr Snoh's statement is quoted in an advertisement placed by the Thai Government in *Asian Wall Street Journal*, 13–14 March 1987.

31. On the history of the House of Mitsui, see John Roberts, *Mitsui: Three Centuries of Japanese Business*, New York, Weatherhill, 1973.

32. Fernand Braudel, *Civilization and Capitalism, 15th–18th Century*, Vol. 2: *The Wheels of Commerce*, New York, Harper & Row, 1982.

33. Simon Kuznets, *Economic Growth of Nations*, Cambridge, Mass., Harvard University Press, 1971, Chapter 1.

Chapter 6
Conclusion

Foreign Capital

It is no longer true that foreign capital dominates the superlayer of the economy of South-East Asia. After the Pacific War, the environment for foreign capital changed dramatically with the independence of former colonies and the rise of economic nationalism. South-East Asian governments sometimes became hostile, but, more generally, they were cautious towards foreign capital. They nationalized or took over a number of foreign companies; imposed many regulations on those which remained; and restricted new entrants wishing to take advantage of the domestic market. At the same time, they took measures to promote domestic capital by offering protection and financial assistance, and in the sectors where domestic capital was unwilling or slow to respond, the governments set up state enterprises. As a consequence, there has been a dramatic decline of foreign capital and, conversely, a rise of domestic capital in the post-war period.

Foreign capital remains important in the sectors where South-East Asia still lacks expertise. One area is oil exploration. Another concerns the sectors of manufacturing that require some technological sophistication. The capital-intensive sector of manufacturing used also to be dominated by foreign capital, but has ceased to be so since the South-East Asian governments began channelling into the sector royalties from resource exploitation, economic aid, and other external funds. For example, petroleum refining, on which foreign capital had a monopoly for some time, is now largely handled by domestic capital. As a result, the major industrial sectors in which foreign capital is still significant are those which were promoted by the government but for which there is insufficient technological base.

Under some circumstances, foreign capital is necessary. Singapore, for example, welcomes foreign capital more than do the other South-East Asian countries. It welcomes foreign capital that is looking for an offshore production base. The American electronics industry first used Singapore for this purpose, and more recently Japanese companies came for the same purpose, especially manufacturers of household electrical appliances. The island-state also welcomes foreign capital that wants to use the island as a regional centre. Having served as the centre of entrepôt trade in the region, Singapore has the necessary infrastructure and a more attractive environment for foreign expatriates. A number of foreign banks, trading companies, and manufacturing companies have set up their regional headquarters there (in the case of the manufacturing companies, for regional co-ordination and marketing). Oil companies have built large refineries and made Singapore the third largest oil-refining centre in the world, using Singapore partly as a regional base and partly as a link in their global networks. In addition, Singapore's interest in attracting foreign capital seems to have been motivated by security considerations. After all, it is a Chinese island in a 'sea of Muslims', and a large amount of foreign capital from developed countries can act as a deterrent against attack.

Advocates of foreign capital often cite Singapore's situation to support their case, but even Singapore restricts the entry of foreign capital aimed at the domestic market. For example, a foreign bank wishing to set up a branch there has little chance of getting a licence for full commercial banking. The situation is very different from that in Hong Kong, where the government maintains a fairly *laissez-faire* policy even on banking. While it is true that Singapore is more open to foreign capital than some other South-East Asian countries, the fact remains that it is cautious about the entry of foreign capital directed at the domestic market.

All the other South-East Asian countries are also open to export-oriented investment. Recently, for example, Thailand has been attracting a large amount of the Japanese capital that is actively looking for an offshore production base because of the large revaluation of the Japanese yen. As discussed in Chapter 5, Thailand has succeeded on its own in making its textile industry export-oriented, but in upgrading its export composition and successively developing new major products, it has been relying on foreign capital. This is because Thailand cannot rely on domestic capital to move into the next phase of export development. If domestic capital could do what foreign capital can, there would be no need to depend on foreign capital.

It is better to regard foreign capital as a necessary evil, and the sooner a country gets rid of it, the better, since the country can enjoy more economic benefits. For example, Japan made little use of foreign capital (meaning direct investment). More recently, probably because of its speed of industrialization, Korea depended on foreign capital more than Japan in the earlier stage of development, but as the Korean economy matured, it gradually phased out foreign capital, and now little remains. Thus, in South-East Asia, there is great need for domestic capital to be more dynamic.

Apologists for foreign capital would argue that it played an important role in the development of the West. If foreign capital is broadly interpreted to include foreign loans, then it is true that foreign capital played an important role in the early phase of the development of many Western countries as well as Japan. However, the role of direct investment—the typical interpretation of foreign capital—was much more limited. The only countries in which direct foreign investment was important would be former British colonies. The United States depended on British capital in the early phase of its development, as did Canada and Australia, though in Canada, American capital later became more important. One has, however, to remember that these countries are cultural offshoots of Britain, and the cultural and political conflicts that direct foreign investment entailed were much less than in the developing countries which today receive foreign investment from culturally and, in the case of Western investment, racially different countries.

If foreign investment is a necessary evil to be used only to fill the gaps that domestic capital cannot, a country may need foreign capital much more in an economic crisis than during normal times. The Philippines, for example, is in the midst of a serious economic crisis, and has to revive the economy quickly to prevent hunger from spreading further and to ensure a more decent living standard for the masses. The Philippine Government has acquired many major companies it has to privatize in the near future: some are state enterprises created by Marcos, others are Marcos's and his cronies' companies that the government sequestered after Marcos fled, and the rest are companies which defaulted on government or government-guaranteed loans. The remaining private capitalists have been considerably weakened by the economic turmoil of the past few years, and the only effective way to stimulate the economy seems to be through an infusion of foreign capital. The government, however, is reluctant to liberalize the entry of foreign capital for the domestic market. It is more open to export-oriented foreign investment, but since other countries also want to attract this and the Philippines is not presently very attractive to foreign export-oriented investors, the only quick way to attract foreign capital is to let it in for the domestic market. Then, when the economy recovers, the government can encourage private capital to grow in new or expanding areas and let the position of foreign capital gradually decline. Given the economic trouble the country is in, the government seems to be too cautious towards foreign investment. Contrary to what some critics contend, foreign capital need not be politically powerful or uncontrollable as long as the government maintains its autonomy and is determined to pursue its own chosen course for recovery and development.

Technology

Dependence on foreign capital for export or for the development of a technologically sophisticated industry needed for import substitution is not a happy solution. Nevertheless, because the South-East Asian countries do not have a strong technological base, they need foreign capital. The only way to replace foreign capital with domestic capital in these fields is to raise the level of technology, but the South-East Asian governments do not seem to be too concerned. The plea of Roger Posadas, Dean of the College of Science at the University of the Philippines, that much greater funds should be allocated to science and technology because the Philippines is seriously behind in this field, has been largely ignored. Damrong Lathaphipat, a former Minister of Science, Technology and Energy in Thailand, was serious about the problem and wanted to do something about it, but became very frustrated because the government was unwilling to fund his ministry (and it is alleged that he committed suicide partly for this reason).

B. J. Habibie champions the cause of science and technology in Indonesia. He is more fortunate than Damrong, because he is a protégé of President Suharto, and so has access to more funds and is more effective in carrying out what he wants to do. For example, he has undertaken a number of projects to upgrade Indonesian technology (e.g. aeronautics, machine tools, and shipbuilding) and aroused the interest of bright Indonesian students in science and technology. Despite his accomplishments, however, he has many critics, especially among economists, who claim that he ignores economic efficiency.

An engineer by training, Habibie seems to pay little attention to economic costs and tends to be extravagant. His critics tend to focus on the aircraft manufacturing company, Nusantara Aircraft Industry, which he started and still heads. They argue that it is much beyond the level of Indonesian technology and that he increased Nusantara's staff to more than 12,000, which is too large for an industry that will never 'mature'. He even talks of expanding the work-force to 60,000 by the year 2000. It might also be argued that he should be using secondary schools and universities to upgrade the level of technology instead of state enterprises such as Nusantara Aircraft Industry.

Besides being a little extravagant, he may have his priorities wrong.

He emphasizes high technology, whereas agricultural, textile, and other much lower technologies are equally, if not more, relevant to the present-day Indonesian economy and should therefore be equally emphasized. Besides, it is important and often more effective to stream-line the education system rather than use state enterprises for techno-logical training. None the less, in his defence, it should be stated that since he has no authority over education (which comes under the Ministry of Education), he is at least using the state enterprises he can control. Also, to encourage people to study agriculture is less inspiring than to ask them to study more glamorous technologies such as space science, aeronautics, and computers.

Priorities are important, and economic costs should be kept in mind. But what is important for South-East Asia is a more concerted effort towards technological progress. To this end, it is important to reorient the emphasis of education towards science and technology and away from humanities and social sciences, and to set up training institutes of different levels to meet the demands of industry. Scientists and high-tech engineers are important, and there should be educational institutions to train them; but at the same time, South-East Asia needs agricultural technicians, textile engineers, as well as skilled workers. The problems of educational reforms and backing them up with adequate funds are enormous, so rather than criticize what Habibie is doing in Indonesia, it is more important to nurture people like him so that they may tackle these problems more effectively.

Government Intervention

Hong Kong is the darling of the *laissez-faire* economist. He would argue that if the South-East Asian governments followed Hong Kong and did not intervene in the economy, there would be no rent-seekers, economic efficiency would improve, and thus the capitalism of South-East Asia would perform better. The flaw in this argument, how-ever, is that Hong Kong is a colony. Although it may not be entirely true that its people are exploited by their British rulers, their ambitions and expectations are not reflected in government economic policy, and therefore it is not a politically viable model: even if it makes sense economically, politically it does not make sense for the independent South-East Asian countries to accept a colony as a model.

The *laissez-faire* economist would then take the case of Singapore and make a similar pitch. However, the trouble is that the Singapore Government is much more interventionist than the Hong Kong Govern-ment. The Singapore Government, for example, owns shares in about

450 companies, many of which it controls, and is the dominant force in a number of industries. Although it is much less interventionist than the other South-East Asian governments, this is not necessarily the reason for Singapore's higher growth. Korea, Taiwan, and Japan have been more interventionist, but their economic performance has been better (although, for various reasons, Japan's performance has declined somewhat in the past decade).

According to the *laissez-faire* economist, the private sector does everything better than the government. Thus, if a country like Japan has done well, it has to be due to the performance of the private sector acting without government direction or intervention. According to this premise, Meiji Japan has to have been a free-trade country, and MITI, which directed post-war industrialization, and the Ministry of Finance, which regulated the banking industry, have to be either ignored or regarded as non-autonomous agencies that were highly penetrated by the interests of the private sector. But this is far from the truth. Government intervention was a major factor in Japanese industrialization and economic development, especially in the post-war period.

Given the gap between themselves and developed countries and their peoples' ambitions, it is unreasonable to expect the governments of South-East Asia to do nothing. By intervening, governments can accelerate growth, as Japan did, and realize economic development much faster than by relying solely on private initiative. It is true that in a later phase of development, when the private sector has accumulated capital and gained experience, the government may not have to intervene much, but in an earlier phase, government intervention is both necessary and desirable. Therefore, government intervention in South-East Asia can be at least theoretically justified.

The problem is not government intervention versus non-intervention. Certainly, government intervention gives rise to some inefficiency and rent-seekers, but this can be easily outweighed by the benefits of such intervention. If it has turned out to be more harmful than beneficial, it is not because *laissez-faire* policy is theoretically better than government intervention; rather, it is because the intervention was badly formulated and/or poorly implemented. If government intervention is of low quality, it will result in great inefficiency and huge losses—and if it is implemented by politicians such as Marcos, it will enable them to siphon a huge amount of money from the economic system and cause disaster. Without government intervention in the economy, he would not have made it in the Guinness Book of World Records as the world's biggest thief.

What determines the quality of intervention is the quality of government, which is in turn determined by the political system, the quality of the government leaders, and the bureaucracy. The problem facing South-East Asia is to decide whether the quality of government intervention will tend to be so poor that it is bound to bring more harm than good, or, under some circumstances, the government can become more purposive, autonomous, and clean, and intervene to accelerate economic development. Those who argue for less government intervention assume implicitly that their government is not capable of improving itself. Whether or not they are right is an empirical, not theoretical, question.

Chinese Capital

The problem of the Chinese does not exist in some countries. Singapore is essentially a Chinese state, so Chinese dominance of its capitalism is not a problem. In Thailand, also, there is little problem, for although the Chinese are a minority (possibly accounting for 10–15 per cent of the population), they are fairly well integrated. There may be some degree of latent anti-Chinese feeling, but there is no mechanism by which it can be translated into political action. For all practical purposes, the Chinese question is a dead issue.

The Philippines harbours more anti-Chinese sentiment than does Thailand. One of the few good legacies of the Marcos period, however, is that most Chinese obtained Philippine citizenship and discrimination against them (at least in business) ceased. Some Filipinos would object to this statement, perhaps wishing to revive the Chinese question; but before doing so, they should realize the enormity of the problem of rejuvenating their economy. It is true that the Chinese are not as well integrated in the Philippines as in Thailand, but there is no sharp dividing line between the Chinese and the indigenous like that perceived to be drawn by Islam in Indonesia and Malaysia. Certainly there are points of friction in Chinese–Filipino relations, but these should be forgotten for the sake of overcoming the present economic difficulties and then making up for the losses the country has suffered in the past several years. This proposition would not be viable if there were a great divide between the Filipinos and the Chinese; but there is none, and whatever problems may exist between them should be socially and politically controllable.

The Chinese problem in Indonesia is more serious, for Islam divides the Chinese from the indigenous. One should not, however, be too pessimistic about this division. For one thing, Islam is not as strong a force in Indonesia as it is in Malaysia. For another, since Chinese immigration stopped after the Pacific War, this will work for integration. The descendants of Chinese immigrants several generations ago remain Chinese today because a fresh supply of immigrants in the past kept alive the Chinese community, but with the supply now cut, the Chinese will drift more and more towards indigenous society. In the meantime, if a dictatorial military government remains in power and continues its present pragmatic policy, anti-Chinese activities will be kept under control. Despite these hopeful signs, however, the pariah status of the Chinese capitalists has imposed enormous costs on the economic system. The *de jure* and *de facto* pribumi policy has produced many rent-seekers among the indigenous, while the social background which gave rise to this policy required the Chinese to seek protective patrons among the political power holders (who, of course, receive a fee for this). For the Chinese who are successful today, it meant uncertainty about the future, which forced them to become rent-seekers, speculators, or predators, in order to make quick money to send abroad.

The Chinese problem is most serious in Malaysia. This is not because it has been most costly to the economic system. Certainly, the New Economic Policy discriminates against the Chinese and imposes large costs on the economy, but it is not clear whether these costs exceed those which the pribumi policy and anti-Chinese feelings have imposed on the Indonesian economy. The Chinese problem of Malaysia is, however, more serious because it seems to lack a solution. The chances are that anti-Chinese discrimination will worsen, due partly to the Malaysian political system and partly to the rise of Islamic fundamentalism. Unlike Indonesia, Malaysia is a democracy, and Malay political leaders have to go periodically to the people for a fresh mandate. This means that if a Muslim fundamentalist group becomes popular (which is the present trend), Malay political leaders have to accommodate their demands; and the more influential such a group becomes, the more demands it will make on the political leaders. And many of their demands could be for discrimination against the Chinese. Unlike the NEP, this may not necessarily work for the Malay capitalists, but it will definitely work against the Chinese capitalists. The NEP has produced a number of rent-seekers among Chinese capitalists, yet relatively speaking, the Chinese capitalists have still been a more dynamic force than the bumiputra capitalists. Thus, if discrimination becomes stronger, Malaysian capitalism will suffer. Of course, it is not certain how the Malaysian political situation will evolve in the future, but, to put it mildly, the future of Malaysian capitalism is uncertain.

Summing Up

The capitalism that has emerged in South-East Asia has some intractable problems. One arises from a low level of technology. Even though past industrialization looks impressive on the surface, the level it has reached is not commensurate with the region's own level of technology. Essentially, South-East Asia has relied on foreign companies to make up for its technological deficiency. This has produced such technologically dependent capitalists as comprador capitalists and also allowed foreign capital to come in, in order to generate new exports. This is not a desirable situation from the nationalistic point of view, but the situation cannot be changed within a short period. There is a great need for South-East Asia to make concerted efforts to upgrade the level of technology and encourage technological progress. Without this, capitalism will never become an autonomous propelling force of economic development.

In the Philippines, Malaysia, and Indonesia, another problem arises from the low quality of government intervention. This has created massive inefficiency in the economy and a large number of rent-seekers. Given the developmental gap between South-East Asia and the West and Japan and the people's ambition to close this gap, it is difficult to argue that the government should not intervene, since government intervention can accelerate development, as Japan and, more recently, Korea and Taiwan have successfully demonstrated. In fact, the South-East Asian governments have intervened extensively and are unlikely to reduce the level of intervention in the near future (the Philippines, of course, is an exception; but even after the massive scale of government intervention as occurred during the Marcos period has been reduced, it is not certain that the level of government intervention will be lower than the average level in the other South-East Asian countries). Some people might argue that government intervention should be kept at a minimum level, but since this view implies that the governments are incapable of a high quality of intervention, it would not be politically acceptable. The Philippines, Malaysia, and Indonesia will therefore continue to intervene, but whether they can improve the quality of intervention is left to be seen. If they cannot, intervention will continue to bog down the economy.

The last difficult problem is the problem of the Chinese. In Singapore, the Chinese-dominated island-state, there is no problem. In Thailand, for all practical purposes, the Chinese problem does not arise. The Philippines has more problems than Thailand, but in view of the enormity of the problem of reviving the economy, the Chinese problem should not surface. Since most Chinese now have citizenship (a good legacy from the Marcos period) and discrimination in the Philippines has been based largely on citizenship, the chances are that the Chinese problem will disappear. In Indonesia and Malaysia, however, the Chinese problem has imposed enormous costs on the economy; and given the prevalence of anti-Chinese feelings, socially and politically acceptable measures to alleviate the Chinese problem are difficult to formulate. The present anti-Chinese measures will likely remain (if not get stronger), enabling a number of indigenous capitalists to become rent-seekers and forcing the Chinese into rent-seeking, speculative, and predatory activities in order to gain quick returns to invest in havens abroad.

Technological backwardness, the low quality of government intervention, and Chinese discrimination are the three most difficult problems afflicting the capitalism of South-East Asia. Because of these problems, the region has been dependent on the market economy and the government for its growth, rather than being the vanguard of economic change. This type of capitalism is very different from what arose in the West and Japan, where capitalism has spearheaded economic development, at least since the Industrial Revolution. Despite industrial progress, its role has been far from dynamic. Rather, the capitalism that has emerged in South-East Asia is a new brand: ersatz capitalism.

Appendices

NOTE

1. The purpose of Appendices 1–4 is to give the reader some factual information on major capitalists and capitalist institutions in the region and any further references available. In Appendix 1, foreign companies are grouped by industry and country (in some cases, by industry alone), for to list them individually would require inordinate space; thus, for example, for 'Ford', see 'American Motor Vehicle Manufacturers'. Only when more information is necessary for understanding the text, or when classification by industry is not meaningful, does an individual company have its own entry.

2. In Appendices 2 and 3, the entries are by the names of capitalists. If more than one member of a family is active in business, the most prominent among them is listed, and the others are discussed under the same entry. Their major companies are discussed, but there are no entries by company besides those in Appendix 4. All companies discussed appear in the Name Index. The author's attempts both to limit the number of entries and to cover major capitalists and different types of capitalist mean that while the listing is not comprehensive, it is nevertheless quite extensive for the region as a whole, and the profiles are necessarily brief. These appendices are not meant to provide exhaustive information on these capitalists: for those who want to know more, references are given, whenever available, at the end of each write-up.

3. In Appendices 1–4, references available are cited as follows. If the author is known, only his surname is given: full bibliographical information appears in the Bibliography. For different authors with the same surname, given names are also cited. If the author has more than one publication, the year of publication is shown in parentheses. If he has more than one publication in the same year, the title, abbreviated if necessary, is also given. If the author is an organization and its name is long, only the first few words are given whenever this is adequate for identification. If there is no author, the abbreviated title is given unless the full title is absolutely necessary. If the reference is the oral history programme of Singapore, it is cited as 'Oral History' followed by the name of the person who gave the interview: for example, 'Oral History, Ang Keong Lan' (this oral history programme is explained in Appendix 5). In Appendix 5, full bibliographical information is given for each reference, so that it is readable by itself.

4. In Appendices 1–4, the following abbreviations are used in giving references:

ACCJ	*American Chamber of Commerce Journal* (Philippines)
AF	*Asia Finance*
AS	*Apa & Siapa*
AWSJ	*Asian Wall Street Journal*
BP	*Bangkok Post*
BR	*Business Review* (Thailand)
BT	*Business Times* (Malaysia)
CKJ	*Chusho Kigyo Jigyo-dan*
FEER	*Far Eastern Economic Review*
ICN	*Indonesian Commercial News*
KK	*Kokusai Keizai*
LAC	The Life and Career of
MB	*Malaysian Business*
NBS	*Nihon Boeki Shinko-kai*
NR	*Nation Review* (Thailand)
NST	*New Straits Times* (Malaysia)
TB	*Thailand Business*
WWT	*Who's Who in Thailand*

Appendix 1
Major Foreign Investors

AJINOMOTO

This Japanese producer of the taste enhancer, monosodium glutamate, operates in all five ASEAN countries. Entry barriers into this industry are rather high for South-East Asian entrepreneurs, for production is capital-intensive and marketing costs are heavy. There are no Western companies in this field. As a consequence, Ajinomoto's market share is high in each of the ASEAN countries. In April 1987, Ajinomoto acquired a 50 per cent stake in each of CPC International's subsidiaries in the Philippines, Thailand, Malaysia, and Singapore (CPC International is an American food company known for the 'Knorr' brand). This is the only major Japanese food producer that is operating successfully in the region.

AMERICAN MOTOR VEHICLE MANUFACTURERS

The first American assembly plant was set up in Singapore by Ford in 1926. A year later, this was followed by General Motors' plant in Jakarta. These were the only assembly plants in the pre-war period. In the post-war period, Ford, General Motors, and Chrysler set up assembly plants in the other ASEAN countries. In the 1970s, however, in the face of increasing competition from Japanese cars, American manufacturers began withdrawing and currently there are no American-owned assembly plants in the region. If American cars are assembled, this is done under licensing on a small scale.

AMERICAN BANKS

Bank of America has branches in all five ASEAN countries, Citibank in all but Thailand, and Chase Manhattan in all but the Philippines. First National Bank of Chicago has a branch in Singapore. A few other banks participate in domestic banks as minority partners. Bank of America began setting up branches in the late 1940s, whereas Chase Manhattan began in the 1960s. First National Bank of Chicago's branch in Singapore was the latest (set up in 1970). Among the American banks, Citibank has the longest history in the region. Its predecessor, the National City Bank of New York, set up a branch in Singapore in 1902 and in the Philippines in 1915. Its Indonesian operation also started in the pre-war period. Partly because of this long involvement, Citibank is the biggest private bank in the Philippines and Indonesia.

AMERICAN MINING COMPANIES

In the pre-war period, some American residents of the Philippines organized companies for gold mining. One of these companies, Benguet Consolidated, was directed by John Haussermann, who was dubbed the 'gold king' of the Philippines. Andres Soriano, who is known for having built up San Miguel, also invested in gold mining in the 1930s. In the post-war period, however, he switched to copper mining and set up Atlas Consolidated. There were some other American mining companies earlier, but by around 1970, those two were the only American companies left in the Philippines. After the Laurel–Langley Agreement expired in the mid-1970s, their controlling interests were transferred to Filipinos. Outside the Philippines, there have been no American mining companies (oil exploration is not included).

AMERICAN PLANTATIONS

Soon after the United States took over the Philippines from Spain, it imposed a 1 000-hectare limitation on corporate landownership. In the early 1910s, however, the American Administration sold the friars' lands which it had acquired to American investors, and two sugar plantations were created (Calamba Sugar Estate and Mindoro Sugar Co.). After this, the only way to set up a plantation was to lease public land from the government. California Packing Corp. (known for 'Del Monte') set up a pineapple plantation in the late 1920s and Castle & Cooke (known for 'Dole') did the same in the 1950s. From the 1960s, however, with the rise of nationalism, leasing a large tract of public land for plantations became impossible. The two pineapple plantations are still American-owned, but the sugar plantations are no longer so. Mindoro Sugar Co. no longer exists; while Calamba Sugar Estate was taken over by the Filipino businessman, Vicente Madrigal, who changed its name to Canlubang Sugar Estate. In Sumatra, there were a few American-owned rubber plantations. Two of these were owned by American tyre producers, Goodyear and United States Rubber (the present Uniroyal). The Sumatra plantation of United States Rubber was the biggest rubber plantation in South-East Asia in the pre-war period. This plantation was recently taken over by the Bakrie group. United States Rubber also had plantations in Malaya in the pre-war period.

AMERICAN SEMICONDUCTOR COMPANIES

In the late 1960s, American companies such as National Semiconductor, Texas Instruments, Fairchild, and Hewlett-Packard, invested in Singapore in plants to assemble electronic components, especially semiconductors. Singapore's attraction was the availability of cheap but productive labour, which was essential in keeping down the cost of this labour-intensive operation. Later, this type of investment spread to Malaysia, Thailand, and the Philippines, but Singapore is still the centre of American semiconductor production in the region.

AMERICAN SUGAR MILLS

Calamba Sugar Estate and Mindoro Sugar Co. (see *American Plantations*) had their own mills. In addition to these, there were several other American-owned sugar mills in the Philippines—for example, San Carlos, Hawaiian-Philippine, Bogo-Medellin, and Pampanga Sugar Mills. Pampanga Sugar Mills was set up jointly by Calamba Sugar Estate and the American sugar company, Spreckels, whereas the other three were set up by Hawaiian investors. In the 1950s, Pampanga Sugar Mills and in the 1970s, San Carlos and Bogo-Medellin were sold to Filipino interests. In the early 1980s, Hawaiian-Philippine was the only American-owned sugar mill left.

AMERICAN TYRE MANUFACTURERS

As the sales of motor vehicles increased in the region, American tyre manufacturers set up sales offices. Then, in the mid-1930s, Goodyear began production in Indonesia. Its operations were interrupted during the Sukarno period, but were resumed in the New Order period. In other ASEAN countries, tyre production did not start until the post-war period when import-substitution policy began. In the Philippines, Goodyear, B.F. Goodrich, and Firestone; in Thailand, Goodyear and Firestone; and in Malaysia, Goodyear set up factories. In the recent period, American car manufacturers withdrew from the region, and this caused problems to the American tyre-makers, but Goodyear is still doing well (better than the largest Japanese tyre manufacturer, Bridgestone), producing in the four ASEAN countries now mostly for Japanese car manufacturers.

AMERICAN TRADING COMPANIES

In pre-war Philippines, Pacific Commercial Co. (PCC) was the biggest American trading company. It was set up in 1911 by a few American traders in the Philippines with financial help from investors in the United States. PCC exported sugar, copra, abaca, and other Philippine produce, and imported textiles, motor vehicles, food, and other goods into the Philippines. In the late 1930s, when war with Japan became imminent, the shareholders decided to liquidate the company. Theo. H. Davies is a British-owned trading company, but since it is based in Hawaii, it is normally considered as an American company. It came to the Philippines in the late 1920s, and from the beginning was heavily involved in the sugar business. In the pre-war period, it was the agent for Bogo-Medellin, and in the early post-war years, it brought two other sugar mills (Hawaiian-Philippine and San Carlos) under its management. It was also active in setting up factories to manufacture construction materials (e.g. paint, cement). In the 1970s, Theo. H. Davies's interests in the Philippines were sold to Jardine of Hong Kong. *References*: Gleeck (1975); 'LAC Gerald Hugh Wilkinson'; *ACCJ*, June 1969.

ASAHAN PROJECT

This project in Indonesia is Japan's biggest direct investment in the region (the total amount invested is $2 billion). In its operating company, Indonesia Asahan Aluminium, which produces aluminium ingots with its own electricity, the Japanese Government holds 50 per cent of the equity (through the Overseas Economic Cooperation Fund, OECF), twelve Japanese companies 25 per cent, and the Indonesian Government the remaining 25 per cent of the total equity. Production began in 1982.

ASAHI GLASS

This Japanese glass manufacturer is operating a large joint-venture factory (Asahimas Flat Glass) in Indonesia. It has a monopoly on sheet glass production, and has been one of the most profitable Japanese joint ventures in the region. At present, the Japanese company is planning to move into production of ethylene dichloride and vinyl chloride monomer, together with Tan Siong Kie, who is also the Indonesian partner of Asahimas Flat Glass.

ATLANTIC, GULF AND PACIFIC (A G & P)

This was a subsidiary of A G & P of New York until it was sold to a Filipino group led by Robert Villanueva in 1970. A G & P operated in the Philippines from the very beginning of the American period, building wharves, docks, piers, bridges, and roads. It also installed water and sewer systems and undertook land reclamation in Manila. In the second decade of its operation, it built sugar mills and became an engineering firm as well. In the mid-1930s, it took over the management of the Philippine Iron Mines, which was supplying iron ore to Japan. *References*: Gleeck (1975); *ACCJ*, April 1960.

BATA SHOE

This company came first to Malaya and Indonesia to market the shoes it made in Europe. Then, in the 1930s, it set up factories in Selangor (Malaysia), Singapore, and near Jakarta. In Thailand, Bata became directly involved only in the post-war period: in the early 1950s, it set up a sales office, and several years later, started production. Although the shoe industry is competitive and the market is rather fragmented, Bata is the largest shoe producer in South-East Asia. Named after its Czech founder, the company is now an international company operating in various parts of the world.

BEER COMPANIES

Neither American nor Japanese beer companies have invested in the region (although there was a Japanese-owned beer factory for a short time in pre-war Philippines). Even European companies did not invest in the Philippines and Thailand, where strong domestic companies grew up (for example, San Miguel of the Philippines, and Boon Rawd, which produces 'Singha' beer, in Thailand).

European companies have been involved only in Singapore, Malaysia, and Indonesia. These include Guinness in Singapore and Malaysia, and Heineken in all the three countries. In Indonesia, Heineken owns the largest beer company, Multi Bintang, while another Dutch beer company, Delta Djakarta, produces 'Anker'. These two beer companies are among the several Dutch companies still operating in Indonesia.

BRITISH BANKS

The Chartered Bank and the Hongkong and Shanghai Bank have been the major British banks in the region in the past century. Chartered Bank was organized in England in 1853 by British investors, whereas Hongkong and Shanghai Bank was set up by British merchants in China in 1864, in order to buy the bills of exchange which arose in the regional trade as well as in the trade with Europe. Both Chartered Bank and Hongkong and Shanghai Bank had several branches in the region by the end of the nineteenth century, and in Malaya and Thailand, they were the note-issuing banks and dominated commercial banking. In the post-war period, however, with the rise of domestic banks, their relative importance declined. Nevertheless, among the British companies, they are the most active in the region today. They have branches in all five ASEAN countries—a privilege other foreign banks cannot enjoy. *References*: Mackenzie; King (1983).

BRITISH TRADING COMPANIES

Guthrie, Harrisons & Crosfield, and Sime Darby operated in the region, with Singapore as their base. Guthrie's history goes back to the early 1820s, when Alexander Guthrie came to Singapore as a trader. The firm grew as a family enterprise based in Singapore. Harrisons & Crosfield was a partnership in England importing tea from China, and moved to the region as the organizer of rubber plantations. Sime Darby was set up as a partnership of British residents in Malaya (the Sime brothers and Darby) to manage rubber plantations in Melaka. Despite the different ways in which they first became involved in the region, all of them became trading companies with strong interests in rubber. They were often called agency houses because they were management agencies for the plantation companies organized in England. Today, however, none of these companies operates in the region. Guthrie sold its plantations to the Malaysian Government, and its trading division to the Chinese-owned Multi-Purpose Holdings. Harrisons & Crosfield also sold its plantations to the Malaysian Government, and pulled out from the region. Sime Darby, too, was taken over by the Malaysian Government.

The Borneo Co. was another British trading company operating in the region. Unlike the other British trading companies, its major operations were in Sarawak and Thailand, and it was little involved in rubber. In Malaya, it was involved in trading, but its strength lay in motor vehicles and other technical goods. The Borneo Co. no longer exists as an independent entity: in 1967, it merged with the British international trading company, Inchcape. In 1975, Inchcape also took over another old British company based in Thailand, Anglo-Thai Corp. Despite these take-overs, however, Inchcape has not been doing very well in the region. For example, its share of the motor vehicle market has become minuscule under the onslaught of Japanese car manufacturers, since its business is mostly with Western car manufacturers. Until the early 1980s, it had the Toyota agency in Singapore and Malaysia, but lost it to a Chinese company (United Motor Works). *References*: Cunyngham-Brown; Longhurst; *One Hundred Years as East India Merchants*; Drabble and Drake; Allen and Donnithorne; Jones.

CALTEX

Caltex has been operating in the region since 1936 when it was formed as a joint venture between Texaco and Standard Oil of California. In Indonesia, it started exploration in the mid-1930s, but it was not until after the Pacific War that it started oil production. With the discovery of the Minas field in Sumatra, it has become the major oil producer in Indonesia. It has not, however, been involved in refining and marketing there. In the Philippines, in 1921, Texas Co. (now Texaco) set up a subsidiary, Texas Co. (Phil.), to sell petrol and other petroleum products in order to meet the demand created by the increase in the number of motor vehicles. Then in 1936, this company became a subsidiary of Caltex, Caltex (Phil.). In the 1950s, Caltex set up the first refinery in the Philippines, where it is still engaged in refining and distribution. In Thailand, Caltex has a minority interest in Thai Oil Refinery and is engaged in distribution.

CIGARETTE MANUFACTURERS

American brands of cigarettes are produced in the region, under licence— American cigarette companies have never set up factories in the region. On the other hand, a few European cigarette companies have been directly involved in the region for quite some time. British–American Tobacco Co. (BAT) began production in Thailand, Malaya, and Indonesia in the pre-war period. Its production in Thailand was a reaction to the increased tariff on manufactured tobacco, but this was taken over by the Thai Government in 1941. In Malaysia and Indonesia, it still operates (Malaysian Tobacco and BAT Indonesia). Today, there are two more cigarette companies operating in the area: Rothmans in Malaysia and Faroka in Indonesia.

CONTAINER MANUFACTURERS

In the post-war period, Metal Box of Britain set up factories in Singapore, Malaysia, and Thailand, while Continental Can established itself in Indonesia (PT United Can Co.). They are the major suppliers of tin cans and other types of container to the food industry in the respective countries. In the Philippines, Rheem of the Philippines, owned by Rheem International but managed by

Soriano y Cia, began producing steel drums in the mid-1950s. There is no foreign company producing containers for the food industry there.

CULTURE BANKS

Nederlandsche Handel-Maatschappij (NHM), Handelsvereeniging Amsterdam (HVA), Koloniale Bank, and Nederlandsch-Indische Landbouw Maatschappij (NILM) were called 'culture banks'—banks which provided long-term capital to plantations. NHM was also engaged in commercial banking, but the others specialized in long-term investment. In the early years of Dutch banking in Indonesia, banks provided both long- and short-term loans. It was only Koloniale Bank which specialized in long-term loans from the beginning. After the sugar crisis of the early 1880s, however, the two kinds of banking were separated. NILM was set up as a subsidiary of the Dutch Bank, Nederlandsch-Indische Handelsbank, to take over its long-term investment activities. HVA was initially engaged in commercial banking and trading, but these were phased out after the sugar crisis. Among the culture banks, NHM was by far the largest. It had investments in sugar, coffee, tea, and rubber plantations. Its factories accounted for about 25 per cent of sugar production in Indonesia in the early 1930s. See also *Nederlandsche Handel-Maatschappij* and *Dutch Banks. References*: Van Laanen (1980 and 1983); Allen and Donnithorne.

DELI MAATSCHAPPIJ

The largest tobacco company in pre-war Indonesia, it was founded in the late 1860s by Jacob Nienhuys with the financial assistance of Nederlandsche Handel-Maatschappij and investors in the Netherlands. Nienhuys, who was growing tobacco in Java, went to East Sumatra in the early 1860s, where he discovered that its soil and climate were ideal for tobacco cultivation. A few years later, after proving the quality of the tobacco grown there, he obtained the necessary financial help to set up the company. Other companies were set up following Deli Maatschappij. Besides tobacco, Deli Maatschappij was involved in infrastructure construction in the region; it took the initiative in establishing the railway company, Deli Spoorweg Maatschappij. Later, the company diversified into rubber, tea, and coffee production. After the Pacific War it resumed operations in Indonesia, but in 1957 it was nationalized by the Indonesian Government. *References*: Thee; Allen and Donnithorne.

DETERGENT MANUFACTURERS

Unilever is the largest detergent maker, operating throughout the region. Procter & Gamble is the other major foreign detergent maker, but its involvement in the region is limited, and currently it operates only in the Philippines. Unilever and Procter & Gamble were initially involved in the Philippines to buy copra or coconut oil for their plants in the United States, but they soon began producing soap for the local market from coconut oil. Later, production for the local market became their major activity, and in the post-war period, they began producing synthetic detergents. Procter & Gamble is known for 'Tide' and Unilever for 'Breeze' or 'Rinso'. See also *Unilever*. *Reference*: Gleeck (1975).

DUNLOP

This company was founded in England in the late 1890s by John Boyd Dunlop, who is known for the invention of the pneumatic tyre. Its first involvement in the region was the investment in plantations in the 1910s. Later, its plantations were consolidated under Dunlop Plantations Ltd. (subsequently renamed Dunlop Estate Bhd.), which constituted the largest plantation group under a single ownership in Malaya. In the early 1960s, Dunlop set up Dunlop Malaysia Industries Bhd. and began producing tyres and other rubber products. In the early 1980s, Dunlop Estate Bhd. was sold to the Chinese company, Multi-Purpose Holdings. A few years later, Dunlop Malaysia Industries Bhd. was also sold, this time to the government-controlled Sime Darby.

DUTCH BANKS

The sugar crisis of the early 1880s brought a new banking order, leaving only three major Dutch commercial banks. They were NHM (Nederlandsche Handel-Maatschappij), NIHB (Nederlandsch-Indische Handelsbank), and NIEM (Nederlandsch-Indische Escompto Maatschappij). NIEM was established in Indonesia in 1857 by resident merchants, whereas NIHB was set up in the Netherlands by European finance capital, to provide banking services in Indonesia. NHM was organized by the Dutch Government as a trading company, and later became a banking institution. After the Pacific War, the three banks returned to Indonesia, but were nationalized by the Indonesian Government in 1957. NHM became the state bank, Bank Ekspor Impor Indonesia; NIEM, Bank Dagang Negara; and NIHB, Bank Bumi Daya. See also *Javasche Bank, Nederlandsche Handel-Maatschappij*, and *Culture Banks*. *References*: Allen and Donnithorne; Van Laanen (1980).

DUTCH TRADING COMPANIES

The 'Big Five' Dutch trading companies in the pre-war period were Jacobson, George Wehry, Borsumij, Internatio, and Lindeteves. The first three grew in Indonesia as trading companies in the second half of the nineteenth century. Internatio was originally established in the Netherlands to undertake commercial banking in Indonesia, but it got into trouble during the sugar crisis of the early 1880s and was subsequently reorganized as a trading company. Lindeteves entered Indonesia as a technical importer (handling machinery) after the First World War. Besides trading, George Wehry and Borsumij had investments in plantations, manufacturing, and mining. These trading companies re-entered Indonesia after the Second World War but were nationalized by the Indonesian Government in late 1957, and no longer operate in the region. *Reference*: Allen and Donnithorne.

EAST ASIATIC CO.

This company was founded in 1897 by H. N. Andersen together with investors in Denmark. Andersen once worked for King Chulalongkorn as captain of one of his trading vessels. In 1884, he came ashore and started a trading company—importing European goods into Bangkok and exporting Thai goods, especially teak. It was one of the first companies to be given teak concessions in northern Thailand. After it had become East Asiatic Co., its headquarters was moved to Copenhagen, and the company grew with the trade between Europe and Bangkok. In this, teak played an especially important role. It also started rice milling and trading, and became involved in the regional trade. Perhaps because of H. N. Andersen's earlier profession, the company made shipping one of its mainstays in its early years and became a trading-cum-shipping company. As a result, its operations extended beyond South-East Asia, and its dependence on the region declined, which saved the company from the fate of other European trading companies in the post-war period. Within South-East Asia, Bangkok still remains its largest base of operation. *Reference*: Laugesen *et al.*

ENGINEERING COMPANIES

In the pre-war period, the need to import, install, and service the machines needed in the processing and mining industries was met by such engineering companies as United Engineering (Malaya) and Honiron (the Philippines). In the post-war period, these companies imported industrial machinery and did various engineering jobs for factories. United Engineering expanded and has operated mainly in Malaya, whereas Honiron, a Hawaiian-based company, has operated in various parts of the world.

ISHIHARA SANGYO

In 1916, Ishihara Hiroichiro, the founder of this company, went to British Malaya to set up a rubber plantation. Although he failed in this, he became a successful operator of iron mines in Johor and Terengganu, and supplied about half of the iron-ore consumed in Japan in the 1920s and 1930s. Ishihara Sangyo lost its mines in British Malaya at the end of the Pacific War, and became a chemical company in the post-war period. Its only investment in South-East Asia since the war is its participation in Bank Perdania in Indonesia. *Reference*: Yasuba.

JAPANESE MOTOR VEHICLE MANUFACTURERS

Their investment in the region started in the 1960s, and in the next decade, they began dominating the motor vehicle industry of the region. In the 1980s, they account for about 90 per cent of the market. (Their share is larger than

90 per cent for commercial vehicles but less for passenger cars. Commercial vehicles, however, sell much better than passenger cars.) In some cases, they are directly involved in assembling, and in others, through licensing. In Indonesia and Malaysia, they are also producing engines (Daihatsu, Honda, Isuzu, Mitsubishi, Suzuki, and Toyota in Indonesia; and Mitsubishi in Malaysia). Toyota, Mitsubishi, and Nissan are the 'big three' of the Japanese motor vehicle manufacturers involved in the region: Toyota in Malaysia, Thailand, and Indonesia (in the Philippines, Delta Motor was its agent, but the company went bankrupt a few years ago, and Toyota is now planning to return to the Philippines with the Metro Bank group as its Philippine partner); Mitsubishi in the Philippines, Thailand, Malaysia, and Indonesia; and Nissan in Thailand and Malaysia. (Nissan cars are also assembled in the Philippines and Indonesia but only on a very small scale compared with other Japanese cars. In Indonesia, Indokaya was its agent, but this tie-up was terminated in the early 1980s.)

JAPANESE BANKS

The Japanese 'policy bank' Yokohama Specie Bank set up its first branch in the region in Singapore in 1916, and by the end of the 1930s, had branches in Bangkok, Surabaya, Batavia, Semarang, and Manila. Another 'policy bank', the Bank of Taiwan, also had branches and liaison offices in various places in the region. After the Pacific War, the Bank of Taiwan was closed, and Yokohama Specie Bank became the Bank of Tokyo. Today, the Bank of Tokyo has branches in Singapore, Kuala Lumpur, Jakarta, and Bangkok, whereas another bank, the Mitsui Bank, has branches in Singapore and Bangkok. There is no Japanese bank in the Philippines. Other Japanese banks operate in the region as offshore banks or as partners in finance and leasing companies. In a few cases, they are minority shareholders in domestic banks. In general, Japanese banks are weak in the region. This is partly because they lost their pre-war footings after the war and nationalistic banking legislation barred their new entry in the post-war period.

JAPANESE HOUSEHOLD ELECTRICAL APPLIANCE COMPANIES

Matsushita, Sanyo, Hitachi, Toshiba, and Sharp have either joint ventures or licensees in the region. Among these, Matsushita is most heavily involved: it has subsidiaries or joint ventures in all five ASEAN countries. In Malaysia and Singapore, some of these Japanese companies are engaged in production for export. Sanyo is also heavily involved in the region. Its products are popular since their prices tend to be lower than those of the other Japanese brands. In the Japanese market, too, Sanyo competes in price. Recently, Sony entered the region to produce for export.

JAPANESE PETROCHEMICAL COMPANIES

Sumitomo's petrochemical complex in Singapore is the only one of its kind in the region. This is the second biggest Japanese direct investment in South-

East Asia (after the Asahan project). Most of the other Japanese investments in chemicals went to the downstream sector. The only exceptions are two joint ventures producing polyvinyl chloride (PVC) in Indonesia, Standard Toyo Polymer and Eastern Polymer.

JAPANESE SHIPBUILDING COMPANIES

Ishikawajima-Harima's investment in Jurong Shipyard in 1963 was the first Japanese investment in this field. Several years later, Ishikawajima-Harima set up another company (Jurong Shipbuilders), this time to undertake ship-building. Then in the early 1970s, Mitsubishi Heavy Industries and Hitachi Zosen also set up shipyards in Singapore as joint ventures. This was followed by Sumitomo Shipbuilding and Machinery's investment in Johor and Kawasaki Heavy Industries' in the Philippines. Recently, Mitsubishi pulled out from Singapore.

JAPANESE STEEL COMPANIES

The Japanese steel industry's involvement in the region is small, except in the downstream sector producing various steel products (such as galvanized iron (GI) sheets, nuts and bolts, wires, steel rods, structural steel, and steel pipes). The only Japanese investment in integrated steel production is in Malaysia where Nippon Steel, the largest Japanese steel maker, is involved in Malayawata and the sponge-iron plant in Terengganu on a minority basis. Kawasaki Steel has a sintering plant in Mindanao in the Philippines. See also *Philippine Sinter Corp.*

JAPANESE TEXTILE MANUFACTURERS

Toray, Teijin, Kanebo, Kuraray, Shikishima Boseki, etc., have invested in the region. Among these, Toray's involvement is most extensive: some of its joint ventures are direct investments, and others are through TAL in Hong Kong, which Toray took over in the mid-1970s. Among the five ASEAN countries, Japanese textile investment is largest in Indonesia, where, in 1984, there were fourteen Japanese joint ventures engaged in spinning and four in synthetic fibre production. Recently, with the growth of Indonesian companies, the Japanese share in spinning has fallen, but it is still high in synthetic fibres. *References*: Yoshihara (1978); Thee and Yoshihara.

JAPANESE TYRE MANUFACTURERS

Bridgestone is the dominant tyre producer in Japan. Its first investment in the region was a venture in Singapore in the early 1960s for the forthcoming Malaysian common market. After Singapore withdrew from Malaysia, the Singapore factory operated for some time by exporting the products, but eventually it was closed down. Bridgestone also set up factories in Thailand and Indonesia, where it is now the largest tyre producer.

JAPANESE TRADING COMPANIES

There are nine large general trading companies called sogo shosha: they are Mitsubishi Shoji, Mitsui Bussan, C. Itoh, Marubeni, Sumitomo Shoji, Nissho-Iwai, Nichimen, Tomen, and Kanematsu-Gosho. Most of these have branches in all five ASEAN countries (though, legally, they may not be branches in some countries). They are investors as well as traders: they have participated in various Japanese joint ventures. Their history of involvement in the region predates the Pacific War. The first branch was Mitsui's in Singapore in 1891. Mitsubishi Shoji's involvement came much later: its first branch was set up in Bangkok in the 1930s. In the pre-war period, a company called Daido sold textiles in the Philippines and Indonesia. This company was set up from the overseas department of C. Itoh when the latter got into financial trouble after the First World War. After the Pacific War, Daido became part of Marubeni. See also *Mitsubishi Shoji* and *Mitsui Bussan*. *Reference*: Yoshihara (1982).

JAVASCHE BANK (JAVA BANK)

The bank was established in the late 1820s to provide credit to traders in Indonesia. It was promoted by the Dutch colonial government, which also held some equity, but essentially it was privately owned. It was not, however, an ordinary private bank. It was the only note-issuing bank; it was a cashier for the government; and it acted as a central bank in other ways. It was, nevertheless, a commercial bank as well, for although it did not accept deposits, it was engaged in lending and other commercial banking activities. Soon after Indonesia gained independence, it was nationalized and renamed Bank Indonesia. *Reference*: De Bree.

KONINKLIJKE PAKETVAART MAATSCHAPPIJ (KPM)

This company had a virtual monopoly on inter-island shipping in pre-war Indonesia and also offered shipping services to and from Singapore and Penang. The company was set up in 1888 by a consortium of Dutch companies headed by Nederlandsche Handel-Maatschappij, in order to wrest control of inter-island shipping from British and Chinese ships covering the area from Singapore. Under the protection of the Dutch colonial government, which gave it the mail contract and excluded foreign ships from inter-island shipping, KPM became one of the largest Dutch companies. After the Pacific War, it re-entered Indonesia but was nationalized by the Indonesian Government in 1957.

MERCEDES-BENZ

Daimler-Benz, the German producer of Mercedes-Benz cars, has an assembly plant in Indonesia (German Motor Manufacturing, a joint venture with Haji Muhammad Joesoef). In Singapore and Malaysia, its licensee is Cycle & Carriage, and in Thailand, Thonburi Phanich. In the Philippines, the cars were formerly assembled under licence by Universal Motors. Since Mercedes-Benz are luxury cars and do not compete much in price with Japanese cars, they are still strong and are the only non-Japanese cars which sell well in the region.

MITSUBISHI SHOJI

It was during the First World War boom that Mitsubishi Shoji was established as the trading arm of the Mitsubishi zaibatsu. In the post-war period, it became the number one trading company in Japan, supported by the heavy industry of the Mitsubishi group. Its largest investment in the region is its participation in the LNG plant of Brunei. It also participated in the LNG plant of Sarawak, Malaysia, as well as collaborating with Mitsubishi Motor. The latter's strength in the region seems to derive from the strength of Mitsubishi Shoji. Other manufacturers market their cars on their own.

MITSUI BUSSAN

Mitsui Bussan was set up in 1876 by the Mitsui family, and became the largest trading company of pre-war Japan. Its first branch in the region was set up in Singapore in 1891 in order to sell the coal from the Miike mines owned by the Mitsui zaibatsu, though later rubber and tin trading became more important. Then it became involved in sugar buying in Surabaya. After the Pacific War, Mitsui's relative position declined and it became the number two trading company.

NEDERLANDSCHE HANDEL-MAATSCHAPPIJ (NHM)

NHM, commonly called the 'Factorij', was one of two large companies promoted by the Dutch colonial government in the 1820s (the other being the Java Bank). In pre-war Indonesia, it was the largest culture bank as well as the largest commercial bank. It was organized in the 1820s to promote trade between Indonesia and the Netherlands, and during the time of the culture system, it gained the exclusive agency for the government's agricultural products and became the dominant trader in the Indies. At this time, it began extending credit to cultivators and individual traders, and became involved in some banking operations. After the culture system was abolished, NHM lost its trading business with the government and became better known as a financial institution. After the Pacific War, NHM returned to Indonesia but was nationalized by the Indonesian Government in 1957. Its commercial banking division became the government-owned bank, Bank Ekspor Impor Indonesia. NHM retained its operations outside Indonesia, but in 1964 it merged with another Dutch bank (de Twentsche Bank) to become Algemene Bank Nederland. *References*: Allen and Donnithorne; Day; Mansvelt.

NOMURA ZAIBATSU

Nomura Tokuhichi, the founder of the Nomura zaibatsu, was a securities broker who made money in the stock market. Having set up Nomura Bank, he directed his efforts to estate production in South-East Asia. The zaibatsu's investment was first in rubber production in Borneo, and then, several years later, in coffee production in Sumatra. It also set up a rubber trading company in Singapore. After the Pacific War, all of its assets in the region were confiscated, and the Nomura zaibatsu was dissolved. Unlike other zaibatsu, former Nomura companies never regrouped: Nomura Securities, Daiwa Bank (the former Nomura Bank), and Nomura Trading do not form a group. Today, Daiwa Bank is a minority partner in Bank Perdania in Indonesia. Nomura Trading has often tied up with Shikishima Boseki (a Japanese spinner) and invested in Thailand and Indonesia. *Reference*: Yoshihara (1981).

OIL COMPANIES

Western oil companies came to the region to sell kerosene, fuel oil, lubricating oil, petrol, and other petroleum products. Among these, kerosene had the largest demand in the late nineteenth century, but with the spread of motor vehicles in the early years of the twentieth century, petrol became the number one product. In the pre-war period, Western oil companies were engaged only in marketing in most of the region. In Indonesia, however, Shell and Stanvac were engaged in oil production and refining as well. In the post-war period, the two companies also began constructing refineries outside Indonesia, and in Malaysia, oil production began in the 1960s. Recently, LNG production began in Indonesia and Malaysia. Major oil companies operating in the region are Caltex, Shell, Esso, and Mobil. Esso is engaged in oil production in Indonesia and Malaysia, and refining in Malaysia, Singapore and Thailand. Mobil has a refinery in Singapore, and in Indonesia, it is the largest producer of LNG. See also *Caltex*, *Shell*, and *Stanvac*.

PHARMACEUTICAL COMPANIES

A number of foreign companies set up plants in the region in the post-war period. European companies tend to dominate in Singapore, Malaysia, and Indonesia, whereas American companies dominate in the Philippines. There are a few Japanese companies (such as Takeda) producing drugs in the region, but their share is small: pharmaceuticals is one of the few major manufacturing industries in which Japanese companies are weak. Some of the foreign companies which have not invested in the region have their products produced by South-East Asian companies under licence. Among those which have invested, none is dominant: each company has a small share of the local pharmaceutical market, though in a particular product, its share may be large.

PHILIPPINE SINTER CORP.

This is one of the largest Japanese companies in the region. It was built in the 1970s by Kawasaki Steel at a total cost of 1.6 billion pesos. The plant, located at Mindanao, produces sintered ore from imported iron ore for Kawasaki Steel's plants in Japan. Kawasaki Steel's involvement in the Philippines started with its supply of a pellet plant to the Philippine Iron Mines. The failure of the plant to operate properly caused a dispute, which was settled by Kawasaki Steel agreeing to set up a company to take over the plant. In the 1960s, this company (Pellet Corp. of the Philippines) was the only company incorporated in the Philippines with Japanese majority.

PUBLIC UTILITIES COMPANIES

Since the colonial administrations and, in Thailand, the Thai Government were actively involved in public utilities, there were only a few large private companies in this field. In Indonesia, Koninklijke Paketvaart Maatschappij (KPM) was engaged in inter-island shipping, Algemene Nederlandsch Indische Electriciteit Maatschappij in electricity supply, and Deli Spoorweg Maatschappij in railroad transportation (in East Sumatra). In the Philippines, Philippine Long Distance Telephone Co. (PLDT) and Manila Electric Co. (Meralco) were the only two privately owned public utilities companies. At first, these companies were not affiliated with major American companies, but later General Telephone and Electronics Corp. acquired a controlling interest in PLDT, while Meralco became a subsidiary of General Public Utilities Corp. Now these companies in Indonesia and the Philippines are all domestically owned. The Indonesian Government began taking over public utilities companies soon after independence, whereas the two companies in the Philippines were sold to private Filipino groups in the 1960s (Eugenio Lopez, the sugar baron, bought the controlling interest in Meralco). *References*: Allen and Donnithorne; Manila Electric Co.

SHELL

The Royal Dutch/Shell group of companies, commonly known as Shell, was formed as a result of the merger in 1907 between Royal Dutch Petroleum and Shell Transport and Trading. Royal Dutch was established in 1890 by a Dutchman in Sumatra with financial help from investors in The Hague, and was producing oil. Shell Transport and Trading was founded by Marcus Samuel, an Englishman who was trading in oil in the region. In the pre-war period, protected by the Dutch colonial administration, Shell was the largest producer of oil in Indonesia, some of which it refined for the regional market. After the Pacific War, however, the refineries were nationalized, and Shell's production declined; in the 1980s its presence is hardly noticeable in Indonesia. In other ASEAN countries, however, Shell is active. It has its own refineries in Singapore, the Philippines, and Malaysia, and in Thailand it participates in a Thai-owned company (Thai Oil Refinery) on a minority basis. Among the Shell refineries in the region, Singapore's is the largest, having been set up as the refinery for the region. In Malaysia, Shell is engaged in oil and LNG production. *Reference*: *Royal Dutch Petroleum Company*.

SOFT-DRINK COMPANIES

Production of soft drinks was started in the nineteenth century, mainly by Chinese. There was, however, one well-known European company covering Malaya and Indonesia in the pre-war period: Fraser & Neave. The company was set up as a partnership in 1883 by John Fraser and D.C. Neave, but several years later, it became a limited liability company. After the Pacific War, its controlling interests were sold to the OCBC group. Coca-Cola is produced in the region, but usually under licence. The only exception is in the Philippines, where, in 1981, Coca-Cola set up a joint-venture bottling plant with San Miguel, which had been its licensee for several decades (since 1927). Coca-Cola's holding in this new company is, however, a minority. *Reference*: *1883–1983: The Great Years.*

SORIANO GROUP

This is a group of companies managed by Soriano y Cia (now called A. Soriano Corp.). In the early 1970s, there were some American-owned companies in the group (for example, Atlas Consolidated Mining), but now most of them are Filipino-owned. Soriano y Cia was founded by Andres Soriano, who was born into a prominent Spanish family in the Philippines. During the Pacific War, he acquired Philippine citizenship and became Secretary of Finance in the Quezon government, but renounced it a few years later and became an American citizen. His sons (Andres Jr. and Jose) also obtained American citizenship. In the post-war period, Andres Soriano and his sons were active in the American Chamber of Commerce and in the American community in the Philippines. Andres Soriano died in 1964, and his son, Andres Soriano Jr., in 1984. The other son, Jose, now lives in the United States. Andres Soriano III is the only family member now conspicuous in the Philippine business community. He is struggling to retain the management of San Miguel. *References*: A. Soriano Corp.; Osborne; *ACCJ*, March 1961; 'LAC Don Andres Soriano'.

SPANISH COMPANIES

In pre-war Philippines, there were some Spanish companies. One was Tabacalera, organized in Spain in 1881. The others were owned by Spaniards in the Philippines. One was owned by the Roxas family, and another by the Elizalde family. After the Elizaldes became Filipino citizens, their businesses ceased to be Spanish companies, but Roxas businesses remained Spanish since the Roxases did not acquire Filipino citizenship. Both the Roxas and Elizalde families were engaged in sugar production and trading. Antonio Roxas, who headed the Roxas family in the post-war period, died in the early 1980s. His children now live in Spain, and the family has little investment left in the Philippines. See also *Tabacalera*. *Reference*: Yoshihara (1985).

STANVAC

Stanvac existed for about three decades from 1933, when it was formed as a joint venture in Asia between Standard Oil of New Jersey (the predecessor of Exxon) and Standard Oil of New York (the predecessor of Mobil). These companies came to the region to sell kerosene initially, and then petrol and other petroleum products. Standard Oil of New York started oil exploration in Indonesia in the early 1910s, and this was continued under Stanvac after 1933. In Indonesia, it also started refining in the 1930s, but this was nationalized in the late 1960s. In the Philippines, Stanvac built a refinery, which was renamed Bataan Refining Co. after Stanvac was dissolved. This was jointly owned by Mobil and Esso until the 1970s, when it was taken over by the national oil company of the Philippines (Philippine National Oil Co.).

STRAITS STEAMSHIP CO.

This company was organized in 1890 by Western merchants in Singapore, with the help of Chinese merchants in Singapore and Melaka who had been involved in local shipping. It specialized in regional shipping (one of its major cargoes being tin ore from Malaya to the smelting plant of the Straits Trading Co. in Singapore) and served over 50 ports in the region in the 1920s. In the process of expansion, more and more capital was raised in England, and its controlling interests shifted there. At the end of 1974, it was a subsidiary of Ocean Transport and Trading of England, but in 1983, the Singapore Government-controlled Keppel Shipyard became its controlling shareholder. *Reference*: Tregonning (1965).

TABACALERA

La Compania General de Tabacos de Filipinas, commonly known as Tabacalera, was founded in Spain in 1881, to take over the export of leaf tobacco and the production of cigars and cigarettes from the Spanish Government, which had decided to discontinue the tobacco monopoly. Tabacalera was not, however, a specialized tobacco trader. By the mid-1880s, it was already handling sugar, abaca, copra, and other Philippine produce. Of these, sugar became the main commodity, and sugar trading led to sugar production: Tabacalera set up two sugar mills (Central Azucarera de Bais and Central Azucarera de Tarlac) and one plantation (Hacienda Luisita). In the post-war period, Tabacalera withdrew from sugar production: it first sold Luisita, then Central Azucarera de Tarlac, and finally Central Azucarera de Bais. *Reference:* Raventos.

TANJONG PAGAR DOCK CO.

This company was engaged in wharfage and ship-repair in Singapore for about four decades from 1864. It was organized as the first joint-stock company in Singapore, by a group of resident merchants (such as Thomas Scott, manager of Guthrie). It was established mainly with capital raised in Singapore, but with the passage of time, as the original shareholders returned to England, the bulk of its equity came to be held by non-residents. As a private enterprise, it was quite successful: within a couple of decades it came to account for the bulk of wharfage business and monopolized major ship-repair services. Since Singapore's trade depended very much on efficient port facilities, this meant that a single company acquired the power to affect the welfare of the whole community, which created pressure on the British Government to take over the company. It was eventually expropriated in 1905. *Reference*: Bogaars (1956).

TIN-MINING AGENCIES

British tin-mining agencies were similar to rubber agency houses in the sense that they organized and managed the companies established in England for venture in Malaya. But unlike rubber agency houses, tin-mining agencies were run basically by engineers, and were heavily involved in mining and prospecting; they had little interest in general trading. Of the major tin-mining agencies in the mid-1950s, Osborne & Chappel was an independent company which grew up in Malaya, like the rubber agency houses, but Anglo-Oriental (Malaya) was a subsidiary of London Tin, which was, in a way, an investment company specializing in tin mining. These tin-mining companies were sold to bumiputra interests under the NEP. London Tin, for example, was bought by the Malaysian Government and became Malaysia Mining Corp.

TIN SMELTERS

Two British-owned companies in Malaya, Straits Trading and Eastern Smelting, dominated tin smelting in the region in the pre-war period. They smelted tin ore from not only Malaya but also Thailand and Indonesia (from 1933, Indonesian ore was sent to the Netherlands). Straits Trading started as a partnership of two merchants in Singapore, James Sword and Hermann Muhlinghaus, in the mid-1880s, but it was soon converted to a public company registered in Singapore. It set up smelters first in Singapore and then in Butterworth, which became the principal smelter in the pre-war period. Chinese were involved in this company as investors from its early years (for example, Loke Yew), and in the post-war period, it was sold to the OCBC group. Recently, the Malaysian Government bought the controlling interest. Eastern Smelting was formed as a public company in 1907 by Chinese business leaders in Penang, such as Eu Tong Sen and Khaw Joo Tok, but as more capital became necessary to remain in this field, they sold the company to British investors (such as Cecil Budd, a metal trader in London, and Ernest Birch, the former Resident of Perak). In 1929, it became a subsidiary of Consolidated Tin, which was formed in the same year to consolidate the Patino interests in tin smelting in the world (Patino was a Bolivian tin trader who built a tin empire). Recently, the Patino empire collapsed, and Eastern Smelting was sold to the German mining company, Preussag. *References*: Allen and Donnithorne; Cushman; Tregonning (1962).

UNION CARBIDE

This American company began production of 'Eveready' dry-cell batteries in all five ASEAN countries in the post-war period, and was a virtual monopolist in this field for some time. It has since lost a substantial part of the market to Japanese and South-East Asian manufacturers. In Indonesia, for example, the Chinese company, Intercallin (a member of the ABC group), has the largest share of the market, followed by the Japanese company, Matsushita; Union Carbide's share is the lowest of the three. In the Philippines, it once set up a joint venture to produce carbide; it pulled out in around 1970. *Reference*: Gleeck (1975).

UNILEVER

The establishment of Philippine Refining Co. was Unilever's first investment in the region. It was set up to produce coconut oil for Unilever's plants in the United States. In the 1930s, it began producing cooking oil and soap for the local market. At around the same time, it also began production in Indonesia for the local market. In the post-war period, it became no longer profitable to produce coconut oil for export, so its Philippine plant, like the one in Indonesia, concentrated on the local market and began producing synthetic detergents and margarine. In Kuala Lumpur and Bangkok, too, production for the local market began in the post-war period. Today, in detergents, soap, and margarine, Unilever has probably the largest market shares in the region. *Reference*: Colayco (1978).

WESTERN HOUSEHOLD ELECTRICAL APPLIANCE COMPANIES

Philips began production of electric bulbs in Indonesia in the pre-war period, but production of household electrical appliances really began in the post-war period when import restriction was imposed. At first, Western companies, like Philips, (English) General Electric Co. (GEC), and General Electric (GE) of the United States, dominated this field, but in the 1960s their position began to be challenged by Japanese manufacturers, and has considerably declined since then. Except for a few products (for example, electric bulbs), Japanese brands are now dominant.

Appendix 2
Major Indigenous Capitalists

The Philippines

ABOITIZ, RAMON

Ramon Aboitiz, the founder of Aboitiz & Co., is the son of Paulino Aboitiz, who migrated from the Basque region of Spain to the Philippines in the nineteenth century. Aboitiz & Co. initially dealt in abaca, then diversified into copra and other Philippine produce. The company brought abaca and copra grown in various parts of the Visayas to Cebu and either sold them to foreign trading companies in the Philippines or exported them directly. This distributional function led to inter-island shipping. In the post-war period, it participated in the establishment of a flour mill in Mindanao. *Reference*: Aboitiz & Co.

AGUINALDO, LEOPOLDO

Leopoldo was born in 1885 in Manila. After completing his school education in the Philippines, he went to study textiles at Nagoya, Japan. Several years later, he returned to Manila and, with some friends, established Philippine Net and Braid Manufacturing Co. In 1921 he resigned and started his own business (importing), and later the first Filipino-owned department store, L. R. Aguinaldo. In the post-war period, his sons took over the business and diversified into logging and agribusiness. None of these businesses are, however, significant today.

ARANETA, AMADO

Amado married his cousin, a daughter of Jorge Araneta, who founded a sugar central in Negros called Ma-ao. In the post-war period, this central came into his possession, together with Talisay-Silay and Bacolod-Murcia. He is said to have made money in the early post-war years by handling US Army surplus goods and used this money to finance Manuel Roxas's campaign for the presidency. This was the beginning of his close relations with political leaders, which continued until the end of the Garcia Administration. Political connections undoubtedly contributed to the expansion of his interests in sugar. He was a large recipient of PNB loans.

ARANETA, SALVADOR

Salvador is the son of Gregorio Araneta, who bought real estate with the money he obtained from his law practice. In 1930, Gregorio Araneta, Inc. was established to manage his property. Originally, it was purely a real estate company, but after the Pacific War, it began trading, and this led to manufacturing at the time of import substitution (G.A. Machineries, Refrigeration Industries, and Republic Flour Mills). Salvador was also active in politics, and held ministerial positions during the Quirino and Magsaysay Administrations. Republic Flour Mills is now managed by his son-in-law, Jose Concepcion, the present Minister of Trade and Industry.

BENEDICTO, ROBERTO

Benedicto was a crony of former President Marcos. Their relations go back to the pre-war period when they were both law students at the University of the Philippines. In the 1965 presidential election, he became Marcos's principal lieutenant, and after Marcos became President, he was appointed to a number of government posts, such as the president of PNB and Ambassador to Japan. At the beginning of the martial law period, Benedicto was appointed chairman of Philippine Sugar Commission, which had a monopoly on sugar trade (the actual trading was done by its subsidiary, National Sugar Trading Corp.), and used his position to amass a large fortune. For example, Benedicto came to own a controlling interest in Republic Planters Bank, Traders Royal Bank, and a number of other companies (some of these were formerly Lopez companies). He also had close ties with the Japanese trading company, Marubeni. *Reference*: 'Some are Smarter than Others'.

CABARRUS, JESUS

Cabarrus, a Spanish mestizo, began working for Elizalde & Co. as an accountant in the mid-1930s, and stayed with the company until the late 1950s, when he left for Marinduque Mining & Industrial Corp. In the next two decades, he was the key figure in Marinduque, which became a major mining company as well as a cement producer. In the 1960s, Marinduque was operating as a major copper producer, but in the 1970s, it diversified into nickel processing. For this, it borrowed heavily abroad through government guarantee, and when the nickel price went down in the early 1980s, it faced serious financial problems. To rescue the company, the government converted the loans to equity and took over the company. *References*: 'Business Profile: Jesus S. Cabarrus, Sr.'; *AWSJ*, 26 April 1983.

COJUANGCO, EDUARDO JR.

Eduardo Jr. is a great-grandson of a Chinese immigrant who came to the Philippines around 1860. He began working as a carpenter and soon became a building contractor. He invested the money he made in building in rice and, later, sugar lands in Tarlac, where he had moved, and laid the foundation for the Cojuangco fortune in Tarlac. He had three children, two daughters and a son (Melicio). The son entered politics, and died suddenly afterwards, but left four sons, Jose, Juan, Antonio, and Eduardo. Of the two daughters, one died young, but the other, Ysidra, remained single and built up the Cojuangco fortune. In the 1950s, Jose bought Hacienda Luisita and Central Azucarera de Tarlac from Tabacalera. His interests are now managed by his son, Jose Jr. Juan did not have children. Antonio's son, Ramon, headed a team to take over PLDT in the 1960s. During the martial law period, he had close ties with Marcos, who was also a major shareholder of PLDT (through Prime Holdings). He died a few years ago. Eduardo's son, Eduardo Jr., was one of Marcos's principal lieutenants in the 1965 presidential election, and worked closely with him afterwards. During the martial law period, he headed United Coconut Oil Mills (UNICOM), which had a monopoly on coconut-oil production and its export, and United Coconut Planters Bank (UPCB), the bank which was created ostensibly for coconut planters but functioned, in effect, as the depository for a production tax on them, which amounted to almost $1 billion before it was repealed in 1981. He also bought a controlling interest in San Miguel from Ayala. In February 1986, when Marcos fell from power, Eduardo Jr. left the country with him. *References*: Carlos Quirino (1968); Yoshihara (1985); Aquino; 'Some are Smarter than Others'.

CONCEPCION, JOSE JR.

Jose Jr. is the son of Jose Concepcion, who was with the American trading company, Edward J. Nell Co., for over thirty years. After this, he worked for Aircon, Inc., a company organized by another American trading company, Theo. H. Davies, to assemble household electrical appliances. He then left this company to establish his own company in the same field, Concepcion Industries. In the late 1950s, when Republic Flour Mills was organized by Salvador Araneta, he took part. Later, his son Jose Jr. married Salvador's daughter and took over the company. His other son, Raul, took over Concepcion Industries after Jose's retirement. Jose Jr. is Minister of Trade and Industry in the Aquino government.

CUENCA, RODOLFO

Cuenca started a construction business in the late 1940s, but he was a small contractor until the mid-1960s, when he formed Construction & Development Corporation of the Philippines (CDCP). Under his aggressive management, the company became one of the biggest companies in the next decade. This success is widely attributed to Cuenca's close ties with President Marcos: especially after martial law was declared, CDCP won practically all major government contracts. However, in late 1983, it got into trouble. That it had a high debt–equity ratio (7 to 1 in 1975) and had to make large interest payments was the immediate cause of the trouble, but behind this were bad business decisions which had been made, in part, because of his ties with Marcos. For example, CDCP got involved in Imelda Marcos's pet project, Manila Bay Land-reclamation Project, which was a constant drain on the company's funds. Also, the entry into international shipping, which CDCP made under the instigation of Marcos, was another costly decision. *References*: *AWSJ*, 10 May 1979 and 24 February and 8 November 1983; *Insight*, September 1979; 'Some are Smarter than Others'.

DE LEON, ALFONSO

Alfonso is the brother of Jose L. de Leon, who in the late 1910s organized the sugar central, Pampanga Sugar Development Co. (PASUDECO). When Jose was shot dead in the late 1930s, Alfonso took charge of the family's interests in PASUDECO, and in the post-war period, he headed the company for over twenty years. It was during his time as head of the company that PASUDECO bought the sugar refinery, Insular Sugar Refining Co. The de Leon family was originally a large sugar planter in Pampanga.

DEL ROSARIO, RAMON

After finishing his studies at De La Salle University in 1938, he joined IBM in the Philippines. In 1950, he became its general manager, but soon left the company for another American company, Philippine American Life Insurance Co. A few years later, he moved again, this time to form the management–investment company called Philippine Investment and Management Corp. In the next few years, this company organized a few major manufacturing companies, but Ramon was able to keep only one under his management: Bacnotan Cement. He also set up the family business, Del Rosario Brothers, and went into the assembling and marketing of household electrical appliances, but later withdrew from assembling. However, Ramon's brother, Jesus, is involved in assembling, independently of Del Rosario Brothers. Precision Electronics, which he set up in 1967, became a joint venture with Matsushita Electric of Japan, and grew into a major producer in this field.

DISINI, HERMINIO

Disini, a Filipino of Italian descent, whose wife is a cousin of Imelda Marcos as well as her personal physician, was a crony of former President Marcos. He worked for F. E. Zuellig, a Filipino trading company, in the 1960s, and in 1970 became independent, setting up Philippine Tobacco Filters Corp. Although this attracted little attention in its first few years, from 1975 it gained control of the cigarette filter market because a 100 per cent import duty was imposed on acetate tow, the main raw material of filters, while Disini paid only 10 per cent. He also set up a number of other firms, and eventually in 1979, his holding company, Herdis Group Inc. One of the companies in the group acted as the agent of Westinghouse, which sold a nuclear power plant to the Philippines. The demise of his group came during the financial crisis of 1981. One of his companies, Atrium, was a finance company which bought commercial papers from Dewey Dee, and collapsed after Dewey fled the country. *References*: Soriano and Retizos; *AWSJ*, 8 November 1983; 'Some are Smarter than Others'.

DURANO, RAMON

Durano, a politician of long standing, built a political and business empire in Danao, about 30 kilometres north of Cebu City. There, he built a sugar mill and a cement factory, and on these, together with the many other businesses he owns, most Danao residents depend directly or indirectly for their living. There are also schools and hospitals bearing his name. Now over eighty years old, Durano recently announced publicly that he has quit politics. This was apparently prompted by the fall of Marcos, whom he had supported. In return for his support he had received various rewards, including government loans for his businesses. For example, in constructing the sugar mill and the cement factory, he depended heavily on the government.

ELIZALDE, MANUEL

The Elizalde business empire was founded by Juan Miguel Elizalde, who came to the Philippines from Spain in the mid-nineteenth century. Juan Miguel's first business was ship chandlery, and later added rope production. The family's business expanded during the American period, when it went into sugar milling and trading. In the post-war period, it diversified further into mining and manufacturing. Manuel Elizalde is the grandson of the founder, and headed the Elizalde group for most of the post-war period. He died in 1985 at the age of eighty-one. *References*: *Tableau*; Yoshihara (1985); 'LAC Don Manuel Elizalde'; *ACCJ*, February 1965; *The Commercial and Industrial Manual*.

FERNANDEZ, RAMON

Ramon was born in 1878 in Manila. After attending Ateneo de Manila University, he went to London to study electrical engineering. In 1904, together with his two brothers (Jose and Vicente), he formed the trading firm, Fernandez Hermanos. In 1912, this company bought Compania Maritima, an inter-island shipping company, from the British trading firm, Smith, Bell & Co. Forty-seven years later (1959), Maritime Company of the Philippines was set up for international shipping. Ramon died in 1964, and the management of Fernandez Hermanos and the two shipping companies was transferred to his nephews (Jose's sons, Jose, Luis, and Carlos).

FLOIRENDO, ANTONIO

Floirendo is a 'banana king' based in Davao, Mindanao. His flagship company is Tagum Agricultural Development Company (Tadeco), which exports bananas under the 'Chiquita' brand through a tie-up with United Fruit Co. Tadeco also went into pineapple production with United Fruit. Floirendo's big break came in the early 1970s when he was awarded the lease of Davao Penal Colony land for banana production, thanks to his close ties with former President Marcos. In 1977, he branched out to sugar. He had been among Marcos's supporters since the latter's first presidential campaign and was the regional head of Marcos's KBL party. He had started off in Davao as a Ford dealer. *Reference*: 'Some are Smarter than Others'.

GUEVARA, GUILLERMO

Guevara set up two large manufacturing companies in the post-war period, Maria Cristina Chemical Industries and Mabuhay Vinyl. He began his career as City Fiscal of Manila, and then became a partner in a prestigious law firm called Guevara, Francisco & Recto. He also taught at the University of the Philippines as professor of law, and was widely regarded as an authority on criminology. His first venture into business was in 1929, after he resigned from the law firm. This venture led several years later to Mabuhay Rubber Corp., which in the post-war period was reorganized as Mabuhay Vinyl. *Reference*: Guevara.

JACINTO, NICANOR

Nicanor was formerly a physician to Jose Cojuangco, Sr. (the grandson of the first Cojuangco) and his family. This contact led him to involvement in the establishment of the Philippine Bank of Commerce. He invited his first cousins, the Rufinos, to join him and Cojuangco. In 1951, Nicanor withdrew from the bank and set up another bank, Security Bank and Trust, with the Rufinos. From banking, Nicanor, together with his son, Fernando, went into steel production (Jacinto Steel, Jacinto Iron & Steel, and Iligan Integrated Steel Mills). However, Iligan Integrated Steel Mills was a business fiasco and was taken over by the government in the early 1970s (becoming National Steel Corp.). To make things worse, Fernando became Marcos's political enemy, so that soon after martial law was declared, the family lost most of their other businesses. Jacinto Steel and Jacinto Iron & Steel were taken over by the military, and Security Bank and Trust by Marcos. The Aquino government recently returned to the family of Fernando Jacinto, Jacinto Iron & Steel and some other businesses Marcos had taken over during the martial law period, but not Security Bank and Trust. *Reference*: 'LAC Don Nicanor S. Jacinto, Sr.'.

LAUREL, JOSE P.

Jose P. Laurel was a prominent politician. His political career began in the pre-war period, and during the Japanese occupation he was President of the Philippines. After the war, he was accused of collaboration with the Japanese, but the charge was soon dropped and he made a political comeback. In the mid-1950s, he founded Philippine Banking Corporation, and died a few years later. His sons have also been active in politics. Jose III, once the Philippine ambassador to Japan, is active in Philippine–Japanese relations. Salvador is today

Vice-President of the Philippines and was Minister of Foreign Affairs in the first Aquino government.

LIRAG, BASILIO

Lirag set up an integrated textile mill in the early 1960s. Starting as a remnant dealer, in the late 1930s he went into the production and marketing of garments. After the war, he started importation and domestic distribution of textiles, and later set up a finishing plant. From finishing, he went into weaving and spinning. In the initial phase of his investment in textile production, he depended heavily on the government for capital. For example, he was a heavy borrower from the Philippine Reparations Commission.

LOPEZ, EUGENIO

Eugenio and Fernando inherited extensive sugar lands in Negros and Pasay, and while Fernando entered politics, Eugenio managed the family business. In the 1950s, Eugenio took over two large sugar centrals, the American-owned Pampanga Sugar Mills and the Filipino-owned Binalbagan-Isabela; and in the 1960s, he took over the American-owned power company, Meralco. However, Eugenio's active business career came to a sudden end with martial law. His brother, who was then Vice-President of the country, was Marcos's major political enemy; and to weaken his enemy's power base, Marcos sequestered Eugenio's businesses. In the mid-1970s, Eugenio died in exile in the United States. The Aquino government returned the control of Meralco and some of Eugenio's other businesses to the family. Eugenio's son, Manuel, now heads Meralco, and another son, Eugenio Jr., heads Philippine Commercial & Industrial Bank (Meralco Pension Funds is the bank's major shareholder).

MADRIGAL, VICENTE

Madrigal, a Spanish mestizo, acquired wealth initially in trading, especially in coal import, and used this money to go into manufacturing. By the end of the 1930s, he had a sugar mill (Calamba Sugar Estate), a cement factory (Rizal Cement), a coconut-oil mill, and a textile mill (Madrigal Cotton Mill). Unlike other Filipino capitalists, he ventured into manufacturing fairly extensively, probably in response to the persuasion of President Quezon, who also gave him financial assistance through the Philippine National Bank. In the post-war period, however, he lost interest in this field, and the only manufacturing company left is the cement factory. *Reference*: Carlos Quirino (1967).

MARCELO, JOSE

Unlike most other Filipino capitalists, Marcelo had a technical background when he went into business. After studying rubber technology in an American university, he went to work for Guillermo Guevara in the 1930s. In the late 1940s, he bought a nail plant from the government and, from this, diversified into other steel products. Marcelo Steel was his flagship company in this field. In the late 1950s, he went into fertilizer production with a fertilizer plant bought from the government (Maria Cristina Fertilizer). In the initial phase as well as for expansion, he borrowed heavily from the government. He was an especially large borrower from the government financial institution, DBP. *Reference*: 'The Marcelo Group ...'.

MONTELIBANO, ALFREDO

Montelibano is a large sugar planter in Negros who has been active in the National Federation of Sugarcane Planters, serving as its president from time to time. He was involved in politics as well: he became mayor of Bacolod City in 1938, and chairman of the National Economic Council in the mid-1950s. He returned to the limelight in the early 1970s, when he organized the take-over of Esso's fertilizer plant, whose name was changed to Planters Products. For this take-over, he organized a group of sugar planters who needed fertilizer.

MONTINOLA, AURELIO

Aurelio is the son of the prominent sugar planter, Ruperto Montinola, who served as Governor of Iloilo Province. After finishing his schooling, Aurelio helped his father run the family business, but in the early 1930s, went into securities trading, first in Iloilo and then in Manila. After the war, he set up a trading company called Amon Trading, which became a major trader of construction materials. In the 1950s, together with the American trading company, Theo. H. Davies, he set up several plants to produce construction materials, the largest of which is Republic Cement. *Reference*: De Jesus (1978), *The Amon Story*.

ORTIGAS, FRANCISCO JR.

His father, Francisco Sr., was the son of a captain in the Spanish Infantry in the Philippines. After graduating from the University of Santo Tomas with a degree in law, he handled many celebrated civil cases and became a famous lawyer. He seems to have made a substantial amount of money in legal practice and invested a large part of it in real estate. He died in 1935. Francisco Jr. also became a lawyer, specializing in insurance law, but is better known as the developer of Greenhills in Metro Manila. In the financial investment field, he tied up with Robert Villanueva and established Trans-Philippines Investment Corp., which came to own Binalbagan-Isabela Sugar and A G & P. *Reference*: 'LAC Don Francisco B. Ortigas, Sr.'.

PUYAT, GONZALO

Puyat started his business career in 1906 as the caretaker of a billiards-hall, and in a few years, became its owner. At this time, he learned the skill of repairing billiard tables, which he later used to go into furniture production. In the mid-1930s, he began diversifying into wooden materials such as doors and parquet floors, and in order to secure a steady supply of wood, obtained a logging concession in Mindoro. Production of construction materials seems to have aroused Puyat's interest in construction itself. In the early post-war years he won several substantial government contracts. His interest in construction materials led him to the production of GI sheets, which were in great demand in the early 1950s. Several years later, Puyat went into a completely unrelated field, flour milling. Thus, by the early 1960s, Gonzalo Puyat & Sons had three manufacturing divisions: furniture, GI sheets (Puyat Steel), and flour (Philippine Flour Mills). In 1960 Puyat also organized Manila Banking Corp. *References*: 'LAC Don Gonzalo Puyat'; *ACCJ*, August 1938.

ROMUALDEZ, BENJAMIN

Benjamin is the brother of Imelda Marcos and belongs to the Romualdez clan, which has produced prominent lawyers and politicians. Benjamin's name was, however, virtually unknown until Marcos helped him become Governor of Leyte in the late 1960s. During martial law, he served as Ambassador to the United States while keeping the governorship of Leyte. Benjamin, only a year younger than Imelda, was apparently the most trusted of her brothers. Eugenio Lopez's major businesses (Manila Electric Co. (Meralco), etc.) that Marcos took over were placed under Benjamin's ownership (through First Philippine Holdings). He also came to control the mining company, Benguet Consolidated. His brother, Alfredo, a former naval officer, was given a monopoly on casinos in Manila and other major cities. He also took over Philippine Jai-Alai & Amusement Corp., which had been operated by Madrigal. Furthermore, he was the key figure behind Bataan Shipyard and Engineering. His sister, Alita, an officer at the Central Bank, together with her husband (Rudolfo Martel) and his brothers, also acquired extensive business interests (the Marsteel group of companies, Harrison Plaza, and Century Park Sheraton). *Reference*: 'Some are Smarter than Others'.

ROXAS, SIXTO

Sixto Roxas headed Bancom Development Corp., an investment–consultant company set up in 1965. He was a modern type of businessman (somewhat similar to Ramon del Rosario): he organized a group of investors to set up Bancom, and hired many professionals to run it. In the late 1970s, Bancom apparently had a substantial part of its capital invested in commercial papers. In early 1981, when Dewey Dee fled the country, causing a financial crisis, Bancom was left with many of his papers, and went bankrupt. *Reference*: *Insight*, April 1973.

SANTOS, DANTE

Dante Santos is the moving force behind Philippine Appliance Corp. (Philacor). He studied engineering in college and, after graduation, worked for Ysmael Steel, where he organized the assembly of refrigerators. In the mid-1960s, together with a few friends, he formed his own company, Philacor. In the initial phase, Philacor received technical assistance as well as equity capital from Westinghouse, but in the mid-1970s, Westinghouse divested its interest, and General Electric became its major partner. Philacor has also been producing Mitsubishi's electric appliances under licence since 1975. *Reference*: Roney.

SARMIENTO, LORENZO

Lorenzo studied civil engineering in college and, after graduation, worked for the Public Works Department. After the Pacific War, he went into a used-clothing business with his brothers, Feliciano and Pablo. This took him to Davao, where, while handling used clothing, he started a contracting business. This seems to have aroused his interest in logging. He obtained logging concessions in Davao and Cotabato in the late 1950s, and later used the money earned from his logging operations to diversify into real estate and manufacturing.

SILVERIO, RICARDO

Silverio became a dealer in textile remnants in the early post-war years, then went into general textile trading. By the late 1950s, it had become difficult to remain in this field without going into production, so Silverio looked for a new field. Around this time, Toyota was looking for an agent in the Philippines, and Silverio seized this opportunity. He set up Delta Motor Corp. to produce Toyota cars under licence. Within several years, Silverio had made Toyota the best-selling car, and his company became a leading company in the Philippines. With this success as leverage, he tied up with several other Japanese manufacturers, to produce air-conditioners, construction machinery, and automotive parts, among others. In the early 1970s, he diversified into air transportation, banking, investment finance, insurance, etc. However, by the end of the 1970s, this diversification had turned out to be a financial burden. Also, the expansion plan of Delta Motor Corp. turned out to be unrealistic. This led to serious financial problems in the early 1980s, and his flagship company, Delta Motor Corp., was taken over by its creditor bank, PNB. At present, PNB is negotiating its sale with Toyota. *References*: Tsuda; *FEER*, 16 April 1982.

TANTOCO, BIENVENIDO

In the early 1950s, Bienvenido's wife, the former Gliceria Rustia, ran a gift shop in Manila. Several years later, the Tantocos incorporated this enterprise as Rustan Commercial Corp.; in the mid-1960s, they stepped up its operations by setting up branches in Quezon City and Makati; and in 1971, they opened a four-storey complex in the Makati Commercial Center. In the mid-1970s, Rustan opened a large shopping complex in Cubao. During the martial law period, they also had a monopoly on duty-free shops. Entry into manufacturing seems to have come from Bienvenido's initiative: in the early 1960s, a factory was set up to produce carton boxes (Rustan Manufacturing), and several years later, another factory was established to produce pulp and paper (Rustan Pulp and Paper Mills). The Tantocos were close to the Marcos family, and Bienvenido was appointed Ambassador to Vatican City in 1983. After Marcos fell from power, he was given political asylum there, but several months later, the Vatican court sentenced him to three years in prison on an arms conviction.

TEODORO, TORIBIO

Teodoro is the founder of Ang Tibay Footwear Factory, the biggest footwear maker in pre-war Philippines. Born in 1887, the son of a poor farmer, he began working in a cigar factory at the age of twelve. Later he moved to a slipper shop where he worked as a cutter. After gaining experience, he set up a slipper shop together with a friend; but about ten years later (in the early 1920s), they parted company and he set up his own factory. In this new venture he was enormously successful, becoming known as the 'slipper king' of the Philippines. *Reference*: *Cornejo's Commonwealth Directory*.

TUASON, NICASIO

The Tuason family's history starts with the immigration of Son Tua from China. His son, a mestizo, fought on the side of Spain when the British invaded the Philippines. After the war, he received a large tract of land from the Spanish king as a reward for his loyalty, which became the foundation for the family's wealth in the twentieth century. In the 1950s, with the money gained from real estate development, the family went into several manufacturing ventures with American companies, and in the 1960s, took over two American-owned desiccated coconut plants (Peter Paul and Blue Bar Coconut). Nicasio, born in 1903, was heading the family business in the early 1980s. *Reference*: Seidman.

VILLANUEVA, ROBERTO

Villanueva started his career as a newspaperman. After the Pacific War, he organized the *Manila Chronicle*, which he sold a few years later (in 1949) to Eugenio Lopez. After this, he began working for Lopez and, in the early 1960s, was instrumental in arranging the transfer of the ownership of Meralco to the Filipino group headed by Lopez. He then went on his own and organized a group of investors to set up Trans-Philippine Investment, the investment company which later bought sugar mills and A G & P. In the early 1980s, this company held controlling interests in Binalbagan-Isabela and A G & P, and Villanueva occupied key positions in these companies.

YANGCO, TEODORO

Teodoro was born in 1861, the son of Luis Yangco, who made a fortune in shipping in the second half of the nineteenth century. Luis, the son of a Chinese mestizo, grew up poor as his father died when he was very young, but was given training in business by his aunt. Starting with a few small boats, Luis eventually created a large shipping company, while engaging at the same time in warehousing and trading (El Bazar Siglo XX). After his death in 1907, Teodoro inherited his businesses, and expanded them further. Under his management, more steamships were bought, and consignment business was given greater emphasis. Teodoro also went into the development of commercial properties (Yangco Market and Bazar Villalobos) and housing estates (Barrio Yangco) in Manila. Thus, while Luis was known for shipping, Teodoro became known more for trading and real estate development. Teodoro did not marry, and died in 1934 without an heir. *Reference*: Ruiz.

YULO, JOSE SR.

Jose Yulo is better known as a lawyer, government official, and politician. During the Commonwealth period, he was Secretary of Justice; during the Japanese occupation, he was Chief Justice of the Supreme Court; in 1953 he stood as the Liberal Party's vice-presidential candidate, and in 1957 as its presidential candidate. In the late 1940s, he bought Canlubang Sugar Estate from Madrigal, which, it appears, would not have been possible without his connections with PNB. In the mid-1970s, his son, Jose Jr., went into car assembling. He is the majority owner of Canlubang Automotive Resources Corp., which is a joint venture with Mitsubishi Motor. It was formerly known as Chrysler Phil. *References*: Olivera; 'LAC Don Jose Yulo'; Yoshihara (1985).

ZOBEL, ENRIQUE

A member of the Zobel de Ayala family, which is of Spanish origin, Enrique headed the family's flagship company, Ayala Corp., until 1983. The family is related to the Roxases and Sorianos, and has been rich and well known since Spanish times. Family founder Jacobo married Trinidad Ayala and inherited Ayala y Cia, the predecessor of the present Ayala Corp. Founded in 1834, this company was engaged primarily in estate agriculture in the pre-war period. The Zobels' entry into modern business began in 1910, when they established Insular Life Assurance. In the following decades, they expanded into non-life insurance, setting up the insurance companies that today form FGU Insurance Corp., a member of the Ayala group.

A few years after the Pacific War ended, Enrique's uncle, Joseph McMicking, came up with the idea of converting the family's Makati hacienda into a modern multizone subcity and, in the next twenty-five years, implemented it with great success. The profits derived from this Makati development was invested in banking, investment finance, hotels, tourism, and manufacturing, and made possible the expansion of the Ayala group in the post-war period. Most of the manufacturing investment went into San Miguel's shares, making Ayala the largest shareholder by the late 1970s, before it sold its shares to the Cojuangco group in 1983. In 1969, Ayala Corp. bought a controlling interest in Bank of the Philippine Islands, which still remains within the group.

The success of the Ayala group owes much to two in-laws. One is Joseph McMicking, a Scot, who was the originator of the Makati development. He was married to Mercedes, the daughter of Enrique (the grandfather of the present Enrique). The other is Antonio Melian, who was instrumental in involving the family in insurance in the pre-war period. Having seen it flourish in Lima, Peru, he founded Insular Life Assurance in 1910. As explained above, this led later to non-life insurance as well. He was married to Margarita, the daughter of Jacobo, the founder of the family. *References*: Carlos Quirino (1975); Lachica.

ZUELLIG, FREDERICK

Frederick Edward Zuellig arrived in the Philippines in 1901 from Switzerland. At first, he was associated with the trading company, A. C. Lutz & Co., in which he became a partner about ten years later. In 1924, he established his own trading company, F. E. Zuellig. He died in 1943 without being naturalized. After the Pacific War, his sons (Stephen and Gilbert) took over his business. They were naturalized, and F. E. Zuellig became a Filipino company. In the 1950s, when it became difficult to obtain foreign exchange for pharmaceuticals and textiles, two of the principal products it had been handling, F. E. Zuellig established Pharmaceutical Industries and International Textile Mills.

Thailand

BHIROMBHAKDI, PHRAYA

Bhirombhakdi was a Thai of Chinese ancestry who worked as a bureaucrat for the king, rising eventually to the rank of *phraya* (the second highest rank conferred on bureaucrats and soldiers before 1932). In 1933, he organized, with the assistance of the government, the first brewery in Thailand, Boon Rawd Brewery, which is known for 'Singha' beer and now controls over 90 per cent of the beer market. Boon Rawd remains a privately owned family company, currently headed by Phraya Bhirombhakdi's son, Prachuab, who received a 'Diploma Braumeister' in Munich. This training enabled Prachuab to operate the beer factory during the Pacific War by finding a substitute for hops which were in short supply.

KARNASUTA, CHAIJUDH

Chaijudh heads the Ital-thai group which centres around Italian–Thai Development Corp., the largest civil engineering contractor. Chaijudh, a medical doctor born in 1921 to a prominent Thai family, was reluctantly brought into business in the mid-1950s. He had guaranteed the bonds placed by his brother-in-law to undertake a salvage job, but it appears that his brother-in-law was not able to complete the work. He tied up with the Italian, Giorgio Berlingieri, who had been working in Saigon as a contractor and had to look for work elsewhere in South-East Asia when the government in Saigon changed in 1954.

This tie-up worked well, and after doing some more salvage work, they expanded into construction. Their construction company, Italian–Thai Development Corp., was an important subcontractor of American construction companies building military facilities in Thailand during the Vietnam War and also the largest highway builder in the country. In the 1960s, they expanded into the hotel business, first by taking equity in a hotel they built (today they own controlling interests in Oriental Hotel and Royal Orchid, among others). In December 1981 the Italian partner died, and since then Chaijudh has been managing the group with the assistance of his children and sons-in-law. Italian–Thai Development is currently constructing the new international air terminal at Bangkok's Don Muang airport. *References*: *AWSJ*, 17–18 May 1985; Beal.

Malaysia

ABDUL AZIZ BIN MOHAMED ZAIN

Abdul Aziz was born in 1922, the son of a schoolteacher in Kedah. After completing his education at the government English school, Sultan Abdul Hamid College in Alor Setar, he first worked for the Kedah State Service and later moved to Taiping. There he studied law on his own, and in 1951 he went to England for formal law studies at his own expense (he had some savings, but later obtained a scholarship). He returned to Malaya in 1953 to begin a successful career in the government. He retired from the government as a Federal Judge in 1971, and set up his own legal practice. His first business venture was Azira and Company, a mining company. Eventually, he sold this company, but later went back into business when he bought Malaysia British Assurance together with Low Keng Huat. Then he bought controlling interests in Renong Tin and Bedford Plantations from Straits Trading. *Reference*: *BT*, 3 October 1983.

ABDUL RAZAK BIN SHEIK MAHMOOD

Abdul Razak was born the son of a religious leader in Kedah. He received his early education in Kedah and Penang, and then went to Pakistan where he completed his bachelor's degree in Islamic Studies. However, he became attracted to the business world, and went to London to study accounting. After returning to Malaya in the early 1950s, he first worked for Jardine Waugh. In 1961 he joined the stockbroking firm, Charles Bradburne, and stayed with the company until 1973, when he decided to strike out on his own. He formed a partnership with Ramli Ismail to set up the stockbroking firm, Razak and Ramli. In December 1982, he was appointed chairman of the Kuala Lumpur Stock Exchange, but about three years later, in the aftermath of the Pan Electric crisis, he was ousted from that position, and in April 1986, his firm was suspended from trading by the Kuala Lumpur Stock Exchange.

ABDULLAH IBNI ALMARHUM TUANKU ABDUL RAHMAN, TUNKU

Tunku Abdullah was born in 1925. His father was the Yang Dipertuan Besar of Negeri Sembilan (so he is a brother of the present Yang Dipertuan Besar). He studied in Japan during the Pacific War, and after the war, at Raffles College in Singapore and then at the University of Glasgow. On returning from Scotland in 1952, he entered the Malay Administrative Service. After working for the government for about ten years, he went into business, starting a joint venture in construction with an Australian. Later, he bought out his partner's shares and renamed the company Binaan Nasional, which is today a major bumiputra-owned construction company. Then he diversified into a number of other fields (e.g. insurance, finance, real estate, tourism), and these companies today constitute the Melewar group (the name 'Melewar' comes from Raja Melewar, a Minangkabau prince who founded Negeri Sembilan in the late eighteenth century). His son, Tunku Iskandar, helps him run the Melewar group. *References*: *BT*, 10 October 1983; *CKJ* (1982).

ARIFF BENDAHARA, TENGKU

Tengku Ariff Bendahara, a brother of the present Sultan of Pahang, headed the TAB group of companies until his death. He was born in 1938. In 1957, after attending Clifford School at Kuala Lipis, he went to London for further studies. On his return to Malaya a few years later, he first served in the army, and then, in the mid-1960s, went into logging business. He made a name for himself as the 'Logging Prince'. Then, in the 1970s, under the NEP, he diversified into new fields. In 1973, he organized United Asian Bank Berhad to take over three Indian banks. In the following year, he set up a joint venture with Tata of India to assemble vehicles (TATAB Industries). Later, he also set up a hotel (Kuantan Beach Hotel). His business interests were co-ordinated by TAB Holdings Sdn. Bhd.

In 1984, United Asian Bank began facing financial problems, and in early 1987, Bank Negara took over its control. In June 1987, Tengku Ariff Bendahara died of cancer.

AZMAN HASHIM

Azman was born in 1939. His father was an office assistant at the National Electricity Board and his mother was a schoolteacher. After finishing his schooling at the Methodist Boys' School, he won a Colombo Plan scholarship and went to Australia. He stayed there for five years, from 1955 to 1959, studying accounting. In 1960, he returned to Malaya and joined the central bank, Bank Negara. A few years later, he resigned from the bank to set up his own accounting firm, which later became Azman, Wong, Salleh & Co. Having succeeded as a chartered accountant, in 1971 he was asked by the government to become executive director of Malayan Banking Berhad. He stayed with this bank until 1980, when he resigned to become chairman of Kwong Yik Bank, in which he held a minority interest. In 1982, he sold his holdings in Kwong Yik

Bank and bought Arab-Malaysian Merchant Bank. In late 1986, he sold 40 per cent of the merchant bank's shares to Tokai Bank of Japan and Antah Holdings, but he is still its controlling shareholder. He also controls Arab-Malaysian Development Berhad, through which he controls the merchant bank. This company is also engaged in real estate and textile production (it was called Taiping Textiles before Azman's take-over in 1981). *References*: *BT*, 15 August 1983; *MB*, August 1978 and November 1982; *AWSJ*, 3 December 1986.

DAIM ZAINUDDIN

Daim was born in Kedah in 1938. After finishing secondary schooling at Sultan Abdul Hamid College in Alor Setar, he went to London to study law. In 1959, at the age of twenty-one, he was called to the Bar. On returning to Malaya he practised law, then worked for the government. In the late 1960s, he decided to embark on a business career. After a few years of unsuccessful ventures, a break came. He acquired over 100 hectares of mined-out land on the outskirts of Kuala Lumpur from Harun Idris, then Menteri Besar (Chief Minister) of Selangor, and developed part of it into a very successful housing estate (Taman Maluri). With this success, he went on to acquire a controlling interest in Indosuez Bank's Malaysian operation (which was incorporated as Malaysian French Bank). However, in 1984, he swapped his holdings in the bank for Multi-Purpose Holdings' shares in United Malayan Banking Corporation (UMBC), and became the latter's controlling shareholder. In the early 1980s, he also acquired controlling interests in Raleigh Cycles (M) Berhad and several other companies.

Daim comes from the same village in Kedah as Prime Minister Mahathir, who is about thirteen years senior. It appears, however, that it was not until the late 1970s that his relations with Mahathir became close. In 1979, while Mahathir was Deputy Prime Minister, Daim became chairman of Peremba, a government-owned property developer. After Mahathir became Prime Minister, Daim was given management control of the Fleet group of companies, which acts as an investment arm of the UMNO; and since 1984 he has been serving as Minister of Finance under Mahathir. In 1986, his acquisition of a controlling interest in UMBC became a sensitive political issue (because it was approved by the government after he became Finance Minister), so he disposed of his holdings in the bank. However, he still retains control of a number of other companies (placed under a blind trust), and is considered the wealthiest bumi-putra businessman in Malaysia. *Reference*: *AWSJ*, 9 August 1982, 24–25 August 1984, 30 April 1986, and 26–27 September 1986.

GHAFAR BABA

Ghafar Baba is more of a politician than a businessman. He was born in Negeri Sembilan in 1925, and educated at Sultan Idris Training College. He entered politics in 1945. In 1963 he achieved national prominence by aligning himself with the radical group of the UMNO in condemning Singapore's entry into

Malaysia. Becoming popular with the rank and file of the UMNO, a few years later he was elected one of its three Vice-Presidents. In 1967 he became chairman of MARA, and from 1971 to 1976 he served as Minister of National and Rural Development. In early 1986, he became Deputy Prime Minister— the position he still holds today. In the economic field, he is known as chairman of Kompleks Kewangan, MARA's subsidiary to give financial assistance to small bumiputra investors and businessmen. In addition, he headed Goodyield Plaza, whose subsidiary, Pegi Malaysia, once co-operated with Multi-Purpose Holdings in the take-over of Dunlop Estates.

IBRAHIM BIN MOHAMED, TAN SRI

Ibrahim was born in the east coast town of Kota Bharu. He was educated at the Victoria Institution and University of Malaya. In 1965 he joined Bank Negara, but shortly after, left for England to study law. In 1969 he returned to Malaysia and started his own law practice in Kuantan. His venture into business started in the early 1970s. He first went into real estate, then into logging in Pahang and Trengganu. His biggest break came in 1975, when he was named chairman of Genting Highlands. In 1976 he bought a controlling interest in General Ceramics, but a year later, he sold it to pay for acquisition of another company, Associated Plastic Industries. In 1981 he became the Malaysian partner of Brian Chang in Promet Berhad. Promet went into property development and oil exploration in Malaysia and, for a few years, it did well. In the mid-1980s, however, it ran into financial problems, and a bitter dispute arose between the partners. Ibrahim was finally forced out of the company (later in mid-1986, it faced bankruptcy proceedings). *References*: *MB*, January 1978; *BT*, 5 September 1983.

IKMAL HISHAM ALBAKRI

Ikmal Hisham was born in Perak in 1930, the son of a Malay civil servant. After finishing his secondary education in Malaysia, he went to Sheffield University in England to study architecture on a Perak state scholarship. He returned in 1957 and worked for the government for a few years, then went back to England for further training from 1961 to 1962. Returning to Malaya, he worked for the government again, but in 1964 he decided to go into private business. He tied up with the Chinese architect in Singapore, C. A. V. Chew, and started Kumpulan Akitek in a small way. Since then, by obtaining various government projects, it has grown to be one of the biggest architectural firms in the country, with Hisham owning the controlling interest. In addition, he heads several companies in property development, manufacturing, and servicing fields. *Reference*: *BT*, 17 October 1983.

IMRAN IBNI TUANKU JAAFAR, TUNKU

Tunku Imran was born in 1948 and is a son of the present Yang Dipertuan Besar of Negeri Sembilan and a nephew of Tunku Abdullah of the Melewar group. On his return to Malaysia in 1967 after his studies at Nottingham University in England, he worked for Pernas for several years, and for Haw Par International for a few years. In 1974, he took charge of the relatively inactive family company, Syarikat Pesaka Antah, and a few years later, together with Jardine Matheson, formed Antah Holdings. This became a public company in 1983, and today holds a number of subsidiaries and affiliated companies, which constitute the Antah group of companies (United Orient Leasing, Commercial Union Assurance, etc.). Jardine Matheson's holdings in Antah now constitute less than 15 per cent. The name 'Antah' comes from Yamtuan Antah, the ruler of Negeri Sembilan from 1872 to 1888. *Reference*: *The Star*, 6 October 1983.

MATSHAH SAFUAN

Matshah was born in 1949, and went to Australia to study business administration. After returning to Malaysia, in 1974, he took over the small construction company his father had started in Kuala Lumpur in 1965. In the following several years, using it as the base, he built the Safuan group of companies, whose main activities are property development and construction. He is also active in the affairs of the UMNO and the Malay Chamber of Commerce and Industry.

MOHAMED DESA PACHI

Mohamed Desa was born in 1934. He first attended a Malay-medium school, and then English-medium schools in Penang. In 1954, he entered the Technical College in Kuala Lumpur on a Terengganu state scholarship, but a year later he went to Australia to study accounting on a Colombo Plan scholarship. Returning to Malaya in 1962, he worked for Shell for several years before setting up his own accountancy firm. In 1976, he was asked to head the financial and corporate division of the Fleet group. After two years, he moved to Permodalan Nasional Berhad as its chief executive. Following that he became chairman of another government-owned corporation, Malaysia Mining Corp., the largest tin-mining company in the world. *Reference*: *BT*, 31 October 1983.

MOHAMED NOAH BIN OMAR, TAN SRI HAJI

Tan Sri Noah was born in Johor in 1897. After attending Malay-medium schools in Johor, he went to the American University of Beirut in Lebanon (1914–19). From 1920 to 1950, he worked for the Johor Civil Service. In 1951 he went into politics, becoming a prominent politician in the following years. In 1970, he retired from politics and went into business. Since then he has served on the board of directors of a number of companies. For example, in 1971 he became chairman of Genting Highlands Hotel, a company developed and controlled by Lim Goh Tong. Lim had first met Mohamed Noah while he was still working for the Johor state government. Two of his sons-in-law served as Prime Minister (Abdul Razak Hussein and Hussein Onn). *Reference*: Morais (1976).

MOHAMED SALLEH BIN YUSOF

Salleh was born in Johor Bahru in 1935, and went to Australia on a Colombo Plan scholarship to study accounting. He is today a partner in the prestigious accounting firm, Azman, Wong, Salleh & Co. He once worked for FELDA as chief accountant, and for Malaysian International Merchant Bankers as general manager. In the early 1980s, besides being a partner in the accounting firm, he went into property development, finance, and banking (he had been serving as executive director of Perwira Habib Bank before the bank got into trouble in 1986).

RAJA KHALID

Raja Khalid was born in Negeri Sembilan in 1922. After graduating from Raffles College, he set up and, for a while, operated a small bus company in Kuala Pilah, Negeri Sembilan. He then joined the government service. In 1950, he went to England for further studies on a government scholarship and stayed there until 1954. He was with the Malayan Civil Service until 1960, when he was transferred to Bank Negara. Dissatisfied with service in the bank, in 1964 he resigned, and went into business. After some years of struggle, he acquired over 100 hectares of mined-out land and made money in converting part of it into housing estates. Currently, through his family investment company, Sri Lemak, he has interests in Malaysian Textile Industries and Syarikat Permodalan Kebangsaan, and operates Malayan Commercial Services (MCS).

In early 1987, he was detained by the government for a month under the Internal Security Act, accused of causing large losses to Perwira Habib Bank, in which the Armed Forces Pension Fund has a controlling interest. Representing Syarikat Permodalan Kebangsaan, which holds a 26 per cent interest in the bank, Raja Khalid had been serving on its board of directors and also on its executive committee, which decides on large loans. At the same time, his firm, Malayan Commercial Services (MCS), processed a number of loan applications to the bank. Police charged that many of these applicants had succeeded in getting loans and paid 'substantial fees' to MCS, but that the loans resulted in losses for the bank (about M$600 million, or US$235 million). *References*: *BT*, 8 August 1983; *AWSJ*, 20–21 February 1987.

SHAHRANI HAJI ABDULLAH

Shahrani was born in Kelang in 1947. He went to a Malay primary school and then to an Arabic school for three more years in his hometown. After finishing school, he began working as an office boy for the Ministry of Works in Kelang. Several years later, he left the government, and in 1970, set up a company called Shahrani Hj. Abdullah & Co. to deal in scrap metal and act as a general trader. Then, in 1972, he set up another company to operate a private jetty to handle timber in Port Kelang (the international port for the central region of Peninsular Malaysia), and from this, he diversified into other port-related activities. In 1978, he established Shapadu Holding as the parent company of his companies. Today, the Shapadu group is engaged in various port-related activities (such as container shipping), marine dredging, and construction.

SHAMSUDDIN BIN ABDUL KADIR

Shamsuddin was born in 1931. After obtaining a degree in electrical engineering in England, he worked for the Telecommunications Department for sixteen years, where he eventually became its director. In the early 1970s, he resigned from the government and went into business. Today, he heads the Sapura group of companies which include Malayan Cables Bhd. and Uniphone Sdn. Bhd. The group is particularly strong in telecommunications equipment and does large business with Syarikat Telekom Malaysia Bhd. (which took over the formerly government-operated telecommunications services on 1 January 1987). *Reference*: *BT*, 30 January 1985.

SYED IBRAHIM BIN SYED MOHAMED

Syed Ibrahim was born in Ipoh in 1950. His father was a clerk in the Ipoh Municipality. In 1969, he obtained a federal government scholarship to study abroad, and went to Monash University. While he was a student in Australia, he worked part-time and invested his earnings in stocks. After receiving his degree in the early part of 1973, he worked for an Australian accounting firm. In 1976, when he returned to Malaysia, he had substantial savings. For a while he worked for the government, but he soon resigned and set up a firm in Kuala Lumpur. However, this firm failed, so he went back to Ipoh and joined his brother in his property development business. With the money made in this field, in 1980, they began diversifying. Syed Ibrahim organized the takeover of two public companies (Ulu Benut Consolidation Industries and Unilite Electrical Industries Bhd.). Ulu Benut Consolidated Industries was renamed Construction and Supplies House (CASH) Bhd. *Reference*: *BT*, 29 August 1987.

SYED KECHIK BIN SYED MOHAMED

Syed Kechik was born at Alor Setar, Kedah, in 1928, the son of a minor prison official. He went through various hardships to further his education, and finally obtained a degree in law. In 1964, he began to get involved in politics, becoming Assistant Secretary of the Kedah Alliance. In late 1965, he was sent by Tunku Abdul Rahman, then Prime Minister, to Sabah to arrest the centrifugal tendency of Sabah in the aftermath of Singapore's separation from Malaysia. There, he helped Tun Mustapha Harun rise to power. In these years, Syed Kechik seems to have been busy with politics, but from around 1970 he became involved in business and, in the next several years, amassed a large fortune from logging and its related business.

In the mid-1970s, he began investing in Peninsular Malaysia, and in 1976, when Tun Mustapha was voted out of office, Syed Kechik moved his business headquarters to Kuala Lumpur (he became a persona non grata under the

Berjaya government of Harris Salleh, who defeated Tun Mustapha in the 1976 election, and his assets in Sabah were confiscated). Since then, he has acquired substantial holdings in such public companies as Development & Commercial Bank, Temerloh Rubber Estates, Sri Hartamas, and Castlefield Development. In addition, he owns a number of commercial buildings in Kuala Lumpur (including Syed Kechik Foundation Building) and is involved in housing projects, hotels, and film production and distribution. *References*: *ASEAN Forecast*, January 1986; Ranjit Gill (1985), *The Making of Malaysia Inc.*; Hunter; *MB*, July 1975; *AWSJ*, 7 May 1980 and 15 August 1984.

Indonesia

ABIDIN, RUKMINI ZAINAL

After studying pharmacy, Rukmini, a Minangkabau, set up the first pribumi-owned drugstore in Jakarta, PT Apotek Tunggal, in 1953, and a few years later, the pharmaceutical factory, Abdi. This was the time of the Benteng Programme. In her school-days in Jakarta, Rukmini had lived with the sister of Vice-President Hatta (also a Minangkabau), through whom she seems to have made the necessary government contacts to obtain import licences. In the New Order period, she expanded pharmaceutical production by tying up with Western companies, primarily European companies, such as Hoechst and Beecham. *References*: *AS*; *CKJ* (1971).

AFFAN, WAHAB

Wahab was born in South Sumatra in 1926 and went to school at Padang. During the Benteng Programme, he went into shipping and trading with his brothers. The trading company PT Indokaya was set up at this time. It remained a relatively small concern until 1969, when it became the agent for Nissan. In the following decade, Indokaya went into the assembling and distribution of Nissan cars and became one of the largest concerns in Indonesia. However, trouble began after Wahab died suddenly. Nissan and its Japanese agent, Marubeni, did not like the way the other Affans were managing the car business, and discontinued the supply of parts. This led to a legal dispute in 1980, but the Japanese companies had their way, and the Indokaya group declined thereafter. *References*: *NBS*; *AWSJ*, 11 October 1980 and 21 February 1981.

AFFANDI, SOFJAN

A retired naval officer, Sofjan now heads the Admiral group, which is involved in shipping and cargo handling. The flagship company of the group is PT Admiral Lines. The group seems to be owned by the navy, to generate extra funds and hire retired naval personnel. In the mid-1980s, the group was having difficulty finding enough cargo.

ALISJAHBANA, SOFJAN

Sofjan is the key figure of the Femina group, a leading group in publishing and printing. The group is known widely as the publisher of two ladies' magazines, *Femina* and *Gadis*. Recently, the group has expanded into shrimp cultivation, palm-oil processing, and plantations. Sofjan's brother, Iskandar (a professor at Institute Teknologi Bandung (ITB)), and his father, Sultan Takdir (the Rector of the National University of Jakarta), also have interests in the group.

ARDIE, TONY

Tony Ardie was born in Java in 1930. After finishing his high school education in Surabaya, he went to study in the United States. Since returning to Indonesia, he has been involved in oil-related businesses. He manufactures drilling fluids, offers technical services to oil companies, and operates logistic and supply centres in Batam, Balikpapan, and a few other places. He seems to be interested in expanding into repair and maintenance services, and manufacturing of drilling and refining equipment. His flagship company is PT Indokor Indonesia. He is also active in Kadin, serving as one of its vice-presidents. *Reference*: AS.

AZIZ, ABDUL GHANY

Aziz was born in 1896, the son of a Palembang trader, Kiagoos Abdul Aziz, and began working for his father around 1914. The following two decades saw ups and downs in his career, but by the late 1930s he had become a nationally known pribumi trader. During the Benteng Programme in the early 1950s, his company, Masayu Trading Co., prospered as a pribumi company. At this time, he became the agent for a number of foreign manufacturers, including International Harvester. Towards the end of the Guided Economy period, he retired and left the management of Masayu Trading to one of his professional managers, but in the New Order period, despite the progress of import-substitution industrialization, the company failed to invest in manufacturing and its trading business declined. Thus, in the mid-1970s, aged over eighty, Aziz took charge of Masayu again, but to no avail. It was unfortunate for him that he did not have sons until his later years, so that they were not ready to take over his business when he wanted to retire in the mid-1960s. *Reference*: CKJ (1982).

BAKRIE, ACHMAD

Bakrie was born in 1916, the son of a farmer in Lampung, and became a trader there when he was about twenty years old. In the late 1930s he set up the trading company, Bakrie & Brothers, to deal in rubber, pepper, coffee, and other produce of southern Sumatra. Bakrie is still engaged in this trade and has a rubber processing plant. It was, however, in the post-war period that he became a prominent businessman. During the Benteng Programme he seems to have begun dealing in steel, for after the nationalization of Dutch enterprises he went into steel manufacturing. His steel business prospered under the New Order, and he is, in the 1980s, the biggest pipe manufacturer in Indonesia. He is also one of the very few significant pribumi manufacturers. His son, Aburizal, a graduate of ITB, helps to run the business. *Reference*: AS.

BARAMULI, ARNOLD

Baramuli was born in 1930 to a Bugis family in South Sulawesi. After studying law at the University of Indonesia, he became a government official, working first in Sulawesi and then in Jakarta. In 1972, he resigned from the government to concentrate on business, his involvement in which dates back to the late 1950s, when he was in Sulawesi. His business did not, however, expand until the late 1960s. Around this time, he obtained logging concessions, and a little later he ventured into manufacturing together with foreign, especially Japanese, companies. The largest of these is a joint venture with Toray to produce synthetic fibres (Indonesia Toray Synthetics). These businesses constitute the Poleko group today. There is a rumour that the Department of Interior is the real owner of the group and Baramuli simply its manager. What is certain is that, without his ties with the Department, he would not have succeeded in business. *References*: *CKJ* (1981); *NBS*; *AS*; Robison (1986).

BEKTI, HARLAN

Bekti was born in 1918, the son of an ordinary salaried worker in Bandung, and is said to have studied engineering at THS (the predecessor of ITB) at the insistence of his father, who wanted him to become an engineer so as to have a more comfortable life. In the early 1950s, together with Eddi Kowara and a few other people, he set up PT Teknik Umum, which he headed until 1968. Originally a construction company, the firm obtained import licences during the Benteng Programme and went into trading. Why he left Teknik Umum is not clear, but having done so, he set up his own company (Harlan Bekti Corp.) and entered various fields, though none with great success. PT Elegant Textile Industry, in which Bekti owns about 20 per cent equity, seems to be the only major company in which he is involved now. *References*: *AS*; *CKJ* (1982).

DASAAD, AGUS MUSIN

Dasaad, a Minangkabau born in the Philippines, seems to have entered business in the mid-1930s. Together with Abdul Ghany Aziz, he organized the import of Japanese textiles when the Chinese merchants boycotted them after the China Incident broke out in 1937. Then, in 1940, Dasaad and Aziz bought a textile mill formerly owned by Germans. This textile mill, Kancil Mas, became Dasaad's major business in the early post-war years. During the Benteng Programme. Dasaad went into import trading and became the agent for a number of Western manufacturers, including Lockheed and Westinghouse.

Dasaad survived to the New Order period, but his business declined over time. The textile mill faced increasing competition from foreign joint ventures, and with no strong political ties, he was no longer attractive as an agent to foreign manufacturers. *References*: Robison (1986); Sutter.

DIAH, BURHANUDDIN MOHAMAD

Diah is a prominent figure in Indonesian journalism. He owns *Merdeka*, the oldest newspaper in Jakarta, and also publishes the English-language *Indonesian Observer* and various magazines (*Topik*, etc.). He was close to President Sukarno, who appointed him Ambassador to England, Czechoslovakia, and Thailand, but this did not prevent him from making a successful transition to the New Order period. In the late 1960s, he was appointed Minister of Information. While he was in Thailand, he came up with the idea of starting an international hotel. With his wife, he constructed a hotel in the early 1970s, which is known today as the Hyatt Aryaduta Hotel. The bulk of the capital for this came from a state bank. *Reference*: *CKJ* (1982).

EMAN, FRITZ

Fritz Eman was born in North Sulawesi in 1917. Today, he is the owner of the Indauda-Udatimex group, which is involved in the automotive industry (he has a plant in Surabaya to assemble Holden vehicles), banking, tourism, hotel, distribution and export/import trade. Among these, the manufacturing of automotive components seems to be his main business today. He is a survivor from the Benteng Programme era. *Reference*: *AS*.

GITOSARDJONO, SUKAMDANI SAHID

Sukamdani was born in 1928, the son of a peasant-cum-petty trader in Solo, Central Java. In the early post-war years he began trading on a small scale, and towards the end of the Guided Economy period he became moderately successful, owning print-shops in Jakarta and a hotel in Solo. It was, however, only in the New Order period that he became a large businessman. He is the owner of the Sahid group, which is involved in hotels, construction, trading, and a number of other fields. Among these, Sahid Jaya Hotel at Jalan Jenderal Sudirman is the best known. He is sometimes said to be related to Mrs Suharto, who is also from Solo, but if there is a blood relationship between them, it must be distant. *Reference*: *AS*.

GOBEL, THAYEB

Gobel was born in 1930 at Gorontalo, North Sulawesi. At the age of seventeen, he went to Macassar to work at a trading company. Several years later he moved to Jakarta, and in 1954 he set up PT Transistor Radio Manufacturing, the first transistor radio factory in Indonesia. In 1960, he signed a technical co-operation agreement with Matsushita and began producing 'Radio Cawang'.

In the first few years of the New Order period, his company faced competition from imports and began declining, so he asked Matsushita to set up a joint venture, which resulted in PT National Gobel, which is now the biggest company in the field of household electrical appliances. A devout Muslim, he was active in the 'government-approved' Islamic party, Partai Persatuan Pembangunan. He died in 1984. *References*: *CKJ* (1982); *AS*.

HAMENGKUBUWONO, SRI SULTAN

Hamengkubuwono is one of the few sultans left after independence. He was born in 1912 and installed as Sultan of Yogyakarta in 1940. He has served the central government in various capacities in the past three decades, the highest office being that of Vice-President of Indonesia from 1973 to 1978. He has extensive business interests, among them his investment in a major private bank, Bank Dagang Nasional Indonesia, which ran into trouble in the late 1970s because of mismanagement by his Chinese partner, Wibowo. The bank was rescued by the Central Bank and the newly involved Chinese capitalist, Sjamsul Nursalim, but the Sultan still holds about half of its equity. He owns or holds interests in a number of other companies (such as PT Duta Merlin, a shopping complex in Jakarta), but does not participate in their management. *References*: *AS*; *AWSJ*, 25 August 1979, 14 September 1979, 26 February 1980, and 13 September 1980; Robison (1986).

HARDJOJO, BERNARD IBNU

Bernard Ibnu Hardjojo is Mrs Tien Suharto's brother. He heads the Gunung Ngadeg Jaya group, which is engaged in logging, cement distribution, export/import trade, and offshore supply. He is also the Indonesian partner of the Japanese joint venture, Semen Nusantara, a producer of cement. Together with Bob Hasan, he also set up a holding company, PT Posopati, for various joint undertakings.

HERLAMBANG, SRI MULYONO

Herlambang was born in Solo, Central Java, in 1930. After a successful career in the air force, he retired as Air Vice-Marshal in the mid-1960s and went into the poultry business. Being considered a supporter of Sukarno, he was at first apparently blacklisted by the Suharto government, but later he was cleared of this suspicion and given facilities by the government. From the poultry business, he went into air cargo handling, general trade, agency business (especially fighter planes), and tourism. His businesses constitute the Daria group. *Reference*: *AS*.

HUSODO, SISWONO JUDO

Siswono was born in East Kalimantan in 1943. His father, a medical doctor, later became a Vice-Governor of Jakarta in the 1960s; and his mother is the daughter of a prominent politician. After obtaining a degree in civil engineering from ITB, he started a construction company. From around 1973, when he became a protégé of Ibnu Sutowo and was awarded lucrative contracts by Pertamina, his initially small business began expanding rapidly. The fall of Sutowo in the mid-1970s was a set-back for him, but only a temporary one, for he has continued to receive large government contracts. His flagship company, PT Bangung Tjipta Sarana, is involved in real estate development as well as construction. *References*: *CKJ* (1981); *AS*.

JOESOEF, HAJI MUHAMMAD

In the early 1960s, Joesoef left the Ministry of Trade to head the state trading company, Rajawali, the successor of Kian Gwan after its nationalization, which he still heads. He is also involved in private business. He was close to Ibnu Sutowo, with whom he invested in a few ventures; but in the early 1980s they parted and Joesoef kept their interests in the agency of Mercedes-Benz. He also has interests in spinning mills (Sempurna and Naintex Dua).

KALLA, HADJI

Hadji Kalla was born in 1920 in South Sulawesi. After a few years of schooling, he went into trading, following the Buginese tradition, but it was not until the early 1950s that his business became well established. At that time, he took advantage of the Benteng Programme and went into the importing and distribution business in Ujung Pandang. In the New Order period, he diversified into construction, printing, motor vehicle distribution, meat processing, and feed production, thus building the largest business group in Ujung Pandang. He died in 1982, and his businesses are now managed by his son, Jusuf.

KOWARA, EDDI

Kowara's name is associated with PT Teknik Umum, one of the largest companies in Indonesia, which is engaged in construction, engineering, and general trading. Kowara has been with this company since its founding in 1942, but it was not until 1968 that he became its head. Teknik Umum was by then a well-known construction company, but its real development came after Kowara took over, allegedly made possible by his political connections. One of his sons is married to President Suharto's daughter. Kowara was born to a modest family and did not have much education. As his mother died when he was very young, he went to live with a relative who was engaged in petty trade. It was apparently at this time that he decided to make his career in business. *Reference*: *CKJ* (1982).

LATIEF, ABDUL

Latief is a Minangkabau born in Banda Aceh in 1940. When he graduated from university in 1965, he had already started working. He was dealing in eggs and onions at the age of twenty, and a few years later he joined the state enterprise, Sarinah Department Store. While he was with Sarinah, he was sent abroad a few times for training. In the early 1970s he resigned and set up his own business, which developed into the largest private department store in the country, Sarinah Jaya Department Store. The capital for this seems to have come largely from state banks. *Reference: AS.*

NING, HASYIM

Ning is a Minangkabau who made a name in motor vehicle distribution and assembling. His father was a small trader dealing in produce of Sumatra such as coffee and pepper. In the late 1930s, after finishing high school, he went to Jakarta and worked for a Dutch motor vehicle company. After independence, he obtained import licences and became a leading motor vehicle dealer. In this, he seems to have been helped by Hatta, a fellow Minangkabau and relative. Ning made a successful transition to the New Order and continued to be an important figure in the motor vehicle industry. However, after the mid-1970s, since most of the vehicles he handled were either European or American, his business declined in the face of Japanese competition. He was also the major shareholder of Bank Perniagaan Indonesia, but its controlling interests are now held by Mochtar Riady. Today, there seem to be no major businesses under Ning's control. *References: CKJ* (1981); *AS.*

OETAMA, JACOB

Oetama is the key figure of the newspaper, *Kompas.* He was born in Central Java in 1931. Intending to become a Catholic priest, he entered a seminary, but later he changed his mind and went to Gadjah Mada University. After graduation he began his career in journalism, and in 1965 became the chief editor of *Kompas.* This newspaper was founded by a Chinese, P. K. Ojong, who also happened to be a Catholic. The two worked together and made *Kompas* the leading paper in Indonesia. Since Ojong's death in 1980, Oetama has been heading it. *Reference: AS.*

PARDEDE, TUMPAL DORIANUS

Pardede is a Christian Batak born in 1916. After finishing primary school, he went into petty trading, and during the Japanese occupation he became a fairly successful trader in his home province in Sumatra. During the Benteng Programme he started textile distribution and production, and his success in this business made him a prominent businessman in Indonesia. He was close to Sukarno and was appointed Minister of Berdikari in 1965. He made a successful transition to the New Order, and in the 1970s he diversified into cold storage, plantations, hotels, and real estate, which constitute the largest business group in Medan in the 1980s. *References:* Bangun (1981 and 1987); *CKJ* (1982); *AS.*

PROBOSUTEDJO

Probosutedjo, a brother of President Suharto, was born in Central Java in 1930. After finishing high school, he became a teacher in North Sumatra. In 1963 he started a business in Medan, but soon moved to Jakarta. His success came after his brother became President of the country. He was given one of the two licences to import clove (the other was given to Liem Sioe Liong), logging concessions and special preference in government contracts. In addition to these fields, he is involved in motor vehicle assembling, glassware manufacturing, plantations, real estate development, and agribusiness. His businesses constitute the Mertju Buana group. *References*: *CKJ* (1981); *AS*.

SAID, SJARNOEBI

Sjarnoebi Said was born in Palembang in 1927. After finishing primary school in 1938, he seems to have begun working. During the Japanese occupation he learned Japanese and worked for the Japanese military. After the war, he joined the Indonesian Army as an intelligence officer; and after independence, he joined the staff of General Nasution. In 1966, he transferred to the state oil company, Permina, and worked for Ibnu Sutowo. A few years later, he became the head of the maintenance division, one of whose jobs was to operate and maintain motor vehicles. Through this work, he apparently came into contact with Mitsubishi Motor, and in the early 1970s, together with his brothers, he went into the distribution and assembling of Mitsubishi cars. His companies in the motor vehicle field constitute the Krama Yudha group today. It was not, however, until 1975 that he resigned from the army and Pertamina (the successor of Permina). The capital for his business ventures seems to have come from 'savings' accumulated during the Pertamina period. *References*: *CKJ* (1981); *AS*.

SASTROSATOMO, SOEDARPO

Soedarpo was born in 1920, the son of a Javanese who worked for the Dutch colonial government. He had initially aspired to be a medical doctor, but gave this up and joined the Revolution. After independence, he was sent to the United States to work first at the United Nations and then at the Indonesian Embassy in Washington, DC. He returned to Indonesia in 1951 and resigned from the government to go into business. His first venture was an importing business which took advantage of the Benteng Programme. In obtaining import licences, he probably used his connections with the Partai Sosialis Indonesia, of which his brother was a leader. With the money he made during the Benteng Programme he went into shipping: he bought a controlling interest in the Dutch shipping company, International Shipping & Transport, with the help of US Steel's shipping subsidiary, and learned the shipping business. He now heads the Samudera group of companies, the largest shipping group in Indonesia. He is also involved in banking (he is a major shareholder of Bank Niaga) and the distribution of office equipment and pharmaceuticals through Soedarpo Corporation. *References*: *CKJ* (1981); *AS*.

SOEMITRO

Soemitro was born in 1927. He had a brilliant career in the army and rose to the rank of General. He retired after taking responsibility for the Malari Riot of early 1974, and although soon cleared of the charge of inciting the riot laid by his political enemies, he did not go back to the army. Instead he went into business, and today he owns the Rigunas group, which is engaged in logging, engineering, construction, distribution, and manufacturing. In business, he seems to depend heavily on government connections: he was given logging concessions and other facilities by the government. His son, Andy, a graduate of ITB, helps him. *Reference*: AS.

SOSE, ARDI

Sose, a Bugis, was with the Hasunuddin Division of the Indonesian Army for quite some time. He retired in 1973 and went into business. First, he operated a taxi company (Marante Djaya) in Jakarta, and later diversified into hotels, banking, distribution, and shipping. His businesses (Marante Djaya, Marannu City Hotel, Marannu Bank, Bira Raya, etc.) constitute the Marannu group. Today, he is involved in the establishment of a new university in Ujung Pandang. His entry into business seems to have been prompted by his experience as the manager of a company owned by the West Java provincial authorities. His father-in-law was the governor of the province when he got this appointment.

SUHARTO'S CHILDREN

President Suharto has three sons: Sigit Harjojudanto, Bambang Trihatmodjo, and Hutomo (Tomy) Mandala Putra, from eldest to youngest. All are involved in business. Bambang, together with Indra Kowara who is married to his sister, Siti Hardijanti Hastuti, formed the Bimantara group, one of the fast-growing groups, which is involved in shipping (PT Trikora Lloyd), distribution of machinery and equipment (for example, oil equipment), oil export (PT Samudra Petrindo Asia gets oil allocations from Pertamina to trade on the spot market), the export and import of some petrochemical products (for example, Permindo, which has a monopoly on the import of paraxylene and the export of naphtha), and a number of other fields. Sigit is less systematic, and often ties up with his father's cronies, Bob Hasan and Liem Sioe Liong, to obtain monopoly rights and licences from the government. (For example, Sigit tied up with Bob Hasan in Nusamba, which has a monopoly on the import and distribution of tin plate. Nusamba has been also appointed as the Indonesian partner in the next major expansion of the telephone system, which is valued at roughly one billion dollars.) Tomy ventured into business only recently: his company, PT Humpus, was given a monopoly on the distribution of PTA and methanol, which Pertamina began producing recently. Suharto's daughters do not seem to be much involved in business. It is reported, however, that Siti Hardijanti owns a 16 per cent interest in Bank Central Asia, Indonesia's largest private bank. *References*: Robison (1986); *The Sydney Morning Herald*, 10 April 1986; *AWSJ*, 24 November 1986.

SUDWIKATMONO

Sudwikatmono is a foster brother of President Suharto. After finishing high school in Central Java, he went to Jakarta and began working for the company that later became PT Cipta Niaga, a state trading company. From 1962 to 1965 he was the import manager of this company. After his foster brother became President of the country, Sudwikatmono tied up with Liem Sioe Liong in such ventures as Bogasari Flour Mills and Indocement. He is often regarded as the frontman of Liem Sioe Liong. He also has his own company, PT Subentra Multi Petrokimia, which was awarded a contract by the government in 1982 to construct a petrochemical complex. Furthermore, he heads Panca Holding, which has a monopoly on the import of plastics. *Reference*: AS.

SULISTO, SURYO BAMBANG

Sulisto heads the Satmarindo group, which consists of PT Satmarindo (offshore shipping), PT Indonesia Offshore Contractors (marine construction), PT Bantenbay Fabyard (oilfield construction), and some other companies engaged in shipbuilding and repairing and property development. Sulisto began his business career as an agent for a foreign contractor, and then became an independent contractor with one barge. In subsequent years, his business grew with the help of Pertamina, which wanted to develop national companies in oil-related fields.

SUMUAL, HERMAN NICOLAS

Sumual heads the Konsultasi Pembangunan group, which is involved in logging, construction, and plywood manufacturing and is also a partner in several Japanese joint ventures. Sumual was a career officer in the army and led the Permesta Rebellion in Sulawesi in the late 1950s. When this failed, he left the country, but he returned early in the New Order period. Since the government was willing to help him start in business, he tied up with his former colleagues in the rebellion. He first made money in logging, and later he diversified into other fields. His earliest connections with Japanese companies were made during his trips to Japan in the 1950s to raise money for the rebellion. *Reference*: AS.

SUTOWO, IBNU

Sutowo was born in Central Java in 1914, the son of a *priyayi* (government official), and was educated to become a medical doctor. He joined the Revolution as a medical officer but soon began leading combat troops. After independence he remained in the army, but in 1957 he was appointed head of the new state oil company, North Sumatra Oil Exploration, which later became Permina and then Pertamina. He stayed with Pertamina until 1976, when he resigned after taking responsibility for its payment crisis. While he was with Pertamina, he and his family went into business, and he now heads the Nugra

Santana group which is engaged in hotels (Jakarta Hilton), shipbuilding (Adiguna Shipyard), banking (Pacific Banking), construction and property development. His son, Poncho, is also involved in this group. *References*: *AS*; Bartlett; *CKJ* (1982); *FEER*, 30 May 1975 and 19 March 1976.

TAHIJA, JULIUS

Tahija was born in Surabaya in 1916, the son of Ambonese parents. At the beginning of the Pacific War he fought with the Dutch, and during the Japanese occupation he stayed in Australia. Right after the war, he began working for Caltex Pacific Indonesia, and in the past two decades, has been heading it. Apart from his involvement in Caltex, he has been associated with Soedarpo and is serving as a director in Samudera Indonesia and Bank Niaga. *Reference*: *AS*.

TAMIN, RAHMAN

Tamin started off as a petty trader in the early 1910s in the homeland of the Minangkabaus (the Padang area in Sumatra), and then began exporting Sumatran produce (such as coffee, pepper, and rubber) to Singapore. In the early 1930s, he moved to Jakarta to build a better trading network. During the Benteng Programme he was one of the large recipients of import licences, and during the Guided Economy period, he went into textile production. He survived to the New Order period, but his business has declined with the passage of time.

WIRONTONO

Wirontono was born in Surabaya in 1928 and in his youth lived with his uncle, Dul Arnowo, a well-known political figure in East Java. During the Revolution period, he set up his first company, Surabaya Trading Co., to deal in sundry goods. In the following years, he obtained a sugar factory, and also went into real estate, export and import trade, and manufacturing. His most recent venture is the $75 million project, PT Longam Sari Bearindo, a bearing manufacturing company. In trading, Wirontono's strength lies in technical goods: Wirontono & Co. represents various foreign manufacturers in this field. *References*: *Eksekutif*, October 1985; *AS*.

Appendix 3
Major Chinese Capitalists

The Philippines

ANG, PHILIP

Philip Ang was born in 1941 in the Philippines, the son of Ang Ben Uh. Ang Ben Uh worked for his uncle, Ang Tuan Kai, in his Universal Textile Mills (UTEX) and another Ang family business, Ong Chui & Co. In the early 1980s, Ang Ben Uh was also chairman of another textile company, Solid Mills. Around this time, his son, Philip, was executive vice-president of United Textile Mills. He was one of the young aggressive executives of the textile industry, the so-called 'magnificent seven' (Ramon Siy and Dewey Dee were also among them).

ANG, TUAN KAI

Ang Tuan Kai is the key figure behind Universal Textile Mills (UTEX) and the patriarch of the Ang family (Ong Chui is his brother and Ang Ben Uh is his nephew). He was born in China and came to Manila in 1918. For a while he worked for a Chinese textile firm, but in 1927 he organized his own trading company (textile trading was its major activity), Ang Tuan Kai & Co., together with his brother Ong Chui and two other brothers. In the early 1950s, as the Philippine Government imposed barriers on textile imports and encouraged domestic production, Ang Tuan Kai organized UTEX. It was one of the best-managed textile mills until the economic crisis of the 1980s. Ang Tuan Kai died in 1986.

CAMPOS, JOSE (JOSE C. YAO)

Campos was born in China (possibly in 1922) and came to the Philippines in the pre-war period. After a stint at school, he worked as a drug salesman. In 1946, he set up a drug trading company, United Drug Co., which was incorporated in 1951. In 1953, taking advantage of the government's incentives for drug production, he set up United Laboratories, which became the country's largest pharmaceutical company. He had close ties with former President Marcos, which enabled him to receive large orders from the Ministry of Health and its hospitals. He is married to the daughter of the pre-war lumber merchant, Dee Hong Lue (a brother of Dee C. Chuan). Yao Shiong Shio is his brother.

CHENG, JOHNNY

Johnny Cheng was born in the mid-1920s, the son of Cheng Tsai Jun. Cheng Tsai Jun at first worked with the Telengtan brothers in the cigarette business, but later he separated from them and established La Perla Cigar and Cigarette Factory, which in time became one of the top cigarette manufacturers. Cheng Tsai Jun also set up a steel company, Central Steel Manufacturing. When he died in 1957, his son, Johnny, took over his business. However, the steel business did not do well, and a family dispute arose over the control of La Perla. With the advent of martial law, therefore, he moved to Hong Kong and Taiwan, and under the tutelage of Chang Ming Thien, went into finance (in Hong Kong, Hang Lung Bank). But his ventures in Hong Kong and Taiwan failed, and eventually, he returned to the Philippines. In March 1985, he became President of the Federation of Filipino-Chinese Chambers of Commerce and Industry, but he no longer owns any major company.

CHING, LENG (CHING BAN LEE)

Ching Leng was born in China around 1901 and came to the Philippines before the Pacific War. It is not clear what he did at first, but eventually he set up a trading firm which came to be known as Cheng Ban Yek, together with his 'brothers', Cheng Liu alias Cheng Te, and Cheng Tan. (The three 'brothers' were referred to as the Telengtan brothers from the combination of their given names, but probably they were not brothers but cousins from the same village in Fukien.) Cheng Ban Yek was an importer and distributor of groceries, and later began producing cooking oil under the 'Baguio' brand. Also, Ching Leng organized La Suerte Cigar and Cigarette Factory (a major cigarette company) and Philippine Blooming Mills (the first private steel mill). He died in 1965.

COSETENG, EMERSON

Emerson was born in Manila in 1931, the son of a pre-war lumber merchant, Eduardo Coseteng. After graduating from the University of the Philippines in 1953, he organized Fil-Hispano with Jose Marquez Lim (Emerson is married to his daughter, Alicia) to manufacture ceramic ware, but in the early 1960s they decided to sell the company. A few years later, wanting to return to ceramics production, Emerson organized Mariwasa Manufacturing. Several years later, he tied up with Honda and went into production and distribution of Honda motor cycles. However, in 1984, when the economy got into severe recession in the aftermath of the Aquino assassination, he sold his holding to Honda, and soon afterwards, he died. The only major company left in the family is the ceramics company.

CU-UNJIENG, GUILLERMO

Cu-Unjieng was born in Fukien in 1865. When he was seventeen years old, he came to Manila and began working for a Chinese textile store as a clerk.

Several years later, he was made manager of Hap Hin Dry Goods Store, where he proved his competence by making it a leading textile distributor in Manila. In 1894, he set up his own store, Cu-Unjieng & Co., to deal in textiles. This business prospered, and he became probably the richest Chinese merchant in the early part of the twentieth century. Later, he founded Yek Tong Lin Fire & Marine Insurance and Yek Tong Lin Loan Co. He was also a founder of China Banking Corporation. *Reference*: Rodrigo Lim.

DEE, C. CHUAN

Dee C. Chuan was born in Fukien in China and attended St. Joseph's College in Hong Kong (where Miguel Cuaderno, former Governor of the Central Bank, was also a student). In 1901 he came to the Philippines to join his father, and a few years later, he set up his own company, Dee C. Chuan & Co. This company grew to be the biggest lumber company in the Philippines, and Dee C. Chuan came to be called the 'lumber king' of the Philippines. He was also a founder of China Banking Corporation and its first board chairman. He died in 1940. Dee Hong Lue and Dee K. Chiong (who received university education in Shanghai) are his brothers, and George Dee Sekiat (married to Albino Sycip's daughter, Mary Sycip) and Robert Dee Se Wee (married to Lilian Yu of the Yutivo clan) are his sons.

DEE, DEWEY

Dewey was born in the Philippines around 1940, the son of Rufino Dee Un Hong. Also a Philippine-born Chinese, Rufino once worked in China Banking Corporation, and in the early 1930s he organized the textile trading company, Dee Un Hong & Co. After the war, he organized Continental Manufacturing Corp. to take advantage of the government incentives to promote domestic production. After Rufino retired, Dewey took over his business. Unfortunately for the Dee family, Dewey turned out to be a big speculator. He lost heavily in the stock and commodity markets (it is said that he also gambled in Las Vegas and Macao), and in order to cover these losses, he borrowed a large sum of money by issuing commercial papers. In January 1981 he fled, leaving behind about $80 million in debts and causing a crisis in the Philippine financial market. *Reference*: *AWSJ*, 8 June 1983.

GO, KIM PAH

Go Kim Pah was born in Fukien in 1898, coming to the Philippines in his youth to join his father. At a certain stage in his business career, he joined Kian Lam Finance and Exchange Corp. (in which his father may have had interests), and eventually he became its president. The company became the basis for Equitable Banking Corp., which he organized in 1949. For some time, Equitable Banking Corp. and China Banking Corp. were the only Chinese banks in the Philippines. After his retirement, his son, Go Pailian, took over the management of the bank. *Reference*: *Tableau*.

GOKONGWEI, JOHN

Gokongwei was born in Fukien in 1926 and grew up in Cebu. He ventured into trading there during the Pacific War. After the war, he was first engaged in the import and distribution of second-hand clothing in Cebu, and then went into food manufacturing. He set up Consolidated Foods Corp., Universal Corn Products, and Robina Farms. These companies prospered reasonably well. During the martial law period, he obtained large loans from the government and set up hotels (Manila Midtown Ramada and Manila Garden) and a department store (Robinson's). His hotels, however, began facing financial problems around 1980, because of the oversupply of hotel rooms resulting from too many hotels being built in the second half of the 1970s. His department store and food companies are still faring well.

LU, DO

Lu Do was born in Fukien and came to Cebu in the late nineteenth century. He started a business extracting oil from copra to manufacture soap and candles. Around 1918, when his son, Lu Ym, joined the business, coconut-oil production was increased through the introduction of imported expellers. Lu Do died in 1933, so Lu Ym assumed control. In 1940, the name of the partnership was changed to Lu Do & Lu Ym. Its expansion in the post-war period was carried out by Lu Ym's sons, Cayetano Lu Do, Paterno Lu Ym, and Cipriano Lu. It also started copra trading, and by the late 1970s it had become the country's second largest copra exporter. *References*: Emata; *Corporate Profiles*.

PALANCA, CARLOS (TAN GUIN LAI)

Carlos Palanca was born in Fukien in 1869 and came to the Philippines at the age of fifteen. After working in a Chinese store as an apprentice for several years, he opened a dry goods store. Not long after this, he became a godson of the Chinese capitan, Carlos Palanca, whose name he adopted. In 1902, he branched out into distillery in Tondo, naming his company La Tondena. At this time, alcohol was made from nipa sap, but Palanca turned his attention to sugar molasses and pioneered its use in alcohol production. His business prospered, and he came to be called 'the alcohol king'. After his death in 1950, his son, Carlos Palanca, Jr., took over, expanding La Tondena and becoming involved in a number of other businesses. In 1967, he made a splash with the take-over of the American-owned Lepanto Consolidated Mining Co. *References*: 'Business Profile: Carlos Palanca, Jr.'; 'LAC Don Carlos Palanca, Sr.'.

ROXAS-CHUA, ANTONIO

Roxas-Chua was born in Fukien in 1913, and came to the Philippines with his uncle in 1922. He attended San Beda College, and for university education he went to Jose Rizal College at night. It is not clear what work he did in the early 1930s, but in 1935 he became general manager of Kim Kee, Chua Yu & Co., a wholesale trader of sugar. After the Pacific War, he set up Arca & Co. and became a large sugar exporter. In 1955 he founded the third Chinese bank, Pacific Banking Corp., and became its chairman. Later, he set up several other companies whose names start with 'Pacific' (for example, Pacific Land & Building). In the mid-1970s, when sugar trading became a government monopoly, Arca & Co. wound up its business. Roxas-Chua died in 1978. *References*: *Cai Wen* ...; *Sugar News*, December 1959; *Tableau*.

SIY, RAMON

Ramon Siy was born around 1935. After studying business administration at the University of the East, he appears to have been in the textile business. In 1971, his Solid Factors (in which Ang Ben Uh and his son, Philip Ang, were also involved) obtained a contract from DBP to manage Consolidated Mills, which DBP had seized a few years earlier. Siy's group finally bought the company and renamed it Solid Mills. Under his management, the company did well through its newly introduced denim production. Ramon Siy and the Ang family were also involved in United Textile Mill. Siy had even closer relations with Lucio Tan (for example, he was a director of Tan's Allied Banking Corp.). In the early 1980s, unsavory rumours circulated that he was the godfather of a black-market dollar ring and that he was making money in denim not by producing it but by smuggling it into the country.

SYCIP, ALBINO

Albino Sycip was born in Manila in 1887, the son of a relatively well-to-do Chinese merchant (Jose Zarate Sycip, an immigrant from Fukien). After studying in Fukien for a short time and also in the Philippines under various tutors, he left for the United States in 1905 for further studies. He graduated from the University of Michigan with the degree of LL.B., then returned to the Philippines and practised law. At the same time, he set up the trading company, Yek Hua, with his brother, Alfonso, and he became a founder of China Banking Corp. in 1920. In 1940, he took over the management of this bank from Dee C. Chuan, and headed the bank until the mid-1970s. As a lawyer and a business leader, he was deeply involved in the affairs of the Chinese community until the early 1950s, after which he gradually withdrew. His sons (Washington, David, and Alexander) are virtually cut off from the Chinese community. Alexander has died; Washington is chairman of the accounting firm, SGV; and David is active in the business circle (though his business affiliation is not clear). Albino did not leave any significant business to his sons, but built up China Banking Corp. as a public institution—a feat rarely accomplished in the Philippine Chinese community. *Reference*: *Chronicle Magazine*, 17 December 1967.

TAN, LUCIO

In the early 1960s, Lucio Tan apparently worked at a cigarette factory (some say it was Bataan Cigar and Cigarette Factory). Then he set up a small cigarette factory of his own in Ilocos. His break came when an American business-man came to Manila in search of an agent for 'Champion' cigarettes. Since this brand was not well known in the Philippines, established cigarette manu-facturers were not very much interested. Lucio Tan managed to raise sufficient money to obtain the agency, and in the following years he became a leading figure in the cigarette industry (his company was Fortune Tobacco). It is alleged that his success depended to a great extent on the manipulation of customs' clearance and the evasion of cigarette taxes. In 1977, he took over the financially troubled General Banking and Trust and renamed it Allied Banking Corp. With a large dose of low-interest loans from the Central Bank and an increase in the number of branches in the following years (which the Central Bank also liberally approved), Allied Banking Corp. became a leading bank. Then in the early 1980s, he challenged San Miguel's monopoly on beer by setting up Asia Brewery. After the fall of Marcos, the new government considered his businesses to be 'ill gotten wealth' and confiscated them (except Asia Brewery). In the case of Allied Banking Corp., it turned out that Marcos had been its controlling shareholder.

TAN, YU

Tan Yu was born in Fukien in the early 1930s, and came to the Philippines with his parents when he was very young. He grew up in Albay and Camarines Norte, moving to Manila after the Pacific War. In the early 1950s, together with his elder brother (Jesus Typoco), he went into textile distribution and garment manufacturing. In the 1960s his textile business expanded. In the early 1960s, he organized a group to take over Yupangco Cotton Mills; in the late 1960s, he sold his interest in this company and organized another group to take over International Textile Mills. He also went into other fields, setting up the finance company AIC Development, and investing in real estate (especially in Taiwan) and in Sixto Roxas's finance company, Bancom. By the 1970s, finance and real estate seemed to have become the mainstay of his business. *Reference*: *AWSJ*, 20 September 1980.

TANCHI, ERNESTO

Tanchi was born in Fukien in 1919 and came to the Philippines in 1925. He at-tended school for some time, then went back to China for further education. On returning to the Philippines, he helped in his uncle's textile business. After the Pacific War, he dealt in US Army surplus goods, and with the profits from this business, he set up Pan Asiatic Commercial to engage in the import and distribution of textiles. In the 1950s, as the import of textiles became difficult under the government's import-substitution policy, he set up three companies to produce garments, fabrics, and threads. In 1960 these were merged to form Riverside Mills, which Tanchi developed in the following years into a leading textile company.

TEE, CHIONG PEC

Tee Chiong Pec came to the Philippines in 1909 and undertook various ventures, of which textile trading was the most important. In 1940 he returned to China and established a textile mill (Cheong Textile Mills) in Shanghai. After the Communist Revolution the mill was confiscated, so he went to Hong Kong to start an exporting business. Two years later he returned to the Philippines. What he did during the next few years is not very clear; it is known, however, that he had financial interests in a textile wholesale firm registered in his son's name. In 1956, with his cousins and nephews who had been textile traders since pre-war days, he founded Eastern Textile Mills. He died in 1965. In the 1970s, Patrick Ty (a member of Tee Chiong Pec's family, possibly his grandson) was the principal shareholder of Eastern Textile Mills and its chief executive officer, but he sold his shares to Chung Tiong Tay of the Cheng Ban Yek group in the late 1970s.

TY, ALEJANDRO (TY BIO SUY)

Alejandro was born in Fukien around 1921 and came to the Philippines at the age of eleven. Peddling glassware for some time, he saved enough money to set up a store for selling tableware, kitchen utensils, and other miscellaneous household goods. Around 1955, he became an agent for the Japanese taste enhancer, Ajinomoto, and in the 1960s he went into its production, first under licence and later together with the Japanese company (the name of the joint venture is Union Chemicals). The business in household utensils led to the formation of Union Metal Manufacturing Co., which was later renamed Union Industries. This company also started assembling household electrical appliances under licence from Hitachi. Working with Alejandro in building up these companies was his brother, Leonardo. They also bought a controlling interest in Associated Citizens Bank, but it went bankrupt in the early 1980s. Recently, the brothers decided to split up, and Union Chemicals went to Leonardo.

YAO, SHIONG SHIO

Yao was born in China in 1902 and came to the Philippines in the late 1920s. Having helped his father in copra trading, he set up his own company to import and distribute cigarettes in the mid-1930s. In the post-war period, cigarettes became the mainstay of his business. Columbia Tobacco, which he set up in 1950, began around 1960 to manufacture under licence famous American brands such as 'Lucky Strike', and through this grew to be one of the Philippines' largest cigarette manufacturers. Like his brother, Jose Campos, Yao also went into the trading and manufacturing of drugs (Cathay Drug Co. and YSS Laboratories), but did not do as well as his brother in this field.

YU, KHE THAI

Yu Khe Thai is a grandson of Yu Ti Vo, founder of Yutivo Sons Hardware. He was born in Fukien around 1900 and came to the Philippines when he was small. His grandfather (Yu Ti Vo) had come to the Philippines in the 1860s and worked first as a blacksmith before setting up the hardware store that, by the 1930s, became one of the largest of its kind. Towards the end of the 1930s, the American trading company, Pacific Commercial, which had acted as an agent for General Motors, was dissolved, and Yutivo was given the agency. In the post-war period, as the import of finished cars was banned, Yutivo started assembling GM cars under licence; and in the 1970s, as capital requirements increased with the implementation of a programme to increase the domestic content of the cars produced in the country, General Motors came in as the principal shareholder. However, in 1985, General Motors decided to withdraw from the Philippines, and Yutivo lost its motor vehicle business. It still runs a hardware store, but it cannot be regarded as a large establishment by present-day standards. At one time, Yu Khe Thai was president and chairman of the Philippine Bank of Communications, but the family did not own the bank. He died recently.

YUCHENGCO, ALFONSO

Alfonso Yuchengco was born in the Philippines in 1923, the son of Enrique Yuchengco, who founded China Insurance and Surety in 1930. Enrique's father (Yu Tiaoqui) was originally a lumber merchant, but later diversified into rice, tobacco, and construction. After the Pacific War, China Insurance and Surety was renamed Malayan Insurance Co. Alfonso took over this insurance company from his father. He also went into commercial banking, buying a small regional bank and converting it into a large commercial bank (Rizal Commercial Banking Corp.). He also invested in some other fields, organizing the investment company, House of Investments, and becoming a principal shareholder of the telephone company, PLDT, which shares he sold in March 1986. Under the present Aquino government, he is serving as Ambassador to China.

Thailand

ASSADATHORN, SUREE

Suree was born in Kwangtung in 1911 and migrated to Thailand in his youth. He first worked as an apprentice mechanic and later set up his own workshop. Since he often serviced machinery and equipment for sugar mills and had become familiar with the sugar business, in the late 1940s he decided to go into it on his own. He set up Ruam Kam Larb Co. (a trading company) and Sriracha Sugar Factory. Today, he owns several sugar mills, and his group, Thai Roong Ruang, is one of the two largest sugar groups in the country.

BODHIRATANANGKURA, SUKRI

Sukri was born in Hainan in the mid-1910s and came to Bangkok as a child with his parents. His father died soon afterwards, and Sukri had to struggle to make a living; but by the early 1940s, he had saved enough to set up a textile trading shop (Kim Yong Nguan) in Sampheng. In the 1950s he became a supplier of clothing to the military, and a little later, he went into production by leasing a government-owned textile factory. When the government started its import-substitution programme in textiles, he set up a factory (Thai Blanket Industry), which in 1965 became a joint venture with Japanese companies. In the following years, he set up several other joint ventures with foreign (primarily Japanese) companies and created the country's largest textile group. *References*: Ito; *WWT*, December 1977.

BOONSOONG, JOOTEE

Jootee first made money in tin mining in Phuket, a province in southern Thailand. His tin interests included Boonsoong Tin Dredging and constituted the largest Thai-owned tin group. From tin he diversified into manufacturing and trading. He set up a number of joint ventures with foreign (primarily Japanese, Mitsubishi in particular) companies. Most of these are related to motor vehicles: Isuzu Motor, an assembler of Isuzu trucks; Tri Petch Isuzu Sales, their distributor; Nippon Denso Thailand, a producer of automotive parts; and Thai Bridgestone, a producer of tyres. Jootee died in 1982, and the companies he set up are now managed by his family.

BULAKUL, SIRICHAI

Sirichai was born in Bangkok in 1940 and was educated in Hong Kong and the United States. His father (Mah Bulakul) was an established rice miller and exporter with strong Hong Kong connections, and in the mid-1960s Sirichai began working for the family. Today, he is involved in rice trading, shipping, warehousing, construction, and property development (in particular, Mah Boonkrong Center). The flagship of the group is Mah Boonkrong Drying and Silo Co., a public company, which is located on the east coast of the Gulf of Siam and has a bulk loading facility as well as silo facilities. But this company is now in trouble because its investments in the past several years have turned out to be unprofitable (especially Mah Boonkrong Center). Sirichai still heads the company, but he no longer owns a controlling interest. *Reference*: *AWSJ*, 8 July 1987.

BULPAKDI, AMPHORN

Amphorn is the owner of Thanya Thai Co., a leading rice exporter, and has been President of the Chinese Chamber of Commerce since the early 1960s. He was born around 1909, the son of a Chinese rice trader in Thailand, but whether he was born in China or Bangkok is not certain. When he was young, he was in China, where he went to school for some time. In Bangkok, he first worked for a rice mill, since then he has been connected with the rice business. In the early 1940s, he became deputy general manager of the government-owned Thai Rice Co., and in the mid-1950s he set up his own rice exporting company. *References: BR*, December 1973; *WWT*, October 1976.

CHIARAVANONT, DHANIN

Dhanin heads Thailand's biggest agribusiness group, the C.P. (Charoen Pokphand) group, which was founded by his father (Chia Ek Chaw) and his uncle. In 1921 the two Teochiu brothers opened a store to import seeds and fertilizer from China and export eggs in return. In the following years this business expanded, and in the early 1950s it was incorporated as Chia Tai Seeds and Agricultural Co. Several years later, a feed-mill was established to produce its own feed requirements. This feed-mill and the trading company became the foundation of the present-day integrated chicken and egg production. The group is also engaged in textile production (through C.P. Textile Co.). Chia Ek Chaw died in 1983, and Dhanin succeeded him. *References: BR*, September 1985; *FEER*, 3 March 1988.

CHIRATHIVAT, SAMRIT

Samrit heads the largest department store, Central Department. He was born in Thailand in 1923, and after studying commerce at Assumption College he began working for his father, Tiang Chirathivat (Tae Sim Peng). Prior to the Pacific War, Tiang ran a restaurant in Thonburi, but shortly after the war ended, he opened his first retail business, a small shop on New Road. Through his innovative merchandising, the store prospered, and in 1957 he opened a larger retail store at Wang Burapha, which was the first of the family's department store chain. Samrit has been heading the family since Tiang died in 1968. He opened new branches at Chidlom, Lard Ya, and Lardprao. *References: WWT*, September 1979; *BP* (Supplement), 11 October 1982; *NR* (Supplement), 30 April 1983.

CHOKWATANA, THIAM

Thiam was born in Bangkok in 1916, and after finishing primary school, began helping in the family store, selling consumer goods. In 1943 he established his own business under the name of Hieb Seng Chieng, selling food products, and after the war, he began importing consumer products such as clothes and shoes. From the mid-1950s, he began manufacturing various consumer goods (vacuum flasks, mosquito coils, joss-sticks, soap, dentifrice, cosmetics, underwear, etc.). These trading and manufacturing companies constitute the Saha Pathanapibul group today. Thiam also serves as chairman of Saha-Union Corp., of which the president, Damri Darakananda, is his brother-in-law. *References: WWT*, January 1979 and April 1979; *BR*, October 1984.

DARAKANANDA, DAMRI

Damri is president of Saha-Union Corp., an investment and textile distribution company, whose subsidiaries are engaged in textile production ranging from spinning to garment manufacturing. In the late 1950s, Damri was operating a small importing business, World Trading, which handled, among other things, the zips from YKK of Japan. In the early 1960s, he set up a joint venture with YKK, which was the beginning of his ventures into production of inputs for garments, such as thread, buttons, elastic webbing, etc. In 1972, these operations were put under the newly incorporated Saha-Union, which went public a few years later, and, in 1977, together with creditor financial institutions, took over one of Thai Durable's textile mills, making it a full-fledged textile conglomerate. Relying on professional managers to a large extent, Damri has made Saha-Union one of the best-managed companies in Thailand. *References*: *NR* (Supplement), 20 October 1982; *BR*, September 1984.

KHAW, SOO CHEANG

Khaw Soo Cheang was born in Fukien in 1797 and emigrated to Penang in the early 1820s. Having worked there as a labourer and saved some money, he moved to Phangnga in southern Thailand where he opened a store. In the mid-1840s, he obtained a tin-mining concession at Ranong, and subsequently he founded a tin-based business empire. He also maintained close relations with Penang, where tin was smelted for export, and where he established the shipping company, Koe Guan. After Khaw Soo Cheang's death in 1882, the family was headed by Khaw Sim Bee. He sponsored the Australian tin-dredging project in southern Thailand (Tongkah Harbour Tin Dredging Co.). The family also organized joint-stock companies in Penang, Eastern Shipping and Eastern Smelting, but these Penang-based companies did not do well: the latter was sold to British interests in 1911 and the former to Straits Steamship in 1922. Khaw Sim Bee managed to unify the disparate interests within the family reasonably well, but after he died, the Khaw business empire began disintegrating. His nephew, Khaw Joo Tok, who had headed the family interests in Penang when Sim Bee was alive, was in the best position to succeed him, but he seems to have lacked the strength and drive to lead the family. *Reference*: Cushman.

LAMSAM, BANCHA

Since 1963, Bancha Lamsam has headed Thai Farmers Bank, the flagship company of the Lamsam group of companies, which includes Muang Thai Life Assurance, Phatra Insurance, Loxley Trading, Loxley (Bangkok) (an importer of machinery and hardware), and several other companies in real estate, pineapple growing, and dairy products. Bancha is the great-grandson of a Hakka immigrant, Ng Lamsam, who established himself as a teak and rice trader in the early twentieth century. By the 1930s, by diversifying into shipping and other fields and extending their operations into China, the Lamsams had become a leading family in the Hakka community of Bangkok and enjoyed a sufficiently high reputation to allow them to establish an insurance company (now Phatra Insurance) in 1932. In 1945, Bancha's father, Choti Lamsam, organized Thai Farmers Bank, which, after Choti's death in 1948, was headed by his uncle, Kasem Lamsam, until his death in an airplane accident in 1963. *References*: *WWT*, May 1979 and December 1979; *BR*, February 1979.

LAOHATHAI, SAWANG

Sawang was born around 1941. After finishing high school, he went to Japan to study engineering, then returned to Thailand and worked for about two years at the Bangkok branch of Iwai Sangyo (which later merged with Nissho and is now part of Nissho-Iwai). In 1966, along with friends, he set up the trading company, Metro, the strength of which lay in fertilizer. In the early 1970s he set up Thai Central Chemical, a fertilizer plant, together with the Thai Government and two Japanese companies. Then, in 1974, he merged Metro with three other trading companies and made it a diversified trading company. Today he heads the Metro group of companies, which consists of Metro Co. (trading), Thai Central Chemical (fertilizer producer), United Flour Mill, Bangkok Steel Industry, United Silo and Service, Chao Phya (producer of tapioca pellets and flour), and a few others. Metro is particularly strong in fertilizer and flour: its market share is about 80 per cent in fertilizer and 65 per cent in flour. *Reference*: *Investor*, July 1979.

MAHAGUNA, SAHAT

Sahat was born in China in 1894, the son of a contractor and timber merchant in Bangkok. After coming to Bangkok, Sahat first established himself as a contractor and erected such buildings as the General Post Office on New Road. He also went into the rice business and became a major rice trader in Bangkok. His high stature in the Chinese business community is reflected in the fact that he became president of the Chinese Chamber of Commerce from 1946 to 1947. He was close to Sarit Thanarat, and in the late 1950s, he was asked to organize a company to lease the money-losing, government-owned factory producing the 'Mekong' brand of whiskey. This company (Sura Mahakun) later became a leading company in Thailand. After Sahat's death in 1962, his son, Supasit, took over, but the family has not kept up with economic changes in the past few decades and is no longer identified with any major business in Thailand. *Reference*: Ichikawa.

OSATHANUGRAPH, SVASTI

Svasti was born in Bangkok in 1900. Because his father ran a small drugstore (Teck Heng Yoo Pharmacy), Svasti entered Chulalongkorn University to study medicine; but when his father died in 1918, Svasti had to leave school to run the family business. At this time, the store had five employees; and in the next decade, it grew only a little. In the 1930s, however, under the new name of Osothsapha (Teck Heng Yoo), business began expanding as it began improving its distribution and marketing system in order to reach people in the rural areas. In the post-war period, with economic expansion and production of medicine, Osothsapha has undergone accelerated growth, and it is today one of the top companies in pharmaceuticals. *References: WWT*, December 1977; *BP* (Supplement), 27 January 1980.

PORNPRAPHA, TAWORN

Taworn was born around 1920. His birthplace and his career in the pre-war period are not very clear (there are different versions). However, it is certain that he had little education and began working when he was still very young. During the Pacific War, he dealt in second-hand military vehicles, and in the late 1940s a trade mission from Japan aroused his interest in importing Nissan cars, the agent for which he became. Japanese cars were then hardly known, but he was somehow convinced that they would sell in Thailand. He first confined his activity to marketing, but as import restrictions were imposed, he started assembling and, later, parts production. Today, his Siam Motors group is the largest of its kind. *References*: Ito; *BP* (Supplement), 4 September 1982.

RATANARAK, CHUAN

Chuan was born in China in 1920, and came to Thailand in 1926. He may have returned to China for part of his education. After the Pacific War, he worked on lighters for some time and eventually came to own a lighterage company (Bangkok Lighters Co.) together with Field Marshal Praphat Charusathien. In the mid-1950s, he became a compradore of the Bank of Ayudhya, and when the bank ran into difficulties, he purchased a controlling interest with Field Marshal Praphat and became its managing director. By the early 1970s, he had increased his holdings and become the controlling shareholder. Around this time, he began diversifying into other areas and set up such companies as Siam City Cement, Siam Flour Mill, Siam Silo & Drying, and Ayudhya Warehouse.

SOMPRAKIT, JIAM

Jiam was born in Bangkok in the mid-1920s. At the age of sixteen he started working at a cast iron foundry, and soon after he came to own his own shop. Then, in the mid-1950s, he set up Bangkok Industry Service Co. to import iron and steel products, especially from Japan. Today, this company is the flagship company of the Bangkok Industry Service group, which centres around production and distribution of steel products. Jiam also went into production and distribution of heavy equipment, production of nylon filament yarn, and real estate.

SOPHONPANICH, CHIN

Chin Sophonpanich was born in the early 1910s, either in Bangkok or in Swatow (there are different versions). What is certain is that he went to school at Swatow for some time, and came (or returned) to Bangkok at the age of about seventeen. After doing odd jobs for a few years, he began working for a lumber trading company, and eventually he became an independent lumber merchant. He did well in this trade and, by diversifying into other products, had become a fairly successful merchant by the time of the Pacific War. Soon after the war, he started trading with Hong Kong (through Asia Trading Co.) and set up a remittance and foreign exchange business (Asia Trust Co.). He also became a comprador of Bangkok Bank.

He started a new career in 1952, when he became general manager of Bangkok Bank which had been suffering from mismanagement. Set up in 1944, the bank had substantial dealings in foreign exchange, but it needed a trustworthy and experienced man like Chin. By bringing in professionals like Prasit Kanchanawat and Boonchu Rojanasthien, and by increasing equity by inviting government participation, Chin succeeded in making Bangkok Bank one of the country's leading commercial banks. His strategy of cultivating close government connections backfired, however, when his political patron, General Phao Siryanon, then Director-General of the Police Department, was defeated by his rival, Sarit Thanarat, in 1957. To escape from the ensuing heat of political struggle, he left for Hong Kong and stayed there until Sarit died in 1963.

His stay in Hong Kong turned out to be a blessing in disguise. While his trusted professionals took good care of the bank's domestic operations, he built up its foreign network. In the two decades since his return to Bangkok, he had steered the bank's expansion and made it the biggest commercial bank in the ASEAN region. In the course of equity increase, Chin raised his holdings, and by the early 1970s he had obtained a controlling interest in the bank. Today, Bangkok Bank is the flagship company of the biggest business group in Thailand, the Bangkok Bank group, which consists mainly of finance, insurance, and securities companies. Chin died of heart failure in January 1988. *References*: Hiizumi; Suehiro; Salamon; '40 Years of Bangkok Bank'; *WWT*, October 1975; *BP* (Supplement), 16 February 1982; *TB*, February 1982; Sungsidh; *AWSJ*, 16 April 1985; *Asiaweek*, 15 January 1988.

SRIFUENGFUNG, KIARTI

Kiarti was born in the mid-1910s, either in Thailand or China (there are different versions). After the Pacific War, he became an assistant manager of the Bangkok branch of the Bank of Canton. When this bank closed after the Communist Revolution in China, he arranged the transfer of its banking licence to what was to become Bangkok Metropolitan Bank, of which Kiarti later became a director along with U Chuliang and Udane Techapaibul. He also became managing director of a related insurance company and of South East Asia Trading. In the early 1950s, he started Cathay Theatre Co. together with

U Chuliang, which subsequently evolved into a major finance and securities company, Cathay Trust. In the late 1950s, he started forming joint ventures with foreign companies, and today he is the Thai partner of such major joint ventures as Thai Asahi Glass, Thai Caustic Soda, and Goodyear (Thailand). In the mid-1970s he sold his holdings in Bangkok Metropolitan Bank and withdrew from banking, but in mid-1986 re-entered the field, buying a block of the new shares in First Bangkok City Bank that were issued as part of its reorganization plan (the bank had got into difficulties in early 1986 and the government stepped in to reorganize it). *References*: Beal; *BR*, November 1986.

TAEPHAISITPHONGSE (TAE KING ONG)

Two China-born Teochius, Taephaisitphongse and Leophairatana (Leo Keng Hui), founded a business in Saraburi in the pre-war period, trading first in textiles and later in rice. They then moved to Bangkok and became successful rice traders. Hong Yiah Seng, the company they started, is now one of the top rice traders. In the 1960s, Taephaisitphongse set up Betargo and ventured into animal feed alone, since his partner did not want to join him. Later, he went into chicken and pig farming, eventually building a large agribusiness group. One of the companies in this group, Centaco, was later sold to Niphon Laovoravit, Leophairatana's cousin. Taephaisitphongse died in 1979. Today, two of his sons are involved in Hong Yiah Seng, and two others in Betargo.

TARNVANICHKUL, WALLOP

Wallop, better known among his business friends as Johnny Ma, was born in Bangkok, the son of a textile merchant, and was educated in Shanghai. After the Pacific War, he returned to Thailand and distributed monosodium glutamate. Through this work, he became acquainted with Chin Sophonpanich and soon began working for him. Eventually, Chin placed him in charge of Asia Trust Co., which was engaged in remittance and foreign exchange. During Chin's stay in Hong Kong (1958–63), Wallop seized control of Asia Trust Co. (for this breach of trust, Chin never forgave him), and in 1965 he converted it into a commercial bank. In the subsequent years, Wallop became a leading business figure in Thailand, venturing into other areas as well as extending Asia Trust Bank's operations to Hong Kong. But in mid-1984, Asia Trust Bank began facing serious financial trouble, and the Bank of Thailand stepped in to protect its depositors. Officials who examined the bank after the takeover accused Wallop of fraud, embezzlement, and other violations of Thai banking law, but by this time he had left the country. *References*: Beal; *AWSJ*, 23–24 October 1984.

TECHAPAIBUL, UDANE

Udane was born in the mid-1910s, either in Bangkok or China (there are different versions). His father came from a well-to-do family in China and studied to become a mandarin, but at the age of eighteen he left for Bangkok. There he established himself as a liquor manufacturer and pawnshop operator and became a prominent leader of the Chinese community in Bangkok. Udane was educated in Bangkok and, after graduating from Assumption College, began working for his father.

Udane's entry into modern business started in 1950, when he became managing director of Bangkok Metropolitan Bank. This had been organized by U Chuliang, a prominent leader of the Chinese community and a friend of his father. Udane eventually became a controlling shareholder of this bank. He also participated in the liquor company, Sura Mahakun, organized by Sahat Mahaguna in the late 1950s, and eventually he came to control this company as well. As the exclusive producer of whiskey in the Bangkok Metropolitan area, it was an important source of profit for the Techapaibul family. However, his former partners, who had lost the power struggle in Sura Mahakun, obtained the production licence outside the Bangkok area and in the early 1980s began challenging the supremacy of Suramaharas (the successor of Sura Mahakun), thus starting the so-called 'whiskey war'. As a consequence, Udane lost heavily, and his whiskey business is facing serious difficulties.

The Techapaibul family is also involved in a number of other businesses. One of their companies produces 'Kloster' beer (Thai Amarit Brewery), while several others are involved in finance and securities. Udane's brother, Kamron, headed First Bangkok City Bank until its trouble surfaced in mid-1986. He is considered the main culprit. *References*: Beal; Hiizumi; Suehiro; *WWT*, December 1975; *AWSJ*, 4–5 July 1986.

TENG, ARKON (OR CHIN)

Teng was the owner of Kim Seng Lee & Co., possibly the largest business organization of around 1910, which employed over a thousand workers. Teng was born in China and came to Bangkok at the age of eighteen. With the money he had saved by doing odd jobs in Bangkok, he moved to Chiengmai where he opened a shop. As he grew richer, he got into logging (teak) and tax-farming. Then he moved back to Bangkok and set up Kim Seng Lee & Co. While still engaged in tax-farming and logging, he set up five rice mills, three sawmills and a shipyard, and participated in the formation of a bank (Siam Commercial Bank) and a shipping company (Sino-Siam Shipping). Kim Seng Lee began disintegrating in the mid-1910s. The Mandarin pronounciation of Teng's full Chinese name is Chang Ting. *References*: Hong; Sirilak Sakkri-angkrai; Skinner (1957).

U, CHULIANG

U Chuliang was born in Kwangtung in 1899, and at the age of nineteen, he emigrated to Bangkok. He first worked at a shop dealing in dyestuffs, and a few years later, with the help of one of the partners in the shop, he became independent in the same line of business. In subsequent years, he succeeded in business and, by the time of the Pacific War, had built up extensive business interests not only in Thailand but in other South-East Asian cities (e.g. Penang) as well. In the early post-war years, he organized a number of companies and helped young Chinese businessmen such as Udane Techapaibul and Kiarti Srifuengfung to get started. When he died in the mid-1970s, he was on the board of directors of over twenty companies. *Reference*: Beal.

VIRIYAPRAPAIKIT, PRAPA

Prapa was born in Kwangtung, and after coming to Thailand, attended a Chinese primary school and a Thai junior high school. With her brother, Wit, she set up a small metal shop in the mid-1950s and began dealing in steel locally. A few years later, she began importing steel directly from Europe and Japan. Then, in the early 1960s, she went into steel production. Today, she heads the Saha-viriya group of companies, which centres on the import, distribution, and manufacture of steel products (Sahaviriya Panich, Sahaviriya Steel Works, etc.) and is also engaged in securities and finance (Sahaviriya Trust and Sahaviriya Credit Foncier) and computers (Sahaviriya International Computer).

VONGKUSOLKIT, SOONTHORN

Soonthorn is a leading member of the family that owns the Mitr Phol group of companies, a large sugar group. He is a son of the younger of two Hakka brothers who emigrated to Ratchaburi Province, where they started pro-duction of cash crops such as tobacco and sugar. It was their children, however, who went into sugar production in earnest, beginning with 6.4 acres of land in the mid-1940s. Sugar planting later led to sugar milling, then sugar trading, and warehousing, and finally a bulk handling installation. More recent-ly, the group has diversified into tourism and financial services.

WANGLEE, SUVIT

Suvit heads the Wanglee group of companies, which centres on banking, finance, securities, and insurance (Wanglee Bank, Thai Commercial Insurance, Wanglee Insurance, and Poonphipat Finance & Securities). It is also active in the processing and distribution of agricultural products (rice, maize, and tapi-oca)—the activity from which the group originates. In addition, the group is involved in real estate and property development.

Suvit is a great-grandson of Tan Wanglee, who came to Thailand from Kwangtung in the late nineteenth century and established himself as a rice miller and trader. This business was taken over and developed by his son and his grandsons who, in the 1930s and early 1940s, organized a bank, two insurance companies, and a shipping company and, by the time of the Pacific War, had made the Wanglees a prominent business family. Unlike many other prominent families in the pre-war period, theirs has managed to survive. How-ever, being conservative in its business strategy, it did not grow as rapidly as some others did. For example, despite a relatively long history, Wanglee Bank is one of the smallest banks today. *References*: Beal; Suehiro; *WWT*, January 1976.

Malaysia

CHAN, KEONG HON

Chan Keong Hon was born in Kuala Lumpur in 1923 and received high school education in Singapore. Today he is chairman of Selangor Dredging Berhad, which was formed by a group of Chinese in 1963. Until early 1978, the company was managed by his brother, Chan Kwong Hon, but when he passed away, Keong Hon took over his position. At one time he had served as a Selangor State Assemblyman. Under Chan Keong Hon's management, the dredging company began diversifying into property development. In 1985, it built an office complex (Wisma Selangor Dredging) at Jalan Ampang in Kuala Lumpur.

CHANG, MING THIEN

Chang was born in Fukien in 1917 and, after junior high school, came to South-East Asia in the mid-1930s. His first business seems to have been rubber. After the war, he also handled tin and coconut oil. He seems to have made money by smuggling rubber out of Indonesia. With this money, he set up Overseas Trust Bank in Hong Kong in the mid-1950s and United Malayan Banking Corp. (UMBC) in Malaysia a few years later. Besides banking, he was involved in other fields. He invested in the flour mills (Khong Guan and United Malayan Flour) run by his friend, Chew Choo Keng, and founded the Faber Merlin group. Abroad, he set up the finance company, International Trust and Finance Co., in Thailand, and was apparently a major financier and supporter of George Tan's operation in Hong Kong in the initial stage. In the early 1980s, finding business regulations excessive in Malaysia, he sold his interest in UMBC and Faber Merlin and moved to Hong Kong. He died in 1982. *Reference*: *FEER*, 11 June 1982.

CHEN, LIP KEONG

Chen was born in Kinta Valley, Perak, in 1947. After finishing high school in Penang, he entered the University of Malaya and qualified as a medical doctor. In 1976 he decided to enter property development, starting residential development in Bentong, Pahang. In the following years, he has become a successful property developer and today owns the Lipkland group of companies. In 1983, he took over the publicly listed company, Electrical & Allied Industries (EAI), which had been producing refrigerators and air-conditioners, and added property development to its operation (EAI was renamed First Allied Corp.). *Reference*: *The Star*, 8 November 1983.

CHIA, ERIC (CHIA ENG HOCK)

Eric Chia was born in Singapore in 1933 and received his secondary education there at the Anglo-Chinese School. His father, an immigrant who had started out as a bicycle repairman, owned United Motor Works, a large distributor of motor vehicle spare parts in Singapore. In 1956, Eric came to Kuala Lumpur as a representative of the family to start the distribution of spare parts there.

A few years later, however, he went into the distribution of construction equipment. Being successful in this field, his business, United Motor Works (M), became a large distributor of heavy equipment in general. Then, in 1981, it wrested Toyota's franchise in Malaysia from Inchcape, took over the Fiat plant, and went into motor vehicle assembling. However, this assembly business is now encountering problems because of competition from the Proton Saga that the government began producing in 1985. *References*: Yap Koon See; Pillai; *MB*, January 1973; *AWSJ*, 30 December 1985; *Asiaweek*, 26 July 1987.

CHONG, KOK LIM

Chong Kok Lim is a Hakka born in Swatow, Kwangtung, in 1913. At the age of fifteen, he came to Malaya to join his father. He first worked on rubber plantations and, after saving some money, set up a sundry shop. He then went to Singapore to engage in shipping and trading (in particular, with Indonesia). With the money saved in Singapore, he turned to tin mining in Perak in 1946. After several years of struggle, he hit a motherlode and made a fortune in tin mining. Then, in the 1970s, he diversified into real estate and hotels, building, for example, the Sungei Wang Shopping Plaza and the Regent Hotel. These businesses were put under the newly set up holding company called Landmarks Holdings. The recession of the mid-1980s, however, hit his businesses hard, and he lost control of Landmarks Holdings in June 1987. *References*: *The Star*, 9 August 1984; *Asiaweek*, 21 June 1987; *NST*, 18 November 1985.

CHUA, CHENG BOK

Chua Cheng Bok was born in Melaka, the son of Chua Toh, an emigrant from Fukien in the early 1870s. After attending an English school in Melaka, Chua Cheng Bok went to Kuala Lumpur at the age of fourteen to join his elder brother, Cheng Tuan, who had preceded him. In 1899, they set up Cycle & Carriage to deal in bicycles, horse carriages, and guns. The bicycles were supplied on credit by an engineering company where Cheng Tuan had worked. With Cheng Tuan's death a few years later, Cheng Bok assumed control. Under his management for about forty years, the company became a major dealer in motor vehicles. It was also during his time that the company expanded its business to Singapore. With its increasing requirement for capital, the Singapore operation was separated and incorporated in 1926 as a public company, Cycle & Carriage (1926). Cheng Bok died in 1940, after which his three other brothers took turns in heading the company. In 1957, the youngest brother, Cheng Liat, died after being in charge of the company for several years, and his eldest son, Boon Peng, took over. In 1968, the company started assembling Mercedes-Benz and Mitsubishi products. A year later, the Singapore and Malaysian companies merged into one public company, Cycle & Carriage, Ltd. *Reference*: Jennings (1975).

CHUNG, THYE PHIN

Chung Thye Phin was a tin miner and a founder of Eastern Smelting at Penang in the early part of the twentieth century. He attended the English school, St. Xavier's Institution, in Penang. His father, Chung Keng Kwee (alias Ah Quee), was the head of the Penang-based Hai San secret society, who led a prolonged struggle with the Ghee Hin secret society in the third quarter of the nineteenth century. After British intervention in 1873, however, Chung Keng Kwee concluded a peace agreement with the Ghee Hin, and turned his attention to tin mining. In this business venture, he made use of his organizational power as the head of the Hai San, and died in 1901 a wealthy tin miner. *Reference*: Godley.

EU, TONG SEN

Eu Tong Sen was born in Penang in 1877, the son of Eu Kong. In the early 1870s, Eu Kong came to Penang from Canton and, after setting up a grocery store and a dispensary, went into tin mining. He obtained excellent mining land in Perak, but unfortunately died in 1890 at the age of thirty-eight. At this time, Tong Sen was studying in China. He returned two years later, but did not go into business right away. He first received an English education, taking over the father's businesses at the age of twenty-one. In the following years, he expanded the tin-mining business and became one of the two wealthiest Chinese (the other was Loke Yew) in the field. Some of the money he made in tin mining was invested in rubber plantations, banking, real estate, and trading. He died in Hong Kong in 1941. *References*: Wright (1908), *British Malaya*; Song.

FOO, CHOO CHOON

Foo Choo Choon was born in Fukien in 1860. His grandfather had migrated to the region and his father was born in Penang. The father, however, went back to Fukien to study and never came back. In his place, Choo Choon came to Penang at the age of thirteen and lived with fairly well-established relatives there. One uncle was involved in tin mining, and with his help, Foo opened his first mine in Taiping. He pioneered the use of modern machinery to work the mines others had abandoned as unprofitable. This innovation earned him large profits and made him the first 'tin king'. He later went into rubber plantations (the most important rubber estate he owned was the Tanglin Rubber Syndicate). He was already rich when Loke Yew was still struggling. *References*: Godley; *Historical Personalities of Penang*.

FOONG, SEONG

Foong Seong was born in Kwangtung in 1897, and around 1910, left China for Malaya. In Ipoh, he first worked at a foundry which was producing parts for machines used in tin mines, but later he set up his own foundry (Foong Seong

Foundry). From foundry, he went into tin mining, and by the mid-1960s had become one of the biggest tin miners in Malaysia. He invested part of the profits from tin mining in real estate in Ipoh. He also invested some money in OUB and once served as its director. In the early 1970s, he began withdrawing from business, and today he is completely retired. In the mid-1970s he was kidnapped, but was released after his family paid a ransom. One of his sons has taken over his tin mines. Another son is engaged in property development, and the third in stock brokerage.

HEAH, JOO SEANG

Heah Joo Seang was born the son of Heah Ah Kiah in Penang in 1899, and received his education at St. Xavier's Institution. He started life as a clerk and began to build up a rubber fortune. By the late 1920s, he had become a well-known rubber trader and producer in Penang. He died in 1962. *Reference: Historical Personalities of Penang.*

KHOO, KAY PENG

Khoo Kay Peng was born in Johor in 1938. He began his career as a bank clerk and spent twelve years in banking. After OCBC and Malayan Banking, he moved to Bank Bumiputra, and by winning the confidence of Tengku Razaleigh Hamzah, then chairman of the bank, was appointed general manager. In 1971, he bought an obscure company called Malayan United Industries (MUI), a maker of enamel household utensils, and floated it on the Singapore and Kuala Lumpur stock exchanges. This company became Khoo's vehicle for corporate take-over. From the mid-1970s to the early 1980s, in particular, it took over a large number of companies and became one of the country's biggest conglomerates, consisting of companies in such areas as sugar, cement, rubber, finance, insurance, banking, hotels, real estate, and manufacturing (Malayan United Finance, Malayan United Manufacturing, Pan Malayan Cement, Federal Hotel, Southern Bank, etc.). This meteoric rise was made possible by Khoo's friendship with Tengku Razaleigh, Tan Sri Mohamed Noah, and a few other UMNO politicians and by his close working relations with Multi-Purpose Holdings (especially with Tan Koon Swan). *References*: Ranjit Gill (1985), *The Making of Malaysia Inc.*; *AWSJ*, 26 August 1980; *NST*, 21 November 1985; *BT*, 24 November 1980.

KHOO, TECK PUAT

Khoo Teck Puat was born in Singapore in the mid-1910s, and received his education at St. Joseph's Institution. In 1933, he began working as a junior clerk for OCBC, where he rose to the position of deputy general manager. On finding further promotion within the bank blocked, however, in 1959 he left to form the rival Malayan Banking Corp., of which he was appointed chief executive officer (managing director). In the following several years the bank grew rapidly, but in 1966 the rumour that he was channelling the bank's funds to his own companies caused a run on the bank, after which he lost control. In 1965, however, he had set up in Brunei a bank called the National Bank of Brunei, and for two decades, he used the bank as a money machine for his own business. With the loans from this bank, he acquired large interests in real estate and hotels (for example, Goodwood Park Hotel in Singapore and Southern Pacific Hotel in Australia). However, in 1986 the Brunei Government found out about the heavy exposure of the bank to Khoo companies and took over control of the bank. At the same time, it has sequestered Khoo's assets and stocks which were pledged as security to the loans, and the Khoo business empire is now in serious trouble. *References*: *Insight*, June 1971, May 1983, and December 1983; *AWSJ*, 21–22 November 1986 and 2 February 1987; *FEER*, 11 and 18 December 1986.

KUOK, ROBERT (KUOK HOCK NIEN)

Robert Kuok was born around 1923 in Johor, the son of a Hokkien immigrant who was engaged in the distribution of rice, sugar, and flour. After finishing his secondary education in Johor, he went to Raffles College in Singapore. He seems to have started off his business career during the Pacific War, but success did not come for another fifteen years or so, and the 1950s was a particularly unhappy decade for him. His brother joined the Malayan Communist Party, and even though he was killed in around 1952, the Malayan police kept the family under surveillance. Robert left for London. Several years later, when the problem of communist insurgency had subsided, he returned to Malaya, and went into sugar production (Malayan Sugar Manufacturing, a joint venture with the Federal Land Development Authority, FELDA) and sugar trading (Min Tien). In 1968, he set up Perlis Plantations, again with FELDA. By manoeuvring skilfully in the futures market for sugar, he made a large fortune, and used this to diversify into other fields: flour milling (Federal Flour Mills), shipping (Malaysian International Shipping Corp., a joint venture with the Malaysian Government, and his own company, Kerry Shipping) and hotels (Shangri-la Hotel, Rasa Sayang Hotel, and Fiji Resort Hotel). In the course of about twenty years, he built a large business empire spreading to Singapore, Hong Kong, and several other countries. He has also been serving as chairman of the board of directors of Multi-Purpose Holdings since February 1987 when the company was reorganized in the aftermath of the Tan Koon Swan scandal. *References*: Verchere; *FEER*, 30 October 1986.

LAU, PAK KHUAN

Lau Pak Khuan was born around 1900. He was a leading tin miner in the mid-1960s, and once served as president of the All Malaya Mining Association and as president of the Perak Chinese Mining Association. He invested part of the profits from tin mining in banking and insurance. He was at one time a director of OUB and chairman of Public Insurance Co. in Singapore.

LEE, HAU SHIK (H. S. LEE)

Lee was born in 1900 to a prominent family in southern China. After an education at Cambridge University, he worked in Hong Kong for about a year and came to Kuala Lumpur on a holiday. However, he bought a tin mine offered to him while he was staying at a hotel and decided to live in Malaya. He eventually became a successful tin miner and was elected president of the Selangor Chinese Chamber of Commerce and of the Miners' Association of Negri Sembilan, Selangor and Pahang in the mid-1930s. After the Pacific War, he entered politics and served as the first Minister of Finance in Malaya. In the mid-1960s, he left politics and set up Development & Commercial (D & C) Bank. Today, he is retired, and his family have taken control of his businesses. The family still owns 33.3 per cent of the D & C equity through Roxy Electric Industries (Malaysia) but has been trying to sell its interests in Roxy to pay off its debts to a consortium of banks in Singapore. *References*: Yap Koon See; Ng; *AWSJ*, 15 August 1984; *FEER*, 22 January 1987.

LEE, LOY SENG

Lee Loy Seng was born in Menglembu, Perak, in 1921 to a three-generation Hakka family engaged in tin mining. He went to a Chinese school in Ipoh and then to China for further studies, but his education was interrupted by the Pacific War. After the war, he worked in the family's mining business for about ten years. Then, in the mid-1950s, he moved into rubber plantations. At this time, the prices of plantations were low since synthetic rubber was offering strong competition and the Emergency was scaring away European planters. Today, he heads K.L.–Kepong, one of the largest plantation companies in Malaysia. In addition, he directs some 43 companies and subsidiaries. He served as chairman of Multi-Purpose Holdings from 1975 to 1983. *Reference*: *NST*, 20 November 1985.

LEE, YAN LIAN

Lee Yan Lian was born in Fukien in 1906. In 1926, at the age of twenty, he arrived in Malaya. However, unable to find the right job, he went to Singapore and worked for his uncle in his trading business during the next ten years. Then he came back to Malaya and worked as a clerk at an English trading firm (Harper Gilfillan). While he was with this company, he set up a rubber trading firm with his brother (Ban Lee Sdn. Bhd.). Then, in 1962, he went into the housing industry. In the following years, he became one of the most successful property developers in the country. He passed away in March 1983. *References*: *Housing and Property*, May/June 1983; *MB*, June 1977.

LIM, GOH TONG

Lim Goh Tong was born in 1918 in Fukien and came to Kuala Lumpur at the age of nineteen to join his uncle, who was a government contractor. He worked under him as a carpenter. During the Pacific War and in the early post-war years, he worked as a trader and managed to save enough money to set up a construction company, Kien Huat Construction, which evolved into a large construction company. In addition, he was operating iron mines in the 1950s. In the mid-1960s, he decided to set up a resort hotel on Ulu Kali mountain, and he undertook construction of road and resort facilities in the following several years. This business, incorporated as Genting Highlands Hotel, opened for business in 1971, but further construction of resort facilities went on for several more years. It operates the only casino in Malaysia. Lim shares its ownership with others, especially prominent Malays (the company is now a public company), but he holds a controlling interest. *References*: Ian Gill; Khoo.

LIM, LEAN TENG

Lim Lean Teng was born in Kwangtung in 1870. He came to Penang at the age of twenty-three, and first worked as a coolie. After several years of hard work, he started his own business, and became a pioneer rubber planter. By the mid-1910s, he had come to own several large rubber estates in Kedah. In the late 1940s, he became involved in the establishment of OUB in Singapore and served as its chairman from 1952 to 1963. He was succeeded by his son, Lim Theng Hin, but when Theng Hin died prematurely in 1967, Theng Hin's son, Lim Boon Kheng, took over the family's interests in rubber and in OUB. *Reference*: *Historical Personalities of Penang*.

LOH, BOON SIEW

Loh Boon Siew is chairman of the Penang-based company, Oriental Holdings, which is engaged in housing development, assembling of Honda motor cycles and cars, and estate agriculture. He was born in Fukien in 1916 and came to Malaya at the age of twelve. He first worked as an apprentice car mechanic, and several years later he set up his own repair shop. Then he bought 11 buses and started a bus company, Penang Yellow Bus Company, which three years later owned a fleet of 40 buses. After the Pacific War, he went into housing development in Penang, and having become a successful businessman, he went to Japan on a holiday in the late 1950s. There he saw Honda motor cycles and, recognizing their potential, decided to distribute them in Malaysia. Later, he went into assembling, first of Honda motor cycles and then of Honda cars. In the late 1970s, he bought rubber and oil-palm plantations from Jardine Matheson Holdings (Malaysia). *References*: Yap Koon See; *MB*, January 1974; *NST*, 20 November 1985.

LOKE, YEW

Loke Yew was born in 1845 in Kwangtung and came to Singapore at the age of thirteen in 1858. Within four years, he saved enough money to open his own shop. Then he moved to Larut to engage in tin mining. Despite ups and downs in his tin career, he eventually emerged as one of the most successful tin miners in Malaya. Tin mining was the basis for his fortune, but he also held many of the government farms (the monopoly to sell spirits, opium, etc.) and owned provision stores, plantations, and real estate. He died in 1917. His son, Loke Wan Tho, born in 1915, founded the Cathay group of theatres in 1936 and also served as director of OUB and Straits Trading in the early post-war years. In 1964, he died in a plane crash, and the Cathay group was taken over by his sister's husband. In the late 1970s, its Malaysian assets were sold to bumiputra interests, and since then, its operation has been largely confined to Singapore. *References*: Song; Sim; Gullick; *Asia Magazine*, 2 February 1964.

LOW, YOW CHUAN

Low Yow Chuan was born in Kuala Lumpur in 1932, and he obtained a degree in architecture from the University of New South Wales, Australia. His father, an immigrant from China who made good, was Malaysia's biggest contractor, who also had substantial interests in other fields (for example, real estate and hotels). In 1971, when his father died, Yow Chuan took over his businesses, and today he heads the Plaza Yow Chuan, Federal Hotel, and other companies in the Low Yat group. He also has interests in cement and motor vehicle tyre production.

LOY, HEAN HEONG

Loy Hean Heong was born in Penang in 1937 and grew up on a rubber small-holding in Perak. In the late 1950s he served with the British Army in Singapore. Then, around 1960, he apparently speculated in land and made some money. Around 1970, he became a principal shareholder of a carbide production company (Perak Carbide) and an adhesive manufacturing company (Adhesive Tape Inc.), but neither company lived up to his expectations. In the mid-1970s, he organized a group to acquire Island Hotels & Properties from Khoo Teck Puat and converted it into a financial conglomerate (the name of the company was changed to Malaysia Borneo Finance Holdings). One of its subsidiaries, Malaysia Borneo Finance Corp., is the largest finance company in Malaysia today. Through this company, Loy is now diversifying into plantations, palm-oil refining, and property development. *References*: Ranjit Gill (1985), *The Making of Malaysia Inc.*; *Asiaweek*, 12 July 1987; *NST*, 19 November 1985.

TAN, CHAY YAN

Tan Chay Yan is the grandson of Tan Tock Seng of Singapore. His father, Tan Teck Guan, was based in Melaka, where Chay Yan was born and edu-cated (he went to the High School). He and his brothers inherited a cassava and gambier estate in Melaka. Around 1896 he was persuaded of the profitability of rubber by Henry Ridley, director of the Botanic Garden of Singapore, and became the pioneer of rubber planting in the Chinese community. He was also a founder of the Chinese Commercial Bank (which merged with two other banks in the early 1930s to become OCBC). *References*: Song; Feldwick; Allen and Donnithorne.

TAN, CHIN NAM

Tan Chin Nam was born in Selangor in 1926, and for secondary education, went to the Victoria Institution in Kuala Lumpur. In 1947, having saved some money while working as a clerk, he went into business in Singapore. He first imported vegetables from Indonesia to sell to the British Army. He then diversified into rice and sugar trading. However, he decided to quit the trading business, and in Malaysia, went into property development together with a few friends. In this field he has become immensely successful. Today he is probably the largest property developer in Malaysia. His family controls two large property developing companies, Ipoh Garden Berhad and Parkway Holdings (the latter is based in Singapore). *Reference*: Yap Koon See.

TAN, KAY HOCK

Tan Kay Hock was born in Sabak Bernam, Selangor, in 1947. He studied law at Lincoln's Inn, London, and, on returning to Malaya, became a lawyer. His family had substantial interests in plantations and property in Sabak Bernam. Around 1979, he bought Johan Tin Dredging Bhd., a tin-mining company whose ore was depleting, and converted it into a conglomerate by buying George Kent (M), Jacks International, and Diners Club (M) and absorbing family-owned properties. Johan Tin Dredging Bhd. is now called Johan Holdings, in which Tan Kay Hock and his family have a controlling interest. *Reference*: *AWSJ*, 4 January 1988.

TAN, KEONG SAIK

Tan Keong Saik was born in Melaka in 1850, the son of Tan Choon Sian, and was educated at the Penang Free School. After finishing his schooling, he went to Singapore where he worked initially as a shipping clerk in a Chinese store and later as a storekeeper at Borneo Co. Keong Saik is a great-grandson of Tan Hay Kwan who came to Melaka from Fukien in the late eighteenth century, and whose family eventually established an inter-Straits Settlement shipping company. On the death of his uncle, Tan Choon Bock, in 1880, Keong Saik took over the reins of the family business. The shipping company was, however, absorbed by Straits Steamship Co., on whose board of directors he served until his death in 1909. He also served as director of Tanjong Pagar Dock Co. until the same year. In addition to shipping, his uncle, Tan Choon Bock, had interests in estate agriculture, and this line of business was handed down to his descendants (Tan Cheng Lock, Tan Siew Sin, etc.).

TAN, KOON SWAN

Tan Koon Swan was born in Kuala Lumpur in 1940, the son of a hawker father and construction worker mother. At seventeen, he began working, first for the National Electricity Board as an apprentice clerk, then for the Inland Revenue Department as an officer, and in the late 1960s for Esso Malaysia. At this time his name was virtually unknown to the Chinese community, but in

1971 he made news by becoming general manager of Genting Highlands Hotel. In 1974, while he was still with Genting Highlands, he and a few friends acquired a tin-mining company called Sungei Way Dredging Co. (now called Supreme Corp.) and, in the following several years, converted it into a conglomerate (its subsidiaries are Supreme Housing Development, Supreme Plantation Industries, and Supreme Finance Malaysia). In 1977, he left Genting Highlands to become general manager of Multi-Purpose Holdings. A few years later he entered politics and worked his way up through party ranks to eventually become president of the MCA. A few months later, however, he became involved in the scandal related to the collapse of Pan Electric Industries, and in early 1986 he was arrested for fraud by the Singapore Government. Convicted of the charges brought against him, he was sentenced to two years in Singapore prison. *References*: Gale (1985); Ranjit Gill (1985), *The Making of Malaysia Inc.*; *AWSJ*, 4 September 1986; *FEER*, 12 December 1985.

TAN, SENG KEE

Tan Seng Kee was born in Fukien and came to Malaysia to join the tin-mining company his grandfather had set up. After a few decades of struggle, he became the largest tin miner in Selangor. In the early 1980s, he was operating about 17 mines using the gravel-pump method. He is not identified with any well-known company; all of his companies are relatively small (the best known would be Senky Mining Co. Sdn. Bhd.). He also pioneered marble quarrying, producing the Langkawi marble. His businesses have diversified somewhat recently, into such fields as service restaurants. *Reference*: Yap Koon See.

TAN, SIEW SIN

Tan Siew Sin was born in Melaka in 1916, the son of Tan Cheng Lock and the great-grandson of Tan Choon Bock. He received his education at the High School in Melaka, Raffles College in Singapore, and Middle Temple in London. Following in his father's footsteps, he entered politics in the late 1940s; and he served as Minister of Finance from 1959 to 1969 and President of the MCA from 1961 to 1974. His father and grandfather inherited and expanded the interests in estate agriculture that Tan Choon Bock had started, and Tan Siew Sin today serves as chairman of a number of plantation companies, including Sime Darby Holdings. However, Tan Siew Sin and his family do not own any major company.

TAN, YUET FOH

Tan Yuet Foh was chairman and managing director of Tan Chong Motor Holdings, the main line of business of which is the sale and assembly of Nissan cars and trucks for the Singapore and Malaysian markets. It also has subsidiaries engaged in production of motor vehicle parts, cosmetics distribution (Shiseido cosmetics), real estate, and travel agency. Tan Yuet Foh was born in Selangor in 1925. After finishing school in 1940, he first worked for his father who was running a sundry shop. In the first decade after the war, he formed a company with his brothers to act as a contractor for the supply of food. In 1957, he and his brothers established Tan Chong & Sons Motor Co. to distribute Nissan cars. When vehicle assembling began in the country, Tan Chong did not go into it right away. For some time, Nissan cars and trucks were assembled by other companies, and it was not until the mid-1970s that Tan Chong started assembling. Tan Yuet Foh died in October 1985. *Reference*: Yap Koon See.

TEH, HONG PIOW

Teh Hong Piow was born in Singapore in 1930. In 1950, he began working for OCBC, and later transferred to Malayan Banking Berhad where he became general manager of its Kuala Lumpur branch. In 1965, he resigned from the bank and organized Public Bank. Since then he has been serving as its chief executive officer. Public Bank is the largest Chinese-owned bank in Malaysia today.

TEO, SOO CHENG

The Teo family was originally based in Singapore, engaged in rice trade. Although this line of business had declined in importance by the early 1980s, they had in the meantime diversified into real estate and other fields. Teo Soo Cheng, together with his Singapore-based brother, Teo Soo Chuan, heads the See Hoy Chan group, whose flagship is the public company, Paramount Corporation Berhad, which is engaged in property development, estate agriculture, and finance. Paramount Corporation is the successor of Malaysia Rice Industries Berhad which was incorporated in 1969 as a public company to undertake rice milling.

WEE, BOON PENG

Wee Boon Peng (or Ping) was born in Sarawak in 1932 and first worked for his family's little grocery store there. Today, he heads the Kim Chuan Seng group based in Sarawak and Sabah. This grew out of logging and wood processing, and it has become involved in property development and estate agriculture as well. Recently, Wee extended his operations to Singapore and Peninsular Malaysia, taking over International Wood Products, Resources Holdings, the Malaysian operation of Sim Lim Finance, and Batu Lintang Rubber Co. The last is a Malaysian-based public company which has divested itself of rubber plantations and made property development its major line of business. *Reference*: *BT*, 15 July 1984.

YEAP, CHOR EE

Yeap Chor Ee was born in China in 1867 and came to Penang around 1884. He first worked in a sundry shop, but six years later he opened his own shop (Chop

Ban Hin Lee). He first dealt in sugar, then diversified into rubber, rice, tapioca, and tin trading. He later added banking and shipping, and became a leading merchant of Penang. In 1932, he became a director of OCBC, but he does not seem to have invested much in this bank. Instead, he recruited a capable manager from OCBC (the third son of Dr Lim Boon Keng) and formed Ban Hin Lee Bank in 1935. He died in 1952. Ban Hin Lee Bank is still controlled by his descendants. His grandson, Jimmy Yeap Leong Aun, who headed the bank, was shot dead in a kidnap bid on 23 October 1985. *References*: Singh; Tan Ee Leong (1961); *Historical Personalities of Penang*.

YEOH, TIONG LAY

Yeoh Tiong Lay was born in Selangor in 1929 and graduated from Hin Hua High School, Kelang, in 1948. Soon afterwards he took over his father's construction company, which later became Pembenaan Yeoh Tiong Lay. He is now a leading contractor as well as property developer. In late 1984, he took over the publicly listed company, Hongkong Tin Corp. (M). Some of the construction-related companies he had owned (such as Yeoh Tiong Lay Brickworks) are now placed under Hongkong Tin.

Singapore

ANG, KEONG LAN

Ang is a Hokkien born in China in 1920. He came to Singapore at the age of five to live with his father. After primary school, he began helping in his father's grocery store. In 1948, he set up Joo Seng Co. to deal in rice and animal feed, and several years later, he began importing rice and other food products directly from other South-East Asian countries. In the 1960s, he started production of animal feed, and a few years later, went into production of flour, vegetable oil, and some other food products. In the mid-1970s, he sold the vegetable oil factory (United Vegetable Oil Factory) and bought Asia Commercial Banking Corp. He also has investments in Hong Kong, Thailand, and Indonesia. His businesses form the Joo Seng group. *Reference*: Oral History, Ang Keong Lan.

AW, BOON HAW

Aw Boon Haw, known as the 'Tiger Balm King', was a Hakka born in 1882 in Rangoon, where his father, Aw Chu Kin, was running a medicine shop. At the age of about fifteen, he began helping his father and learned about Chinese medicine. After his father's death in 1908, he built up a medicine business in Rangoon with his younger brother, Aw Boon Par. In the mid-1920s they moved to Singapore. With money he had made in medicine, Aw Boon Haw started newspapers in China and South-East Asia (for example, *Sin Chew Jit Poh*), and in 1950 he formed the first Hakka bank, Chung Khiaw Bank. Boon Par died in 1944 and Boon Haw in 1954. None of the major businesses Boon Haw left remain with the Aw family, though the bank still exists and Boon Haw's and Boon Par's names are commemorated in the company name of Haw Par Brothers International, a major pharmaceutical company today, producing, among others, the Tiger Balm brand of medicine. *References*: Oral History, Aw Kow; Lee Poh Ping (1974); Sim.

CHANG, BRIAN

Brian Chang was born in 1943 and received his university education in Britain. After obtaining a degree in electrical engineering in 1965, he returned to Singapore and worked for a few foreign companies until 1970. A year later, with his savings and financial assistance from his brother (a medical doctor), he set up Promet to assemble offshore oil equipment. Promet soon became a rising star in the Singaporean and Malaysian business world. Chang was able to expand the oil equipment business, and in a tie-up with Ibrahim bin Mohamed, an influential bumiputra lawyer, he went into construction and property development in Malaysia. However, with the economic recession in the early 1980s, the company began experiencing trouble, and in September 1986, it was in the process of liquidation. *References*: *Insight*, February 1982; *AWSJ*, 11 September 1986; *Asia Finance*, November 1984; *FEER*, 31 March 1983.

CHEE, SWEE CHENG

Chee Swee Cheng, the first chairman of OCBC, is the grandson of a prominent nutmeg planter in Melaka, Chee Yam Chuan. He was born in Melaka in 1866 and educated at the High School there. At the age of sixteen, he came to Singapore. After working for a few merchant houses, he became a partner in the General Spirit and Opium Farm in British North Borneo and was appointed its manager. While he was there, he developed his own businesses in tapioca and rubber production and a sawmill. Coming back to Singapore, he set up an ice factory. In 1917, when Ho Hong Bank was set up, he became one of its incorporators; and fifteen years later, when it got into difficulties, he became its chairman. The bank was soon merged with two others to form OCBC. *References*: Song; Dick Wilson.

CHEW, CHOO KENG

Chew Choo Keng owns the Khong Guan group, which is engaged in biscuit manufacturing (Khong Guan Biscuit Factory), flour production (Khong Guan Flour Mill and United Flour Mill), and cooking-oil refining (Khong Guan Oil Refinery). Chew is a Hokkien born in China in 1916. At the age of twenty-one, he came to Singapore and worked in Tan Kah Kee's biscuit factory. In 1938, he resigned and went to Malaya. After the Pacific War, he returned to Singapore and set up Khong Guan Biscuit Factory. After establishing himself in this business, he diversified into related fields. *Reference*: Oral History, Chew Choo Keng.

GAW, KHEK KHIAM

Gaw Khek Khiam was born in Semarang in 1885, the second son of Go Boon Chan. Having come to Singapore when he was small, he received an English education at Raffles Institution, then went to England for further studies. His father, together with his uncle, Go Boon Kwan, established a large biscuit factory, Ho Ho Biscuit Factory. After his father died, Khek Khiam assumed control. He was also a director of the first Chinese insurance company, Eastern United Assurance Corp., and the managing director of the Chinese Commercial Bank, one of the three banks which merged to become OCBC. *Reference*: Song.

GOH, TJOEI KOK

Goh is a Hokkien born in China in 1906. At the age of sixteen, he emigrated to Indonesia, and in the 1930s, he was engaged in rubber business. After the Pacific War, he came to Singapore to set up a rubber trading company. In the early 1960s, he set up a steel manufacturing company, National Iron and Steel, together with Soon Peng Yam. Later, Soon withdrew, and Goh became its controlling shareholder. He also owns Tat Lee Bank, the fifth largest private bank in Singapore.

KHOO, CHENG TIONG

Khoo Cheng Tiong was the owner of the trading company, Khoo Cheng Tiong & Co., a large importer of rice from Saigon, where it owned rice mills. A Hokkien born in China, he emigrated to Singapore and, around 1850, began dealing in rice, eventually becoming one of the most successful dealers in this field. When he died in 1896, his wealth was estimated at over a million Straits dollars.

KHOO, KOK WAH

Khoo Kok Wah is Khoo Cheng Tiong's nephew. He was the principal organizer of Oversea-Chinese Bank and in 1919 when it was set up, he became its managing director. (Oversea-Chinese Bank was one of the three banks which merged to become OCBC in 1932.) Kok Wah's father, Khoo Cheng Teow, used to work for his brother, Cheng Tiong, but later started his own rice trading business under the name of Aik Seng & Co. His business prospered, but after his death in 1896, it was closed as a result of bad management. His son, Kok Wah, later went into rice trading on his own and became a large rice trader in Singapore (he did business under the name of Aik Seng & Co.). With the money he earned from rice trading, he organized Oversea-Chinese Bank. In the late 1920s, however, the bank ran into trouble, and Kok Wah left the bank in 1930. At the time of the merger, it was headed by Tan Ean Kiam. *References*: Song; Dick Wilson.

KO, TECK KIN

Ko Teck Kin grew up in Palembang, Sumatra. After the Pacific War, he smuggled a lot of rubber to Singapore, where he soon settled down and set up a rubber trading company. Initially, he was helped by Tan Lark Sye. With the Korean War boom of the early 1950s, he was well prepared and made a large fortune. In the late 1950s, he was elected president of the Chinese Chamber of Commerce of Singapore. His rubber trading was essentially a one-man show, however, and after his death the business declined.

KWEK, HONG PNG

Kwek Hong Png is the head of the Kwek family, which owns the Hong Leong group in Singapore and Malaysia. Large companies in the group are Hong Leong Finance (a finance company), City Development (a real estate company which owns King's Hotel and a number of other properties), Hume Industries (a producer of concrete pipes), and Singapore Cement. The group also owns Dao Heng Bank and several other companies in Hong Kong. Kwek is a Hakka born in China in the mid-1910s. He came to Singapore in the late 1920s and began working as a clerk in a firm supplying building materials. After the Pacific War, together with his brothers, he set up a trading company specializing in construction materials. Then he went into real estate and production of construction materials. In the mid-1960s, he set up Hong Leong Finance. He has close relations with several Japanese companies. *References*: *FEER*, 5 December 1985; Oral History, Kwek Hong Png.

LEE, CHOON GUAN

Lee Choon Guan served as the first chairman of the Chinese Commercial Bank (which merged with two other banks to become OCBC) and as a director of Straits Steamship Co. and Straits British Insurance Co. (Malaya). He was born in 1868 in Melaka, the son of Lee Cheng Yan, owner of the trading company Lee Cheng Yan & Co., which operated in the Straits Settlements. Cheng Yan also engaged in coastal shipping to strengthen his trading operations. Choon Guan worked for his father and took over his business when he died in 1911. He also held substantial interests in rubber and tin. After his first wife died, he married Tan Teck Neo, a daughter of Tan Keong Saik, who had succeeded to the shipping business of Tan Choon Bock (a grandfather of Tan Cheng Lock) and became a founder–director of Straits Steamship Co. *References*: Dick Wilson; Song; Tregonning (1965), *Home Port Singapore*.

LEE, KIM TAH

Lee Kim Tah is a Hokkien born in Singapore in 1902. His father was an army contractor. He was sent to St. Joseph's Institution to learn English so that he could help his father after completing his schooling, but he first worked as a clerk at Ho Hong Bank in 1918, and then at Goodyear's Singapore office. He eventually took over his father's business in 1928, but ten years later, he set up Lee Kim Tah & Co. to undertake building construction in the private sector. In the post-war period, the company evolved into a large building contractor.

LEE, KONG CHIAN

Lee Kong Chian was a Hokkien born in China in 1893. He came to Singapore at the age of ten, but five years later, he won a scholarship from the Chinese Government to study in China. He returned to Singapore in 1912 where he studied English and worked as a translator for a Chinese newspaper and a Chinese trading company. In 1916 he began working for Tan Kah Kee's rubber company, becoming one of Tan's most able lieutenants and eventually marrying his daughter. In 1927 he started his own rubber business. A few years later the Depression started in the US, and in the 1930s the rubber business in Singapore was badly hit; but during this period Lee expanded his company, Lee Rubber, by buying up the factories and plantations which faced financial ruin. Then, during the Korean War boom, he raked in large profits, and succeeded in making Lee Rubber the largest company of its kind in South-East Asia. Today, it is engaged in rubber plantations, trading, and processing and has investments in Malaysia, Thailand, and Indonesia.

Lee also invested in a number of other fields. Among these, his largest investment was in OCBC. Around 1930, his friend, Yap Twee, the managing director of Chinese Commercial Bank, invited him to become a director. When it merged with two other banks to form OCBC, Lee took part in the merger negotiations; and when the new bank was incorporated, he became its vice-chairman. Several years later, when the first chairman died, Lee took over the post. This he did despite his small holding of the bank's equity, because he had influential backers among the major shareholders. In the post-war period, however, he increased his holding, probably with the money he amassed during the Korean War boom, and became the largest shareholder. He remained chairman until 1964, and died in 1967. *References*: Oral History, Tan Ee Leong; Sim; Dick Wilson.

LEE, WEE NAM

Lee Wee Nam was a Teochiu born in China in 1881, who came to Singapore in his youth. After trying various jobs in Singapore and Kuala Lumpur, he began working for the newly formed Teochiu bank called Sze Hai Tong Banking and Insurance Co. There he had a successful career, becoming its chairman and managing director in 1932. After the Pacific War, when OUB was formed, he became a founding director. *References*: Lee Poh Ping (1974); Sim.

LIEN, YING CHOW

Lien Ying Chow is a Teochiu born in China in 1906. At the age of fourteen, he came to Singapore and became apprenticed to a trading house. In 1928 he started his own trading company, Wah Hin & Co., and became a leading merchant in the next decade. In 1941, he was elected president of the Chinese Chamber of Commerce. During the Pacific War, he stayed in Chungking and worked for the Chinese Government. After the war, he returned to Singapore and organized OUB, where he served as vice-chairman in its first twenty years and has since then served as chairman. The OUB group is formed around the bank, with extensive investments in real estate and hotels. For example, OUB Centre, the tallest office building in Singapore, and Mandarin Hotel belong to this group. *References*: Overseas Union Bank; Sim.

LIM, PENG SIANG

Lim Peng Siang was a Hokkien born in China in 1872. He came to Singapore as a child and for a short time received an English education at St. Joseph's Institution. Then he began working for his father in Wee Bin & Co., a shipping company founded by his maternal grandfather. In 1904 he founded Ho Hong Co. and went into trading and food processing (rice and cooking oil). He added shipping to this a few years later, and in 1911 he took over the greater part of the assets of Wee Bin & Co. and founded Ho Hong Steamship Co. His businesses grew rapidly in the next several years, benefiting from the First World War boom, and expanded into banking (Ho Hong Bank) and cement production (Ho Hong Portland Cement Works). Cement production turned out to be a bad investment, however, and the Ho Hong group began declining in the 1920s. The Depression at the end of the decade was a further blow, and in the 1930s the Ho Hong group virtually disappeared. Lim Peng Siang died in 1944. *References*: Feldwick; Oral History, Tan Ee Leong; Song; Sim; Dick Wilson.

LIM, TECK KIN

Lim Teck Kin was born in Fukien in 1886. At the age of eighteen, he came to Singapore and began working at a pineapple factory. About fifteen years later, in 1920, he set up his own trading company to deal in Malayan produce. It is not clear how contacts were made, but two years later he became an agent for Asiatic Petroleum Co. In the early 1930s he organized another company, United Malayan Pineapple Growers & Canneries, and within a few years he became the leading businessman in this field. Today, the pineapple business is managed by his son, Lim Kay Hua. *Reference*: Sim.

LOH, ROBIN

Loh is a Hakka born in Indonesia in 1929. After finishing primary school, he began helping in his father's jewellery shop. He seems to have made some money during the Pacific War; but in 1947, penniless, he left for Singapore and, in the next decade or so, he tried his hand at a number of jobs, such as being a taxi driver and photographer. His break came when he went to West Irian just before the Indonesian Army launched an attack, and he became rich by selling to the army the heavy equipment abandoned by the Dutch. What he did after this is not clear; but by the mid-1970s he was engaged in shipbuilding, shipping, and dredging. He had by then developed close ties with Ibnu Sutowo and done a lot of business with Pertamina. He also had financial backing from Chin Sophonpanich of Bangkok Bank. The fall of Sutowo in 1976 was a severe blow to him, but he managed to overcome this. His businesses, however, do not seem to be going as well as before. *Reference*: *Insight*, March 1978.

NG, QUEE LAM

Ng Quee Lam was born in Fukien in 1919, and came to Singapore at the age of five. He received his primary and high school education in China. He returned to Singapore around 1936 and joined his father's rubber trading company. After the Pacific War, he organized Hiap Hoe Rubber Co. and made large profits during the Korean War boom. In the 1960s, he began diversifying into banking (Far Eastern Bank), shipping (Singapore–Soviet Shipping Co., a joint venture with the Soviet Government), and real estate. In the early 1980s he built President Merlin Hotel in Singapore. He is one of the few rubber traders whose wealth, acquired in the 1950s, has not dissipated. *References*: Oral History, Ng Quee Lam; Sim.

OEI, TJONG IE

Oei Tjong Ie is the son of Oei Tiong Ham. Although Kian Gwan, the family's company, was nationalized by the Indonesian Government in 1961, its overseas subsidiaries remained with the Oei family. Oei Tjong Ie was in charge of Kian Gwan (Malaya) in Singapore at the time of nationalization. He continued to manage this company thereafter as well as the family's assets in Singapore. He collaborated with Khoo Teck Puat in setting up Malayan Banking Corp., and became its first chairman. He currently heads the relatively small Kian Gwan group of companies in Singapore (Kian Gwan Engineering, etc.). *Reference*: Liem.

ONG, TJOE KIM

Ong is a Hokkien born in China in 1911. After finishing high school, he went to Indonesia at the age of sixteen. After working at a textile shop, he began working at the Aurora Department Store, where he remained until 1952. In the following year, he set up his own department store, Metro, in Surabaya, and two years later, he opened a branch in Jakarta. In 1960, when anti-Chinese feelings were running high in Indonesia, he set up a store in Singapore and made it his permanent base. In the following years, he built Metro into a leading department store chain in Singapore. *Reference*: Oral History, Ong Tjoe Kim.

QUEK, SHIN

Quek Shin was born in Hainan in 1886. After graduating from Canton Fong Yan College, he went to Melaka to help his elder brother in tapioca production. Later, seeing a better future in rubber, he started rubber planting and eventually became a large plantation owner (he developed more than 20,000 acres of plantation from the virgin jungle). He also went into real estate, trading, and banking. In banking, he was a director of United Chinese Bank (the present UOB) in the mid-1930s; and after the war, he was a director of OUB. *References*: Oral History, Quek Kai Teng; Sim.

SHAW, RUNME

Shaw was born in Shanghai in 1901. After finishing high school there, he joined his eldest brother's film company as sales manager. In 1924, he came to Singapore alone to start a film business. Together with his younger brother (Run Run), who followed him a year later, he succeeded eventually in building an entertainment empire. Part of the fortune he made in the film industry was invested in banking, hotels, and real estate: he was a director of OCBC and Shangri-la Hotel and was the owner of Shaw House and Shaw Centre. He died in March 1985. His businesses in Singapore and Malaysia are now controlled by the Shaw Foundation. *Reference*: Oral History, Runme Shaw.

SOON, PENG YAM

Soon, chairman of the Sim Lim group of companies, is a Hokkien born in China in 1912. At the age of fourteen he came to Singapore with his family. After working at a sundry-goods store and a pineapple factory, he set up his own company, Sim Lim, in 1932, to deal in timber. This company eventually became a large trader of timber, cement, and other construction materials in Singapore and Malaysia. In the 1960s, he diversified into construction, finance, plantations, and palm-oil processing. *References*: Oral History, Soon Peng Yam; Sim.

TAN, CHIN TUAN

Tan Chin Tuan is a Hokkien born in Singapore in 1908. After finishing his education at the Anglo-Chinese School, he joined Chinese Commercial Bank at the age of seventeen as a junior clerk. (At this time, his father was general manager of Oversea-Chinese Bank.) When the bank merged with Oversea-Chinese Bank and Ho Hong Bank to become OCBC, he became assistant manager and began climbing up the corporate hierarchy. He worked under Lee Kong Chian when Lee was chairman; and soon after Lee's retirement in the mid-1960s, he was appointed chairman and managing director, in which capacity he became the chief architect of OCBC's growth in the 1970s. He remained as chairman until 1983. *References*: *Insight*, December 1983; Sim; Dick Wilson.

TAN, EAN KIAM

Tan Ean Kiam was a Hokkien born in China in 1881. At the age of eighteen, he came to Singapore with his father, and ten years later established Joo Guan Co.

in partnership with a friend. This business flourished, and he invested in rubber estates and factories, eventually making a fortune in this field (his rubber trading company was Bin Seng & Co.). He was also a founder of Oversea-Chinese Bank and its chief decision-maker on the merger with the other banks. At the new bank, he served as managing director until his death in 1943. His son, Tan Tock San, who began working in the bank during the Pacific War, became a director in 1968. *References*: Sim; Dick Wilson.

TAN, GEORGE

George Tan was born in Sarawak in 1933 and grew up there. His father was an unlicensed dentist who supplemented his income by renting out a taxi he owned. Sometime in the mid- or late 1950s, he left for Singapore, where he acquired citizenship and worked for a construction company. However, he did not do very well, so in 1971 he left for Hong Kong, where, after working at a construction company for a few years, he became independent and went into property development. Much of the money for this investment seems to have been the flight capital of South-East Asian Chinese, such as Chang Ming Thien, who trusted him. Then in the late 1970s, he succeeded in persuading Bank Bumiputra's finance company subsidiary in Hong Kong (BMF) to lend him a big sum of money (over HK$1 billion), and his company made a meteoric rise in the Hong Kong property market. However, in 1982, when property prices began falling following the visit to Peking of the British Prime Minister, Mrs Margaret Thatcher, he began facing trouble. A year later he went bankrupt and his group of companies, the Carrian group, was liquidated. *Reference*: Ranjit Gill (1985), *The Carrian Saga*.

TAN, KAH KEE

Tan Kah Kee built the biggest business empire of all Chinese in pre-war Malaya. He was a Hokkien born in China in 1874, who came to Singapore at the age of seventeen to assist in his father's rice business. Later, his father also apparently owned a pineapple factory. In 1904, Tan Kah Kee took over his father's rice and pineapple businesses. Two years later, he also went into rubber planting, and for some time, rice, pineapple, and rubber were the three pillars of his business. Later, however, he withdrew from rice, and made rubber, which had turned out to be quite profitable, his mainstay. He acquired rubber plantations, and processing and manufacturing plants and started exporting rubber directly. His employees at this time included Lee Kong Chian and Tan Lark Sye, who later became famous rubber traders. In the late 1920s, because of increased competition and the decline of rubber prices, he began encountering trouble, and his businesses were eventually liquidated in 1934. *References*: Tan Kah Kee; Yong (1987).

TAN, KIM SENG

Tan Kim Seng was a Hokkien born in Melaka in 1805. At the age of twenty-nine, he moved to Singapore. It is not clear what he did at first, but later he set up the trading company, Kim Seng & Co. He seems to have sold tin and the agricultural produce of the area to Western merchant houses, and in return, bought Western goods from them. By 1850, he had apparently become a prominent merchant, for in that year he began assuming socially responsible positions in the Chinese community. On his death in 1864, his wealth was estimated at about (Straits) $2 million. Kim Seng & Co. continued to flourish thereafter, under the management of, first, his sons and then his grandson, Tan Jiak Kim, who invested in and became a director of Straits Steamship Co. in order to strengthen his trading activities. *References*: Lee Poh Ping (1974); Song; Tregonning (1965), *Home Port Singapore.*

TAN, LARK SYE

Tan Lark Sye was a Hokkien born in China in 1896. He went to primary school for about three years in his village, Chip Bee (also Tan Kah Kee's village) in Fukien. When he was older, he joined his elder brothers in Singapore, where they worked for Tan Kah Kee's rubber business. In 1924, together with his brothers, Tan Lark Sye founded Aik Hoe Co., a rubber trading company. Under his management the company flourished, and in the 1950s it became the largest rubber exporter in Singapore. Some of the profits he made in rubber were invested in other fields: he was at one time a director of OCBC and chairman of Tasek Cement in Malaysia. He died in 1972. *References*: Sim; Oral History, Tan Ee Leong; Dick Wilson.

TAN, SIAK KEW

Tan Siak Kew, a Teochiu who was once called the 'pepper king', was governing director of Buan Lee Seng (a dealer in pepper, coffee, and copra) and chairman and managing director of Four Seas Communications Bank in the early 1970s. His elder brother, Tan Siakuang, served as general manager of the bank for some time in the pre-war period; but he left in the early 1930s to go into business, and by the late 1940s he was heading a leading rubber company. He then joined the newly formed OUB (a bank organized by another Teochiu, Lien Ying Chow) and became its first chairman. Tan Siakuang was born in China and came to Singapore at the age of thirteen. Before working, he studied English briefly and became bilingual. *Reference*: Overseas Union Bank.

TAN, TOCK SENG

Tan Tock Seng was a Hokkien born in Melaka in 1798. He came to Singapore shortly after it became a British colony, and there he peddled agricultural produce. With the money he earned, he opened his own store and became an agent of Shaw, Whitehead & Co. He died in 1850, by which time he seems to have become fairly wealthy, as evidenced by the fact that in 1844, he made an initial donation of (Straits) $5,000 to a hospital which bears his name today, Tan Tock Seng Hospital. He was also an unofficial Capitan China. His son, Tan Kim Ching took over his business, but placed a greater emphasis on rice. He bought steamships and set up rice mills in Saigon and Siam to facilitate rice imports. He also had close relations with the Thai Government, acting as its consul-general in Singapore. Kim Ching died in 1892. Tan Tock Seng's grandson, Tan Chay Yan, invested part of the wealth he inherited in rubber and became the first Chinese rubber planter. Chay Yan died in 1916. *References*: Lee Poh Ping (1974); Song.

TANG, CHOON KENG

C. K. Tang was born in 1901, the son of a pastor in Swatow, and at the age of twenty-one, came to Singapore to sell embroideries made in his home province. In the next few decades, he sold Chinese embroideries and curios to European residents and tourists in Singapore. Even as late as 1958, when he moved to Orchard Road, it was largely to attract European residents in the Tanglin area. However, in the following years, as the Singapore economy became prosperous, his store, C. K. Tang, diversified the products it handled, becoming essentially a department store, and began attracting more and more Singaporean customers. In the early 1980s, C. K. Tang rebuilt the store at the same site, and behind it, built Dynasty Hotel. Both store and hotel were built in the style of a Chinese pagoda, with green roof and red columnades. *Reference*: Oral History, Choon Keng Tang.

TAY, KOH YAT

Tay was born in Quemoy, Fukien, in 1880 and orphaned at the age of eight. At the age of twenty-two he came to Singapore, and in the next twenty-eight years, he was associated with several trading companies (Guan Seng Hin, Guan Soon Co., Aik Seng Hin Co., and Chin Joo Seng Co.), most of which seem to have dealt in the produce of the area. In 1930, he founded Tay Koh Yat Bus Co., which subsequently became the largest private bus company. *Reference*: Sim.

WEE, CHO YAW

Wee Cho Yaw is a Hokkien born in China in 1929. His father, Wee Kheng Chiang, exported pepper and rubber from Sarawak to Singapore and also operated a coffee-shop type of bank in Kuching. In 1935, his father formed United Chinese Bank in Singapore. Wee Cho Yaw received his education at Chung Cheng High School and St. Andrew's High School. After completing his schooling and visiting England for several months, in around 1950 he began working for the family commodity trading company, Kheng Leong, where he stayed until the late 1950s. In 1958, his father asked him to become a director of the bank, and he was made its managing director two years later. His father stayed on as chairman of the bank until 1974, but it was Cho Yaw who was the chief architect of the bank's rapid growth in the 1960s and 1970s. The name of the bank was changed to United Overseas Bank (UOB) in 1965. UOB, which has been listed on the Singapore and Kuala Lumpur stock exchanges since 1970, is now the second largest private bank in Singapore and the core of the UOB group of companies. This group includes Chung Khiaw Bank (a bank set up by Aw Boon Haw), Lee Wah Bank, United Overseas Land (a real estate company), Plaza Hotel, Haw Par Brothers International (which was formerly owned by the Aw family), Setron (a producer of household electrical appliances), and United Overseas Insurance. Wee Cho Yaw is the largest shareholder of the group. *References*: *Insight*, May 1980 and March 1983; *FEER*, 20 August 1982.

WHAMPOA (HOO AH KAY)

Whampoa was a Cantonese born in China in 1816. He came to Singapore in 1830 to assist his father in his provision store. He learned English and became a provisioner for European ships which called at Singapore. He got along well with Western merchants and officials and sometimes participated in their projects, such as Tanjong Pagar Dock Co. His provision store, Whampoa & Co., prospered, and he went into some other businesses (for example, he set up an ice plant and a bakery). In 1880, he died a wealthy and respected merchant. *References*: Lee Poh Ping (1974); Song.

WONG, AH FOOK

Wong Ah Fook was born in China in the mid-1830s and came to Singapore in the early 1850s, where he worked in a carpenter's shop. Later he became successful as an independent contractor, operating in both Singapore and Johor, and he also went into estate agriculture. The use of his own paper currency to pay his workers seems to have aroused his interest in banking. In 1903 he organized the first Chinese bank in the region, Kwong Yik Bank, and became its managing director. Unfortunately, this bank got into difficulties in 1913 and was later liquidated. One of his sons, S. Q. Wong, served as a director of OCBC for over four decades from its inception. *References*: Song; Tan Ee Leong (1961).

YEO, THIAN IN

Yeo Thian In first worked in Amoy in the soy sauce factory his father, Yeo Keng Lian, had set up in 1901. In 1938, after his father's death, Thian In, together with his brothers, moved the factory to Singapore and set up the company, Yeo Hiap Seng Sauce Manufactory. He diversified into canning in the early 1950s, and later into soft drinks, food seasoning, and instant noodles, thus transforming his company from a soy sauce maker to a food conglomerate. Then, in the 1960s, he began expanding outside Singapore, into such countries as Malaysia and Indonesia. Today, Thian In still heads the group, assisted by his sons and nephews (for example, his nephew, Michael Yeo Chee Wee, and his son, Alan Yeo Chee Yeow). *Reference*: Iwasaki.

Indonesia

ANG, KOK HA (HADI BUDIMAN)

Ang Kok Ha seems at first to have dealt in various goods, but in the late 1960s, textile trading was his major activity. This led to joint ventures with Toray (Easterntex and Century Textile Industry). With the money made in textiles, he went into the distribution and assembling of motor vehicles as the agent of Honda (Imora Motor and Prospect Motor). Later he set up a joint venture with Honda (Imora Honda) to manufacture vehicle parts and components. His nephew, Ang Kang Ho, is helping him in his business.

CHANG, PI SHIH (THIO THIAU SIAT)

Chang was a Cantonese born in China in 1840. At the age of fifteen he migrated to Jakarta, and in the next twenty years, he became one of the wealthiest Chinese in Java. When the Dutch moved into Sumatra, Chang followed; and from Sumatra he expanded first to Penang and then to Singapore. His success in Indonesia and, to some extent, Penang depended greatly on his ability to work well with Westerners: he obtained a number of lucrative tax-farms from the colonial governments; he was the major provisioner of the Dutch Army when it fought in Aceh, and he was an important supplier of labour for Western plantations. He also had interests in plantations, shipping, and trading. In his later years, he shifted his attention to China. Complying with the request of the Ch'ing dynasty which wanted to modernize the economy with the assistance of overseas Chinese capital and know-how, he invested extensively in China: for example, he was one of the promoters of the Canton–Hankow railroad. Even after the fall of the Ch'ing government, he stayed in China and, until his death in 1916, tried to help the Republican government in economic modernization. *References*: Godley; *Historical Personalities of Penang*.

CIPUTRA (TJIE SIEM HOAN)

Ciputra was born in Central Sulawesi in 1931 and graduated from ITB with a degree in architecture. He first became prominent as the head of PT Pembangunan Jaya, now one of the largest construction and real estate companies. The Jakarta Government has a controlling interest in the company, but its management is entrusted to him. He was a confidant of Ali Sadikin, the Governor of Jakarta from 1966 to 1977. Ciputra is also a co-owner of the Metropolitan group, a large real estate group (his partners in this group are Liem Sioe Liong and Budi Brasali). *References*: *NBS*; *AS*.

DARMADI, JAN

Jan Darmadi is the son of Dady Darmadi (Darma?), a casino operator during the Sukarno period. In the New Order period, Jan managed to forge close relations with some of the political élites, and obtained a monopoly on casino operation in Jakarta in the late 1960s. Casinos were banned in the early 1980s, but with the money derived from them, he had bought real estate and now owns Skyline Building. He is also the Indonesian partner of the Japanese textile joint venture, Unilon Textile Industries, and the owner of PT Kodel, a trading and investment company. *References*: Nihon Keizai; *KK*, January 1982.

DJOJONEGORO, HUSAIN

Djojonegoro was born in Central Java in 1949. He is today the owner of the ABC group. International Chemical Industrial Co., which produces dry-cell batteries under the ABC brand, is Indonesia's largest dry-cell battery producer. The group also includes two food manufacturing companies, Perindustrial Bapak Jenggot and Central Food. The former is engaged in wine processing and bottling, the latter in ketchup manufacturing. Both market their products under the ABC brand. *Reference*: *AS*.

GO, KA HIM (SUHARGO GONDOKUSUMO)

Go Ka Him is the owner of the Dharmala group, one of the twelve largest groups in Indonesia, which is engaged, among other things, in animal feed-milling, housing development, and produce trading. Go originally traded in the produce of Lampung in Sumatra, such as coffee, rubber, and pepper, and later he developed close connections with Bulog. With the profits from trading, he diversified into other fields. He recently erected a large building, Wisma Dharmala, at Jalan Jenderal Sudirman. His son, Triono, is married to a daughter of Go Swie Kie.

GO, SWIE KIE (DASUKI ANGKOSUBROTO)

Go Swie Kie is the owner of the Gunung Sewu group, whose activities include trading and real estate. He had close connections with Bulog, acting as its exclusive agent for the import of rice and sugar, and through this he seems to have developed close relations with Chin Sophonpanich of Thailand and Robert Kuok of Malaysia. This group is linked to Go Ka Him's Dharmala group by marriage. Go Swie Kie is one of the wealthiest Chinese in Indonesia.

GUNAWAN, MU'MIN ALI (LIE MO MENG)

Mu'min was born in East Java in 1939. He and his brother, Gunadi Gunawan (Lie Mo Kwang), control the Panin group, which is engaged in banking (Pan Indonesia Bank), spinning (Maligi Spinning Mills), life insurance (Asuransi Jiwa Panin Putra), and general insurance (Pan Union Insurance). The Gunawan brothers are related to Mochtar Riady of the Lippo group: their sister is his wife. General Yusuf seems to be their political patron: the president of Pan Indonesia Bank, Andi Gappa, is said to be General Yusuf's brother. *References*: *AWSJ*, 30 June 1986; *KK*, January 1982; *AS*.

HARTONO, MICHAEL BUDI

Michael Budi Hartono is the key figure behind PT Djarum Kudus, one of the three largest kretek cigarette companies. PT Djarum Kudus was founded by his father in 1950. At this time, the company was known as Perusahaan Tembakau Djarum. The father died in 1963. Rapid growth came thereafter, especially in the New Order period, under the management of Budi Hartono. In the second half of the 1970s, he diversified into electronics and textile manufacturing, setting up Hartono Istana Electronic in 1976 to assemble 'Polytron' colour television sets, and Busana Rama Textile & Garment in 1979 to produce garments for export.

HALIM, MINTARDJO

Mintardjo is the present owner of one of Indonesia's largest textile mills, Sandratex (founded by Boediharto Halim (Liem Boen Hwa), who died in 1976). Recently he formed Tri Rempoa Solo Synthetics (the first Indonesian-owned company to produce polyester fibres) together with Handoko Tjokrosaputro of Batik Keris and the Panin group, which owns Maligi Spinning Mills. With technology from West Germany (Lurugi), Tri Rempoa Solo Synthetics began production in Tangerang in the mid-1980s. Halim is also active in CBTI, a government-sponsored organization which has a monopoly on the import of raw cotton.

HASAN, BOB (THE KIAN SENG)

Bob Hasan was born in Semarang in 1931. He later became the 'adopted' son of Gatot Subroto, who is said to have saved Suharto when he was being dismissed by General Nasution for his involvement in smuggling in the late 1950s. Bob Hasan seems to have made use of his adoptive father's relations with Suharto when he went into business. He is sometimes called 'the king of the forest' because of his many logging concessions. He is also engaged in shipping, manufacturing, trading, and construction. His business depends heavily on government connections. *Reference*: *AS*.

JANANTO, SOETOPO (YAP SWIE KIE)

Jananto was the founder of the Berkat group, which is involved in trading, pulp and paper manufacturing (PT Indah Kiat Pulp & Paper Corp.), and tyre manufacturing (PT Bridgestone Tire Indonesia). He first made money in logging (he had a number of logging concessions in Kalimantan and Sumatra), and then diversified into manufacturing. He is dead now, and the group is controlled by his family.

JAUW, TJONG KIE

Jauw was a throwster in the early 1970s, twisting polyester filament imported from Japan and selling the finished product to weavers and knitters. In the late 1970s, he set up Yasinta Poly and went into production of polyester filament. The technology for this venture came from the German company, Zimmer. Jauw has another company, Yasonta, which produces household electrical appliances under licence from Sharp of Japan.

KOH (KHOUW), KIM AN

Koh Kim An was a Hokkien born in Batavia in 1876. The Dutch colonial government appointed him Lieutenant in 1905 and several years later promoted him to Major. In the late 1910s, he formed Batavia Bank together with a few other Chinese (Capitan Lie Tjien-Tjoen, Lie's brother-in-law, and Tjong A Fie). The bank was apparently formed at the wish of Chang Pi Shih, which was conveyed to them after his death by Tjong A Fie, who went to Jakarta to execute his will. The bank did not fare very well at first and had to reduce its capital by half in the mid-1920s (from 10 million to 5 million guilders). Koh headed the bank for some time and died in 1945. *References*: Chang; Suryadinata.

LIE, SIONG THAY (SUSANTA LYMAN)

Lie Siong Thay had a number of large logging concessions and later went into wood processing. In the past several years, he has diversified into coal mining, manufacturing of car chassis, and production of ceramic materials. His companies form the Satya Djaya Raya group, one of Indonesia's largest groups in logging and wood processing.

LIEM, BIAN KHOEN (SOFJAN WANANDI)

Liem Bian Khoen was born in West Sumatra in 1941 and moved to Jakarta in 1957. While attending the University of Indonesia, he was active in the student organization, KAMI. He became close to Ali Murtopo and Sudjono Humardani and was involved in their policy research institute, CSIS. Later he ventured into business, and today he heads the Wanandi group, one of the fast-growing groups in Indonesia. He seems to have some Japanese connections: he is a partner in the Japanese joint venture Eastern Polymer, which produces polyvinyl chloride (one of the Japanese partners is Mitsubishi Corp.). He is also a partner in the Pakarti group, whose other partners are Panglaykim and Humardani's son-in-law. The Pakarti group has several joint ventures with Japanese companies. *Reference*: AS.

LIEM, ENG HWAY (ADIL NURIMBA)

Liem Eng Hway is the owner of the Gesuri group, one of the three largest shipping groups in Indonesia. Its flagship company is Perusahaan Pelayaran

Samudera Gesuri Lloyd, or Gesuri Lloyd for short. He was born in Sumatra in 1922, the son of a Chinese who was engaged in coastal shipping there. During the Japanese occupation, Liem Eng Hway also engaged in shipping, which he continued after the war in Medan. He later moved to Jakarta, and in the New Order period, he went into international shipping. He now has several companies engaged in different kinds of shipping. *Reference*: *AS*.

LIEM, SIOE LIONG (SUDONO SALIM)

Liem Sioe Liong has the biggest business group in Indonesia. Born in Fukien in 1916, he came to Indonesia at the age of twenty-two and first worked at his uncle's store in Central Java. In the first two decades of the post-war period, he was not a nationally known businessman. However, he had developed close relations with Suharto when the latter was Commander of the Diponegoro Division, and after Suharto came into power, Liem obtained a number of monopolies (cloves, flour, etc.) and was also given government facilities. The Liem Sioe Liong group today consists of several subgroups: the Bank Central Asia, Metropolitan, Bogasari, Indocement, Tarumatex, First Pacific, Sinar Mas Inti Perkasa, Indosteel, Indomobil Utama, and Waringin Kencana groups. Bank Central Asia is the biggest private commercial bank; the Metropolitan group is one of the largest real estate groups; Bogasari Flour Mills has a monopoly on flour production and distribution; Indocement's cement complex in Cibinong is the biggest in Asia, accounting for about 40 per cent of Indonesia's cement production in 1985; First Pacific is the offshore centre of the group, based in Hong Kong; Sinar Mas Inti Perkasa, a joint venture with Eka Cipta Widjaya, has a large share of the food oil market; Indosteel is constructing a cold rolling mill with Krakatau Steel; Indomobil Utama is producing the best-selling car of 1986, Suzuki; and Waringin Kencana is a large trading company that has a monopoly on a few products, including cloves. The textile company, Tarumatex, is the only lacklustre member of the group. *References*: *Insight*, May 1978; *FEER*, 7 April 1983; *NBS*; *AS*; *Sydney Morning Herald*, 10 April 1986; Mihira.

LIEM, SOEI LING

Liem Soei Ling is the owner of PT Sampoerna in Surabaya, which produces the 'Dji Sam Soe' brand of kretek cigarettes and is the oldest of the major kretek cigarette producers (Gudang Garam, Bentoel, Djarum Kudus, and Sampoerna). It was founded in 1913 by Soei Ling's father, Liem Seng Tee. Soei Ling is now old, and the company is managed by his sons.

NURSALIM, SJAMSUL (LIEM TJOEN HO)

Nursalim was born in 1942. He is today the owner of a major tyre manufacturing company, Gadjah Tunggal, which produces its own brand of tyres as well as a Japanese brand under licence from Yokohama Rubber. He is also the Indonesian partner in a Japanese joint venture, Indonesia Kansai Paint, and the co-owner of Bank Dagang Nasional Indonesia, the oldest private bank in Indonesia. In the late 1970s, the bank was owned by the Sultan of Yogyakarta (Hamengkubuwono) and his two Chinese partners; but because of mismanagement by the Chinese partners, the bank got into trouble. In 1980, Nursalim injected new capital to save the bank and acquired a 50 per cent interest. The Sultan holds the remaining share. *Reference*: AS.

NYOO, HAN SIANG

Nyoo Han Siang was born in Yogyakarta in 1930 and left for China in 1946, but came back to Indonesia in 1950. He first worked as a journalist, and later went into business. In the New Order period, he developed close relations with Indonesian political élites, especially Ali Murtopo. In 1968 he bought the Bank Umum Nasional (now the third largest private bank) from some members of the PNI (Partai Nasional Indonesia) which he later sold. He died in 1985. The bank is owned today by Kaharuddin Ongko. *Reference*: Suryadinata.

OEI, TIONG HAM

Oei Tiong Ham built the biggest Chinese business group, the Oei Tiong Ham group, in pre-war South-East Asia. Around 1930, it consisted of the following companies: N.V. Handel Mij. Kian Gwan, a large trading company with branches in Bombay, Calcutta, Karachi, Shanghai, Hong Kong, Amoy, Singapore, and London; N.V. Algemeene Mij. Tot Exploitatie der Oei Tiong Ham Suikerfabrieken, which owned five sugar factories producing about 10,000 tons of sugar a year; N.V. Heap Eng Moh Steamship Co., a shipping company which plied between Java ports and the Straits Settlements; N.V. Bank Vereeniging Oei Tiong Ham, the first Chinese bank in Java; N.V. Bouw Mij. Randoesarie, a construction and real estate development company; and N.V. Midden Java Veem, a large warehousing company operating in Semarang, Surabaya, and a few other cities in Java.

Tiong Ham's father, Oei Tjie Sien, migrated from Fukien to Semarang in the late 1850s and started sugar trading a few years later under the name of Kian Gwan, becoming a fairly successful merchant. His eldest son, Tiong Ham, began helping him in the 1880s and eventually took charge of the family business. Like other big Chinese merchants at this time, Tiong Ham also prospered from dealing in opium, but unlike them, he was not content with what had been accomplished and went on to build a business empire that could compete with Western companies. In the early 1920s he moved to Singapore, where he died in 1924. After his death, the Oei Tiong Ham group was managed jointly by two of his sons, Tjong Hauw and Tjong Swan. In the early 1930s, Tjong Swan decided to pull out, so Tjong Hauw assumed full control thereafter. In 1950, he died suddenly, after which his youngest brother, Tjong Tjay, headed the group until it was nationalized by the Indonesian Government in 1961. By this time, having gone through the Pacific War, the Revolution after the war, and the nationalistic measures of the 1950s, the Oei Tiong Ham group had been considerably reduced in size. The Indonesian Government could not touch its assets outside the country. One of Tiong Ham's sons is heading the Kian Gwan group in Bangkok, and another in Singapore. The Kian Gwan group in Bangkok is fairly large. *References*: *The Story of Krebet*; Liem; Panglaykim and Palmer; Tjoa.

ONG, SIN KING

Ong was a director of Coopa (a trading company) and Bank Ramayana in the late 1960s. He was involved in a scandal in the early 1970s, accused of having received several million dollars from the government for fertilizer that was never delivered. He seems to have been involved in a number of irregular practices. He was close to Major-General Soerjo and, through him, President Suharto. He died in 1976. *Reference*: May.

ONGGO, HENRY (LIEM HEN SIN)

He is the owner of the Ratu Plaza Complex, which consists of a modern office building, a shopping centre, and a luxurious apartment building. He is also building another complex called Landmark Center. He seems to have made money originally in stone quarrying, then gone into cement distribution. It was only recently that he entered real estate development in a big way. He also has an interest in the Japanese joint-venture textile firm, Unitex.

ONGKO, KAHARUDDIN (ONG KA HUAT?)

Ongko is the owner of the Arya Upaya group, which comprises Bank Umum Nasional (the third largest private bank), Indikisar Djaja (a construction and real estate development company), Manufacturer Hannover Leasing Indonesia (a leasing company), and Keramika Indonesia Assosiasi (a joint venture with American Standard and the largest manufacturer of ceramic tableware and sanitary ware). He seems to have started business in North Sumatra and then moved to Jakarta.

RAHARDJA, HENDRA (TAN TJIE HIN)

Hendra was born in Ujung Pandang in 1943. In the early 1960s, he began a business with friends to deal in European-made motor cycles. Several years later, he became the agent for Yamaha Motor and made money in the distribution and assembling of Yamaha motor cycles. In the 1970s, he went into real estate, banking, and hotels. He built Harapan Building at Jalan Jenderal Sudirman and Gajah Mada Plaza at Jalan Gajah Mada; he bought a few small banks in Surabaya and Medan; and he began a huge hotel project in Singapore (he had plans to build six hotels and finished building two, one of which is Hotel Meridien). However, the Singapore project got into trouble because of the economic recession there, and this in turn caused financial difficulties for his

Indonesian businesses. Some are rumoured to have been taken over by Liem Sioe Liong. *References*: *AS*; *Management Journal*, March/April 1982; *AWSJ*, 29 February 1984.

RIADY, MOCHTAR (LEE MO SING?)

Mochtar Riady was born in Malang in 1929. He was first educated in Chinese schools and, in the early post-war years, in China. He returned in 1950 and went into business. His banking career began soon after, when he became the manager of a small bank that was in trouble. In 1964 he left for another bank, and in the early 1970s he joined the newly formed Pan Indonesia Bank. A few years later, he was invited by Liem Sioe Liong to manage Bank Central Asia (BCA). In the following several years, Mochtar Riady made BCA the top private bank. He is still the chief executive officer of BCA, but he also has his own business group, the Lippo group, whose flagship company is Bank Perniagaan Indonesia, which he jointly owns with Hasyim Ning (though control seems to lie with Mochtar Riady). The Lippo group first concentrated in the financial field, but has recently gone into manufacturing, producing household electrical appliances in a tie-up with Mitsubishi Electric Co. Mochtar Riady's wife is the sister of the Gunawan brothers of Pan Indonesia Bank, but he is said to have left this bank for BCA because he could not work well with them. *References*: *AS*; *ICN*, 17 June 1985; *Asia Finance*, 15 September 1983.

SETIAWAN, AKIE (KHO KIE PIANG)

Akie Setiawan is the key figure behind the Hutrindo group. This group grew with logging concessions, and while still engaged in logging, it now also produces plywood and other wood products (Hutan Raya Indonesia Timber, Hutrindo Prajen Plywood, etc.). It is also involved in manufacturing; one of its companies, Serinco Djaya Marmer Industries, produces tiles and other ceramic ware; and two others, Willi Antariksa Electronics and Natric Jaya Industries, produce household electrical appliances in a tie-up with Toshiba.

SIE, ROBBY (ROBBY CAHYADI)

In the early 1970s, despite his youth, Robby Sie was one of the well-known *cukong* in Jakarta. He hails from Solo, where he seems to have made the acquaintance of Bernard Ibnu Hardjojo, Mrs Suharto's brother. After moving to Jakarta, he and Hardjojo did business together. However, he was caught smuggling in expensive European cars. Although tried and convicted, he seems to have been released soon after. He is no longer heard of today.

SOERYADJAYA, WILLIAM (TJIA KIAN LIONG)

William is the present head of the Astra group, the second largest group in Indonesia. Astra has been appointed the sole agent of a number of Japanese motor vehicle and heavy equipment manufacturers, such as Toyota, Daihatsu,

Honda, and Komatsu. In motor vehicles, Astra is engaged in assembling as well as engine production. It is also the sole agent of Japanese office equipment and agricultural machinery producers, such as Fuji Xerox and Kubota. With the profits made in this area, the Astra group began diversifying in the 1970s into such areas as plantations, wood processing, fishery, construction, real estate, financial services, and general trading.

William was born in West Java in 1923 and was orphaned at an early age. He seems to have started his business career in the early 1940s. The present core company of the group, Astra International, was founded as early as 1957, but its development came in the New Order period. Its success was partly a matter of business strategy. Astra International concentrated on heavy equipment and motor vehicles, an area which other Chinese businessmen were reluctant to enter but which grew rapidly with new development projects. The architect of the development of the Astra group was William's brother, Tjia Kian Tie. He was instrumental in mapping out strategy and developing the necessary government connections in the second half of the 1960s. However, he died suddenly in the late 1970s, and since then William has been heading the group with the help of his younger brother, Benjamin. *References: AS; NBS;* Nihon Keizai Shinbun-sha; *Asia Finance,* 15 November 1983.

SOETANTYO, TEGUH (TAN KIONG LIEP)

Soetantyo was born in Yogyakarta in 1918. Soon after finishing junior high school (MULO), he apparently started his business career. Today he owns the Mantrust group, which is strong in food processing and distribution. He is the Indonesian partner in a European joint venture to produce condensed and powdered milk, Friesche Vlag Indonesia. One of the companies in the Mantrust group is the trading company PT Borsumij Wehry Indonesia—a company named after two pre-war Dutch companies.

SOSRODJOJO, SUTJIPTO (LIEM HWAY HO ALIAS SOUW HWAY HO)

Sutjipto is one of the three brothers who own PT Sinar Sosro, which produces a soft drink (bottled sweetened tea) under the trademark 'Teh Botol Sosro'. The other brothers are Sugiharto and Surjanto. (Surjanto studied business administration in West Germany.) They come from Slawi, Central Java. Their father began dealing in various food products about forty years ago, but eventually made dried tea his speciality. It was, however, only after his death that the tea business flourished: the three brothers ventured into bottled tea in 1975 and made it a tremendous success. In terms of quantity, Teh Botol Sosro has the largest share of the soft-drink market—bigger than Coca-Cola or any other foreign brand. *References: Indonesian Observer,* 30 April 1986; *AS.*

SUMENDAP, JARRY ALBERT

Sumendap owns the Porodisa group, which is engaged in logging, transportation (Bouraq Indonesia Airlines), plywood manufacturing, construction, and trading. He is a Catholic Chinese from Menado, North Sulawesi. Poorly educated, he first made money in logging (he has had large concessions in West Kalimantan, Central Sulawesi, and West Irian) and diversified into other areas in the 1970s. *Reference: NBS.*

TAN, SIONG KIE

Tan Siong Kie is the owner of the Roda Mas group, which is Indonesia's largest producer of GI sheets, has a monopoly on sheet glass production (through a joint venture with Asahi Glass of Japan), is the largest producer of the taste enhancer, monosodium glutamate (MSG) (the brand name is 'Sasa'), has a detergent manufacturing company competing with Unilever (its brand name is 'Dino'), owns Summitmas Building at Jalan Jenderal Sudirman (jointly with Sumitomo Corp.), and controls Bank Buana Indonesia, the sixth largest private Indonesian bank. The group has been also planning to go into petrochemicals (production of vinyl chloride monomer). Tan Siong Kie was born in Semarang in the mid-1910s. Among his contemporaries, he is well educated, having graduated from Shanghai University. He returned to Indonesia after the Pacific War. In the late 1950s, he set up PT Roda Mas to import construction materials such as steel and sheet glass. This company is the holding company of the group today. *Reference: NBS.*

THE, NING KING

The Ning King was born in Bandung in 1931. After high school, he began helping his father, who was dealing in textiles in Bandung. In 1949, he moved to Jakarta with his father, and a few years later he set up a small textile factory in Salatiga, Central Java. He is now the owner of the Damatex group, which includes Indonesia's largest textile mill, Daya Manunggal Textile Manufacturing; Budidharma Jakarta, a large steel company with an open-hearth furnace; Fumira, a GI sheet manufacturing company; and the joint venture with a Japanese company, Kuraray Manunggal Fiber Industries, which produces polyester fibres. His manufacturing businesses grew through tie-ups with Japanese companies, but Kuraray Manunggal is the only major one left. *Reference: AS.*

TJIOE, YAN HWIE (BUDHIWIDJAYA KUSUMANEGARA)

Tjioe is the president director of Perusahaan Rokok Tjap Bentoel, a major clove cigarette producer. His personal background is not very clear, but he was probably born in the mid-1920s and joined Perusahaan Rokok Tjap Bentoel in the 1950s as a shareholder. Bentoel's history goes back to before the war, but rapid growth and the modernization of production methods came in the

New Order period, especially in the 1970s. Its equity is spread among a number of families. Although not the largest shareholder, Tjioe is the key figure in management.

TJOA, JIEN HWIE (SURYA WONOWIDJOJO)

Tjoa Jien Hwie was the founder of Gudang Garam, the largest clove cigarette company. It is not clear when he went into the tobacco business, but PT Gudang Garam was founded in the late 1950s. Like other cigarette companies, growth and the modernization of production came in the New Order period. Tjoa died in 1985, and PT Gudang Garam is now managed by his son, Rachman Halim (Tjoa To Hing).

TJOKROSAPUTRO, HANDOKO

Handoko was born in Surabaya in 1949 and grew up in Solo. He went to ITB to study mechanical engineering but had to quit to help in the family business. His father, Kasom Tjokrosaputro (Kwee Som Tjiok), was close to President Suharto and founded PT Batik Keris, an integrated textile company engaged in spinning, weaving, garment manufacturing and retailing. After his death, Handoko, together with younger brother, Handiman, took over and formed the Batik Keris group, which includes another large textile company, PT Dan Liris. *Reference*: AS.

TJONG, A FIE

Tjong A Fie was a Hakka born in Kwangtung. At the urging of his successful cousin, Chang Pi Shih, he and his brother, Tjong Yong Hian, left for Medan in the late 1870s and in the next few decades became immensely wealthy. Yong Hian died in 1911, and A Fie in 1921. A Fie was a founder of the first Chinese bank in Indonesia, Deli Bank; he owned about 16 000 hectares of plantation; and he invested in railroads in China, like Chang Pi Shih. When he died, the Dutch colonial government estimated his wealth to be about 40 million guilders (the market value of his assets was probably twice as much). *References*: Chang; Feldwick; Godley; Wright (1909); *A Memorandum for Thirty Year's Cultivation in Nanyang.*

URAY, BURHAN (BONG SUNG ON)

In the mid-1960s, Burhan was an obscure employee of a logging firm in South Kalimantan; but in 1969, he somehow raised the capital to set up a company called Djajanti Djaja. With the backing of powerful friends, this company obtained large logging concessions in Kalimantan and became a major log exporter. He also started production of plywood in the mid-1970s by setting up Nusantara Plywood, and several years later he set up another large factory in Seram. In 1984, he also wanted to venture into production of sheet glass, challenging the monopoly of Asahimas, but this plan did not materialize. He was, however, able to diversify into fishing. His businesses constitute the Djajanti group. In the mid-1980s, his plywood factories seem to be facing financial problems because of a depressed market. *Reference: AWSJ*, 27 June 1985.

WIBAWA, HALIM (NG BOEN HWA)

Wibawa is the owner of Telesonic Electric & Development, a producer of household electrical appliances and sewing machines. Its 'Telesonic' brand of television sets is well known and competes with foreign brands; being cheaper, it is popular among people with low income, especially in the rural areas.

WIDJAYA, EKA CIPTA (OEI EK TJHONG)

Widjaya is the owner of the Sinar Mas group, which is engaged in production of cooking oil, pulp and paper and GI sheets, shipping, trading, and real estate. Bimoli, Indonesia's largest producer of cooking oil, belongs to this group. Widjaya recently bought a controlling interest in Bank International Indonesia, the seventh largest private bank. Recently, Liem Sioe Liong seems to have bought an interest in the group.

Appendix 4
Some Public Companies

WHILE the preceding two appendices focused on people, certain companies were also discussed that are or were associated with particular individuals in South-East Asia. There are, however, other types of company. Some were from the outset organized as public companies with widely distributed ownership. Some are mutual insurance companies with no shareholders. Others may have been associated with different individuals at different times because of changes in ownership. This appendix will cover some of the companies belonging to these categories that are referred to in the text.

Since this book deals with capitalists and capitalist institutions (privately owned companies), no profiles are given of state and military enterprises. When they interact with the capitalist sector and some discussion of them becomes unavoidable, information on them is either given in the text or a note. There are, however, some companies in Thailand which are neither completely government-controlled nor privately controlled. These are the companies controlled by the royal family. Their profiles are included in this appendix.

ASURANSI JIWA BERSAMA BUMIPUTERA 1912

AJB Bumiputera 1912, which means Bumiputera 1912 Mutual Life Insurance Company, is the oldest and largest life insurance company in Indonesia today. It operates throughout the country and has over 600,000 policy-holders and total assets of over 60 billion rupiahs. It also controls a life insurance company for people with low incomes (Pertanggungan Jiwa Jaminan), a non-life insurance company (Asuransi Umum Bumiputera Muda 1967), a pension trust company (Asuransi Pensiun Bumiputera 1974), a real estate company (Wisma Bumiputera, which owns an office building on Jakarta's main street, Jalan Jenderal Sudirman), a printing company (Percetakan Mardi Mulyo in Yogyakarta), and a construction company (Macadam Indonesia). It is also a major shareholder in Bumi Hyatt Hotel in Surabaya and Nusa Dua Hotel in Bali. These companies constitute the Bumiputera 1912 group.

AJB Bumiputera 1912 was established in 1912 by R. Dwidjosewojo, together with M. K. H. Soebroto and M. Adimidjojo. Dwidjosewojo, who became chairman of the board, had been the first secretary of the board of Budi Utomo (an early nationalist organization set up in 1908) and a schoolteacher at Yogyakarta. He later became a member of the Volksraad (People's Council). The launching of this insurance company was a manifestation of Budi Utomo's nationalist ideals in the economic field.

At first, under the name of 'Onderlinge Levensverzekering Mij. P.G.H.B.', it limited its policy-holders to Indonesian schoolteachers, a group the founders had some contact with because of their background; but later, under the new name of 'O. L. Mij. Boemi Poetera', it extended insurance cover to the general public. By around 1940, it had issued about 13,000 policies covering about ten million guilders in insurance, and it owned several small subsidiaries in trading and industry.

As a *mutual* insurance company, this company does not have shareholders but is owned jointly by the policy-holders. At the time of its establishment, for example, there was no equity capital. Its capital came from the premiums of the founders, and this could only be increased by increasing the number of policy-holders. At this time also, the members of the board worked voluntarily, without salary, for the success of the company. Even after this arrangement became impractical with the growth of the company, there was a great deal of idealism in such people as Dwidjosewojo and Roedjito, who headed the company.

The company at first had its headquarters in Magelang in Central Java, where it was formed. Then, in 1921, the head office was moved to Yogyakarta; and in 1958, it was moved to Jakarta, where it remains. *References*: *Sejarah dan Perkembangan Bumiputera 1912*; Sutter; *ICN*, 15 November 1982.

BANK OF THE PHILIPPINE ISLANDS (BPI)

BPI was established in 1851 as Banco Espanol Filipino de Isabella II. In 1869, a year after Isabella II had been dethroned in Spain, 'de Isabella II' was dropped from the bank's name. Then, early in the American period (1903), this was changed to the present name.

During the Spanish period, it was a quasi-government bank. It had a monopoly on note issue, and the government, although it was not a major shareholder, appointed a board of directors who shared management with the board appointed by the shareholders. Also, the government had the right to borrow from the bank, free of interest for six months each year, up to one-third of the bank's paid-up capital.

The bulk of this capital came from the Catholic Church. It had a fund called Obras Pias, which was created from the private funds left to the Church by wealthy people. This fund was often invested in the Manila–Acapulco trade and other commercial ventures during the Spanish period. In the mid-nineteenth century, in response to the need for a bank to finance trade with Spain and other European countries and to provide money for increasingly frequent transactions in the Philippines, the Church became a major financier of the country's first bank.

During the American period, the bank became separated from the government and became purely a private bank, but the Catholic Church remained its major shareholder. Post-war, this situation persisted until 1969, when the Church sold its holding to Ayala Corporation.

During Ayala's time, the bank merged two other small banks. In 1974 it merged with Peoples Bank and Trust Co., a bank Ayala had acquired from American owners about a decade earlier; and in 1981 it absorbed another bank, Commercial Bank and Trust Company. With these mergers and under Ayala's capable management, it became one of the country's leading banks. *Reference*: Colayco (1984).

CHINA BANKING CORPORATION (CBC)

CBC was organized in 1920 by a group of Chinese businessmen in the Philippines (some capital came from outside; for example, the sugar merchant in Java, Oei Tjoe, was an important subscriber). The first board of directors consisted of Dee C. Chuan, chairman and president; Albino Sycip, vice-president; Benito Siy Cong Bieng; G. A. Cu-Unjieng; Carlos Palanca; Dy Buncio; Uy Yetco; Go Jocco; Vicente Gotamco; Antonio Limgencio; and Yu Biao Sentua. Dee C. Chuan remained as chairman until his death in 1940. After that, Albino Sycip became chairman and remained in this position until the mid-1970s.

Unlike the other banks set up in South-East Asia in the 1910s and the early 1920s, CBC was a rather modern Chinese organization. First of all, the organizers sought the help of an American banker in setting up the bank, and, in order to avoid the risk of mismanagement due to inexperience, hired American bankers as general manager until the mid-1930s. Secondly, the bank was headed for over five decades by two Chinese businessmen with Western education, who had a modern outlook for Chinese at that time. Dee C. Chuan studied at St. Joseph's College in Hong Kong, and Albino Sycip had a law degree from the University of Michigan and had been practising law before he joined the bank. In other countries, in Singapore in particular, there were Western-educated Chinese, but they were not well-established businessmen and did not command the trust of their fellow merchants. In contrast, Dee C. Chuan was one of the richest Chinese merchants in the Philippines (he was called the 'lumber king'), and Albino Sycip was involved in the family trading business, Yek Hua.

For the first three decades of the post-war period, the bank was headed by Albino Sycip. His family business, run by his brother Alfonso in the pre-war period, did not survive the Pacific War, so there were no family businesses for him to help in even if he had wanted to; nor did he set up his own companies to enrich himself or his family. This professionalism and the reputation in the Chinese community he had earned over time seem to have enabled the bank to avoid the disputes and mismanagement which have often afflicted jointly-owned Chinese companies.

After Albino Sycip resigned in the mid-1970s, CBC was headed by members of the Dee family (George Dee Sekiat, Dee K. Chiong and Robert Dee Se Wee). Several Dee family members are still involved in the management of the bank, but the family does not hold a controlling share—its holding does not seem to amount to much more than 10 per cent of the total equity. The holding of the Sycip family is insignificant, and none of Albino's children are involved in the management of bank.

For some time (until Equitable Banking Corporation was set up in 1949), CBC was the only Chinese bank, and until the early 1970s, was the largest Chinese bank in the Philippines. However, since then, the relative position of the bank has declined. One problem was that it had become a foreign-owned company and became subject to the government regulation restricting the operation of foreign banks. Because of this, as late as 1975, the bank had only four branches. The second problem was that its management became less modern and professional, compared with newly formed Chinese-controlled banks, such as Metro Bank and Rizal Commercial Banking Corp. (for example, until the mid-1980s, the board meeting was conducted in Chinese). As a result of being unable to take advantage of new opportunities, CBC lagged behind other banks. However, in the past few years, the management has become less Chinese (for example, the board meeting is now in English) and more professional (for example, the present chairman is a professional banker). The problem of foreign ownership was rectified in the late 1970s, and since then, the number of branches has increased substantially. *References: Chronicle Magazine,* 17 December 1967; 'China Banking Corporation: Golden Anniversary'; 'China Banking Corporation: 60th Year'.

MULTI-PURPOSE HOLDINGS (MPH)

MPH was organized in 1975 by members of the Malaysian Chinese Association (MCA), as a response to the establishment of large-scale, government-owned bumiputra companies. It was to cut across family and clan associations and raise a large amount of capital from the public to increase Chinese participation in the modern business sector. The first public issue of about 30 million shares (of M$1 each) in 1977 drew an overwhelming response from the Chinese community, which had been worried over the increasing bumiputra share of business in Malaysia; and in the following several years, supported by the enthusiasm of the Chinese community, more shares were issued, raising the paid-up capital to about M$450 million at the end of 1983. There are now over 40,000 shareholders, but their ownership is fragmented. Control rests with the MCA-related co-operative, Koperatif Serbaguna Malaysia (KSM) (which probably holds over 50 per cent of the total equity, if indirect holdings are counted).

In the first few years of its operation, MPH acquired controlling interests in Bandar Raya Developments (a property developer), Malaysian Plantations (which was created by separating the plantation division of the British company, Plantation Holdings, from its engineering division), and Magnum Corp. (which was engaged in various activities, but whose profit source was a licence to operate a lottery).

Then, in the early 1980s, MPH went on an acquisition spree. It bought the Singapore-based British trading company, Guthrie Bhd. (and renamed it

Mulpha International Trading Corp.), and took over Dunlop Estates Bhd., and Promptship Holdings, which had a fleet of more than 30 vessels totalling about one million tons. MPH also acquired a 40 per cent interest in United Malayan Banking Corp. (UMBC), but since this was a co-ownership with Pernas (a state enterprise), MPH relinquished its UMBC holdings in exchange for a controlling interest in Malaysian French Bank.

Entry into shipping and trading, however, turned out to be a costly decision. In 1985, MPH lost about M$190 million, the largest recorded loss by a listed company in Malaysia. Of this, M$150 million came from the shipping division, and most of the rest came from trading. To make things worse, in January 1986, Tan Koon Swan, who had been heading the company since 1977, was arrested in Singapore on charges including criminal breach of trust in connection with the collapse of Pan Electric Industries in late 1985. Then, in mid-1986, suspecting large losses and corrupt management, Bank Negara Malaysia suspended the operation of MPH's controlling shareholder, KSM, along with twenty-three other co-operatives, and after a few months of investigation, placed it under receivership.

In February 1987, the board of directors was reorganized, the former MCA-related directors being replaced with non-politicians. The new board includes the business tycoon Robert Kuok (chairman) and Lee Loy Seng (of K.L.–Kepong). This is an attempt to revive MPH as a professionally managed, more business-oriented concern. See also *Tan Koon Swan. References*: Gale (1985); *AWSJ*, 9 June 1986 and 16 February 1987.

OVERSEA-CHINESE BANKING CORPORATION (OCBC)

OCBC was established in 1932 through the merger of three Hokkien banks in Singapore. One of these was Chinese Commercial Bank, which, although having the distinction of being the first Hokkien bank to be established (in 1912), was the smallest of the three. The outbreak of the First World War two years after its establishment had caused a run on the bank, along with others, which led it to adopt a conservative policy that resulted in slower growth in the following years. However, when the Great Depression came in the late 1920s, it was least affected of the three banks.

Another of the three, Ho Hong Bank, was organized in 1917 by Lim Peng Siang. He had been an architect of the development of the Chinese Commercial Bank, which he left to set up Ho Hong Bank as one of the Ho Hong group of companies (based on trade and shipping). This bank was oriented more towards foreign trade and set up branches in other South-East Asian countries and China. Because of this orientation, it became the first Chinese bank to engage in foreign exchange operations.

The third bank was Oversea-Chinese Bank. It was organized in 1919 by a prosperous rice merchant, Khoo Kok Wah, with the help of other Hokkien merchants in Malaya and Indonesia (such as Oei Tiong Ham of Semarang). Like Ho Hong Bank, it was oriented towards foreign trade and set up branches in other South-East Asian countries and China in its early years.

All these three banks were in trouble by the early 1930s, as a consequence of which their major shareholders had changed. At that time, Chinese Commercial Bank was headed by Yap Twee, Ho Hong Bank by Chee Swee Cheng, and Oversea-Chinese Bank by Tan Ean Kiam. These men got together in the early 1930s to tide themselves over the difficulties brought about by the Depression and the British abandonment of the gold standard, and came up with a merger plan.

Lee Kong Chian, who headed OCBC for about twenty-five years until the mid-1960s, does not seem to have played a major role at the time of the merger, for he was then not very rich and was only vice-chairman of the smallest bank, Chinese Commercial Bank. But when OCBC was incorporated, he was appointed vice-chairman. This was primarily to prevent the new chairman, Chee Swee Cheng, from becoming too dominant a figure in the bank. In this, Lee Kong Chian was supported by some major shareholders based in Melaka. When Chee Swee Cheng died, there was pressure on Lee Kong Chian to resign, but he resisted and succeeded in getting elected as chairman. By this time, he had greater financial resources and had the backing of the Hongkong and Shanghai Bank.

It was during Lee Kong Chian's term as chairman that OCBC began taking over British companies. Starting with the take-over of Fraser & Neave in 1957, OCBC bought controlling shares of such British companies as Malayan Breweries, Robinson & Co. (department store), Raffles Hotel, Straits Trading, Wearne Brothers, and United Engineering. Most of these companies today form part of the OCBC group.

After Lee Kong Chian resigned, Tan Chin Tuan became the leading figure in the bank. As its chairman for about eighteen years from the mid-1960s, he steered the bank's expansion in the 1970s and early 1980s. He was not, however, a major shareholder in the bank: any shares he may have owned amounted to no more than a few per cent of the total. The largest shareholder was Lee Kong Chian's family, owning about 20 per cent of the total equity. Tan Chin Tuan was supported by the Lee family and other shareholders, thus making it possible for a professional manager to head the bank. One of Lee Kong Chian's sons (Lee Seng Wee) sits on the board, representing the family interests, but does not participate in management. Tan Chin Tuan was succeeded by Yong Pung How, another professional manager who owns practically no shares. *References*: Dick Wilson; Oral History, Tan Ee Leong; Ranjit Gill (1982); Ranjit Gill (1983), 'The Super Duper Rich'; Lim Mah Hui.

SAN MIGUEL CORPORATION (SMC)

SMC was established in 1890 as Fabrica de Cerveza de San Miguel, by the Spanish merchant Enrique Ma. Barretto. A few years later, when it was incorporated, the Spanish mestizo Pedro Roxas joined Barretto and became general manager. In the next 25 years, this beer factory expanded under the management of Pedro and his son, Antonio, and its products came to replace imported beer. In the meantime, the Roxases acquired Barretto's holdings and became the dominant shareholders of San Miguel.

In 1918, Antonio Roxas brought his nephew, Andres Soriano, into the company, and a year later, entrusted the management to him in order to devote more time to other family businesses. In the next 45 years, Soriano transformed the beer company into one of the top companies in the Philippines. Beer production was modernized and expanded, and San Miguel beer came to enjoy a virtual monopoly of the market. At the same time, the company diversified into soft drinks (it became the licensee of Coca-Cola in 1927) and ice-cream and dairy products (by acquiring Magnolia Ice Plant). In the late 1930s, it set up its own glass factory to produce beer bottles. Post-war, the diversification continued. In the mid-1950s it went into feed manufacturing, and several years later into production of packaging materials. Today, it is also engaged in chicken farming and food oil production. Reflecting the diversified interests of the company, in 1963, its name was changed from San Miguel Brewery to San Miguel Corp.

Andres Soriano succeeded in controlling the management of the company without owning much equity. It is true that he came to head the company with the backing of the Roxas family (his mother came from the Roxas family), and its continued support was important in his controlling the management. However, in order to expand the capital base of the company, he began inviting others to invest in the company and eventually had its shares listed on the Manila Stock Exchange. As more shares were issued, the holdings of the Roxas family declined proportionately, but neither he nor his management company (Soriano y Cia) increased their holdings. As a consequence, he had to depend more and more on the confidence of new investors in his management capability.

Andres Soriano died in 1964 and was succeeded by his son, Andres Soriano, Jr. To control the management, Andres Jr. also had to depend on shareholders' confidence in him; but during his time, Ayala Corp. emerged as an important shareholder (the Zobels, who own Ayala Corp., are related to the Sorianos). In the early 1980s, as Ayala Corp. increased its holdings and began threatening his position, Andres Jr. countered by increasing his own holdings (mostly through A. Soriano Corp.). Then his health deteriorated, and when Ayala Corp., worried by this and at the same time realizing the unlikelihood that it could take over the management, sold its holdings (which then amounted to no more than 20 per cent), Andres Jr. did likewise. These shares were bought by Eduardo Cojuangco, President Marcos's crony, who was probably fronting for Marcos. With this, Cojuangco became chairman of the board. Andres Jr. remained as president, but his role was nominal. About a year later (1984) he died. In early 1985, when President Marcos fled the country, Cojuangco went with him, and his (or Marcos's) holdings were sequestered by the Aquino government. Thus, the government is now the largest shareholder of SMC. Andres Jr.'s son, Andres III, is heading the management, and also trying to buy the government's holdings. *References*: San Miguel Brewery; Andres Soriano, Jr.; *AWSJ*, 28–29 January 1983, 25–26 February 1983, 2 March 1983, and 10 May 1986; Yoshihara (1985).

SIAM COMMERCIAL BANK (SCB) AND SIAM CEMENT CO. (SCC)

The Crown Property Bureau (CPB) is the dominant shareholder of these two companies. CPB owns 36 per cent of the total equity of SCB and 37 per cent of that of SCC, plus another 4 per cent through SCB. CPB has been involved in these companies since their beginning (SCB was set up in 1906 and SCC in 1913) but has never been the sole owner: both companies have had other investors. Since the mid-1970s, when the Bangkok Stock Exchange was created, they have been listed on the exchange.

During the period of absolute monarchy (which ended in 1932), there was no clear separation between the government and the royal household. During that time, businessmen approached the king for financial assistance, as they do the government today. Also, as the government often does, the king took the initiative in forming companies. When the monarchy became constitutional, however, the royal household was separated from the government, and its corporate holdings were placed under CPB. Today, it is technically tied to the Ministry of Finance, but in reality it functions as an autonomous body, and is under the supervision of the chamberlain of the royal household.

CPB has been influential in choosing the top management of the companies it controls and in the past two decades, it has recruited competent men from the bureaucracy. Once the choice was made, however, and as long as no major problems arose, CPB does not seem to have interfered in the management. Those chosen as top managers have based recruitment and promotion largely on merit and have built up a professional management team. Besides, since their companies have enjoyed royal patronage, they have had considerable leverage in negotiating with the government.

SCB was created to break the monopoly of the British in commercial banking. Since the Thais had no expertise in this field, however, they set up SCB as a joint venture with Danish and German banks. Although the financial participation of these banks was not large, SCB had to depend on European managers until the end of the pre-war period. Post-war, a Thai became general manager, but the bank did not grow as fast as some others did. When he died in 1972, his successor was recruited from the Bank of Thailand, and under his management, the bank expanded more rapidly and now ranks as the fourth largest commercial bank in the country.

Today SCC is not merely a cement producer. Besides being the largest cement producer, it is also a holding company with investments in various industrial fields. The companies it controls constitute the Siam Cement group.

This group can be divided into five subgroups. One is the construction material group, which consists of Siam Fibre-Cement (producer of asbestos cement products), Concrete Products and Aggregate, Siam Iron and Steel, and Thai Ceramic. Another is the machinery subgroup, which consists of Siam Nawaloha Foundry and Siam Kubota Diesel. The third is the pulp and paper subgroup, which consists of Siam Kraft Paper, Thai Paper, and Thai Container. The fourth is the trading subgroup, which consists of SCT, International

Engineering, and Pan Supplies. The last subgroup includes all other companies, namely SCG Corp., Siam Tyre Co., and Thai Polyethylene Co.

Until the late 1950s, diversification was confined to cement-related products. However, in 1960, SCC went into iron and steel, and this department became independent as Siam Iron and Steel in 1965. In the same year, SCC went into production of paper products. Then in the second half of the 1970s, the two companies in the machinery subgroup were set up. In the last few years, Siam Nawaloha Foundry has become the major partner for Japanese motor vehicle manufacturers who want to produce engines in Thailand for export. Also, in the second half of the 1970s, the trading division of the group was reorganized. In 1978, a former concrete marketing company was reorganized as SCT, subscribing to the government's drive to create international trading companies like Japanese sogo shosha. *References*: King (1984); *BIT*, September 1976 and January 1986; Chatthip Nartsupha *et al.*; *Thailand Profiles 1985*; Beal; '70th Anniversary of the Siam Cement Company'; 'Towards a Brighter Tomorrow with Siam Cement'; Suehiro; *AWSJ*, 20 August 1987.

Appendix 5
A Bibliographical Note

THE major stumbling block in studying big business in South-East Asia is the paucity of information. First, printed information is scarce, especially compared with advanced countries such as Japan, where thousands of company histories and biographies and numerous business journals and newspapers are available. Second, attempts to compensate for the lack of information by interviewing prominent businessmen often fail because they are inaccessible. Questionnaire surveys are not of much help either, since most questionnaires are not returned.

There is, however, some literature on ASEAN business, and this note is an attempt to survey what is available. It is not, however, a comprehensive survey. First, in the case of magazine articles, only those which were thought to be useful for this study were included. Another problem concerns newspapers: the newspaper supplements which came to the author's attention are all included, but newspaper articles are not, since it was impossible for the author to cover them thoroughly (some newspaper companies have files of clippings on major companies and businessmen, so if one is interested in a particular company or businessman, he might approach a newspaper company instead of going through newspapers; the author sometimes used the files of the *New Straits Times* in Malaysia). Likewise, the coverage of directories is not comprehensive, but those which came to the author's attention have been listed.

Most of the references listed here are in English. There are also several in Japanese and Indonesian, and a few in Thai, Chinese, and Dutch. The coverage on Japanese and Indonesian sources may be considered to be fairly good, but that of Thai sources is poorer. However, in the Thai case, further sources are contained in some of the references listed here. There must be more Chinese and Dutch sources than have been listed, but the author has no further information at present.

Among the writings on business, those which give factual information have been included. Those which offer a theoretical framework or conceptualization but little or no factual information have been excluded.

This note is essentially an unannotated bibliography. A note is added only when the importance of a reference is not clear or the contents are not clear from the title (especially if the title is not in English).

The list below is divided by country and category. This was done for the convenience of the reader, but some classification problems arose. They were settled in the following way:

a) Writings on the pre-war period that cover Singapore and Peninsular Malaysia without particular emphasis on either are put under 'Malaya'. Those covering the Netherlands East Indies and Malaya were put under both 'Indonesia' and 'Malaya'. Those about a particular company operating in more than one country were put under the country where its head office (or regional headquarters) is or was located.

b) Not all references listed under 'company histories' are what one might expect from the classification. One of them, for example, explains largely how the company operates and why it was established, for public relations purposes, but since it includes the word 'history' in its title and deals with company history to some extent, it was put in this category. Another consists largely of short profiles of former company directors.

c) There is some ambiguity in the distinction between the following categories: company histories, biographies, books, and other publications. 'Company histories' includes only books dealing with a particular company. (If it is not in book form, it appears under another category.) If a book deals with only the founder of a company, it is put under 'biographies', but if it deals with more than one person related to a company, it is put under 'company histories'. All other books appear under 'books'. In some cases, it was not clear whether a publication could be considered as a book. Government and semi-government publications are usually put under 'other publications'.

d) 'Academic papers' includes articles in academic journals, conference papers, chapters in books, and discussion papers.

Company Histories

The Philippines

Aboitiz & Co., *The Story of Aboitiz & Co., Inc., and the Men behind It*, Cebu, 1973.

Maria Colayco, *The Ropemakers: The Story of Manila Cordage Co.*, Makati, Manila Cordage Co., 1975.

____, *Seeds and Suds: The History of Philippine Refining Company*, Manila, Philippine Refining Co., 1978.

____, *A Tradition of Leadership: Bank of the Philippine Islands*, Makati, Bank of the Philippine Islands, 1984.

Ed. de Jesus, *Fit at Fifty: 1931–1981, Engineering Equipment, Inc.*, Makati, Engineering Equipment, Inc., 1981.

____, *The Amon Story*, Makati, Amon Trading Corp., 1978.

____, *Benguet Consolidated, Inc. 1903–1978, A Brief History*, Makati, Benguet Consolidated, Inc., 1978.

Lachica, Eduardo, *Ayala: The Philippines' Oldest Business House*, Makati, Filipinas Foundation, 1984 (reprinted in *Fookien Times Philippines Yearbook 1984–85*).

Manila Electric Co., *Manila Electric Company: A Brief History*, Metro Manila, 1976.

Emili Raventos, *La Compania General de Tabacos de Filipinas, 1881–1981*, Barcelona, La Compania General de Tabacos de Filipinas, 1981. (This is a fairly comprehensive history of Tabacalera.)

San Miguel Brewery, Inc., *Golden Jubilee, 1890–1940*, Manila, 1940.

Under Four Flags: The Story of Smith, Bell & Co. in the Philippines, n.d.

Bernardo Villegas, *Strategies for Crisis: The Story of the Philippine National Oil Company*, [Manila], Center for Research & Communication, 1983.

Thailand

How It Happened: A History of the Bangkok Bank Ltd., Bangkok, Bangkok Bank, 1981.

Malaysia

Doh Joon Chien, *Public Bank: Entrepreneurship and Corporate Citizenship*, Kuala Lumpur, Public Bank Berhad, 1987.

Eric Jennings, *Wheels of Progress: 75 Years of Cycle and Carriage*, Singapore, Meridian Communications, 1975.

One Hundred Years as East India Merchants: Harrisons and Crosfield, 1844–1943, London, 1943.

Public Bank Group: 15th Anniversary, 1966–1981, Kuala Lumpur, 1981.

Singapore

Sjovald Cunyngham-Brown, *The Traders: A Story of Britain's South-East Asian Commercial Adventure*, London, Newman Neame, 1971. (This is a story of Guthrie and Co.)

1883–1983: The Great Years, Singapore, Fraser & Neave, 1983.

The First Hundred Years of the Post Office Savings Bank of Singapore, Singapore, 1977.

Growing with Singapore, Singapore, United Overseas Bank, 1985.

Stephanie Jones, *Two Centuries of Overseas Trading: The Origins and Growth of the Inchcape Group*, London, Macmillan, 1986.

Henry Longhurst, *The Borneo Story: The History of the First 100 Years of Trading in the Far East by the Borneo Company Limited*, London, Newman Neame, 1956.

Compton Mackenzie, *Realms of Silver: One Hundred Years of Banking in the East*, London, Routledge & Kegan Paul, 1954.

Overseas Union Bank Limited, *25th Anniversary, 1949–74*, Singapore, 1974.

Sim Lim 50 Years, Singapore, Sim Lim Investments Ltd., 1983.

K. G. Tregonning, *Straits Tin: A Brief Account of the Straits Trading Company Limited, 1887–1962*, Singapore, The Straits Times Press, 1962.

_____, *Home Port Singapore: A History of Straits Steamship Co., Ltd., 1890–1965*, Singapore, Oxford University Press, 1965.

_____, *The Singapore Cold Storage 1903–1966*, Singapore, Cold Storage Holdings Ltd., 1967.

Dick Wilson, *Solid as a Rock: The First Forty Years of the Oversea-Chinese Banking Corporation*, Singapore, Oversea-Chinese Banking Corporation, 1972.

Indonesia

Bank Bumi Daya 1950–1984, Jakarta, [1984].

Bank Negara Indonesia 1946: 25 Years, Jakarta, [1971?].

Bank Negara Indonesia 1946: 5 July 1946–1981, Jakarta, [1981?].

Bank Negara Indonesia 1946: 5 July 1946–1986, Jakarta, [1986?].

Anderson Bartlett *et al.*, *Pertamina: Indonesian National Oil*, Jakarta, Amerasian, 1972.

L. de Bree, *Gedenkboek van de Javasche Bank: 1828–24.1.1928*, 2 parts, Weltevreden, G. Kolff, 1928. (This is a standard work on the history of the Java Bank.)

W. M. F. Mansvelt, *Geschiedenis van de Nederlandsche Handel-Maatschappij*, 2 vols., Haarlem, n.d. (This is the history of Netherlands Trading Co.)

Royal Dutch Petroleum Company, 1890–1950, The Hague, 1950.

Sejarah dan Perkembangan Bumiputera 1912, 1912–1982, Jakarta, Yayasan Dharma Bumiputera, 1982.

The Story of Krebet, [Semarang], Handel Maatschappij Kian Gwan, 1932.

Biographies

The Philippines

Cai Wen Hua Xian Sheng Ji Nian Ji, Manila, Don Antonio Roxas Chua Foundation, 1980. (This contains biographical data on Antonio Roxas-Chua.)

Ed. de Jesus and Carlos Quirino, *Earl Carroll: Colossus of Philippine Insurance*, Manila, The Underwriters Publications Co., 1980.

Guillermo Guevara, *Across Four Generations*, Manila, United Publishing Co., 1973.

Oscar Lopez, *The Lopez Family*, Vol. I, Pasig, Eugenio Lopez Foundation, 1982. (This gives the family tree of the Lopez family in Western Visayas. With this, for example, it is possible to see how Eugenio Lopez was related to other Lopezes who owned sugar centrals and haciendas in Western Visayas and to Lopez women who married prominent Filipino leaders in Manila.)

Baldomero Olivera, *Jose Yulo: The Selfless Statesman*, Mandaluyong, The UP-Jorge B. Vargas Filipiniana Research Center, 1981.

Carlos Quirino, 'Philippine Tycoon: The Life and Times of Vicente Madrigal', 1967 (unpublished).

_____, 'The Cojuangco Family', 1968 (unpublished).

____, 'Ayala and the Zobel Families', 1975 (unpublished).

Teofilo Reyes, *Taginting ng Kampana*, Quezon City, R.P. Garcia Publishing Co., 1973. (This is the autobiography of Teofilo Reyes, who founded Reyes Auto Supply, a manufacturer of 'Triple A' batteries.)

Malaysia

Ranjit Gill, *Khoo Teck Puat: Tycoon on a Tightrope*, Singapore, Sterling Corp. Services, 1987.

S. M. Middlebrook, 'Yap Ah Loy, 1837–1885', *Journal of the Malayan Branch of the Royal Asiatic Society*, July 1951.

Victor Morais, *Without Fear or Favour, A Biography of Tan Sri Mohd. Noah*, Kuala Lumpur, published by the author, 1976.

____, *Tun Tan: Portrait of a Statesman*, Kuala Lumpur, published by the author, 1981. (Tun Tan is Tan Siew Sin. The book does not discuss his involvement in business, but is still useful as background reading.)

Singapore

Tan Kah Kee, *Nanqiao Huiyi-lu*, Hong Kong, Caoyuan Chuban-she, 1979. (This is his autobiography. Like other books on him, this book discusses his political and social activities at great length; but at the end it also contains a section on his business career.)

C. F. Yong, *Tan Kah-kee: The Making of an Overseas Chinese Legend*, Singapore, Oxford University Press, 1987.

Indonesia

Tridah Bangun, *Dr. T. D. Pardede: Wajah Seorang Pejuang Wiraswasta*, Jakarta, Gunung Agung, 1981.

____, *Dr. T. D. Pardede 70 Tahun*, Jakarta, CV Haji Masagung, 1987.

Mara Karma, *Ibnu Sutowo*, Jakarta, Gunung Agung, 1979.

Liem Tjwan Ling, *Raja Gula: Oei Tiong Ham*, Surabaya, published by the author, 1979.

A Memorandum for Thirty Year's [sic] *Cultivation in Nanyang of Dr. Chang Yoh Shen*, privately printed, October 1921 (in Chinese). (This book describes the life and accomplishments of Tjong A Fie. There is a short summary in Dutch.)

Magazines

The Philippines

The Philippines has a long history of journalism, in the course of which too many magazine articles have been written to list them all, so the names of the magazines worth going through are first listed, with some comments.

Industrial Philippines. (This magazine was started by the Philippine Chamber of Industry, and often gives profiles of people who were active in post-war industrialization.)

American Chamber of Commerce Journal. (Started in the 1920s, this journal is an important source of information on American businesses in the Philippines. It also covers some Filipino people and companies. The August 1938 issue contains a good write-up on Gonzalo Puyat, and the February 1965 issue, a good profile of Joaquin Miguel Elizalde.)

Sugar News. (This magazine was also started in the early 1920s. Concerned primarily with the sugar industry, to some extent it also covers people who are linked to the industry through buying and selling. Some of the older issues afford a good glimpse of people who were normally publicity-shy. The June 1940 issue, for example, contains a good profile of Ysidra Cojuangco, the main architect of the Cojuangco empire.)

Philippine Journal of Commerce. (The September 1933 issue contains an article on prominent Filipino business leaders such as Leopoldo Aguinaldo, Luis Yangco, Teodoro Yangco, Ramon Fernandez, and Toribio Teodoro.)

Philippine business also receives coverage abroad. The following is a select list of articles which have appeared in foreign magazines.

'Bancom: Bankers' Banker', *Insight*, April 1973.

Dan Coggin, 'Herminio Disini: Friends in High Places', *Insight*, February 1978.

'Cuenca Flees Overseas', *Insight*, September 1979.

John Osborne, 'The Business Passions of Andres Soriano', *Fortune Magazine*, March 1956.

John Peace, 'The Bank and the Philippines', *StanChart Magazine*, April 1985.

Thailand

The past decade or so has seen an increasing number of magazine articles on Thai business. The magazines in English worth going through are *Business in Thailand, Business Review, Who's Who in Thailand* (publication of which ceased in October 1982), *Investor* (which was renamed *ASEAN Investor* in 1982), *Thailand Business*, and *Thai–American Business* (the journal of the American Chamber of Commerce in Thailand). In Japanese, the monthly *Shoho* published by the Japanese Chamber of Commerce in Bangkok is also worth going through. Noteworthy among these magazine articles are 'The Empire Builders', by Peter Beal in *Investor*, February and March 1981, and the series of articles on Thai Chinese by Hiizumi Katsuo in *Shoho*, March 1984–October 1985.

Foreign magazines have also begun giving coverage to Thai business. One such article is Rob Salamon, 'Chin Sophonpanich: The Bangkok Connection', *Insight*, June 1978.

Malaysia

Ian Gill, 'Lim Uses Gambling Profits to Expand Genting', *Insight*, June 1980.

'Interview: Datuk Eric Chia of United Motor Works', *Malaysian Business*, January 1973.

'Interview: Senator Datuk Syed Kechik bin Syed Mohamed', *Malaysian Business*, July 1975.

Khoo Hock Aun, 'Tan Sri Lim Goh Tong: Long, Hard Climb to Success', *Malaysian Business*, March 1981.

'Kuok Connections', *Far Eastern Economic Review*, 30 October 1986.

Peter Lee, 'Banking for the People: The Story of Malayan Banking Limited', *Singapore Trade & Industry*, September 1965.

'The Malaysian Equation' (advertisement), *Fortune*, 28 December 1981.

'The Man who Brought the Honda to Malaysia', *Malaysian Business*, January 1974. (This is an article on Loh Boon Siew in Penang.)

Ng Poh Tip, 'The Amazing Tun Sir Henry H. S. Lee', *Malaysian Business*, July 1980.

Ngam Su May, 'Azman Hashim: A Dream Realized', *Malaysian Business*, November 1982.

'Personality Profile: Datuk Haji Ibrahim bin Mohamed', *Malaysian Business*, January 1978.

'Personality Profile: Azman Hashim', *Malaysian Business*, August 1978.

'Petronas: More Fuel for Growth', *Malaysian Business*, 16 August 1984.

M. G. G. Pillai, 'Ecstasy at UMW over Eric Chia's Toyota Coup', *Insight*, December 1981.

'PNB: On the Road to 1990', *Malaysian Business*, January 1982.

'Promet Plunges into Property Market, Oil Prospecting', *Insight*, February 1982.

Ian Verchere, 'The Changing World of Robert Kuok', *Insight*, August 1978.

Singapore

Robert Cottrell, 'Keeping Business in the Extended Family', *Far Eastern Economic Review*, 5 December 1985. (This article is about Hong Leong Finance and other businesses of the Kwek family.)

Ian Gill, 'The Challenge from Wee Cho Yaw's UOB', *Insight*, May 1980.

Margo Gill, '40 Years of Progress (Ford Motor in Singapore)', *Singapore Trade & Industry*, July 1966.

Ranjit Gill, 'OCBC: On Course with Banking Baron TCT at the Helm', *Insight*, September 1982. (TCT is Tan Chin Tuan.)

——, 'KTP: The All-weather Banker Runs His Rivals to the Ground', *Insight*, May 1983. (KTP is Khoo Teck Puat.)

——, 'The Super Duper Rich', *Insight*, December 1983. (This article gives a profile of rich people in various countries in Asia.)

Iwasaki Ikuo, 'Futatsu no Kajin Kigyo-ka: Meimon Ginko OCBC to Kindai Gijutsu YHS', *Ajiken News*, No. 74 (1986).

'Reaching for the Sky with United behind Him', *Insight*, March 1983. (This is an article on Wee Cho Yaw.)

Barun Roy, 'Promet's Brian Chang: Pioneer and Pace-setter', *Asia Finance*, November 1984.

Rob Salamon, 'The Secret World of Robin Loh', *Insight*, March 1978.

Ilsa Sharp, 'The "Show-Biz" King of South-East Asia', *Singapore Trade & Industry*, May/June 1969. (This is an article on the Shaw brothers.)

Indonesia

'Bagaimana Mereka Jadi Kaya Raya', *Fokus*, 10 May 1984.

Amitabha Chowdhury, 'Mochtar Riady: The Master Builder of an Asian Banking Empire', *Asia Finance*, September 1983.

——, 'William Takes Astra Back to Grassroots', *Asia Finance*, November 1983.

'Daftar Perusahaan Raksasa Indonesia', *Fokus*, 12 April 1984.

'Liem Sioe Liong: Suharto's Secret Agent', *Insight*, May 1978.

'Mengenal Perusahaan Raksasa Indonesia', *Fokus*, 5 April 1984.

James Michener, 'Chinese Success Story', *Life*, 31 December 1951. (This is an article on Kian Gwan.)

Mihira Norio, 'Kokusai-ka ni Mukau Liem Sioe Liong Gurupu', *Ajiken News*, No. 74 (1986).

Anthony Rowley, 'Birth of a Multinational', *Far Eastern Economic Review*, 7 April 1983. (This article gives an overview on Liem Sioe Liong's business empire.)

PN Sondang, '100 Milyarder Indonesia: Apa & Siapa Mereka?', *Expo*, 4 January and 18 January 1984. (This article discusses 44 wealthy Chinese businessmen, but is full of mistakes. A great deal of caution has to be exercised to use it as a source of information.)

Barry Wain, 'Pertamina and the Incredible World of Ibnu Sutowo', *Insight*, October 1976.

Academic Papers

The Philippines

Mary Grace Ampil-Tirona, 'Financial Entrepreneurship and Monopoly Capitalism', A paper presented at the 6th National Conference on Local-National History (11 December 1984, University of the Philippines). (This paper discusses the Filipino-owned commercial banks of the pre-war period and the people behind them.)

Marcelino Foronda, 'Eusebio S. Garcia and the Chemical Industries of the Philippines', *Anuaryo/Annales*, Vol. 3, No. 1 (1984–5).

H. Parker Lewis, 'The Philippine National Bank', *Journal of Political Economy*, May 1917.

Tsuda Mamoru, 'Firipin ni okeru Kindaiteki Kogyo no Hatten to Shinko Zaibatsu no Keisei', in Ito Teiichi, ed., *Tonan Ajia ni okeru Kogyo Keieisha no Seisei*, Tokyo, Ajia Keizai Kenkyu-sho, 1980. (This is an article on Ricardo Silverio before his collapse.)

Roy Ybanez, 'The Hongkong Bank in the Philippines, 1899–1941', in Frank King, ed., *Eastern Banking: Essays in the History of the Hongkong and Shanghai Banking Corporation*, London, The Athlone Press, 1983.

Thailand

J. Cushman, 'The Khaw Group: Chinese Business in Early Twentieth-century Penang', *Journal of Southeast Asian Studies*, March 1986. (The Khaw group included Eastern Shipping Co., Tongkah Harbour Tin Dredging Co., and Eastern Smelting Co.)

Kevin Hewison, 'The Financial Bourgeoisie in Thailand', *Journal of Contemporary Asia*, Vol. 11, No. 4 (1981).

Ito Teiichi, 'Taikoku Sen'i Sangyo ni okeru Ishoku no Keieisha', in Ito Teiichi, ed., *Tonan Ajia ni okeru Kogyo Keieisha no Seisei*, Tokyo, Ajia Keizai Kenkyu-sho, 1980. (This article deals with the early years of Sukri Bodhiratanangkura.)

Ichikawa Kenjiro, 'Chou Ran Shin to Gekido-ki no Tai Kakyo', *Southeast Asian Studies*, December 1970. (This paper discusses Sahat Mahaguna.)

Frank King, 'Foreign Exchange Banks in Siam, 1888–1918 and the National Bank Question', *Proceedings* of the International Conference on Thai Studies, 22–24 August 1984, Bangkok, Vol. 1.

Krirkkiat Phipatheritham and Kunio Yoshihara, 'Business Groups in Thailand', Research Notes and Discussions Paper No. 41, Singapore, Institute of Southeast Asian Studies, 1983.

Malaya

Tan Ee Leong, 'The Chinese Banks Incorporated in Singapore and the Federation of Malaya', in T. H. Silcock, ed., *Readings in Malayan Economics*, Singapore, Eastern Universities Press, 1961.

Malaysia

Chee Peng Lim *et al.*, 'The History and Development of the Hongkong and Shanghai Banking Corporation in Peninsular Malaysia', in Frank King, ed., *Eastern Banking: Essays in the History of the Hongkong and Shanghai Banking Corporation*, London, The Athlone Press, 1983.

J. Cushman, 'The Khaw Group: Chinese Business in Early Twentieth-century Penang', *Journal of Southeast Asian Studies*, March 1986. (The Khaw group included Eastern Shipping Co., Tongkah Harbour Tin Dredging Co., and Eastern Smelting Co.)

J. Drabble and P. Drake, 'The British Agency Houses in Malaysia: Survival in a Changing World', *Journal of Southeast Asian Studies*, September 1981.

Singapore

G. Bogaars, 'The Tanjong Pagar Dock Company, 1864–1905', *Memoirs of the Raffles Museum*, II (1956). (The Tanjong Pagar Dock Company was a large private company until 1905 when it was taken over by the Colonial Administration.)

Saruwatari Keiko, 'Igirisu Shosha no Keiei Senryaku to Soshiki: Guthrie & Co. no Jirei (1821–1981)', *Keiei Shigaku*, Vol. 17, No. 4 (1983).

Lim How Seng, 'Tan Kah Kee's Business Philosophy and Corporate Management', *Journal of Humanities and Social Sciences* (Singapore), Vol. VI (1986) (in Chinese).

———, 'The Business Empire of Lee Kong Chian', *Asian Culture* (Singapore), April 1987 (in Chinese).

Tan Ee Leong, 'Biography of Lee Kong Chian', *Journal of the South Seas Society*, Parts 1 and 2, 1967 (in Chinese).

K. G. Tregonning, 'Straits Tin: A Brief Account of the First Seventy-Five Years of the Straits Trading Company Ltd.', *Journal of the Malaysian Branch of Royal Asiatic Society*, May 1963.

———, 'The Origin of the Straits Steamship Company in 1890', *Journal of the Malaysian Branch of the Royal Asiatic Society*, July 1966.

———, 'Tan Cheng Lock: A Malayan Nationalist', *Journal of Southeast Asian Studies*, Part 1, 1979.

Indonesia

Charles Coppel, 'Liem Thian Joe's Unpublished History of Kian Gwan (Oei Tiong Ham Concern)' (unpublished).

J. Panglaykim and I. Palmer, 'Study of Entrepreneurship in Developing Countries: The Development of One Chinese Concern in Indonesia', *Journal of Southeast Asian Studies*, March 1970. (This article discusses the evolution of Kian Gwan, a large conglomerate founded by Oei Tiong Ham in the pre-war period.)

Tjoa, Soe Tjong, 'OTHC: 100 Jaar—Een Stukje Economische Geschiedenis van Indonesia', *Economische-Statistische Berichten*, June 1963. (This is a 100-year history of Oei Tiong Ham Concern.)

J. T. M. Van Laanen, 'A Preliminary Look at the Role of the Hongkong Bank in Netherlands India', in Frank King, ed., *Eastern Banking: Essays in the History of the Hongkong and Shanghai Banking Corporation*, London, The Athlone Press, 1983.

Newspaper Supplements

The Philippines

'Business Profile: Carlos Palanca, Jr.', Special Report of *The Manila Chronicle*, 6 September 1970.

'Business Profile: Jesus S. Cabarrus, Sr.', *Chronicle* Special Report, 10 March 1970.

'China Banking Corporation: Golden Anniversary', *Chronicle* Business Report, 16 August 1970.

'China Banking Corporation: 60th Year', Supplement to *Times Journal*, 16 August 1980.

Chronicle Magazine (A Special Issue on Albino Z. Sycip), 17 December 1967.

'The Life and Career of Don Andres Soriano', Special Issue of *The Manila Chronicle*, 30 September 1966.

'The Life and Career of Don Antonio De Las Alas, Sr.', Special Issue of *The Manila Chronicle*, 15 October 1968.

'The Life and Career of Don Carlos Palanca, Sr.', Special Issue of *The Manila Chronicle*, 31 December 1968.

'The Life and Career of Earl D. Carroll', Special Issue of *The Manila Chronicle*, 27 September 1970.

'The Life and Career of Don Francisco B. Ortigas, Sr.', Special Issue of *The Manila Chronicle*, 24 October 1969.

'The Life and Career of Gerald Hugh Wilkinson', Special Issue of *The Manila Chronicle*, 29 November 1968.

'The Life and Career of Don Gonzalo Puyat', Special Issue of *The Manila Chronicle*, 31 May 1967.

'The Life and Career of Don Jose Yulo', Special Issue of *The Manila Chronicle*, 31 March 1969.

'The Life and Career of Don Manuel Elizalde', Special Issue of *The Manila Chronicle*, 31 January 1968.

'The Life and Career of Don Nicarnor S. Jacinto, Sr.', Special Issue of *The Manila Chronicle*, 15 June 1968.

Thailand

'Bangkok's Newest Landmark: Bangkok Bank's New Head Office', Supplement to *Bangkok Post*, 16 February 1982.

'Centaco Group of Companies: A 12 Year Success Story', Supplement to *Bangkok Post*, 12 October 1981.

'Central Department Store Lardprao Grand Opening', Supplement to *Nation*, 30 April 1983.

'Central Plaza', Supplement to *Bangkok Post*, 11 October 1982.

'80th Anniversary: Osothsapha (Teck Heng Yoo) Co. Ltd.', Supplement to *Bangkok Post*, 27 January 1980.

'40 Years of Bangkok Bank', Publication of *Nation Review*, December 1984.

'The Hongkong Bank Yesterday', Supplement to *Bangkok Post*, 2 August 1977.

'Saha Union Corp., Ltd. New Head Office', Supplement to *Nation*, 20 October 1982.

'70th Anniversary of the Siam Cement Company', Supplement to *Nation*, 8 December 1983.

'Standard Chartered: A New Name in Asia', Supplement to *Nation Review*, 8 January 1985.

'Thai Farmers Bank: Grand Opening of New Head Office', Supplement to *Bangkok Post*, 7 February 1983.

'Thai Farmers Bank: 40th Anniversary', Publication of *Nation Review*, [1985].

'30th Anniversary, Siam Motors Co. Ltd.', Supplement to *Bangkok Post*, 4 September 1982.

'Towards a Brighter Tomorrow with Siam Cement', Supplement to *Bangkok Post*, 23 July 1981.

Directories

The Philippines

The Commercial and Industrial Manual of the Philippines, Manila, Publishers, Inc., 1938.

Cornejo's Commonwealth Directory of the Philippines, Manila, 1939.

Corporate Profile, Quezon City, Business Day, 1981.

Demetrio Flaviano, *Business Leaders and Executives: Inspiring Biographies of Men and Women who Became Successful,* Manila, Fal Service and Trading Co., 1950.

S. H. Gwekoh, *Distinguished 100: The Book of Eminent Alumni of the University of the Philippines,* Manila, Apo Book Co., 1939.

Rodrigo Lim, ed., *Who's Who in the Philippines (Chinese Edition),* Quezon City, University of the Philippines Press, 1930.

E. Aresenio Manuel, *Dictionary of Philippine Biography,* Vol. I, Quezon City, Filipiniana Publications, 1955, and Vol. II, Quezon City, Filipiniana Publications, 1970.

George Nellist, ed., *Men of the Philippines,* Manila, Sugar News, 1931.

The Outstanding Leaders of the Philippines, 1980, Manila, Asia Research Systems, Inc. and Press Foundation of Asia, n.d.

Pioneers of Philippine Businessmen: 1935, 2nd ed., Manila, Rojadi Publishing Company, 1934.

Eliseo Quirino, *NEPA Handbook,* Manila, National Economic Protectionism Association, 1938.

D. H. Soriano and Isidro Retizos, eds., *The Philippines Who's Who,* 2nd ed., Makati, Who's Who Publishers, 1981.

Tableau: Encyclopedia of Distinguished Personalities in the Philippines, Manila, National Souvenir Publications, 1957.

Olimpio Villasin, *Tops in Philippine Business,* Manila, Superprom, 1962.

Frank Weissblatt, ed., *Who's Who in the Philippines,* Manila, Ramon Roces, Inc., 1937.

Thailand

Directory of Thailand's 1000 Largest Companies, 1979–1981, Bangkok, Faculty of Commerce and Accountancy, Thammasat University, n.d.

Million Baht Business Information Thailand 1986, Bangkok, International Business Research (Thailand), n.d.

Thailand Profiles 1985, Bangkok, A. Tawanna Publications, n.d.

Who's Who: Finance & Banking in Thailand, 1981–1982, Bangkok, Advance Media Co., n.d.

Malaysia

Historical Personalities of Penang, Penang, The Historical Personalities of Penang Committee, 1986.

Who's Who in Malaysia & Singapore 1983–4: Vol. 1, Malaysia, Petaling Jaya, Who's Who Publications Sdn. Bhd., 1983. (Only a few businessmen are covered. Practically all Chinese businessmen are missing.)

Yap Koon See, ed., *Who's Who in Malaysian Business & Directory (1985–86)*, Kuala Lumpur, Budayamas Sdn. Bhd., 1985. (This gives profiles of practically all major Chinese businessmen in Malaysia today. More information is given in Chinese than in English.)

Singapore

Victor Sim, comp., *Biographies of Prominent Chinese in Singapore*, Singapore, Nan Kok Publication Co., 1950. (This gives good profiles of many prominent Chinese businessmen in Singapore at the time of its publication.)

Who's Who in Malaysia & Singapore 1983–4: Vol. II, Singapore, Petaling Jaya, Who's Who Publications Sdn. Bhd., 1983. (Coverage of businessmen is poor, but this is the only biographical directory available for the contemporary period.)

Indonesia

Apa & Siapa: Sejumlah Orang Indonesia 1985–1986, Jakarta, Tempo, 1986.

Gunseikanbu, *Orang Indonesia yang Termuka di Java*, reprinted Yogyakarta, Gadjah Mada University Press, 1986.

The Indonesian Military Leaders: Biographical and Other Background Data, 2nd ed., Jakarta, Sritua Arief Associates, 1979.

Leo Suryadinata, *Eminent Indonesian Chinese: Biographical Sketches*, Singapore, Institute of Southeast Asian Studies, 1978.

Orang-Orang Tionghoa jang Terkemoeka di Java, Solo, The Biographical Publishing Centre, 1935. (This is a directory of well-known Chinese in the 1930s.)

Who's Who in Indonesia, Jakarta, Gunung Agung, 1971.

Who's Who in Indonesia, 2nd ed., Jakarta, Gunung Agung, 1980. (Coverage of businessmen in these *Who's Who* is poor. For those who can read Indonesian, *Apa & Siapa* is much better.)

Who's Who in Indonesian Business, 2nd ed., Jakarta, Sritua Arief Associates, 1976. (Mainly small businessmen are included.)

Books

The Philippines

Central Bank of the Philippines, *Central Bank of the Philippines: January 3, 1949–January 3, 1974*, Manila, 1974. (This book discusses the early years of several commercial banks.)

Lewis Gleeck, *American Business and Philippine Economic Development*, Manila, Carmelo & Bauermann, 1975.

——, *The Manila Americans (1901–1964)*, Manila, Carmelo & Bauermann, 1977.

Abraham Hartendorp, *History of Industry and Trade of the Philippines*, Manila, American Chamber of Commerce of the Philippines, 1958.

——, *History of Industry and Trade of the Philippines: The Magsaysay Administration*, Manila, Philippine Education Co., 1961.

Carlos Quirino, *History of the Philippine Sugar Industry*, Manila, Kalayaan Publishing Company, 1974. (This book discusses a number of sugar centrals.)

Rigoberto Tiglao, *The Philippine Coconut Industry*, [Manila], ARC Publication, 1981. (This explains the formation of United Coconut Planters' Bank and United Coconut Oil Mills (UNICOM).)

Yoshihara Kunio, *Philippine Industrialization: Foreign and Domestic Capital*, Quezon City, Ateneo de Manila University Press, and Singapore, Oxford University Press, 1985. (This book discusses large manufacturing companies around 1970 and the people behind them.)

Thailand

Chuphong Maningi, *Chiwit 25 Mahasetthi: Chuthhi 2*, Bangkok, Kanngoenthanakhan, 1986. (This book gives profiles of 25 leading businessmen.)

Lysa Hong, *Thailand in the Nineteenth Century: Evolution of the Economy and Society*, Singapore, Institute of Southeast Asian Studies, 1984. (This book discusses a few Chinese bureaucratic capitalists of the nineteenth century.)

Krirkkiat Phipatheritham, *Wikhro Laksana Kanpenchaokhong Thurakit Khanatyai Nai Prathetthai*, Bangkok, Faculty of Economics, Thammasat University, 1982. (This book is the first comprehensive book on Thai business groups. Some of its main features appear also in Krirkkiat Phipatheritham and Kunio Yoshihara, 'Business Groups in Thailand', Research Notes and Discussions Paper No. 41, Singapore, Institute of Southeast Asian Studies, 1983.)

Mary Laugesen *et al.*, *Scandinavians in Siam*, [Bangkok], [1980]. (This book gives a short history of East Asiatic Co.)

Phaanachak Thurakit 25 Trakun Mahasetthi, 2nd ed., Bangkok, Samapharn, n.d. (This book gives profiles of 25 leading businessmen. Chuphong's book is, in a way, a follow-up of this.)

Sirilak Sakkriangkrai, *Ton Kamnoed Khong Chonchan Naithun Nai Prathet Thai (B.E. 2398–2453)*, Bangkok, Sang San, 1980. (This book discusses several Chinese bureaucratic capitalists in the late Chulalongkorn period.)

Akira Suehiro, *Capital Accumulation and Industrial Development in Thailand*, Bangkok, Chulalongkorn University, 1985. (This book discusses a number of Western companies, Chinese businessmen, and contemporary business groups. It also contains a comprehensive bibliography on Thai businesses.)

A. Wright, ed., *Twentieth Century Impressions of Siam*, London, Lloyd's Greater Britain Publishing Co., 1908. (The section on Chinese enterprises and businessmen is useful.)

Malaya

G. C. Allen and Audrey Donnithorne, *Western Enterprise in Indonesia and Malaya*, London, George Allen & Unwin, 1954.

W. Feldwick, ed., *Present Day Impressions of the Far East and Prominent & Progressive Chinese at Home and Abroad*, London, The Globe Encyclopedia Co., 1917. (One section gives profiles of various Chinese businessmen in Malaya in the 1910s.)

Michael Godley, *The Mandarin-capitalists from Nanyang*, Cambridge, Cambridge University Press, 1981. (This book discusses rich Chinese in the Netherlands East Indies and British Malaya who contributed to the development of the Chinese economy in the late Chi'ng period.)

A. Wright, ed., *Twentieth Century Impressions of British Malaya*, London, Lloyd's Greater Britain Publishing Co., 1908. (The section on Chinese enterprises and businessmen is useful.)

Malaysia

Bruce Gale, *Politics and Public Enterprise in Malaysia*, Singapore, Eastern Universities Press, 1981.

____, *Politics & Business: A Study of Multi-Purpose Holdings Berhad*, Singapore, Eastern Universities Press, 1985.

Ranjit Gill, *The Making of Malaysia Inc.*, Petaling Jaya, Pelanduk Publications, 1985. (This book discusses a number of prominent Malaysian (Chinese and bumiputra) businessmen and their businesses in the contemporary period.)

J. M. Gullick, *The Story of Kuala Lumpur (1857–1939)*, Singapore, Eastern Universities Press, 1983. (This book contains some information on Eu Tong Sen, which cannot be found anywhere else.)

Ed Hunter, *Misdeeds of Tun Mustapha*, [Hong Kong?], Ed Hunter Enterprise, [1976]. (This book is banned in Malaysia. It discusses how money was made in Sabah by Mustapha and his Political Secretary, Syed Kechik.)

Lim Mah Hui, *Ownership and Control of the One Hundred Largest Corporations in Malaysia*, Kuala Lumpur, Oxford University Press, 1981.

Bruce Ross-Larson, *The Politics of Federalism: Syed Kechik in East Malaysia*, Singapore, published by the author, 1976.

Supriya Singh, *Bank Negara Malaysia: The First 25 Years, 1959–1984*, Kuala Lumpur, Bank Negara Malaysia, 1984. (This book discusses the early years of UMBC, Malayan Banking Berhad, and other commercial banks.)

Singapore

Ranjit Gill, *George Tan: The Carrian Saga*, Petaling Jaya, Pelanduk Publications, 1985.

Song Ong Siang, *One Hundred Years' History of the Chinese in Singapore*, reprinted Singapore, Oxford University Press, 1984. (This book discusses numerous prominent Chinese businessmen up to the 1910s.)

Yap Pheng Geck, *Scholar, Banker, Gentleman Soldier*, Singapore, Times

Books International, 1982. (In one section, the author discusses his career at OCBC and Chinese banking in the pre-war period.)

Indonesia

G. C. Allen and Audrey Donnithorne, *Western Enterprise in Indonesia and Malaya*, London, George Allen & Unwin, 1954.

Queeny Chang, *Memories of a Nonya*, Singapore, Eastern Universities Press, 1981. (Queeny Chang is the daughter of Tjong A Fie.)

W. Feldwick, ed., *Present Day Impressions of the Far East and Prominent & Progressive Chinese at Home and Abroad*, London, The Globe Encyclopedia Co., 1917. (One section gives profiles of prominent Chinese businessmen in the Netherlands East Indies in the late 1910s.)

Michael Godley, *The Mandarin-capitalists from Nanyang*, Cambridge, Cambridge University Press, 1981. (This book discusses rich Chinese in the Netherlands East Indies and British Malaya who contributed to the development of the Chinese economy in the late Chi'ng period.)

Hui-lan Koo (Madame Wellington Koo), *An Autobiography as told to Mary Van Rensselaer Thayer*, New York, Dial Press, 1943. (Hui-lan Koo is Oei Tiong Ham's daughter, Oei Hui-lan. Part of this book records her reminiscences of life with her father in Java.)

Mrs Wellington Koo and Isabella Taves, *No Feast Lasts Forever*, New York, Quadrangle, 1975.

Richard Robison, *Indonesia: The Rise of Capital*, North Sydney, Allen & Unwin, 1986. (This book is an important source of information on entrepreneurs in the post-war years, especially those during the Benteng and Guided Economy periods. It also has a good discussion on the businesses owned by the military.)

John Sutter, *Indonesianisasi; Politics in Changing Economy, 1940–1955*, Data Paper No. 36, Southeast Asian Program, Cornell University, 1959. (This book contains data on business in Indonesia around 1940 and in the early post-war years.)

A. Wright, ed., *Twentieth Century Impressions of Netherlands India*, London, Lloyd's Greater Britain Publishing Co., 1909. (The section on Chinese enterprises and businessmen is useful.)

Theses

The Philippines

Marietta Jayme, 'Andres Soriano, Sr.', Master of Business Management thesis, De La Salle University, 1972.

Mariano Marante, 'Corporate Strategy for Associated Anglo-American Tobacco Corporation', Master of Management thesis, Asian Institute of

Management, 1979. (This thesis also discusses La Perla and La Suerte, major cigarette companies around 1970.)

Demetrio Ruiz, Jr., 'Teodoro Rafael Yangco: His Life and Business Career (1861–1939)', MA thesis, University of Santo Tomas, 1975.

Samuel Seidman, 'Enterprise and Entrepreneurship in the Philippine Republic, 1949–1959', Ph.D. thesis, New York University, 1963. (This thesis contains a great deal of information on Filipino entrepreneurs, such as Salvador Araneta, Tuasons, and Ramon del Rosario, who were active in the 1950s. It also discusses the Chinese entrepreneur, James Huang, and the American businessman, Harry Stonehill.)

Thailand

Sungsidh Piriyarangsan, 'Thai Bureaucratic Capitalism, 1932–1960', Master of Economics thesis, Thammasat University, 1980. (This thesis discusses various bureaucratic capitalists from the mid-nineteenth century to the early 1960s.)

Singapore

Lee Poh Ping, 'Chinese Society in Nineteenth and Early Twentieth Century Singapore: A Socioeconomic Analysis', Ph.D. thesis, Cornell University, 1974. (The appendix contains profiles of prominent merchants at the turn of this century.)

Other Publications

The Philippines

A. Soriano Corp., '1980 Annual Report'. (This gives a good profile of Andres Soriano, Sr.)

Bankers Association of the Philippines, *History of Banking in the Philippines*, Manila, 1957. (This discusses the history of several commercial banks.)

Caltex (Phil.), 'Caltex in the Philippines: Pathway to Progress', [Manila], [1981].

Renato Emata, *Coconut Processing*, Vol. II, Manila, United Coconut Association of the Philippines, April 1971.

The Hongkong and Shanghai Banking Corporation, 'The History of the Hongkong Bank, Manila', [Makati], [1985].

'Some are Smarter than Others', [Metro Manila], [1979], (unpublished). (This underground paper circulated in 1979. It gives profiles of a number of former President Marcos's cronies.)

'Victorias Milling Company, Inc. 1919–1979, 60th Anniversary'.

The Zaibatsu in the Philippines, A study prepared for Japan Trade Center in Makati, August 1977.

Malaya

United States Department of Commerce, *Netherlands East Indies and British Malaya: A Commercial and Industrial Handbook*, Washington, Government Printing Office, 1923.

Malaysia

Chusho Kigyo Jigyo-dan, *Chusho Kigyo Kaigai Toshi Partners Chosa: Malaysia*, March 1982. (This is not as good as the work on Indonesia in the same series, but contains useful information on Tunku Abdullah and his Melewar group.)

Indonesia

Chusho Kigyo Jigyo-dan, *Chusho Kigyo Kaigai Toshi Partners Chosa: Indonesia*, 1981.
____, *Chusho Kigyo Kaigai Toshi Partners Chosa: Indonesia (Hokan)*, 1982.
Nihon Boeki Shinko-kai, *Indonesia ni okeru Minzoku-kei Kigyo to Kajin Shihon*, 1975. (These three Japanese sources give fairly detailed information on a number of Indonesian business élites, and are the most useful sources of factual information on major business élites in Indonesia.)
United States Department of Commerce, *Netherlands East Indies and British Malaya: A Commercial and Industrial Handbook*, Washington, Government Printing Office, 1923.

Oral History

The Philippines

Michael Onorato, interviewer and ed., 'Salvador Araneta: Reflections of a Filipino Exile', The Oral History Program, California State University, Fullerton, 1979.

Singapore

In the Pioneers of Singapore Project, many prominent businessmen and their close relatives were interviewed in the period from January 1980 to February 1984, and many of the transcripts of the tapes taken in the interviews are available for public inspection. The names of those interviewed and the contents of the interviews are published in *Pioneers of Singapore: A Catalogue of Oral History Interviews*, Singapore, Archives & Oral History Department, 1984.

This source of information is important for those interested in Singapore business, partly because it is the only source of information on many of the businessmen covered by the oral history programme. The other reason is that, while much of the literature on business is for public relations purposes and gives information that is too 'shallow' to be used for analysis, this oral history programme seems to have elicited from interviewees fairly frank answers to a number of questions relating to business modernization and economic change.

Most transcripts are in English, but some are in Chinese. For Kwek Hong Png (of Hong Leong), Ng Quee Lam (a large rubber dealer), and Ong Tjoe Kim (of Metro Department Store), for example, the transcripts are in Chinese.

The transcripts are divided into two categories. Those in category A are available for public inspection and are quotable. Those in category B are available only if permission to use them is obtained from the interviewees.

Unfortunately, Singapore is the only country in the ASEAN region which has an oral history programme covering major businessmen.

Bibliography

Aboitiz & Co., *The Story of Aboitiz & Co., Inc., and the Men Behind It*, Cebu, 1973.

Adler, Jacob, *Claus Spreckels: The Sugar King in Hawaii*, Honolulu, University of Hawaii Press, 1966.

Akin Rabibhadana, *The Organization of Thai Society in the Early Bangkok Period, 1782–1873*, Data Paper, Number 74, Southeast Asian Program, Department of Asian Studies, Cornell University, July 1969.

Alburo Florian *et al.*, 'Towards Recovery and Sustainable Growth', School of Economics, University of the Philippines, September 1985.

Allen, G. C. and Donnithorne, Audrey, *Western Enterprise in Indonesia and Malaya*, London, George Allen & Unwin, 1954.

Alzona, E., trans. and ed., *Selected Essays and Letters of Jose Rizal*, Manila, Rangel & Sons, 1964.

Ampil-Tirona, Mary Grace, 'Financial Entrepreneurship and Monopoly Capitalism', Paper presented at the 6th National Conference on Local-National History (11 December 1984, University of the Philippines).

Amyot, Jacques, *The Manila Chinese: Familism in the Philippine Environment*, IPC Monographs, No. 2, Quezon City, Ateneo de Manila University, 1973.

———, *The Chinese and the National Integration in Southeast Asia*, Bangkok, Institute of Asian Studies, Chulalongkorn University, October 1972.

Anderson, Benedict, 'The Idea of Power in Javanese Culture', in Claire Holt, ed., *Culture and Politics in Indonesia*, Ithaca, Cornell University Press, 1972.

———, 'Old State, New Society: Indonesia's New Order in Comparative Historical Perspective', *Journal of Asian Studies*, May 1983.

Aquino, Belinda, 'The Philippines under Marcos: Political Decay', Paper presented at the Annual Conference of the American Political Science Association, 30 August–2 September 1984.

Apa & Siapa: Sejumla Orang Indonesia 1985–1986, Jakarta, Tempo, 1986.

A. Soriano Corporation, '1980 Annual Report'.

'Bagaimana Mereka Jadi Kaya Raya', *Fokus*, 10 May 1984.

'Bancom: Bankers' Banker', *Insight*, April 1973.

'Bangkok's Newest Landmark: Bangkok Bank's New Head Office', Supplement to *Bangkok Post*, 16 February 1982.

Bangun, Tridah, *Dr. T. D. Pardede: Wajah Seorang Pejuang Wiraswasta*, Jakarta, Gunung Agung, 1981.

____, *Dr. T. D. Pardede 70 Tahun*, Jakarta, CV Haji Masagung, 1987.

Bank Bumi Daya 1959–1984, Jakarta, [1984].

Bank Negara Indonesia 1946: 25 Years, Jakarta, [1971?].

Bank Negara Indonesia 1946: 5 July 1946–1981, Jakarta, [1981?].

Bank Negara Indonesia 1946: 5 July 1946–1986, Jakarta, [1986?].

Bank Negara Malaysia, Economics Department, *Money and Banking in Malaysia*, Kuala Lumpur, 1984.

Bankers Association of the Philippines, *History of Banking in the Philippines*, Manila, 1957.

Bartlett, Anderson G. *et al.*, *Pertamina: Indonesian National Oil*, Jakarta, Amerasian, 1972.

Barton, Clifton, 'Trust and Credit: Some Observations Regarding Business Strategies of Overseas Chinese Traders in South Vietnam', in Linda Lim and Peter Gosling, eds., *The Chinese in Southeast Asia*, Vol. 1, Singapore, Maruzen Asia, 1983.

Beal, Peter, 'The Empire Builders', *The Investor*, February and March 1981.

Behn, Meyer & Co. and Arnold Otto Meyer, Hamburg, Hans Christians Verlag, 1981.

Bello, Walden *et al.*, *Development Debacle: The World Bank in the Philippines*, San Francisco, Institute for Food and Development Policy, 1982.

BMF: The People's Black Paper, Petaling Jaya, Institute for Social Analysis, 1986.

Boeke, J. H., *Indische Economie*, Vol. 1, Haarlem, H. D. Tjeenk Willink, 1940.

Bogaars, George, 'The Effect of the Opening of the Suez Canal on the Trade and Development of Singapore', *Journal of the Malayan Branch of the Royal Asiatic Society*, Vol. 18, Pt. 1 (1955).

____, 'The Tanjong Pagar Dock Company, 1864–1905', *Memoirs of the Raffles Museum*, II (1956).

Botan, *Letters from Thailand*, translated by Susan Fulop Morell, Bangkok, D. K. Book House, 1977.

Bowring, John, *The Kingdom and People of Siam*, reprinted Kuala Lumpur, Oxford University Press, 1969.

Boxer, C. R., *The Dutch Seaborne Empire, 1600–1800*, London, Hutchinson & Co., 1965.

Braudel, Fernand, *Civilization and Capitalism, 15th–18th Century*, 3 vols., New York, Harper & Row, 1981–4.

Budiman, Arief, 'The State and Industrialization in Indonesia', July 1985 (unpublished).

'Business Profile: Carlos Palanca, Jr.', Special Report of *The Manila Chronicle*, 6 September 1970.

'Business Profile: Jesus S. Cabarrus, Sr.', *Chronicle* Special Report, 10 March 1970.

Cai Wen Hua Xian Sheng Ji Nian Ji, Manila, Don Antonio Roxas Chua Foundation, 1980.

Callis, Helmut, *Foreign Capital in Southeast Asia*, New York, Institute of Pacific Relations, 1942.

Caltex (Phil.), 'Caltex in the Philippines: Pathway to Progress', [1981] (mimeographed).

Carino, Ledivina, ed., *Bureaucratic Corruption in Asia*, Manila, College of Public Administration, University of the Philippines, 1986.

Carroll, John, *The Filipino Manufacturing Entrepreneur: Agent and Product of Change*, Ithaca, Cornell University Press, 1965.

Castles, Lance, 'Socialism and Private Business: The Latest Phase', *Bulletin of Indonesian Economic Studies*, No. 1, 1966.

_____, *Religion, Politics, and Economic Behavior in Java: The Kudus Cigarette Industry*, New Haven, Southeast Asian Studies, Yale University, 1967.

Cator, W. J., *The Economic Position of the Chinese in the Netherlands Indies*, Chicago, University of Chicago Press, 1936.

'Centaco Group of Companies: A 12 Year Success Story', Supplement to *Bangkok Post*, 12 October 1981.

Central Bank of the Philippines, *Central Bank of the Philippines: January 3, 1949–January 3, 1974*, Manila, 1974.

'Central Department Store Lardprao Grand Opening', Supplement to *Nation*, 30 April 1983.

'Central Plaza', Supplement to *Bangkok Post*, 11 October 1982.

Chang, Queeny, *Memories of a Nonya*, Singapore, Eastern Universities Press, 1981.

Charlesworth, Harold, *A Banking System in Transition*, Jakarta, The New Nusantara Publishing Coy, [1959].

Chatthip Nartsupha and Suthy Prasartset, eds., *The Political Economy of Siam, 1851–1910*, Bangkok, The Social Science Association of Thailand, n.d.

Chatthip Nartsupha *et al.*, eds., *The Political Economy of Siam, 1910–1932*, Bangkok, The Social Science Association of Thailand, [1978].

Chee, Peng Lim *et al.*, 'The History and Development of the Hongkong and Shanghai Banking Corporation in Peninsular Malaysia', in Frank King, ed., *Eastern Banking: Essays in the History of the Hongkong and Shanghai Banking Corporation*, London, The Athlone Press, 1983.

_____, 'The Proton Saga—No Reverse Gear: The Economic Burden of Malaysia's Car Project', in Jomo, ed., *The Sun Also Sets: Lessons in 'Looking East'*, Petaling Jaya, Institute for Social Analysis, 1985.

Cheng, Lim Keak, *Social Change and the Chinese in Singapore*, Singapore, Singapore University Press, 1985.

Chiang, Hai Ding, 'Sino-British Mercantile Relations in Singapore's Entrepot Trade 1870–1915', in Jerome Ch'en and Nicholas Tarling, eds., *Studies in Social History of China and South-East Asia*, Cambridge, Cambridge University Press, 1970.

_____, *A History of Straits Settlements Foreign Trade, 1870–1915*, Singapore, National Museum, 1978.

'China Banking Corporation: Golden Anniversary', *Chronicle* Business Report, 16 August 1970.

'China Banking Corporation: 60th Year', Supplement to *Times Journal*, 16 August 1980.

Choi, Kee Il, 'Tokugawa Feudalism and the Emergence of the New Leaders of Early Modern Japan', *Explorations in Entrepreneurial History*, December 1956.

Chronicle Magazine (A Special Issue on Albino Z. Sycip), 17 December 1967.

Chuphong Maningi, *Chiwit 25 Mahasetthi: Chuthhi 2*, Bangkok, Kanngoenthanakhan, 1986.

Chusho Kigyou Jigyo-dan, *Chusho Kigyo Kaigai Toshi Partners Chosa: Indonesia*, 1981.

_____, *Chusho Kigyo Kaigai Toshi Partners Chosa: Indonesia (Hokan)*, 1982.

_____, *Chusho Kigyo Kaigai Toshi Partners Chosa: Malaysia*, March 1982.

Chowdhury, Amitabha, 'Mochtar Riady: The Master Builder of an Asian Banking Empire', *Asia Finance*, September 1983.

_____, 'William Takes Astra Back to Grassroots', *Asia Finance*, November 1983.

Clammer, John, *Straits Chinese Society*, Singapore, Singapore University Press, 1980.

Coble, Parks M., Jr., *The Shanghai Capitalists and the Nationalist Government, 1927–37*, Cambridge, Council on East Asian Studies, Harvard University, 1980.

Coggin, Dan, 'Herminio Disini: Friends in High Places', *Insight*, February 1978.

Colayco, Maria, *The Ropemakers: The Story of Manila Cordage Co.*, Makati, Manila Cordage Co., 1975.

_____, *Seeds and Suds: The History of Philippine Refining Company*, Manila, Philippine Refining Co., 1978.

_____, *A Tradition of Leadership: Bank of the Philippine Islands*, Makati, Bank of the Philippine Islands, 1984.

Cole, Arthur, 'Entrepreneurship and Entrepreneurial History', in Joseph T. Lamble and Richard V. Clemence, eds., *Economic Change in America: Readings in the Economic History of the United States*, Harrisburg, The Stackpole Co., 1954.

Collier, David, ed., *The New Authoritarianism in Latin America*, Princeton, Princeton University Press, 1979.

The Commercial and Industrial Manual of the Philippines, Manila, Publishers, Inc., 1938.

Company Handbook 1986, Bangkok, Securities Exchange of Thailand.

Coppel, Charles, 'Liem Thian Joe's Unpublished History of Kian Gwan (Oei Tiong Ham Concern)', Paper presented at the ASAA (Asian Studies Association of Australia) Conference on Minority Groups in Southeast Asia, May 1976.

_____, *Indonesian Chinese in Crisis*, Kuala Lumpur, Oxford University Press, 1983.

Cornejo's Commonwealth Directory of the Philippines, Manila, 1939.

Corporate Profile, Quezon City, Business Day, 1981.

Cottrell, Robert, 'Keeping Business in the Extended Family', *Far Eastern Economic Review*, 5 December 1985.

Cowan, C. D., ed., *The Economic Development of South-East Asia*, London, George Allen & Unwin, 1964.

Crawfurd, John, *Journal of an Embassy to the Courts of Siam and Cochin China*, reprinted Kuala Lumpur, Oxford University Press, 1967.

Crouch, Harold, 'Generals and Business in Indonesia', *Pacific Affairs*, Winter, 1975–6.

_____, *The Army and Politics in Indonesia*, Ithaca, Cornell University Press, 1978.

_____, 'Patrimonialism and Military Rule in Indonesia', *World Politics*, July 1979.

'Cuenca Flees Overseas', *Insight*, September 1979.

Cunyngham-Brown, Sjovald, *The Traders: A Story of Britain's South-East Asian Commercial Adventure*, London, Newman Neame, 1971.

Cushman, J., 'The Khaw Group: Chinese Business in Early Twentieth-century Penang', *Journal of Southeast Asian Studies*, March 1986.

'Daftar Perusahaan Raksasa Indonesia', *Fokus*, 12 April 1984.

Davies, D. W., *A Primer of Dutch Seventeenth Century Overseas Trade*, The Hague, Martinus Nijhoff, 1961.

Day, Clive, *The Policy and Administration of the Dutch in Java*, reprinted Kuala Lumpur, Oxford University Press, 1966.

de Bree, L., *Gedenkboek van de Javasche Bank: 1828–24.1.1928*, 2 parts, Weltevreden, G. Kolff, 1928.

de Cruz, Peter, 'The Small Man's Banker: Dato Lee Chee Shan, Managing Director of the Chung Khiaw Bank', *Singapore Trade & Industry*, November 1968.

de Jesus, Ed., *The Tobacco Monopoly in the Philippines*, Quezon City, Ateneo de Manila University Press, 1980.

_____, *Fit at Fifty: 1931–1981, Engineering Equipment, Inc.*, Makati, Engineering Equipment, Inc., 1981.

_____, *The Amon Story*, Makati, Amon Trading Corp., 1978.

_____, *Benguet Consolidated, Inc. 1903–1978, A Brief History*, Makati, Benguet Consolidated, Inc., 1978.

_____ and Quirino, Carlos, *Earl Carroll: Colossus of Philippine Insurance*, Manila, The Underwriters Publications Co., 1980.

Directory of Thailand's 1000 Largest Companies, 1979–1981, Bangkok, Faculty of Commerce and Accountancy, Thammasat University, n.d.

Doh, Joon Chien, *Public Bank: Entrepreneurship and Corporate Citizenship*, Kuala Lumpur, Public Bank Berhad, 1987.

Drabble, J. H., *Rubber in Malaya*, Kuala Lumpur, Oxford University Press, 1973.

Drabble, J. and Drake, P., 'The British Agency Houses in Malaysia: Survival in a Changing World', *Journal of Southeast Asian Studies*, September 1981.

Drake, P., *Financial Development in Malaya and Singapore*, Canberra, Australian National University, 1969.

1883–1983: The Great Years, Singapore, Fraser & Neave, 1983.

'80th Anniversary, Osothsapha (Teck Heng Yoo) Co. Ltd.', Supplement to *Bangkok Post*, 27 January 1980.

Emata, Renato, *Coconut Processing*, Vol. II, Manila, United Coconut Association of the Philippines, April 1971.

ESCAP, *Patterns and Impact of Foreign Investment in the ESCAP Region*, Bangkok, ESCAP, 1985.

Evans, Peter, *Dependent Development: The Alliance of Multinational, State, and Local Capital in Brazil*, Princeton, Princeton University Press, 1979.

Feldwick, W., ed., *Present Day Impressions of the Far East and Prominent & Progressive Chinese at Home and Abroad*, London, Globe Encyclopedia Co., 1917.

Fenner, Bruce, *Cebu under the Spanish Flag (1521–1896); An Economic–Social History*, Cebu City, University of San Carlos, 1985.

The First Hundred Years of the Post Office Savings Bank of Singapore, Singapore, 1977.

Fisk, E. K. and Osman-Rani, H., eds., *The Political Economy of Malaysia*, Kuala Lumpur, Oxford University Press, 1982.

Flaviano, Demetrio, *Business Leaders and Executives: Inspiring Biographies of Men and Women who Became Successful*, Manila, Fal Service and Trading Co., 1950.

Foronda, Marcelino, 'Eusebio S. Garcia and the Chemical Industries of the Philippines', *Anuario/Annales*, Vol. 3, No. 1 (1984–5).

'40 Years of Bangkok Bank', Supplement to *Nation Review*, December 1984.

Franke, Richard, 'Limited Good and Cargo Cult in Indonesian Economic Development', *Journal of Contemporary Asia*, No. 4, 1972.

Furukawa, Yoshizo, *Davao Kaitaku-ki*, Tokyo, Furukawa Takushoku Kabushiki Kaisha, 1956.

Gale, Bruce, *Politics and Public Enterprise in Malaysia*, Singapore, Eastern Universities Press, 1981.

____, *Politics & Business: A Study of Multi-Purpose Holdings Berhad*, Singapore, Eastern Universities Press, 1985.

Geertz, Clifford, *Peddlers and Princes*, Chicago, The University of Chicago Press, 1963.

Gill, Ian, 'The Challenge from Wee Cho Yaw's UOB', *Insight*, May 1980.

____, 'Lim Uses Gambling Profits to Expand Genting', *Insight*, June 1980.

Gill, Margo, '40 Years of Progress (Ford Motor in Singapore)', *Singapore Trade & Industry*, July 1966.

Gill, Ranjit, 'OCBC: On Course with Banking Baron TCT at the Helm', *Insight*, September 1982.

____, 'KTP: The All-weather Banker Runs His Rivals to the Ground', *Insight*, May 1983.

____, 'The Super Duper Rich', *Insight*, December 1983.

——, *The Making of Malaysia Inc.*, Petaling Jaya, Pelanduk Publications, 1985.

——, *George Tan: The Carrian Saga*, Petaling Jaya, Pelanduk Publications, 1985.

——, *Khoo Teck Puat: Tycoon on a Tightrope*, Singapore, Sterling Corp. Services, 1987.

Girling, John, *The Bureaucratic Polity in Modernizing Societies: Similarities, Differences, and Prospects in the ASEAN Region*, Singapore, Institute of Southeast Asian Studies, 1981.

——, *Thailand: Society and Politics*, Ithaca, Cornell University Press, 1981.

Gleeck, Lewis, *American Business and Philippine Economic Development*, Manila, Carmelo & Bauermann, 1975.

——, *The Manila Americans (1901–1964)*, Manila, Carmelo & Bauermann, 1977.

Godley, Michael, *The Mandarin-capitalists from Nanyang*, Cambridge, Cambridge University Press, 1981.

Golay, Frank *et al.*, *Underdevelopment and Economic Nationalism in Southeast Asia*, Ithaca, Cornell University Press, 1969.

Goldberg, Michael, *The Chinese Connection*, Vancouver, University of British Columbia Press, 1985.

Greenfield, Sydney and Strickon, Arnold, 'A New Paradigm for the Study of Entrepreneurship and Social Change', *Economic Development and Cultural Change*, April 1981.

Growing with Singapore, Singapore, United Overseas Bank, 1985.

Guerrero, Milagros C., 'A Survey of Japanese Trade and Investment in the Philippines, 1900–1941', *Philippine Social Sciences and Humanities Review*, March 1966.

Guevara, Guillermo, *Across Four Generations*, Manila, United Publishing Co., 1973.

Gullick, J. M., *The Story of Kuala Lumpur (1857–1939)*, Singapore, Eastern Universities Press, 1983.

Gunseikanbu, *Orang Indonesia yang Termuka di Java*, reprinted Yogyakarta, Gadjah Mada University Press, 1986.

Guy, John S., *Oriental Trade Ceramics in South-East Asia, Ninth to Sixteenth Centuries*, Singapore, Oxford University Press, 1986.

Gwekoh, S. H., *Distinguished 100: The Book of Eminent Alumni of the University of the Philippines*, Manila, Apo Book Co., 1939.

Hall, Kenneth, *Maritime Trade and State Development in Early Southeast Asia*, Honolulu, University of Hawaii Press, 1985.

Hartendorp, Abraham, *History of Industry and Trade of the Philippines*, Manila, American Chamber of Commerce of the Philippines, 1958.

——, *History of Industry and Trade of the Philippines: The Magsaysay Administration*, Manila, Philippine Education Co., 1961.

Hatten Tojokoku no Denki-Denshi Sangyo, Tokyo, Ajia Keizai Kenkyu-sho, 1981.

Hatten Tojokoku no Jidosha Sangyo, Tokyo, Ajia Keizai Kenkyu-sho, 1980.

Hawes, Gary, *The Philippine State and the Marcos Regime: The Politics of Export*, Ithaca, Cornell University Press, 1987.

Hewison, Kevin, 'The Financial Bourgeoisie in Thailand', *Journal of Contemporary Asia*, 11, No. 4 (1981).

____, 'The State and Capitalist Development in Thailand', in Richard Higgott and Richard Robison, eds., *Southeast Asia: Essays in the Political Economy of Structural Change*, London, Routledge & Kegan Paul, 1985.

Higgins, Benjamin, 'Development Planning', in E. K. Fisk and H. Osman-Rani, eds., *The Political Economy of Malaysia*, Kuala Lumpur, Oxford University Press, 1982.

Higgott, Richard and Robison, Richard, eds., *Southeast Asia: Essays in the Political Economy of Structural Change*, London, Routledge & Kegan Paul, 1985.

Hiizumi, Katsuo, '"Tai no Kakyo" ni tsuite no Arekore', *Shoho* (of the Japanese Chamber of Commerce, Bangkok), March 1984–October 1985.

Hirschmeier, Johannes, 'Shibusawa Eiichi: Industrial Pioneer', in William Lockwood, ed., *The State and Economic Enterprise in Japan*, Princeton, Princeton University Press, 1965.

Historical Personalities of Penang, Penang, The Historical Personalities of Penang Committee, 1986.

Hong, Lysa, *Thailand in the Nineteenth Century: Evolution of the Economy and Society*, Singapore, Institute of Southeast Asian Studies, 1984.

'The Hongkong and Shanghai Banking Corporation: A Century in Singapore, 1877–1977'.

The Hongkong and Shanghai Banking Corporation, 'The History of the Hongkong Bank, Manila', [1985] (mimeographed).

'The Hongkong Bank Yesterday', Supplement to *Bangkok Post*, 2 August 1977.

Horie, Yasuzo, 'Modern Entrepreneurship in Modern Meiji Japan', in William Lockwood, ed., *The State and Economic Enterprise in Japan*, Princeton, Princeton University Press, 1965.

____, 'Business Pioneers of Modern Japan: Ishikawa Masatatsu and Oshima Takato', *Kyoto University Economic Review*, October 1960.

How It Happened: A History of the Bangkok Bank Ltd., Bangkok, Bangkok Bank, 1981.

Hunter, Ed, *Misdeeds of Tun Mustapha*, [Hong Kong?], Ed Hunter Enterprise, [1976].

Hyde, Francis, *Far Eastern Trade: 1860–1914*, London, Adam & Charles Black, 1973.

Ichikawa, Kenjiro, 'Chou Ran Shin to Gekido-ki no Tai Kakyo', *Southeast Asian Studies*, December 1970.

The Indonesian Military Leaders: Biographical and Other Background Data, 2nd ed., Jakarta, Sritua Arief Associates, 1979.

Indonesian Sociological Studies: Selected Writings of B. Schrieke, Parts One and Two, The Hague, W. van Hoeve, 1957.

Informasi Financial Profile 84/85, Jakarta, Pusat Data Business Indonesia, 1985.

International Bank for Reconstruction and Development, *A Public Development Program for Thailand*, Baltimore, The Johns Hopkins Press, 1959.

'Interview: Datuk Eric Chia of United Motor Works', *Malaysian Business*, January 1973.

'Interview: James Reid Scott, Group Chief Executive of Sime Darby Holdings Ltd.', *Malaysian Business*, November 1978.

'Interview: Senator Datuk Syed Kechik bin Syed Mohamed', *Malaysian Business*, July 1975.

Ito, Teiichi, ed., *Tonan Ajia ni okeru Kogyo Keieisha no Seisei*, Tokyo, Ajia Keizai Kenkyu-sho, 1980.

Iwasaki, Ikuo, 'Futatsu no Kajin Kigyo: Meimon Ginko OCBC to Kindai Gijutsu YHS', *Ajiken News*, No. 74 (1986).

Jackson, Karl, and Pye, Lucian, eds., *Political Power and Communications in Indonesia*, Berkeley, University of California Press, 1978.

Japan External Trade Organization, *List of Japanese Investment Projects in Indonesia, 1985*, Jakarta.

Japan Overseas Enterprises Association, 'Indonesian Partners in Japan–Indonesia Joint Venture Companies', Jakarta, May 1983.

Jayme, Marietta, 'Andres Soriano, Sr.', MBM thesis, De La Salle University, 1972.

Jenkins, David, *Suharto and His Generals: Indonesian Military Politics 1975–1983*, Ithaca, Cornell Modern Indonesian Project Monograph No. 64, 1984.

Jennings, Eric, *Mansfields: Transport & Distribution in South-East Asia*, Singapore, Meridian Communications, [1973?].

_____, *Wheels of Progress: 75 Years of Cycle and Carriage*, Singapore, Meridian Communications, 1975.

Jensen, Khin Khin Myint, 'The Chinese in the Philippines during the American Period: 1896–1946', Ph.D. thesis, University of Wisconsin, 1956.

Joaquin, Nick, *The Aquinos of Tarlac*, Mandaluyong, Cacho Hermanos, 1983.

Jomo, ed., *The Sun Also Sets: Lessons in 'Looking East'*, Petaling Jaya, Institute for Social Analysis, 1985.

Jones, Stephanie, *Two Centuries of Overseas Trading: The Origins and Growth of the Inchcape Group*, London, Macmillan, 1986.

Junid Saham, *British Industrial Investment in Malaysia, 1963–1971*, Kuala Lumpur, Oxford University Press, 1980.

Karma, Mara, *Ibnu Sutowo*, Jakarta, Gunung Agung, 1979.

Kawabe, Toshio, *Kakyo*, Tokyo, Ushio Shuppan-sha, 1972.

Khoo, Hock Aun, 'Tan Sri Lim Goh Tong: Long, Hard Climb to Success', *Malaysian Business*, March 1981.

Khor, Eng Lee, 'The Case for Heavy Industry', *Investors Digest*, May 1985.

Khor, Kok Peng, *Malaysia's Economy in Decline*, Penang, Consumers' Association of Penang, 1987.

King, Frank, ed., *Eastern Banking: Essays in the History of the Hongkong and Shanghai Banking Corporation*, London, The Athlone Press, 1983.

———, 'Foreign Exchange Banks in Siam, 1888–1918 and the National Bank Question', *Proceedings* of the International Conference on Thai Studies, 22–24 August 1984, Bangkok, Vol. 1.

Koo, Hui-lan (Madame Wellington Koo), *An Autobiography as told to Mary Van Rensselaer Thayer*, New York, Dial Press, 1943.

Koo, Mrs Wellington and Taves, Isabella, *No Feast Lasts Forever*, New York, Quadrangle, 1975.

Kraisak Choonhavan, 'The Growth of Domestic Capital and Thai Industrialization', *Journal of Contemporary Asia*, 1984.

Krirkkiat Phipatseritham, *Wikhro Laksana Kanpenchaokhong Thurakit Khanatyai Nai Prathetthai*, Bangkok, Faculty of Economics, Thammasat University, 1982.

———, 'The Push and Pull of Economics and Politics in Thailand' (unpublished).

——— and Yoshihara, Kunio, 'Business Groups in Thailand', Research Notes and Discussions Paper No. 41, Singapore, Institute of Southeast Asian Studies, 1983.

'Kuok Connections', *Far Eastern Economic Review*, 30 October 1986.

Kuznets, Simon, *Economic Growth of Nations*, Cambridge, Mass., Harvard University Press, 1971.

Lachica, Eduardo, *Ayala: The Philippines' Oldest Business House*, Makati, Filipinas Foundation, 1984 (reprinted in *Fookien Times Philippines Yearbook 1984–85*).

Landa, Janet, 'The Political Economy of the Ethnically Homogeneous Chinese Middleman Group in Southeast Asia: Ethnicity and Entrepreneurship in a Plural Society', in Linda Y. C. Lim and Peter Gosling, eds., *The Chinese in South-east Asia*, Vol. 1, Singapore, Maruzen Asia, 1983.

Laugesen, Mary *et al.*, *Scandinavians in Siam*, [Bangkok], [1980].

'Lee Kim Tah Holdings Ltd.: A Profile', [1984?].

Lee, Peter, 'Banking for the People: The Story of Malayan Banking Limited', *Singapore Trade & Industry*, September 1965.

Lee, Poh Ping, 'Chinese Society in Nineteenth and Early Twentieth Century Singapore: A Socioeconomic Analysis', Ph.D. thesis, Cornell University, 1974.

———, *Chinese Society in Nineteenth Century Singapore*, Kuala Lumpur, Oxford University Press, 1978.

Lee, Sheng-Yi, *The Monetary and Banking Development of Malaysia and Singapore*, Singapore, Singapore University Press, 1974.

Lewis, H. Parker, 'The Philippine National Bank', *Journal of Political Economy*, May 1917.

Li, Dun Jen, *British Malaya: An Economic Analysis*, reprinted Petaling Jaya, Institute for Social Analysis, 1982.

'Liem Sioe Liong: Suharto's Secret Agent', *Insight*, May 1978.

Liem, Tjwan Ling, *Raja Gula: Oei Tiong Ham*, Surabaya, published by the author, 1979.

'The Life and Career of Don Andres Soriano', Special Issue of *The Manila Chronicle*, 30 September 1966.

'The Life and Career of Don Antonio De Las Alas, Sr.', Special Issue of *The Manila Chronicle*, 15 October 1968.

'The Life and Career of Don Carlos Palanca, Sr.', Special Issue of *The Manila Chronicle*, 31 December 1968.

'The Life and Career of Earl D. Carroll', Special Issue of *The Manila Chronicle*, 27 September 1970.

'The Life and Career of Don Francisco B. Ortigas, Sr.', Special Issue of *The Manila Chronicle*, 24 October 1969.

'The Life and Career of Gerald Hugh Wilkinson', Special Issue of *The Manila Chronicle*, 29 November 1968.

'The Life and Career of Don Gonzalo Puyat', Special Issue of *The Manila Chronicle*, 31 May 1967.

'The Life and Career of Don Jose Yulo', Special Issue of *The Manila Chronicle*, 31 March 1969.

'The Life and Career of Don Manuel Elizalde', Special Issue of *The Manila Chronicle*, 31 January 1968.

'The Life and Career of Don Nicarnor S. Jacinto, Sr.', Special Issue of *The Manila Chronicle*, 15 June 1968.

Lim, Chong-yah, *Economic Development of Modern Malaya*, Kuala Lumpur, Oxford University Press, 1967.

Lim, How Seng, 'Tan Kah Kee's Business Philosophy and Corporate Management', *Journal of Humanities and Social Sciences* (Singapore), Vol. VI (1986) (in Chinese).

_____, 'The Business Empire of Lee Kong Chian', *Asian Culture* (Singapore), April 1987 (in Chinese).

Lim, Kim Liat, 'The Deli Tobacco Industry: Its History and Outlook', in Douglas Paauw, ed., *Prospects for East Sumatra Plantation Industries: A Symposium*, New Haven, Southeast Asian Studies, Yale University, 1962.

Lim, Kit Siang, *BMF: Scandal of Scandals*, Petaling Jaya, Democratic Action Party, 1986.

Lim, Linda Y. C. and Gosling, L. A. Peter, eds., *The Chinese in Southeast Asia*, 2 vols., Singapore, Maruzen Asia, 1983.

Lim, Mah Hui, *Ownership and Control of the One Hundred Largest Corporations in Malaysia*, Kuala Lumpur, Oxford University Press, 1981.

Lim, Rodrigo, ed., *Who's Who in the Philippines (Chinese Edition)*, Quezon City, University of the Philippines Press, 1930.

Longhurst, Henry, *The Borneo Story: The History of the First 100 Years of Trading in the Far East by the Borneo Company Limited*, London, Newman Neame, 1956.

Lopez, Oscar, *The Lopez Family*, Vol. I, Pasig, Eugenio Lopez Foundation, 1982.

Low, James, *The British Settlement of Penang*, reprinted Singapore, Oxford University Press, 1972.

Lubis, Mochtar, *The Indonesian Dilemma*, trans. F. Lamoureux, Singapore, Graham Brash, 1983.

Mackenzie, Compton, *Realms of Silver: One Hundred Years of Banking in the East*, London, Routledge & Kegan Paul, 1954.

Mackie, J. A. C., ed., *The Chinese in Indonesia*, Honolulu, University Press of Hawaii, 1976.

Mahathir bin Mohamad, *The Malay Dilemma*, Kuala Lumpur, Federal Publications, 1970.

Mak, Lau Fong, *The Sociology of Secret Societies: A Study of Chinese Secret Societies in Singapore and Peninsular Malaysia*, Kuala Lumpur, Oxford University Press, 1981.

Makarim, Nono Anwar, 'Companies and Business in Indonesia', Doctor of Juridical Science thesis, Harvard Law School, November 1978.

'The Malaysian Equation' (advertisement), *Fortune*, 28 December 1981.

'Malaysian Resources Corporation Berhad: Our Corporate Profile', [1983?].

'The Man who Brought the Honda to Malaysia', *Malaysian Business*, January 1974.

Manila Electric Co., *Manila Electric Company: A Brief History*, Metro Manila, 1976.

Mansvelt, W. M. F., *Geschiedenis van de Nederlandsche Handel-Maatschappij*, 2 vols., Haarlem, n.d.

_____ et al., *Changing Economy in Indonesia: A Selection of Statistical Source Material from the Early 19th Century up to 1940*, Vols. 1–5, The Hague, Martinus Nijhoff, 1975–9.

Mantetsu Toa Keizai Chosa-kyoku, *Taikoku ni okeru Kakyo*, Tokyo, [published by the author], 1939.

_____, *Firipin ni okeru Kakyo*, Tokyo, [published by the author], 1939.

_____, *Ranryo Indo ni okeru Kakyo*, Tokyo, [published by the author], 1940.

_____, *Eiryo Marei Biruma oyobi Goshu ni okeru Kakyo*, Tokyo, [published by the author], 1941.

Manuel, E. Aresenio, *Dictionary of Philippine Biography*, Vol. I, Quezon City, Filipiniana Publications, 1955, and Vol. II, Quezon City, Filipiniana Publications, 1970.

Marante, Mariano, 'Corporate Strategy for Associated Anglo-American Tobacco Corporation', Master of Management thesis, Asian Institute of Management, 1979.

'The Marcelo Group of Corporations', Special Report of *The Manila Chronicle*, 5 April 1970.

Mauzy, Diane and Milne, R. S., 'The Mahathir Administration: Discipline through Islam', in Bruce Gale, ed., *Readings in Malaysian Politics*, Petaling Jaya, Pelanduk Publications, 1986.

Mavro, Alex P., Jr., 'Thailand's Security Exchange: Change is Slow', *Insight*, January 1985.

McVey, Ruth, 'The Post-Revolutionary Transformation of the Indonesian Army', *Indonesia*, No. 11 (1971).

Meilink-Roelofsz, M. A. P., *Asian Trade and European Influence*, The Hague, Martinus Nijhoff, 1962.

A Memorandum for Thirty Year's [*sic*] *Cultivation in Nanyang of Dr. Chan Yoh Shen*, privately printed, October 1921 (in Chinese).

'Mengenal Perusahaan Raksasa Indonesia', *Fokus*, 5 April 1984.

Michener, James, 'Chinese Success Story', *Life*, 31 December 1951.

Middlebrook, S. M., 'Yap Ah Loy, 1837–1885', *Journal of the Malayan Branch of the Royal Asiatic Society*, July 1951.

Mid-Term Review of the Fourth Malaysia Plan, 1981–1985, Kuala Lumpur, Government Press, 1984.

Mihira, Norio, 'Kokusai-ka ni Mukau Liem Sioe Liong Gurupu', *Ajiken News*, No. 74 (1986).

Mijares, Primitivo, *The Conjugal Dictatorship of Ferdinand and Imelda Marcos I*, San Francisco, Union Square Publications, 1976.

Million Baht Business Information Thailand 1986, Bangkok, International Business Research (Thailand).

Ministry of Finance (Capital Market Executive Agency), 'The Indonesian Capital Market', Jakarta, 1983.

Ministry of Finance (of Japan), 'Nihonjin no Kaigai Katsudo ni Kansuru Rekishi-teki Chosa: Nanpo-hen' (unpublished), 1947.

Ministry of International Trade and Industry (MITI), *Keizai Kyoryoku no Genjo to Mondaiten 1983*, Tokyo, Tsusho Sangyo Chosa-kai, 1984.

Mitsui Ginko Hyakunen no Ayumi, Tokyo, Mitsui Ginko, 1976.

'Mobil in Singapore',1982.

Mohamed Amin and Caldwell, Malcolm, eds., *Malaya: The Making of a Neo-Colony*, Nottingham, Bertrand Russell Peace Foundation, 1977.

Mohamed Ariff and Hill, Hal, 'Protection for Manufactures in ASEAN', *Asian Economic Journal*, March 1987.

Morais, Victor, *Without Fear or Favour, A Biography of Tan Sri Mohd. Noah*, Kuala Lumpur, published by the author, 1976.

_____, *Tun Tan: Portrait of a Statesman*, Kuala Lumpur, published by the author, 1981.

Morison, S. *'Old Burin': Commodore Matthew C. Perry, 1794–1858*, Boston, Little, Brown & Co., 1967.

Myrdal, Gunnar, *International Economy*, New York, Harper & Row, 1956.

Nellist, George, ed., *Men of the Philippines*, Manila, Sugar News, 1931.

Navarro-Pedrosa, Carmen, *The Untold Story of Imelda Marcos*, Rizal, Tandem Publishing Co., 1969.

Ness, Gayl, *Bureaucracy and Rural Development in Malaysia*, Berkeley, University of California Press, 1967.

Nippon Tekko Renmei, 'Indonesia', 1984.

Ng, Poh Tip, 'The Amazing Tun Sir Henry H. S. Lee', *Malaysian Business*, July 1980.

Ngam, Su May, 'Azman Hashim: A Dream Realized', *Malaysian Business*, November 1982.

Nihon Boeki Shinko-kai, *Indonesia ni okeru Minzoku-kei Kigyo to Kajin Shihon,* 1975.

Nihon Keizai Shinbun-sha, ed., *Kakyo,* Tokyo, Nihon Keizai Shinbun-sha, 1981.

Olivera, Baldomero, *Jose Yulo: The Selfless Statesman,* Mandaluyong, The UP-Jorge B. Vargas Filipiniana Research Center, 1981.

Omohundro, John, *Chinese Merchant Families in Iloilo: Commerce and Kin in a Central Philippine City,* Quezon City, Ateneo de Manila University Press, 1981.

One Hundred Years as East India Merchants: Harrisons and Crosfield, 1844–1943, London, 1943.

Onorato, Michael, interviewer and ed., 'Salvador Araneta: Reflections of a Filipino Exile', The Oral History Program, California State University, Fullerton, 1979.

Ooi, Jin Bee, *The Petroleum Resources of Indonesia,* Kuala Lumpur, Oxford University Press, 1982.

Orang-orang Tionghoa jang Terkemoeka di Java, Solo, The Biographical Publishing Centre, 1935.

Osborne, John, 'The Business Passions of Andres Soriano', *Fortune Magazine,* March 1956.

The Outstanding Leaders of the Philippines, 1980, Manila, Asia Research Systems, Inc. and Press Foundation of Asia, n.d.

Overseas Union Bank Limited, *25th Anniversary, 1949–74,* Singapore, 1974.

Paauw, Douglas S., 'From Colonial to Guided Economy', in Ruth McVey, ed., *Indonesia,* New Haven, Southeast Asian Studies, Yale University, 1963.

_____, 'The Economic Legacy of Dutch Colonialism to Independent Indonesia', Paper presented at the Conference on Indonesian Economic History in the Dutch Colonial Period, Australian National University, 16–18 December 1983.

'Pacific Banking Corporation: Fifteenth Year', *Chronicle* Business Report, 24 June 1970.

Pannee Ouansakul, 'Trade Monopoly in Ayudhya', *Social Science Review* (Bangkok), 1976.

Panglaykim, J., *Japanese Direct Investment in ASEAN: The Indonesian Experience,* Singapore, Maruzen Asia, 1983.

_____ and Palmer, I., 'Study of Entrepreneurship in Developing Countries: The Development of One Chinese Concern in Indonesia', *Journal of Southeast Asian Studies,* March 1970.

Patrick, Hugh and Moreno, Honorata, 'Philippine Private Domestic Commercial Banking, 1946–1980, in the Light of Japanese Experience', in Kazushi Ohkawa and Gustav Ranis, eds., *Japan and the Developing Countries: A Comparative Analysis,* Oxford, Basil Blackwell, 1985.

Peace, John, 'The Bank and the Philippines', *StanChart Magazine,* April 1985.

'Personality Profile: Datuk Haji Ibrahim bin Mohamed', *Malaysian Business,* January 1978.

'Personality Profile: Azman Hashim', *Malaysian Business*, August 1978.

Petras, James, *Critical Perspectives on Imperialism and Social Class in the Third World*, New York, Monthly Review Press, 1978.

'Petronas: More Fuel for Growth', *Malaysian Business*, 16 August 1984.

Phaanachak Thurakit 25 Trakun Mahasetthi, 2nd ed., Bangkok, Samapharn, n.d.

Philippine National Bank, *Philippine Commercial Banking System in 1983*, Manila.

Phitsanes Jessadachatr, 'A History of Sugar Policies in Thailand: 1937–75', Master of Economics thesis, Thammasat University, 1977.

Pillai, M. G. G., 'Ecstasy at UMW over Eric Chia's Toyota Coup', *Insight*, December 1981.

Pioneers of Philippine Businessmen: 1935, 2nd ed., Manila, Rojadi Publishing Company, 1934.

Pioneers of Singapore: A Catalogue of Oral History Interviews, Singapore, Archives & Oral History Department, 1984.

'Pioneers in Trade: They Contributed So Much', *Business in Thailand*, August 1977.

'PNB: On the Road to 1990', *Malaysian Business*, January 1982.

Poole, Fred and Vanzi, Max, *Revolution in the Philippines: The United States in a Hall of Cracked Mirrors*, New York, McGraw-Hill Book Co., 1984.

Prebisch, Raul, *Towards a New Trade Policy for Development*, New York, United Nations, 1964.

'Prima Limited: 1961–1986'.

'Promet Plunges into Property Market, Oil Prospecting', *Insight*, February 1982.

'Prudential Bank', *Manila Chronicle* Special Report, 7 December 1969.

Public Bank Group: 15th Anniversary, 1966–1981, Kuala Lumpur, 1981.

Purcell, Victor, *The Chinese in Malaya*, Kuala Lumpur, Oxford University Press, 1967.

_____, *The Chinese in Southeast Asia*, reprinted Kuala Lumpur, Oxford University Press, 1980.

Puthucheary, J. J., *Ownership and Control in the Malayan Economy*, reprinted Kuala Lumpur, University of Malaya Cooperative Bookshop, 1979.

Quirino, Carlos, 'Philippine Tycoon: The Life and Times of Vicente Madrigal', 1967 (unpublished).

_____, 'The Cojuangco Family', 1968 (unpublished).

_____, *History of the Philippine Sugar Industry*, Manila, Kalayaan Publishing Company, 1974.

_____, 'Ayala and the Zobel Families', 1975 (unpublished).

Quirino, Eliseo, *Nepa Handbook*, Manila, National Economic Protectionism Association, 1938.

Ranis, Gustav, 'The Community-centered Entrepreneur in Japanese Development', in *Explorations in Entrepreneurial History*, December 1965.

Raventos, Emili, *La Compania General de Tabacos de Filipinas, 1881–1981*, Barcelona, La Compania General de Tabacos de Filipinas, 1981.

'Reaching for the Sky with United behind Him', *Insight*, March 1983.

Reid, Anthony, 'Pre-colonial Economy of Indonesia', Paper presented to the Conference on Indonesian Economic History in the Dutch Colonial Period, Australian National University, 16–18 December 1983.

Report of the Public Sector Divestment Committee, Singapore, February 1987.

Reyes, Teofilo, *Taginting ng Kampana*, Quezon City, R. P. Garcia Publishing Co., 1973.

Rieffel, Alexis and Wirjasuputra, Aninda, 'Military Enterprises', *Bulletin of Indonesian Economic Studies*, July 1972.

Riggs, Fred, *Thailand: The Modernization of a Bureaucratic Polity*, Honolulu, East-West Center Press, 1966.

Rivera, Temario, 'Rethinking the Philippine Social Formation: Some Problematic Concepts and Issues', in *Symposium: Feudalism and Capitalism in the Philippines*, Quezon City, Foundation for Nationalist Studies, 1982.

Rizal, Jose, 'The Indolence of the Filipinos', in E. Alzona, trans. and ed., *Selected Essays and Letters of Jose Rizal*, Manila, Rangel & Sons, 1964.

Roberts, John, *Mitsui: Three Centuries of Japanese Business*, New York, Weatherhill, 1973.

Robertson, Denis, *Essays in Monetary Theory*, St. Albans, Staples Press, 1948.

Robison, Richard, 'Capitalism and the Bureaucratic State in Indonesia; 1965–75', Ph.D. thesis, University of Sydney, November 1977.

_____, 'Toward a Class Analysis of the Indonesian Military Bureaucratic State', *Indonesia*, No. 25 (1978).

_____, 'Culture, Politics, and Economy in the Political History of the New Order', *Indonesia*, No. 31 (1981).

_____, *Indonesia: The Rise of Capital*, North Sydney, Allen & Unwin, 1986.

Roeder, O. G., *The Smiling General: President Soeharto of Indonesia*, Jakarta, Gunung Agung, 1969.

Roney, Donna, *The Golden Nipa Hut: Success Stories from the Philippines*, [Manila], Vera-Reyes, Inc., 1978.

Ross-Larson, Bruce, *The Politics of Federalism: Syed Kechik in East Malaysia*, Singapore, published by the author, 1976.

Rowley, Anthony, 'Birth of a Multinational', *Far Eastern Economic Review*, 7 April 1983.

Roy, Barun, 'Promet's Brian Chang: Pioneer and Pace-setter', *Asia Finance*, November 1984.

Royal Dutch Petroleum Company, 1890–1950, The Hague, 1950.

Ruiz, Demetrio, 'Teodoro Rafael Yangco: His Life and Business Career (1861–1939)', MA thesis, University of Santo Tomas, 1975.

Rush, James, 'Opium Farms in Nineteenth Century Java: Institutional Continuity and Change in a Colonial Society, 1860–1910', Ph.D. thesis, Yale University, 1977.

Sadli, Mohammad, "The Private Sector in Indonesia', February 1986 (unpublished).

'Saha Union Corp., Ltd. New Head Office', Supplement to *Nation*, 20 October 1982.

Salamon, Rob, 'The Secret World of Robin Loh', *Insight*, March 1978.

———, 'Chin Sophonpanich: The Bangkok Connection', *Insight*, June 1978.

San Miguel Brewery, Inc., *Golden Jubilee, 1890–1940*, Manila, 1940.

Sarasin Viraphol, *Tribute and Profit: Sino-Siamese Trade, 1652–1853*, Cambridge, Mass., Council on East Asian Studies, Harvard University, 1977.

Saruwatari, Keiko, 'Igirisu Shosha no Keiei Senryaku to Soshiki: Guthrie & Co. no Jirei (1821–1981)', *Keiei Shigaku*, Vol. 17, No. 4 (1983).

Schurz, William, *The Manila Galleon*, reprinted Manila, Historical Conservation Society, 1985.

Seaports of the Far East, London, Allister Macmillan, 1907.

Second Malaysia Plan, 1971–1975, Kuala Lumpur, Government Press, 1971.

Seidman, Samuel, 'Enterprise and Entrepreneurship in the Philippine Republic, 1949–1959', Ph.D. thesis, New York University, 1963.

Sejarah dan Perkembangan Bumiputera 1912, 1912–1982, Jakarta, Yayasan Dharma Bumiputera, 1982.

'75 Years at Bukom', *Singapore Trade & Industry*, July 1966.

'70th Anniversary of the Siam Cement Company', Supplement to *Nation*, 8 December 1983.

Shaplen, Robert, 'Letter from the Philippines', *The New Yorker*, 8 June 1963 and 4 February 1985.

Sharp, Ilsa, 'The "Show-Biz" King of South-East Asia', *Singapore Trade & Industry*, May/June 1969.

Sieh, Lee Mei Ling and Chew, Kwee Lyn, 'Redistribution of Malaysia's Corporate Ownership in the New Economic Policy', in *Southeast Asian Affairs 1985*, Singapore, Institute of Southeast Asian Studies, 1985.

'The Silverio Group of Companies', Special Report of *The Manila Chronicle*, 30 September 1969.

Sim Lim 50 Years, Singapore, Sim Lim Investments Ltd., 1983.

Sim, Victor, comp., *Biographies of Prominent Chinese in Singapore*, Singapore, Nan Kok Publication Co., 1950.

Simbulan, Dante, 'A Study of the Socio-economic Elite in Philippine Politics and Government, 1946–1963', Ph.D. thesis, Australian National University, 1965.

Singh, Supriya, *Bank Negara Malaysia: The First 25 Years, 1959–1984*, Kuala Lumpur, Bank Negara Malaysia, 1984.

Siregar, Arifin, 'Indonesian Entrepreneurs', *Asian Survey*, May 1969.

Sirilak Sakkriangkrai, *Ton Kamnoed Khong Chonchan Naithun Nai Prathet Thai (B.E. 2398–2453)*, Bangkok, Sang San, 1980.

Skinner, G. William, 'Report on the Chinese in Southeast Asia', Southeast Asian Program, Cornell University, 1950.

———, *Chinese Society in Thailand: An Analytical History*, Ithaca, Cornell University Press, 1957.

———, *Leadership and Power in the Chinese Community of Thailand*, Ithaca, Cornell University Press, 1958.

'Some are Smarter than Others', [Metro Manila], [1979] (unpublished).

Sondang, PN, '100 Milyarder Indonesia: Apa & Siapa Mereka?', *Expo*, 4 January and 18 January 1984.

Song, Ong Siang, *One Hundred Years' History of the Chinese in Singapore*, reprinted Singapore, Oxford University Press, 1984.

Soriano, Andres Jr., 'San Miguel Corporation: 90 Years of Growth and Diversification', *1980 Fookien Times Philippines Yearbook*.

Soriano, D. H. and Retizos, Isidro, eds., *The Philippines Who's Who*, 2nd ed., Makati, Who's Who Publishers, 1981.

'Standard Chartered: A New Name in Asia', Supplement to *Nation Review*, 8 January 1985.

'Standard Chartered: 125 Years of Service to Singapore', [1984?].

Stifel, Laurence, *The Textile Industry: A Case Study of Industrial Development in the Philippines*, Ithaca, Cornell University Press, 1963.

'Stock Exchanges Stir in New Manila", *Insight*, April 1973.

The Story of Krebet, [Semarang], Handel Maatschappij Kian Gwan, 1932.

Suehiro, Akira, *Capital Accumulation and Industrial Development in Thailand*, Bangkok, Chulalongkorn University, 1985.

Sungsidh Piriyarangsan, 'Thai Bureaucratic Capitalism, 1932–1960', Master of Economics thesis, Thammasat University, 1980.

Suryadinata, Leo, *Eminent Indonesian Chinese: Biographical Sketches*, Singapore, Institute of Southeast Asian Studies, 1978.

Sutter, John, *Indonesianisasi; Politics in a Changing Economy, 1940–1955*, Data Paper No. 36, Southeast Asian Program, Cornell University, 1959.

Suyama, Taku *et al.*, *Kakyo*, Tokyo, Nihon Hoso Shuppan Kyokai, 1972.

Swasono, Sri-Edi, 'Some Notes on the Nurturing of the Indonesian Entrepreneur', *The Indonesian Quarterly*, July 1973.

Swettenham, F. A., *British Malaya*, London, Allen & Unwin, 1955.

Syed Hussein Alatas, *The Myth of the Lazy Native*, London, Frank Cass, 1977.

———, *The Problem of Corruption*, Singapore, Times Books International, 1986.

Szanton, Cristina Blanc, 'Thai and Sino-Thai in Small Town Thailand: Changing Patterns of Interethnic Relations', in Linda Y. C. Lim and Peter L. A. Gosling, eds., *The Chinese in Southeast Asia*, Vol. 2, Singapore, Maruzen Asia, 1983.

Tableau: Encyclopedia of Distinguished Personalities in the Philippines, Manila, National Souvenir Publications, 1957.

Taikoku Keizai Gaikyo 1986–87 Nen-ban, Bangkok, Bangkok Nihonjin Shoko Kaigisho, n.d.

Taiwan Ginko-shi, Tokyo, Taiwan Ginko-shi Hensan-shitsu, 1964.

Tan, Boon Kean, 'Foreign Investment and Ownership Trends in the Malaysian Economy, 1970–1980', *Ilmu Masyarakat*, July–September 1984.

Tan, Chwee Huat, *Financial Markets and Institutions in Singapore*, 4th ed., Singapore, Singapore University Press, 1985.

Tan, Ee Leong, 'The Chinese Banks Incorporated in Singapore and the Federation of Malaya', in T. H. Silcock, ed., *Readings in Malayan Economics*, Singapore, Eastern Universities Press, 1961.

_____, 'Biography of Lee Kong Chian', *Journal of the South Seas Society*, Parts 1 and 2, 1967 (in Chinese).

Tan, Kah Kee, *Nanqiao Huiyi-lu*, Hong Kong, Caoyuan Chuban-she, 1979.

Tan, Mely, 'Majority–Minority Situations: Indonesia', *Prisma*, November 1976.

Tate, D. J. M., *The Making of Modern South-East Asia*, 2 vols., Kuala Lumpur, Oxford University Press, 1971 and 1979.

'Thai Farmers Bank: Grand Opening of New Head Office', Supplement to *Bangkok Post*, 7 February 1983.

'Thai Farmers Bank: 40th Anniversary', Publication of *Nation Review*, [1985].

Thailand Profiles 1985, Bangkok A. Tawanna Publications.

Tham, Seong Chee, *Malays and Modernization*, 2nd ed., Singapore, Singapore University Press, 1983.

Thee, Kian-wie, *Plantation Agriculture and Export Growth: An Economic History of East Sumatra, 1863–1942*, Jakarta, National Institute of Economic and Social Research, 1977.

_____ and Yoshihara, Kunio, 'Foreign and Domestic Capital in Indonesian Industrialization', *Southeast Asian Studies*, March 1987.

'30th Anniversary, Siam Motors Co. Ltd.', Supplement to *Bangkok Post*, 4 September 1982.

Tiglao, Rigoberto, *The Philippine Coconut Industry*, [Manila], ARC Publication, 1981.

Tilly, Charles, 'War Making and State Making as Organized Crime', in Peter Evans *et al.*, eds., *Bringing the State Back In*, Cambridge, Cambridge University Press, 1985.

Tjoa, Soe Tjong, 'OTHC: 100 Jaar—Een Stukje Economische Geschiedenis van Indonesia', *Economische-Statistische Berichten*, June 1963.

Toemsakdi Krishnamra, 'Commercial Banking in Thailand', *Journal of Commerce and Accounting*, Vol. 1, No. 4 (1963).

'Towards a Brighter Tomorrow with Siam Cement', Supplement to *Bangkok Post*, 23 July 1981.

Tregonning, K. G., *Straits Tin: A Brief Account of the Straits Trading Company Limited, 1887–1962*, Singapore, The Straits Times Press, 1962.

_____, 'Straits Tin: A Brief Account of the First Seventy Five Years of the Straits Trading Company Ltd.', *Journal of the Malayan Branch of the Royal Asiatic Society*, 1963.

_____, 'The Origin of the Straits Steamship Company in 1890', *Journal of the Malaysian Branch of the Royal Asiatic Society*, 1966.

_____, *Home Port Singapore: A History of Straits Steamship Co., Ltd., 1890–1965*, Singapore, Oxford University Press, 1965.

_____, *The Singapore Cold Storage 1903–1966*, Singapore, Cold Storage Holdings Ltd., 1967.

_____, 'Tan Cheng Lock: A Malayan Nationalist', *Journal of Southeast Asian Studies*, Part 1, 1979.

Tsuda, Mamoru, 'Firipin ni okeru Kindai-teki Kogyo no Hatten to Shinko Zaibatsu no Keisei', in Ito Teiichi, ed., *Tonan Ajia ni okeru Kogyo Keieisha no Seisei*, Tokyo, Institute of Developing Economies, 1980.

Uchida, Naosaku, *Tonan Ajia Kakyo no Shakai to Keizai*, Tokyo, Chikura Shobo, 1982.

Under Four Flags: The Story of Smith, Bell & Co. in the Philippines, n.d.

'United Motor Works (Malaysia) Holdings Berhad', [1983?].

United States Department of Commerce, *Netherlands East Indies and British Malaya: A Commercial and Industrial Handbook*, Washington, Government Printing Office, 1923.

Van Laanen, J. T. M., *Changing Economy in Indonesia*, Vol. 6: *Money and Banking 1816–1940*, The Hague, Martinus Nijhoff, 1980.

_____, 'A Preliminary Look at the Role of the Hongkong Bank in Netherlands India', in Frank King, ed., *Eastern Banking: Essays in the History of the Hongkong and Shanghai Banking Corporation*, London, The Athlone Press, 1983.

Van Leur, J. C., *Indonesian Trade and Society*, The Hague, W. van Hoeve, 1955.

Van Niel, Robert, 'The Legacy of the Cultivation System for Subsequent Economic Development', Paper presented at the Conference on Indonesian Economic History in the Dutch Colonial Period, Australian National University, 16–18 December 1983.

'The Vast Significance of Two New Oil Refineries', *Singapore Trade*, February 1961.

Verchere, Ian, 'The Changing World of Robert Kuok', *Insight*, August 1978.

'Victorias Milling Company, Inc. 1919–1979, 60th Anniversary'.

Villasin, Olimpio, *Tops in Philippine Business*, Manila, Superprom, 1962.

Villegas, Bernardo, *Strategies for Crisis: The Story of the Philippine National Oil Company*, [Manila], Center for Research & Communication, 1983.

Voon, Phin Keong, *Western Rubber Planting Enterprise in Southeast Asia, 1876–1921*, Kuala Lumpur, Penerbit Universiti Malaya, 1976.

Wain, Barry, 'Pertamina and the Incredible World of Ibnu Sutowo', *Insight*, October 1976.

Warnford-Lock, C. G., *Mining in Malaya for Gold and Tin*, London, Crowther & Goodman, 1907.

Warren, Bill, *Imperialism: Pioneer of Capitalism*, London, Verso, 1980.

Weissblatt, Frank, ed., *Who's Who in the Philippines*, Vol. II, Manila, Ramon Roces, Inc., 1937.

Who's Who: Finance & Banking in Thailand, 1981–1982, Bangkok, Advance Media Co., n.d.

Who's Who in Indonesia, 2nd ed., Jakarta, Gunung Agung, 1980.

Who's Who in Indonesian Business, 2nd ed., Jakarta, Sritua Arief Associates, 1976.

Who's Who in Malaysia & Singapore 1983–4, Petaling Jaya, Who's Who Publications Sdn. Bhd., 1983.

'Why Do So Many Chinese Family Businesses Remain Small?', *Malaysian Business*, February 1973.

Wickberg, Edgar, 'The Chinese Mestizo in Philippine History', *Journal of Southeast Asian History*, 1964.

———, *The Chinese in Philippine Life, 1850–1898*, New Haven, Yale University Press, 1965.

Williams, Lea E., 'Chinese Entrepreneurs in Indonesia', *Explorations in Entrepreneurial History*, October 1952.

———, *The Future of Overseas Chinese in Southeast Asia*, New York, McGraw-Hill, 1966.

Wilmott, Donald, *The Chinese of Semarang: A Changing Minority Community in Indonesia*, Ithaca, Cornell University Press, 1960.

Wilson, Constance, 'Ethnic Participation in the Export of Thai Rice, 1885–1890', in Karl Hutterer, ed., *Economic Exchange and Social Interaction in Southeast Asia: Perspectives from Prehistory, History, and Ethnography*, Ann Arbor, Center for South and Southeast Asian Studies, University of Michigan, 1977.

Wilson, David, *Politics in Thailand*, Ithaca, Cornell University Press, 1962.

Wilson, Dick, *Solid as a Rock: The First Forty Years of the Oversea-Chinese Banking Corporation*, Singapore, Oversea-Chinese Banking Corporation, 1972.

Wittfogel, Karl, *Oriental Despotism*, New Haven, Yale University Press, 1957.

Wong, Lin Ken, 'The Trade of Singapore, 1819–69', *Journal of the Malayan Branch of the Royal Asiatic Society*, Vol. 33, Pt. 4, 1960.

———, *The Malayan Tin Industry to 1914*, Tucson, University of Arizona Press, 1965.

Wright, A., ed., *Twentieth Century Impressions of British Malaya*, London, Lloyd's Greater Britain Publishing Co., 1908.

———, ed., *Twentieth Century Impressions of Siam*, London, Lloyd's Greater Britain Publishing Co., 1908.

———, ed., *Twentieth Century Impressions of Netherlands India*, London, Lloyd's Greater Britain Publishing Co., 1909.

Wu, Yuan-li and Wu, Chun-hsi, *Economic Development in Southeast Asia: The Chinese Dimension*, Stanford, Hoover Institution Press, 1980.

Yang, Lien-sheng, *Money and Credit in China: A Short History*, Cambridge, Mass., Harvard University Press, 1952.

Yano, Toru, *Nihon no Nanshin to Tonan Ajia*, Tokyo, Nihon Keizai Shinbun-sha, 1975.

———, *Nihon no Nanyo Shikan*, Tokyo, Chuokoron-sha, 1974.

———, *Nanshin no Keifu*, Tokyo, Chuokoron-sha, 1975.

Yap, Koon See, ed., *Who's Who in Malaysian Business & Directory (1985–86)*, Kuala Lumpur, Budayamas Sdn. Bhd., 1985.

Yap, Pheng Geck, *Scholar, Banker, Gentleman Soldier*, Singapore, Times Books International, 1982.

Yasuba, Yasukichi, 'Ishihara Hiroichiro to Shigen Kakuho-ron', *Southeast Asian Studies*, December 1980.

Ybanez, Roy, 'The Hongkong Bank in the Philippines, 1899–1941', in Frank King, ed., *Eastern Banking: Essays in the History of the Hongkong and Shanghai Banking Corporation*, London, The Athlone Press, 1983.

Yip, Yat Hoong, *The Development of the Tin Mining Industry of Malaya*, Kuala Lumpur, University of Malaya Press, 1969.

Yokohama Shokin Ginko-shi, Yokohama, Yokohama Shokin Ginko, 1920.

Yong, C. F., 'Pang, Pang Organizations and Leadership in the Chinese Community of Singapore during the 1930s', *Journal of the South Seas Society*, Parts 1 and 2, 1977.

_____, *Tan Kah-kee: The Making of an Overseas Chinese Legend*, Singapore, Oxford University Press, 1987.

Yoshihara, Kunio, *Foreign Investment and Domestic Response: A Study of Singapore's Industrialization*, Singapore, Eastern Universities Press, 1976.

_____, *Japanese Investment in Southeast Asia*, Honolulu, University Press of Hawaii, 1978.

_____, 'Nomura Zaibatsu no Nanpo Jigyo', *Southeast Asian Studies*, December 1981.

_____, *Sogo Shosha: The Vanguard of the Japanese Economy*, Tokyo, Oxford University Press, 1982.

_____, 'A Note on Information Sources on Philippine Business History', *Southeast Asian Studies*, December 1984.

_____, 'Indigenous Entrepreneurs in the ASEAN Countries', *Singapore Economic Review*, October 1984.

_____, *Philippine Industrialization: Foreign and Domestic Capital*, Quezon City, Ateneo de Manila University Press, and Singapore, Oxford University Press, 1985.

_____, 'The Problem of Continuity in Chinese Businesses in Southeast Asia', *Southeast Asian Studies*, December 1988.

Young, Ernest, *The Kingdom of the Yellow Robe*, reprinted Kuala Lumpur, Oxford University Press, 1982.

Yu, Chung Hsun, *Kakyo Keizai no Kenkyu*, Tokyo, Ajia Keizai Kenkyu-sho, 1969.

_____, 'Capitalistic Development and the Overseas Chinese Economy: Thailand', *The Developing Economies*, September 1971.

The Zaibatsu in the Philippines, A study prepared for Japan Trade Center in Makati, August 1977.

Zaide, Gregorio, 'Contribution of Aliens to Philippine Economy', *Fookien Times Yearbook 1954*, Manila.

Subject Index

Name Index